Nick Hannes

NEW CAPITAL

Lannoo

NEW CAPITALS AS TROPHY CITIES

At the turn of the 20th century, as empires fell and involuntary unions were dissolved, numerous new capital cities began to be established. In 1900, there were approximately 40 capital cities in existence, but by the dawn of the new millennium, this number had skyrocketed to 200. Astonishingly, around 40% of all nations have contemplated the idea of relocating their capital. Even today, new capital cities are being put forward or actively planned.

This book presents six new capital cities spread across time and cultures: Brasília (Brazil), Abuja (Nigeria), Astana (Kazakhstan), Sejong (South Korea), New Administrative Capital (NAC) (Egypt), and Nusantara (Indonesia). While the first four have been around longer, the last two are very recent. Only a portion of NAC is complete, whilst Nusantara just broke ground.

Gifted with a sharp eye for urban planning details, Nick Hannes has travelled the world to document these cities as they stand in the early 2020s. His is a bottom-up perspective, juxtaposing starchitecture with the lives of those struggling to make a life in new capital cities.

Starchitecture

In theory, building an entire city from scratch provides the most suitable conditions for creating a perfect utopia. Yet the new capitals designed since the turn of the 20th century have been major planning disasters. Centred on large, monumental spaces and their accompanying ego-boosting starchitecture, they are bombastic symbols of male political power: overpowering, underserviced, wasteful and unaffordable. Instead of unifying the people of the respective nations, as envisaged by their patriarchal leaders, the new capitals are rife with social and ethnic inequalities. Dystopian cityscapes are the result. The promise was squandered. Failures can be observed in various contexts, regardless of whether they are democratic or authoritarian, post-colonial or long-established independent nations, socialist or capitalist, and regardless of the racial or ethnic composition of the population. These failures are not confined to either poorer or wealthier countries, early or recent capitals, or those built in greenfield locations or as extensions to existing settlements. They transcend the boundaries of time, encompassing both the modern and postmodern eras, among other factors. Patriarchy is the only common thread that connects these megaprojects in their failures.

New capitals have emerged from political power rather than being developed over time, guided by the residents' needs and wants. 'Trophy cities' show how power and influence driven by ego come to control the national image. Therefore, problems are magnified. New capitals are as, or even more, unfavourable to disadvantaged groups as ordinary cities. They fare worse than cities which are not capitals in the respective countries.

Nationalism on steroids

Brazil, Nigeria and Kazakhstan moved their capitals in the aftermath of independence. The creation of new capitals in these countries was driven by a desire for national unity but also to consolidate the power of the new regimes. However, these projects brought about major challenges, including political instability, ethnic tensions and divisions.

Brasília was the pinnacle of a national mission to conquer and settle Brazil's vast interior. This mission was rooted in colonial-era *bandeirismo*, an ideology of expanding the frontier and taming the wild land. Yet Brasília's construction, which took place in the late 1950s, was framed as a symbol of liberation from Portuguese dominion. The significant expenses associated with building a new city in the savannah led to discontent and finally a military coup in 1964.

Nigeria's quest for national unity was even more urgent than Brazil's due to its diverse ethnic composition. The country was created by British colonisers who arbitrarily drew lines on a map and merged various regions, whose people had little in common except skin colour. The new capital, Abuja, was established to provide a fresh start in the post-colonial era. But the relocation of the capital to the north (a predominantly Muslim region) exacerbated tensions with the Christian south, leading to ongoing strife and division within the country.

In Kazakhstan, the need for a new capital arose after the collapse of Russian control and the demise of Moscow as the capital. Kazakhstan faced major challenges in nation-building due to its diverse population and ethnic Russian dominance. Kazakhs were in fact a minority group in 1990 and concerns for Russian irredentism were running high. The relocation of the capital from Almaty to Astana was seen as a way to assert a new Kazakh national identity separate from Russia and the Soviet Union. Nonetheless, frictions based on ethnicity, language and regional provenance have persisted.

A number of new capitals have been built based on a bellicose image of nationhood. In particular, Abuja and NAC are both brainchildren of the military and reflect their parentage. They have been placed in inaccessible locations, away from water and other resources, supposedly to defend the nation from external 'enemies'. In reality, local generals may have been more concerned with shielding the seat of government from protest movements in the existing capitals.

For example, Nigeria's head of state in the 1970s, General Yakubu Gowon, expressed concerns about the security of Lagos following the Biafran War, citing its vulnerability to bombings. In reality, the ruling junta needed Abuja to create a necessary buffer between itself and all Nigerian people. To safeguard against unrest, General Ibrahim Babangida, responsible for the formal relocation of the capital in 1991, converted the presidential villa into an elaborate fortress with underground tunnels and bomb-proof bunkers.

Apart from these types of extravaganzas, the adoption of generic 'international' templates has stripped the new capitals of contextual individuality. Their designs have not guarded or promoted the national 'culture', despite that often being the stated intention. Instead, interchangeable cities without history have been created.

Grand design schemes

Irrespective of the internal images and perceptions, countries that have built new capitals have consistently endeavoured to project a shiny external image, one that mirrors the competitive and stratified nature of their societies. By creating new capitals, national leaders have aspired to redefine their homelands as bastions of refined culture, economic prowess and discerning taste.

The design of new capitals has often reflected the totalising visions of egotistic politicians, bureaucrats or designers pursuing self-aggrandisement, glorification and immortalisation. Powerful politicians or government bureaucrats, embodying a 'benevolent patriarchy', have served as champions for the construction of the new capitals. Moreover, renowned designers imported from far afield have imposed their own vision and identity on the capital cities they have designed, introducing solutions that are disconnected from the local context.

New capitals are characterised by sprawling plazas and boulevards, anchored by fountains, statues, obelisks and so on. Apart from Sejong, the plans of all cities feature broad linear thoroughfares that run through their centres. This style draws from European urbanism in the Grand Manner — a model that has been evolving since the Renaissance. Locally, it has been rationalised in a variety of ways.

For example, the monumental Nurzhol Boulevard in Astana's pharaonic plan was justified by the belief that Kazakhs have a preference for openness rooted in their nomadic heritage. The Disneyland-like architecture along the boulevard features a mix of styles, with abstract symbols that are not necessarily unique to the region. Locals' opinions about this space are divided, with some perceiving it as vibrant and exciting, akin to a 'foreign' setting; others feel a sense of emptiness, artificiality and even anxiety, finding the area alienating and eerie in its appearance. On the positive side, this ceremonial axis is pedestrian-friendly.

While NAC's autocratic backers wanted the city to feature sleek designs by top Western urban planners and architects, the reality is an unstylish mixture of postmodern styles ranging from rococo-inspired ornamentation to 1980s brutalism, combined with Egyptian and Islamic elements. Even Brasília's Pilot Plan nucleus, the oldest of the case studies, covers a vast space which far surpasses human scale. The primary driver of the city's urban layout was the road transportation infrastructure rather than the three-dimensional urban image. As Jan Gehl has pointed out, the Pilot Plan may look impressive when observed from an aeroplane, but it lacks vibrancy and charm when experienced on foot. Similarly, in Abuja, public space voids dwarf the building mass.

A comparatively less ambitious version of a new capital city, smaller and not majestic, Sejong lacks a grand symbolic boulevard, and its layout does not adhere to a hierarchical grid system. Instead, it is often regarded as the epitome of a 'postmodern' capital due to its decentralised urban plan, featuring a vast green area at its core and a ring road. These are meant to symbolise decentralisation, democracy and equal opportunity. However, Sejong's aesthetics are unappealing. The city is a quiet and nondescript expanse of government structures, encircled by rows of identical residential tower blocks and manicured parks commonly seen throughout urban areas in South Korea.

Modernisation and lifestyle

An agenda of modernisation (of design and society) has been present in new capitals. Automobility is a cornerstone of modernity as conceived in these cities. In Astana, as in Abuja and Brasília, car ownership is a major status symbol. While Astana is automobile-orientated, it lacks the road and parking infrastructure to support a large and growing number of vehicles. Although the city is just a few decades old, many people waste several hours daily battling congestion. During the exceptionally cold winters, a significant portion of the centre becomes impassable outside of a vehicle due to the considerable distances separating destinations. Whilst Abuja's core boasts some of the best road infrastructures in Nigeria, the outer districts are as congested as in the former capital, Lagos. As in Brasília, protracted daily commutes are common for the mass of impoverished workers who live in satellite shanty towns.

A focus on modernity, speed and order has led new capital city planners to give short shrift to issues of liveability, affordability, walkability and accessibility. Strict planning checks have often backfired, leading to high levels of peri-urban informality. Housing inequalities are as severe as differentials in mobility and infrastructure access, even where — as in Brasília — the initial intention is to create an egalitarian city. Brasília's spatial arrangement, with a focus on centralising work and dispersing housing into suburbs, gave rise to class stratification and various social tensions right from its inception. Presently, there is a stark contrast between the privileged centre (the famous Pilot Plan) and the marginalised periphery, reflecting patterns seen in other Brazilian cities, but exacerbated in the case of Brasília. In NAC, an affordable housing policy has already been scrapped.

Sejong, which has fewer than half a million inhabitants, is perhaps the most affordable and family-friendly of the case studies. Compared with Seoul's cramped residential quarters, it provides a safe and secure environment for children with designated car-free public spaces. Children enjoy the freedom to play, cycle and explore without constant adult supervision. The city's population mainly consists of young couples in their 30s and 40s, contributing to the country's highest fertility rates. To support families, a dedicated public facility called the Happy Mom Center offers comprehensive mental and physical health services for pre- and post-natal needs. Additionally, each block of flats comes with its own daycare centre, emphasising a culture of family-centric socialising over interactions centred solely on colleagues, workplaces and after-work drinking. But even in Sejong, the fundamental assumptions around social hierarchies have not been challenged.

Environmental devastation

A recurring trend in the creation of new capital cities involves the notion of controlling and even improving upon nature. Disregarding practicality, these cities have often been constructed on challenging or delicate terrains, ranging from rainforests to arid steppes. Natural elements like mountains and rivers have been subjected to peculiar symbolism serving the interests of political agendas. For example, when developing Abuja, two topographical features, namely Aso Rock and Zuma Rock, were fetishised.

In Brasília, extensive savanna vegetation was cleared to expedite its construction, and subsequently, tropical plants were introduced from Rio to enhance the city's appearance. The selected site for Astana was a desert steppe characterised by an extremely harsh winter climate compared with the major city and former capital, Almaty. The absence of natural barriers allows frigid Siberian winds to blow southward. In terms of historical context, Soviet Gulags were once scattered throughout the area, with interned individuals unable to escape due to the cold.

More recently, NAC is being built in the desert, far from all water sources, whereas Nusantara's construction is invading Borneo's virgin rainforest, a habitat for endangered species. These approaches reflect a perception of nature as a subordinate entity, one that can be tamed and dominated by culture and civilisation.

Far-fetched symbolism

The accounts of the foundation and development of new capitals are rife with myths and far-fetched symbols. Masonic, Egyptian, New Age and feng shui icons and design principles are scattered throughout.

For example, Brasília, despite its bland appearance, exudes an intriguing air of mystery. It continues to captivate enthusiasts of conspiracy theories and remains a popular destination for those interested in New Age beliefs, the occult, mysticism, alternative healing, paranormal activity, metaphysics, ufology and similar subjects. Numerous organisations, communities and communes dedicated to these pursuits have been established in Brasília, becoming an integral part of local pop culture. Their followers are convinced that the city's otherworldly geography and architecture attracts cosmic energies and disembodied spirits. They claim it to be the sole place on Earth destined to survive the final Armageddon.

Astana has gained a reputation as the Masonic capital of the world, primarily due to the presence of occult symbolism intricately woven into its urban design and architecture. There is also speculation that this capital's designers have drawn inspiration from groups like the Illuminati and even the Opus Dei. A conference hall shaped like a square-based equilateral pyramid, which was designed by the renowned British architect Norman Foster, has triggered a plethora of esoteric interpretations. The plan for the main concert hall is purportedly inspired by the Masonic *vesica piscis*. The presidential palace is also framed as a Masonic symbol because it occupies the same position on the left bank of the local river as the chair of a worshipful master in a Masonic lodge.

These are not mere idiosyncrasies but serve to legitimise and sacralise places that lack history. Overall, they have generated a number of intriguing conspiracy theories, but, otherwise, they have been innocuous. Meanwhile, where the iconography of traditional religions has been adopted in the capitals of multi-faith nations, it has often planted discord: some groups have inevitably felt neglected or even spurned. For example, the design of the National Assembly Complex in Abuja, which features a dome, caused displeasure among Christians and other religious groups who viewed the building as a symbol of Islam.

Economic strain

Several of the case study capitals — Abuja, Astana and NAC — have been built by petrodollars. Nigeria and Kazakhstan have large reserves of domestic oil whilst Egypt has relied on loans and investments from oil-rich allies in the Gulf, such as Saudi Arabia and the United Arab Emirates. The latter has also pledged to invest in Nusantara.

Oil-fuelled economic booms have lent confidence to the notion that governments can sustain the construction of such megaprojects from scratch. But oil prices are notoriously volatile, and oil-producing countries which have not diversified their economies have seen their revenues plummet. For example, the oil shock of 1978 crashed the Nigerian economy right at the time when Abuja was being built.

Brazil fell into political and economic turmoil in the 1960s, due to the spiralling deficit accumulated by the government's spending on Brasília. NAC's construction has plunged Egypt into major debt, which future generations will struggle to repay for decades to come. The megaproject was planned and built as the country was experiencing one of the worst financial crises in its recent history.

Nusantara will be built on a separate island, Borneo, which contains only 5% to 6% of the Indonesian population. With nearly 60% of the people concentrated in Java, the new capital will be accessible only by air, financially burdening both locals and visitors. Isolated in Brazil's interior, Brasília suffers from a near-identical problem.

Furthermore, none of the new capitals have supported the economic empowerment and equality of marginalised groups. On the contrary, some capitals have been built by migrant labourers, who were then banned from the city they put together. In Brasília, the authorities believed that the new 'capital of hope' should not be inhabited by illiterate, powerless and hungry people. The construction workers who wished to stay ended up settling in satellite communities beyond the boundaries of the Pilot Plan, forming a more or less permanent underclass.

In no case has a new capital transformed the national economy, even though this was used as a justification for building a capital anew in some places. In recent decades, the advent of globalisation has only deepened the precarious condition of the poor. In South Korea, a developmentalist government has historically viewed megaprojects, including the creation of entirely new cities, as a way to enhance the country's competitiveness on the global stage and boost private investment from both domestic and foreign sources. In this process, the government has interacted closely with the *chaebol* (large industrial conglomerates controlled by powerful families). Now the influence of the latter has been socially discredited and the Korean state is forging new development alliances with foreign capital. But in the realm of urban planning, a combination of strict controls and 'business-friendly' policies has resulted in cookie-cutter master plans that erode local identities and weaken civil society organisations. Therefore, it can be argued that the majority of newly established capitals constitute extremely costly errors.

What would a liveable capital city look like?

Obviously, new capitals need affordable housing, accessible transport and safe public spaces. Albeit crucial, such urban transformations would be only skin-deep. Much bolder steps are required, which involve a rejection of authoritarianism, individualism and neoliberalism in favour of consensus-based planning and design. The capital cities of the future — indeed all cities of the future — should embody principles of equality, classlessness, peace, inclusivity, ecology, beauty and well-being. Nature should serve as a foundation for urban design. Planners ought to consider not only human lives but also the preservation of the local fauna and flora. Existential threats such as climate breakdown, automation, nuclear warfare and pandemics call for audacious thinking that transcends convention.

Dorina Pojani
Author of *Trophy Cities: A Feminist Perspective on New Capitals* (Edward Elgar, 2021)

Selected bibliography

Albo, F. 2017. *Astana: Architecture, Myth & Destiny.* Winnipeg: Vidacom.

Elleh, N. 2017. *Architecture and Politics in Nigeria: The Study of a Late Twentieth-Century Enlightenment-Inspired Modernism at Abuja, 1900–2016.* New York and London: Routledge.

Gordon, D. (ed.). 2006. *Planning Twentieth Century Capital Cities.* New York and London: Routledge.

Holston, J. 1989. *The Modernist City: An Anthropological Critique of Brasília.* Chicago: University of Chicago Press.

Koch, N. 2010. The monumental and the miniature: imagining 'modernity' in Astana. *Social & Cultural Geography* 11(8):769-787.

Lichá, A. 2015. *Songdo and Sejong: Master-Planned Cities in South Korea.* Master's thesis. Paris Institute of Political Studies (Sciences Po), Paris, France.

Minkenberg, M. (ed.). 2014. *Power and Architecture: The Construction of Capitals and the Politics of Space.* New York: Berghahn Books.

Pojani, D. 2021. *Trophy Cities: A Feminist Perspective on New Capitals.* London: Edward Elgar Publishing.

Pojani, D. 9 February 2022. How not to build a capital: what Indonesia can learn from other master-planned cities' mistakes.
The Conversation.

Rossman, V. 2016. *Capital Cities: Varieties and Patterns of Development and Relocation.* New York and London: Routledge.

Sonne, W. 2003. *Representing the State: Capital City Planning in the Early Twentieth Century.* New York: Prestel.

Taweel, S. 2023. *Al-Sisi's bubble in the desert: The political economy of Egypt's new administrative capital.* Washington, DC: Project on Middle East Democracy (POMED).

Vale, L. 2008. *Architecture, Power and National Identity.* New York and London: Routledge.

Warsilah, H., Mulyani, L., Nasution, I.K. 2023. *Assembling Nusantara: Mimicry, Friction, and Resonance in the New Capital Development.* Cham: Springer.

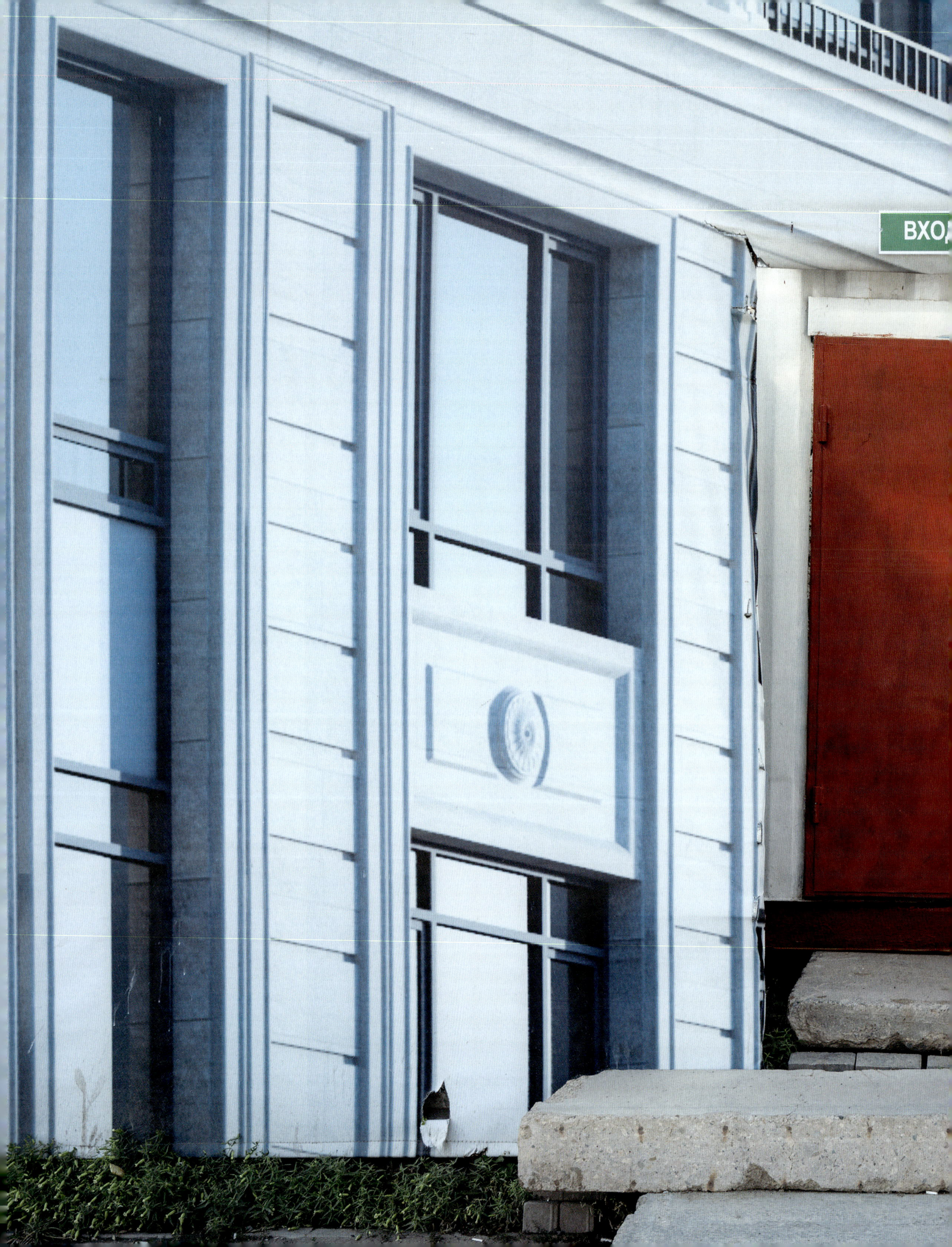

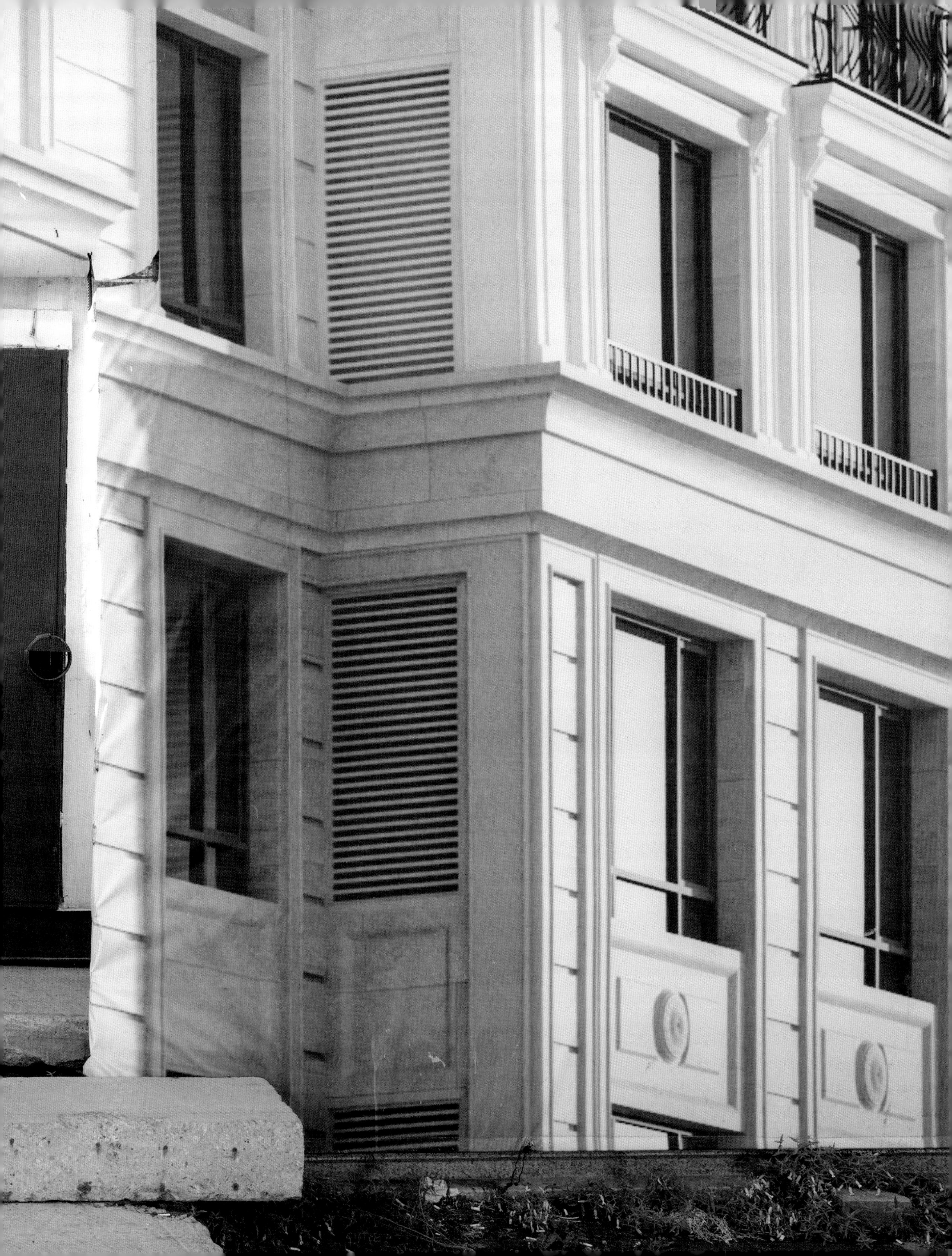

BRAZIL

BRASÍLIA

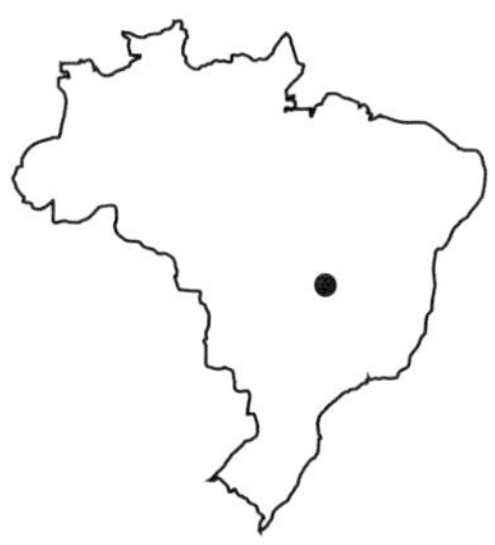

Start of construction: 1956
Inauguration date: 21 April 1960
Initiated by: President Juscelino Kubitschek
Master plan by: Lúcio Costa
Urban agglomeration population in 2023: 3 million
Surface area: 5800 km²
Former capital: Rio de Janeiro

I Uber from the airport to the St Paul Plaza Hotel in the southern hotel sector. It is noon and I barely spot a living soul in the streets. Is this what people mean when they refer to Brasília as the most un-Brazilian city in the country? Or are the streets deserted because it is Sunday?

When Juscelino Kubitschek was elected Brazil's 21st president in 1955, he immediately made good on his promise to build an all-new, centrally located capital. The utopian model city was to become the symbol of a modern nation and to develop Brazil's hinterland economically. Influenced by Le Corbusier's ideas, urbanist Lúcio Costa designed the *Plano Piloto*, the heart of the city. Oscar Niemeyer drew the architectural eye-catchers, which earned the city a place on the UNESCO World Heritage List in 1987. After 41 months of non-stop construction, Brasília was ceremoniously inaugurated in 1960.

The city is rationally divided into sectors. Commercial, residential and government facilities are separated. Hotels, banks and embassies also have their own neighbourhoods. With the car as a benchmark, wide boulevards and large car parks were built. The central Monumental Axis is a 12-lane highway with a sparse grassy area as a wide central reservation. Crossing here requires patience and courage. Or a long diversion to one of the few pedestrian crossings with traffic lights.

In search of people, I make my way to the massive city park, named after Kubitschek's wife Sarah. There, cyclists and joggers in spandex shorts and sports bras circle the artificial pond. Its bank is an ideal location for birthday parties, revelry and make-out sessions. Slurping coconut water with a straw, I listen to the exhilarating rhythms of a Batukenjé drum band. The percussionists' graceful choreography, collective power and joy of playing move me unexpectedly and for the first time in this wide-open, vacuous city.

A few kilometres down the road is Pontão do Lago Sul, an upscale restaurant district on Lake Paranoá. One drives in under a kitschy triumphal arch complete with barrier. Off the coast, macho men on jet skis beg for attention. Security guards on Segways patrol among the dolled-up crowd, strolling past tidy flowerbeds with fake rockery and ditto waterfall. Here, one is not allowed to walk on the grass, let alone have a picnic or BBQ. Taking selfies is the main activity of the majority of those in attendance.

Seen from the air, Brasília is shaped like an aeroplane. The Monumental Axis symbolises the fuselage, along which the ministries are located. At right angles to it are two wings with numbered residential blocks grouped in *superquadras*. The cockpit represents the Three Powers Plaza, referring to the National Congress, the Supreme Court and the Presidential Office.

Every evening, soldiers in ceremonial uniform lower the Brazilian flag there. Tension is in the air. Presidential elections will take place soon. Opposite the palace, a woman holds up a protest sign reading *Fora Bolsonaro!* (Down with Bolsonaro!). 'The people are hungry,' she says. An angry man approaches her and, with clenched fists, loudly chants the name of the incumbent president.

'A capybara has more brains than Bolsonaro,' sighs a third one. 'He's our Trump, a disaster on every front!'

A busload of schoolchildren gets there. The guide wears a general's uniform and orders the children into tight rows with each time an arm's length between them. With their hand on their chest and cap off, they sing the national anthem. They chant slogans of which I understand only the words 'discipline' and 'respect'. Afterwards, each child receives a small Brazilian flag. This square just oozes politics.

Kubitschek has been resting in a black coffin in his darkened mausoleum since 1981, surrounded by historical photographs, badges of honour and all manner of paraphernalia. His library — featuring Shakespeare's complete works — was reconstructed here. His wife Sarah's wardrobe is also on display. She always looked elegant, the caption reveals.

The mausoleum is Niemeyer's umpteenth creation. His modernist architecture has stood the test of time. But Brasília's utopia ultimately led to a segregated society, with an affluent centre for the happy few and impersonal suburbs for the masses. Of metropolitan Brasília's more than 4.5 million residents, only 215,000 live in the *Plano Piloto*. They tend to belong to the upper middle class. The low-rise residential blocks in the *superquadras* stand on elegant pillars, creating a leafy ground-floor communal space surrounded by tidy gardens. It smells of all-purpose cleaner and perfume. A woman with a pink-bowed keeshond passes by, while a man does sit-ups on a yoga mat under the watchful eye of his personal trainer. Caretakers and security cameras provide round-the-clock surveillance. Visible poverty is limited to the many homeless people sleeping in tents in the parks.

In the evening, I look out from my balcony at the deserted streets in the southern hotel sector. A bum with a rattling pushcart goes by. A scantily clad transsexual paces the pavement. From behind an illuminated advertisement, she pulls up her dress and shows her knickers to passing drivers. This city lives in minutiae. You have to pay close attention or you miss them.

May 2022

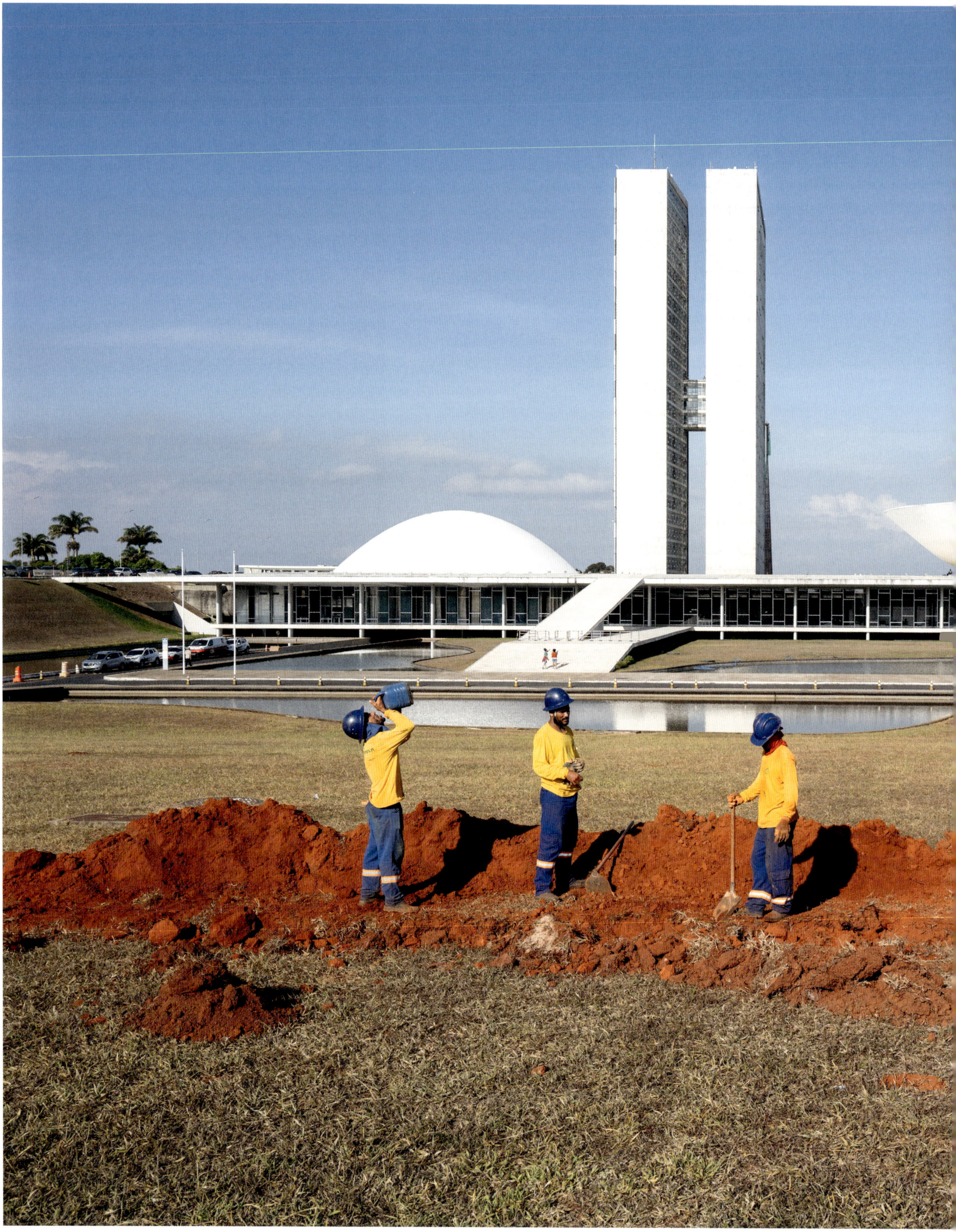

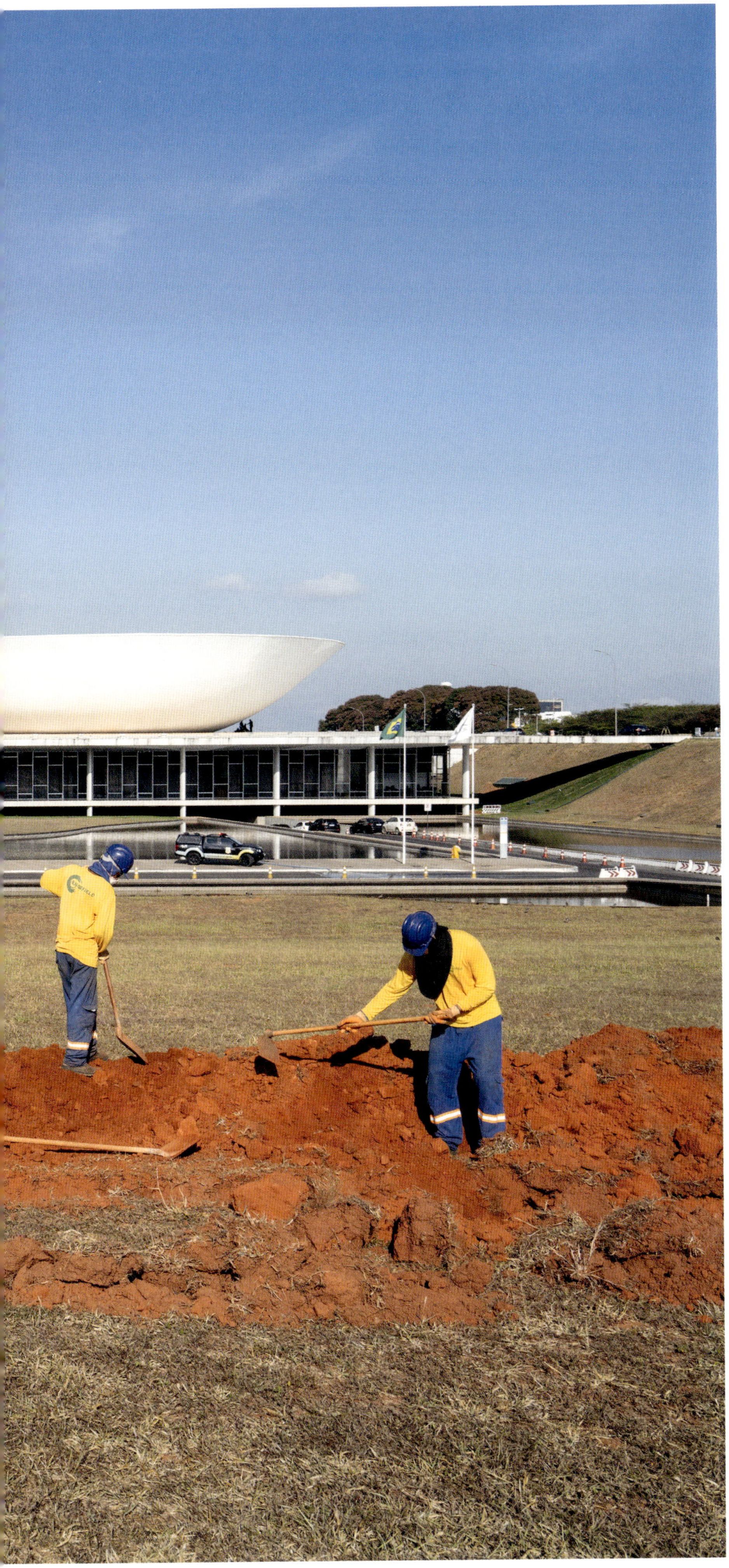

National Congress of Brazil,
designed by Oscar Niemeyer.

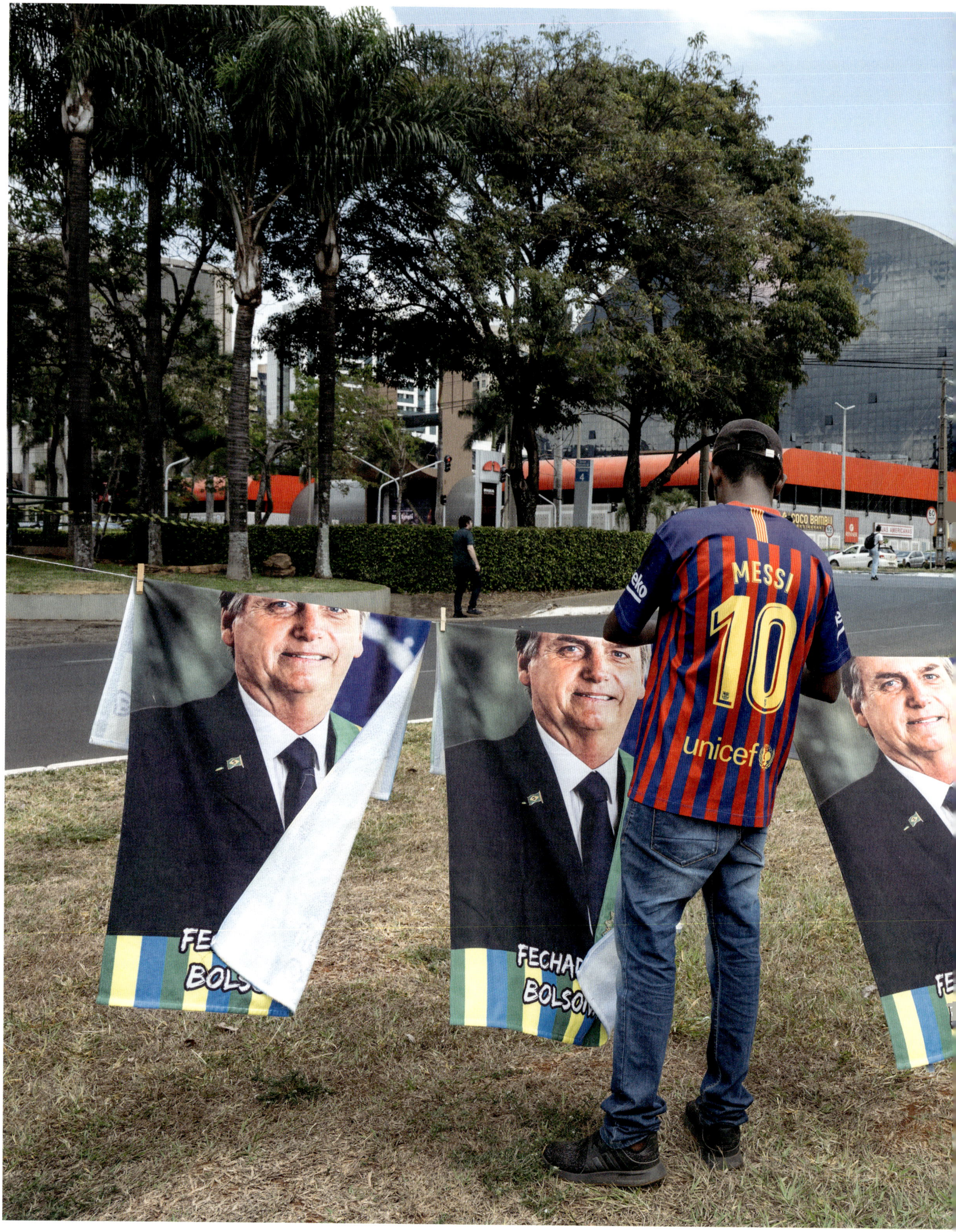
MESSI
10
unicef

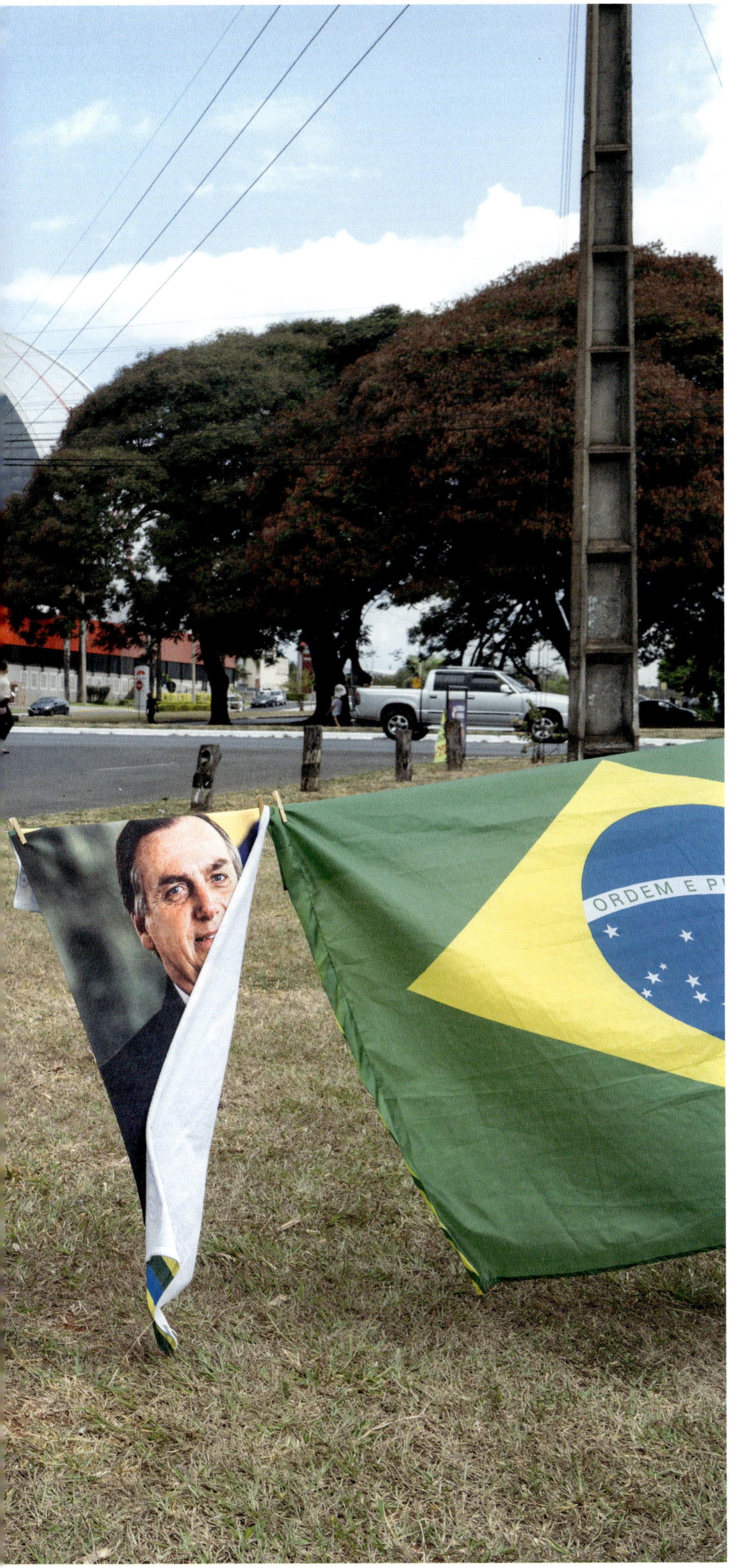

Banners depicting the then
president Jair Messias Bolsonaro.

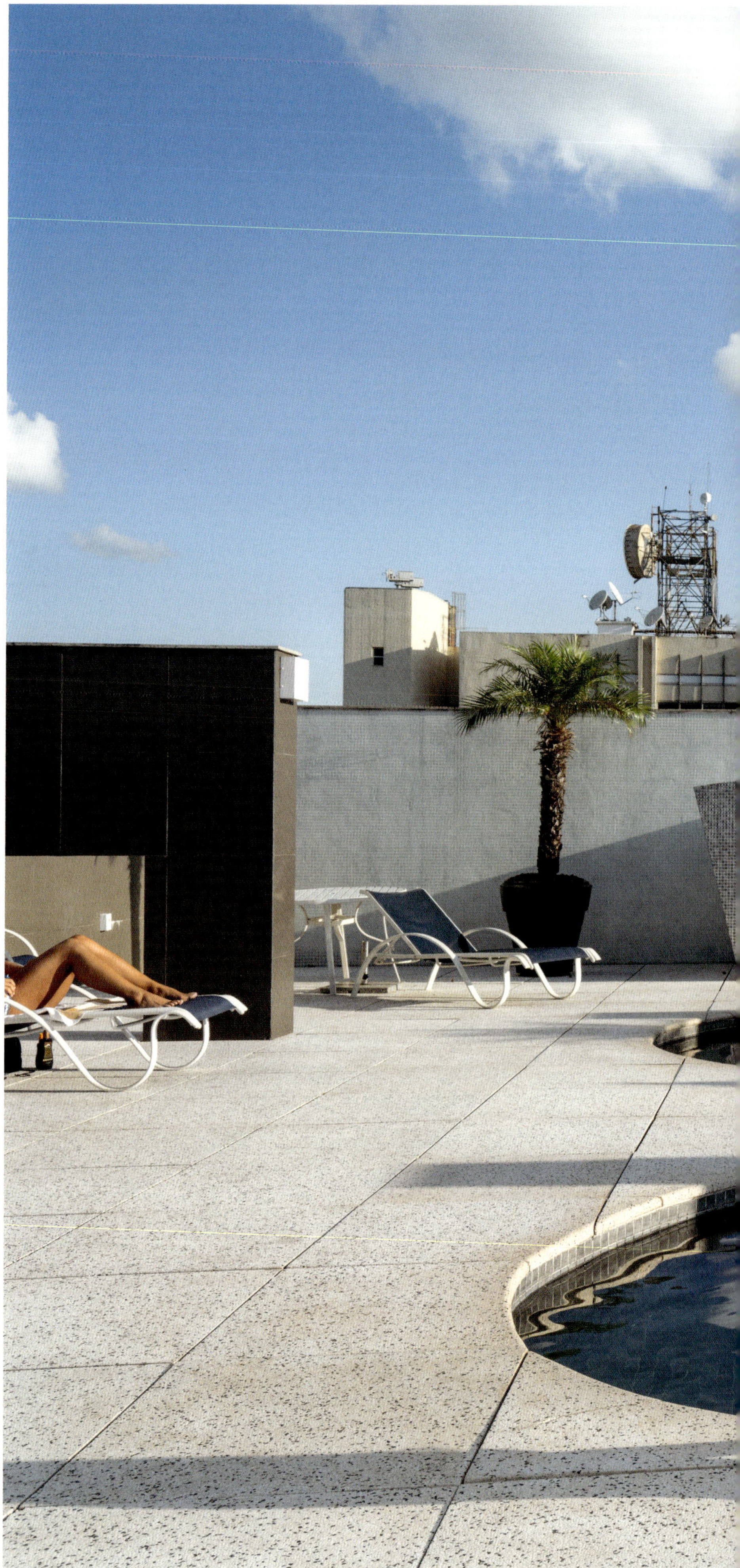

Rooftop pool at St Paul Plaza Hotel.

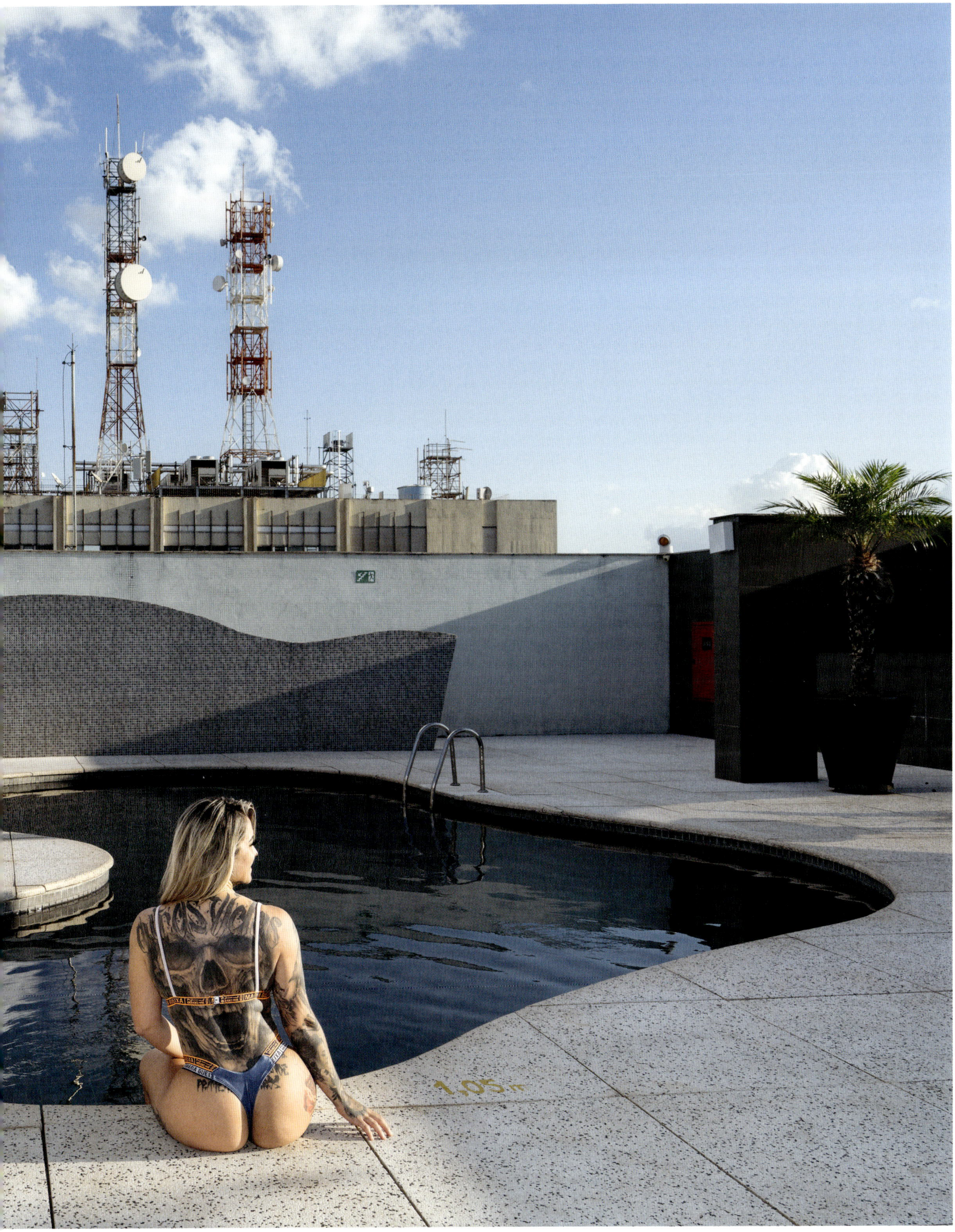

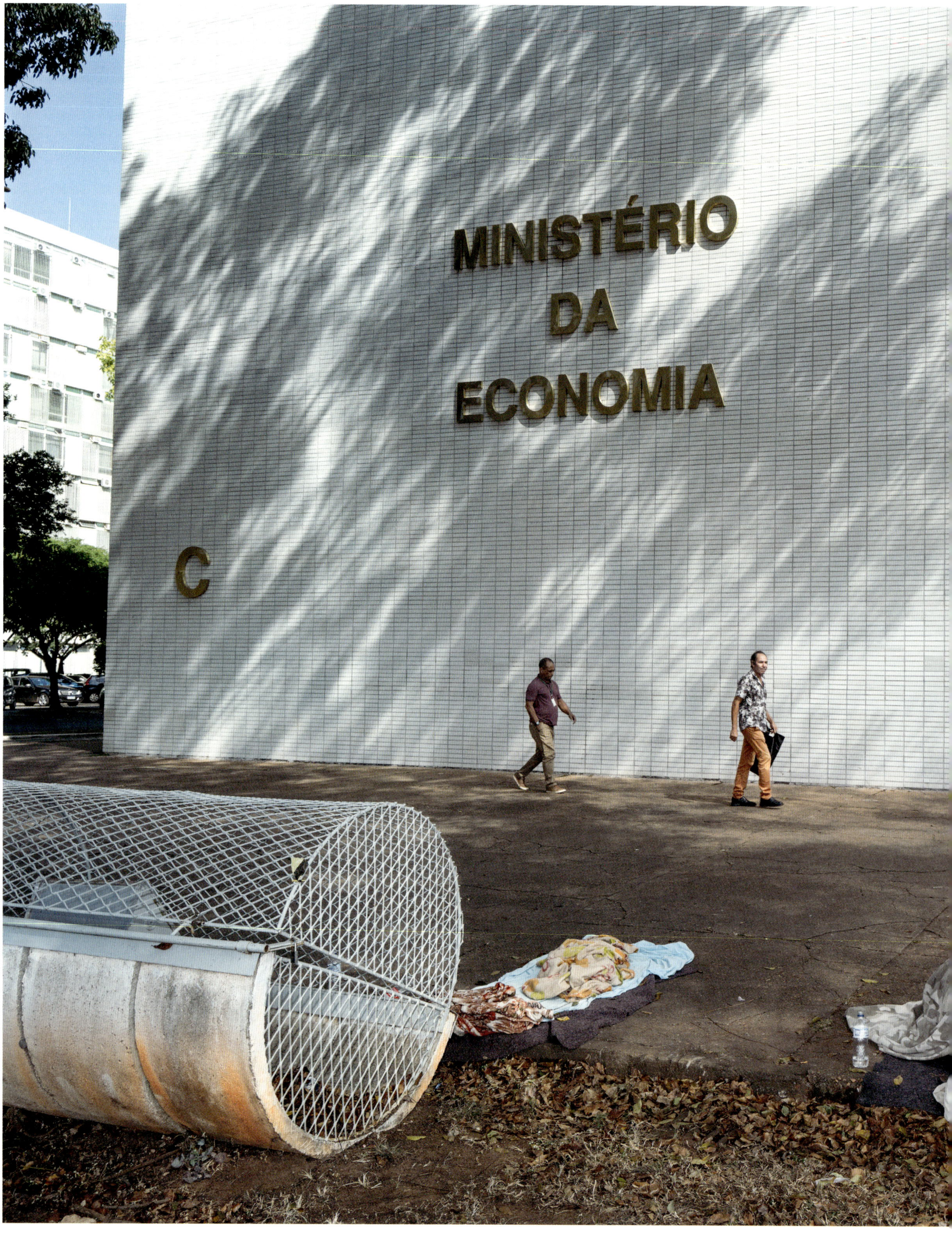
MINISTÉRIO
DA
ECONOMIA
C

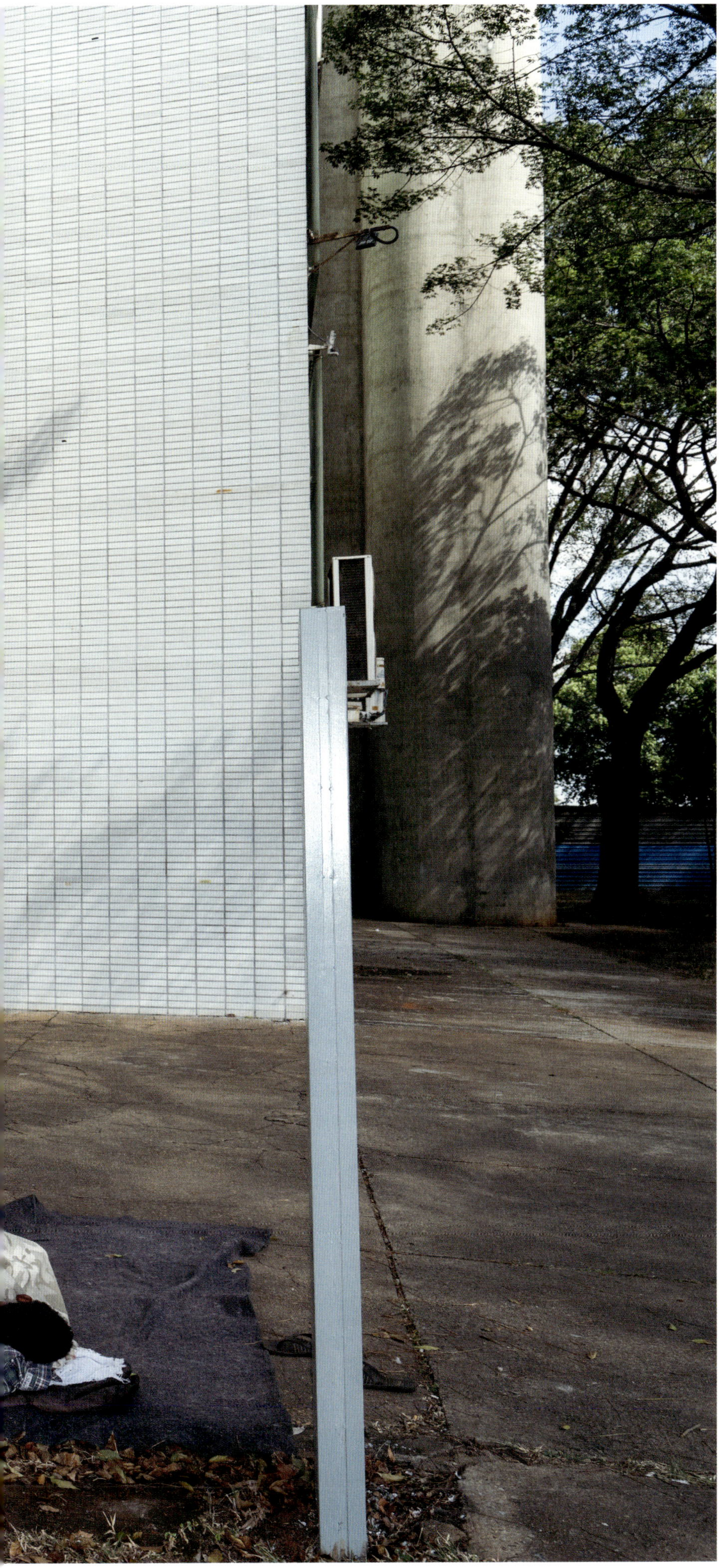

Ministry of the Economy on the Esplanade of the Ministries.

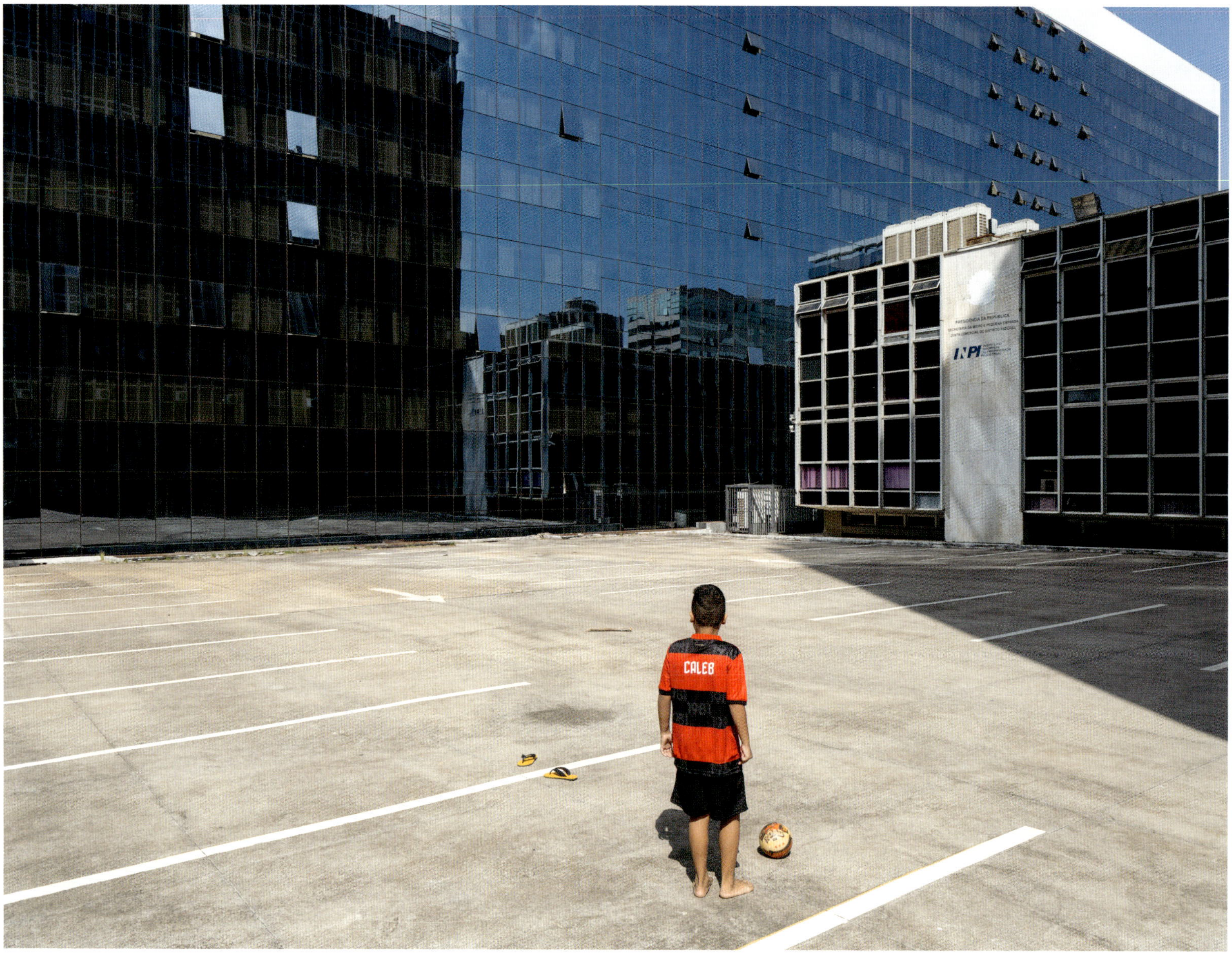

National Social Security Institute.

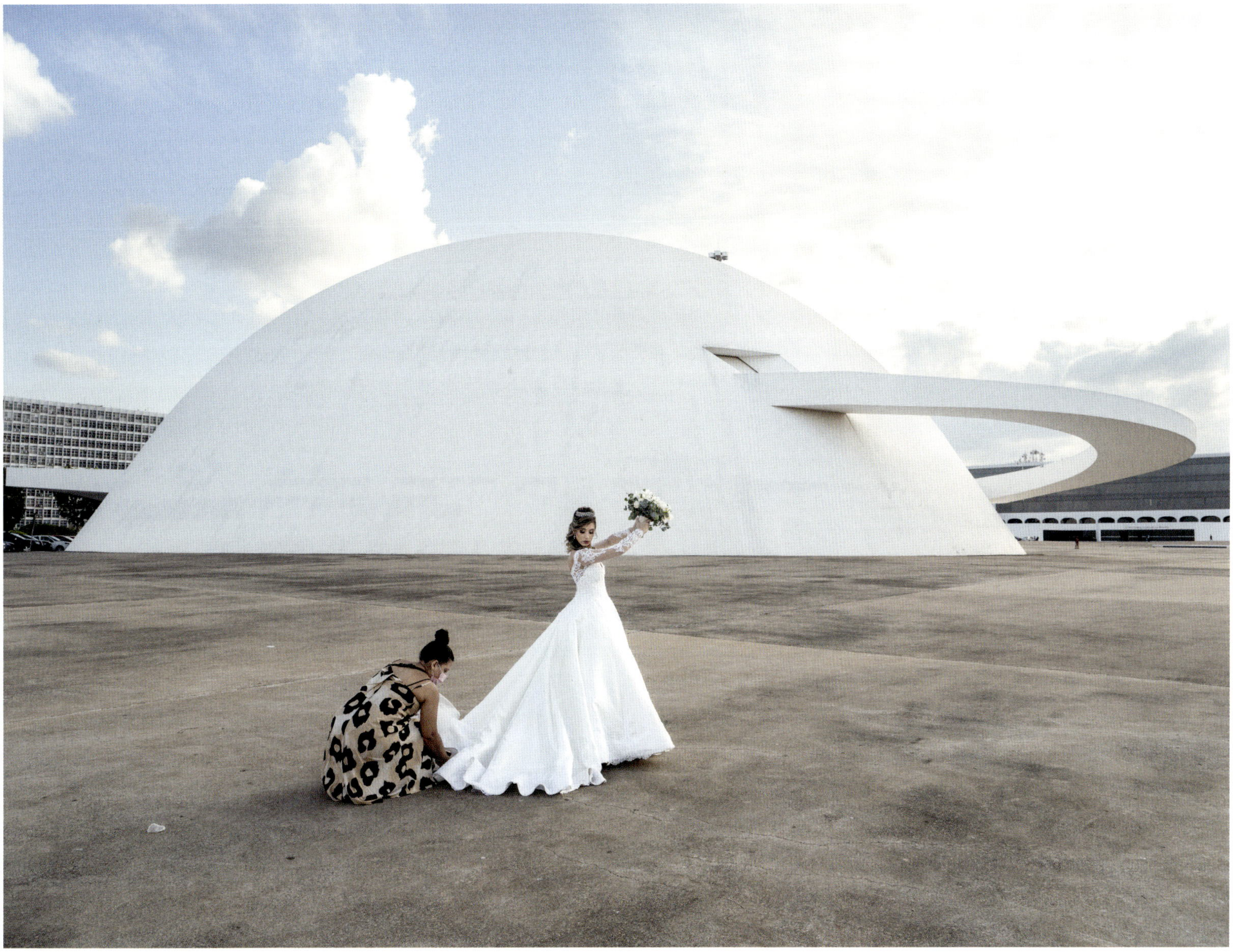

Honestino Guimarães National Museum, designed by Oscar Niemeyer.

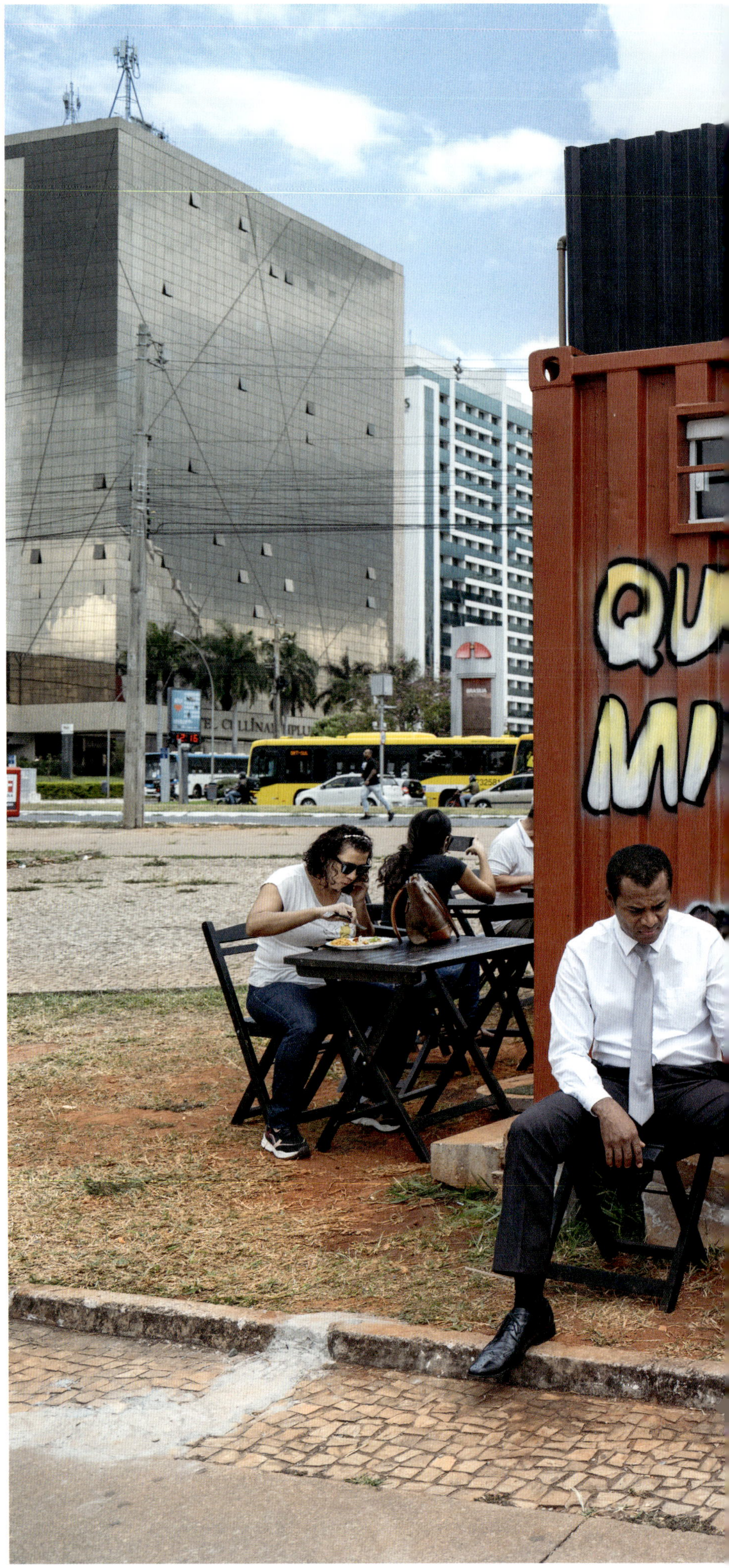

Brasília Shopping.

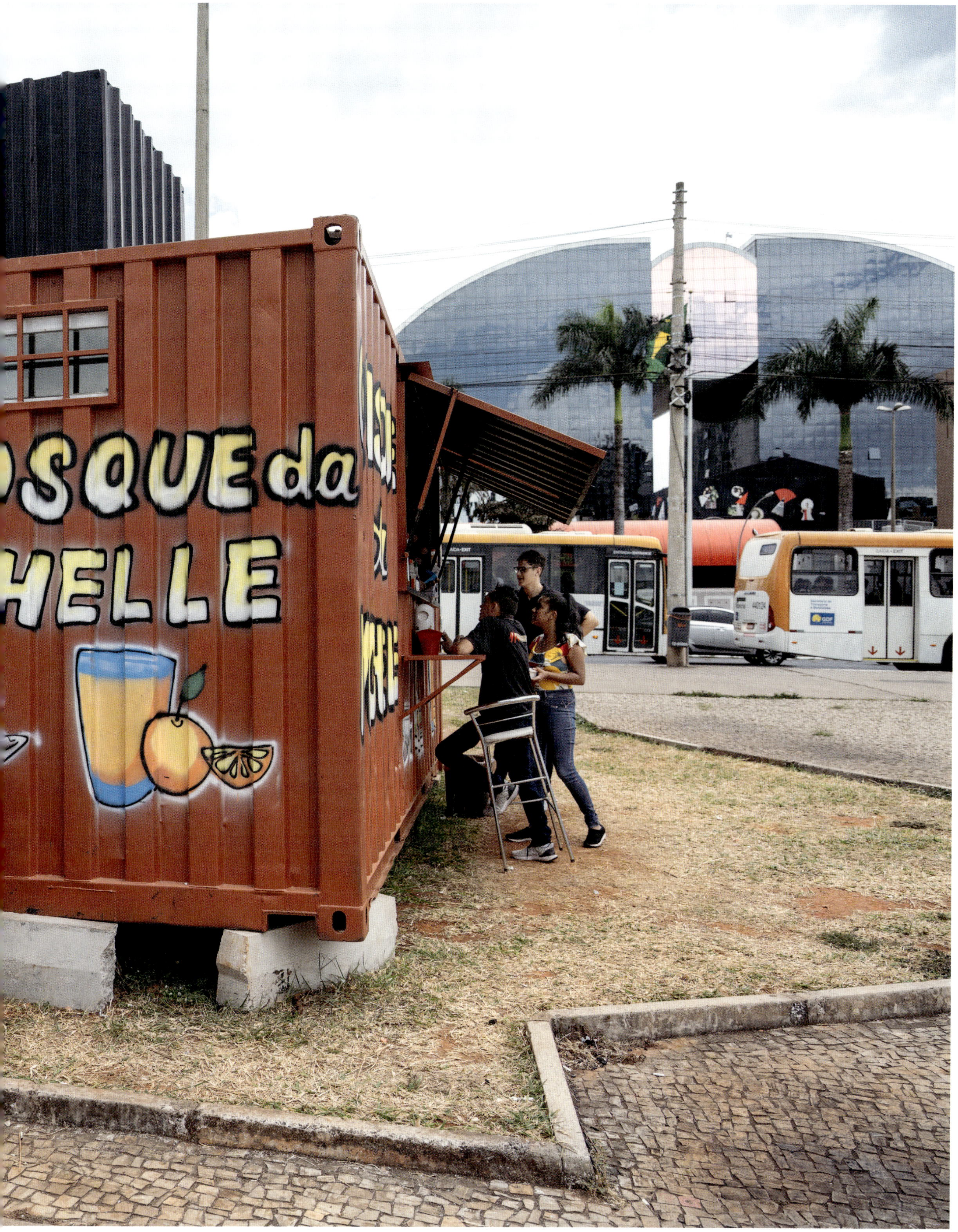

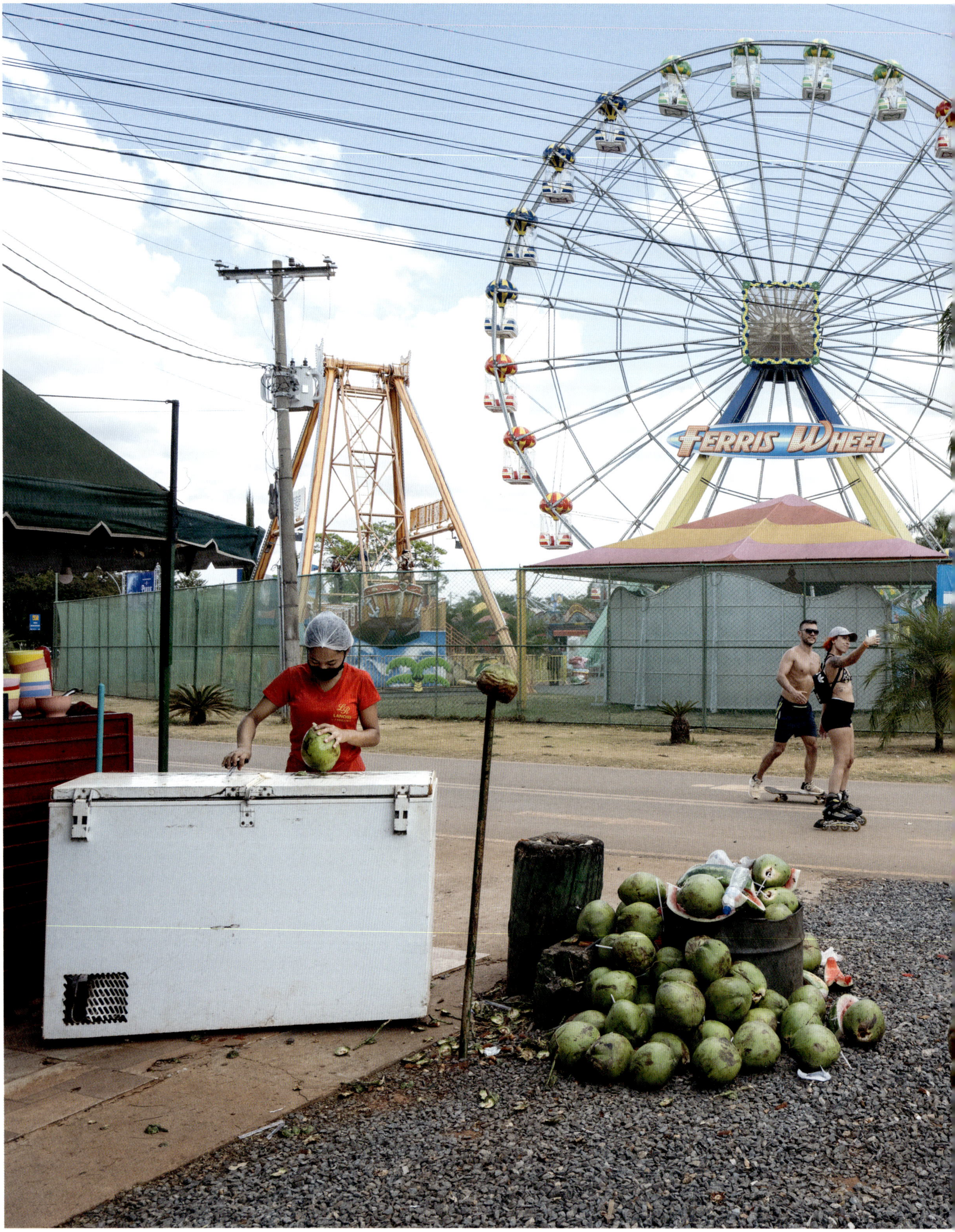
FERRIS WHEEL

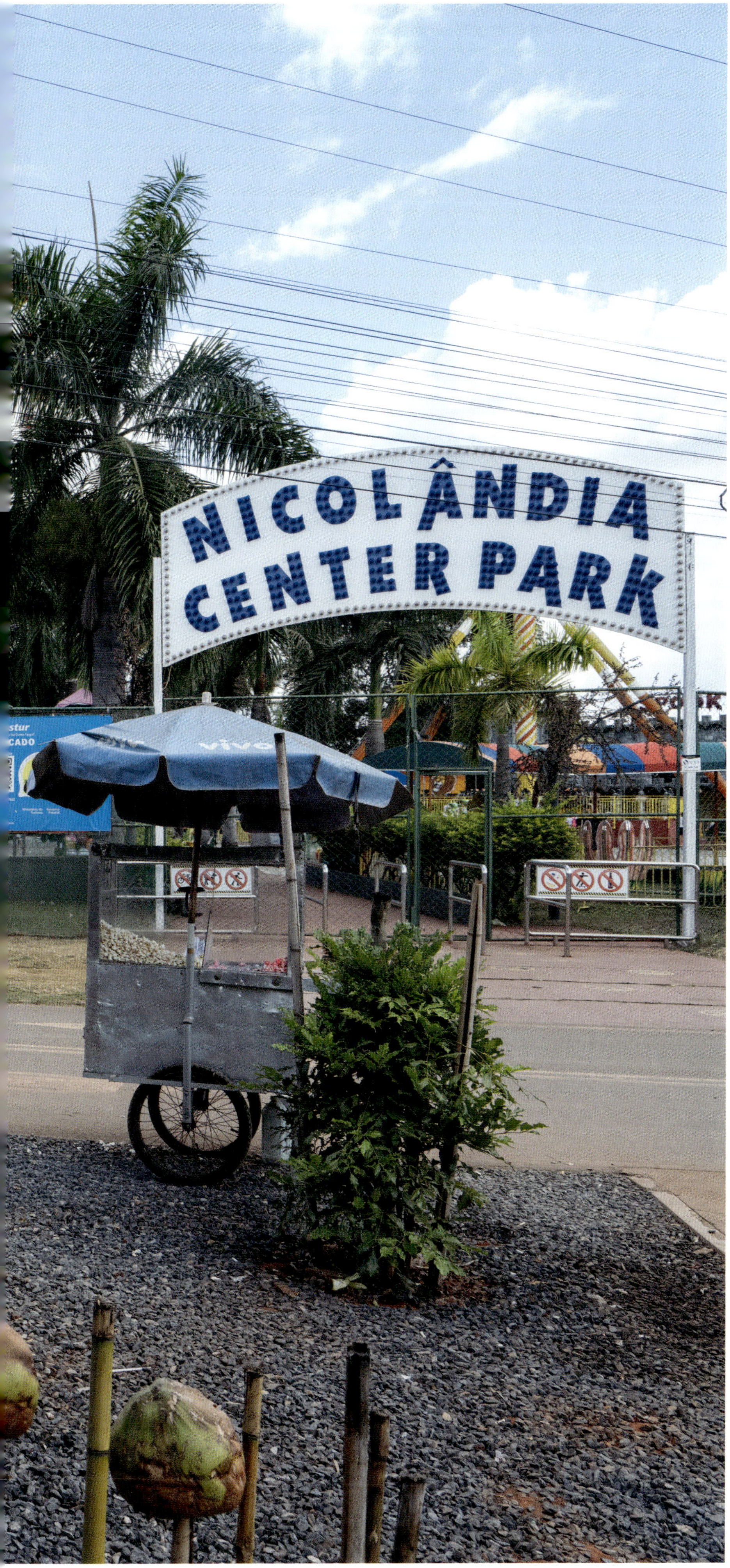

Sarah Kubitschek City Park.

Lake Paranoá.

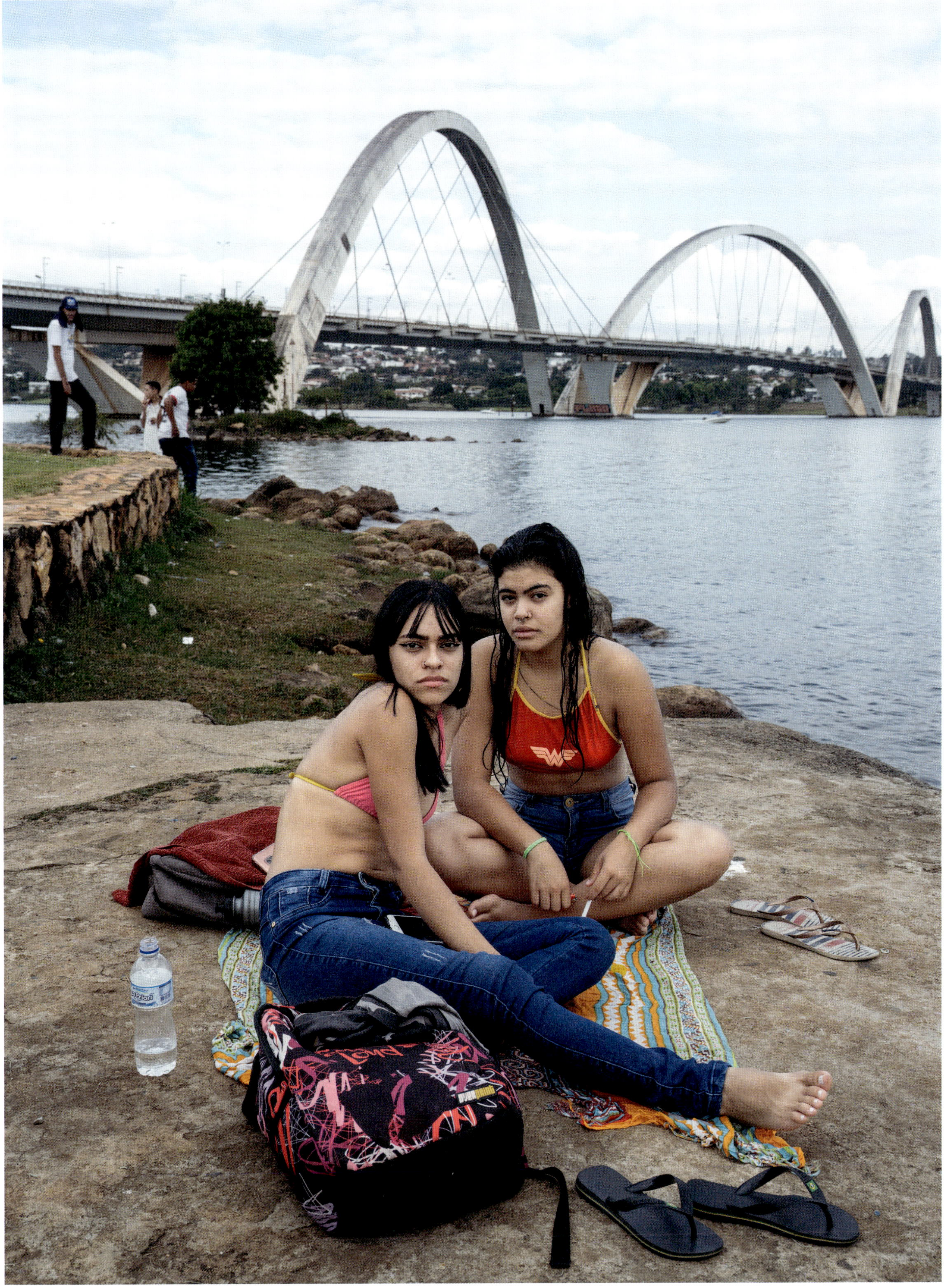

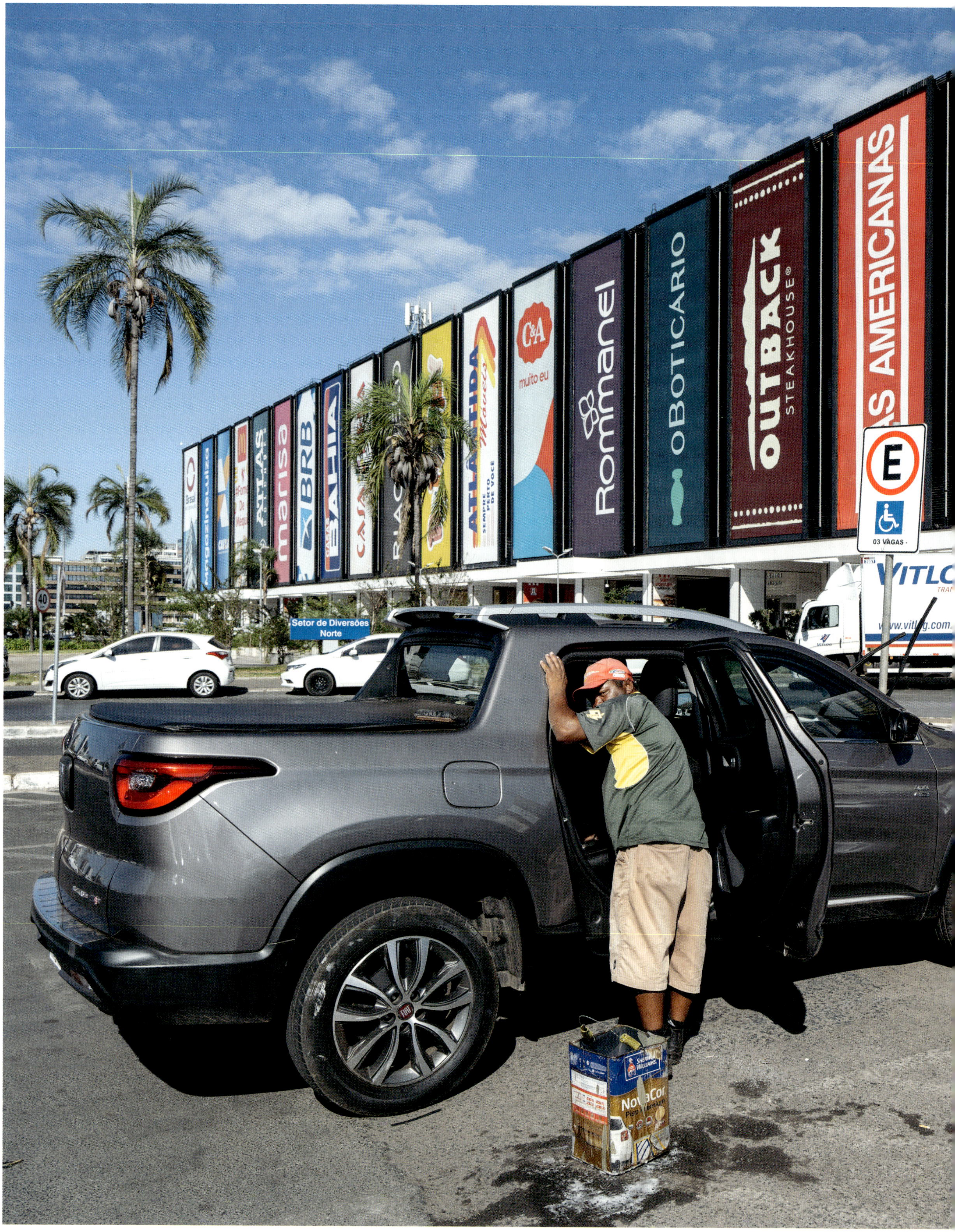
AS AMERICANAS
OUTBACK
STEAKHOUSE
OBOTICÁRIO
Rommanel
C&A
muito eu
marisa
BRB
BAHIA
Setor de Diversões
Norte
E
03 VAGAS
40

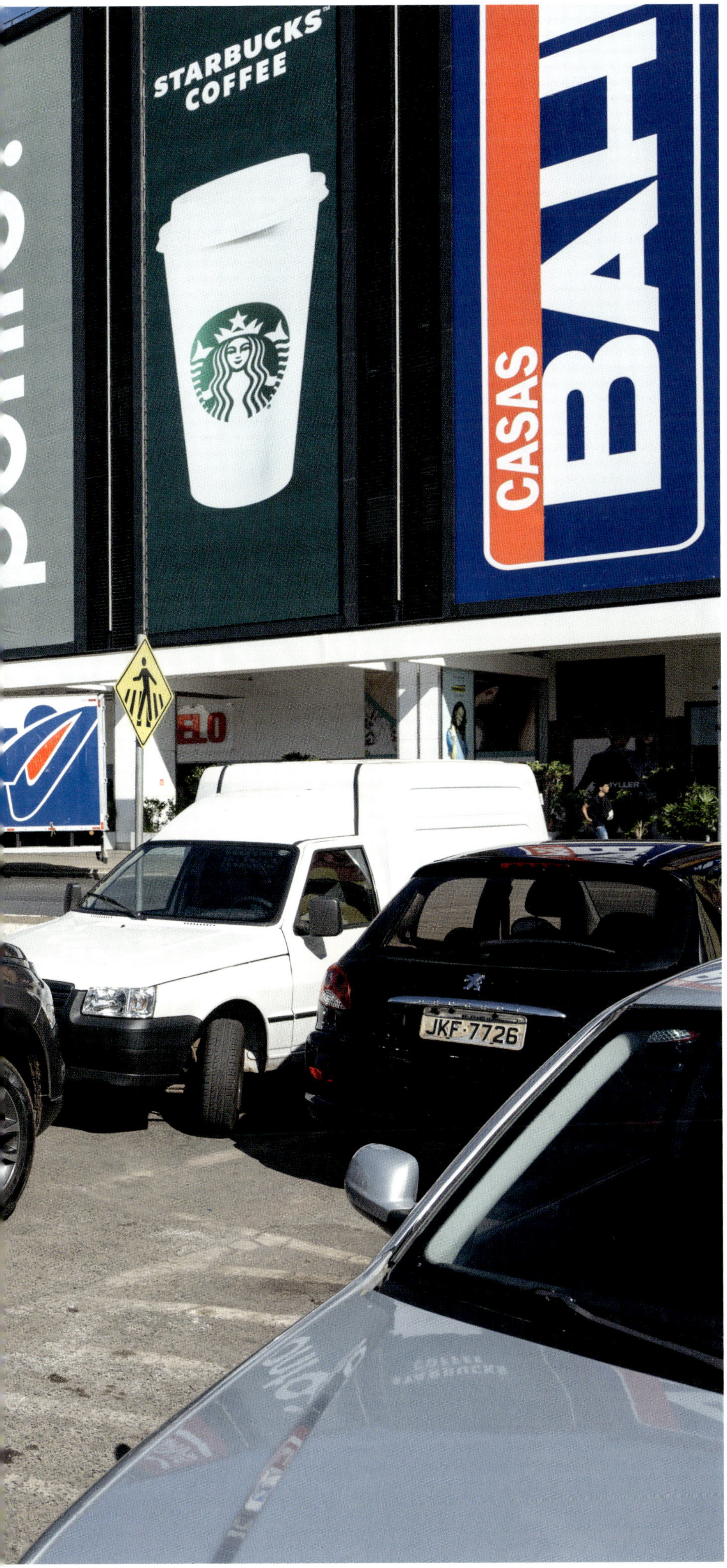

Shopping Conjunto Nacional, Brasília's first shopping mall.

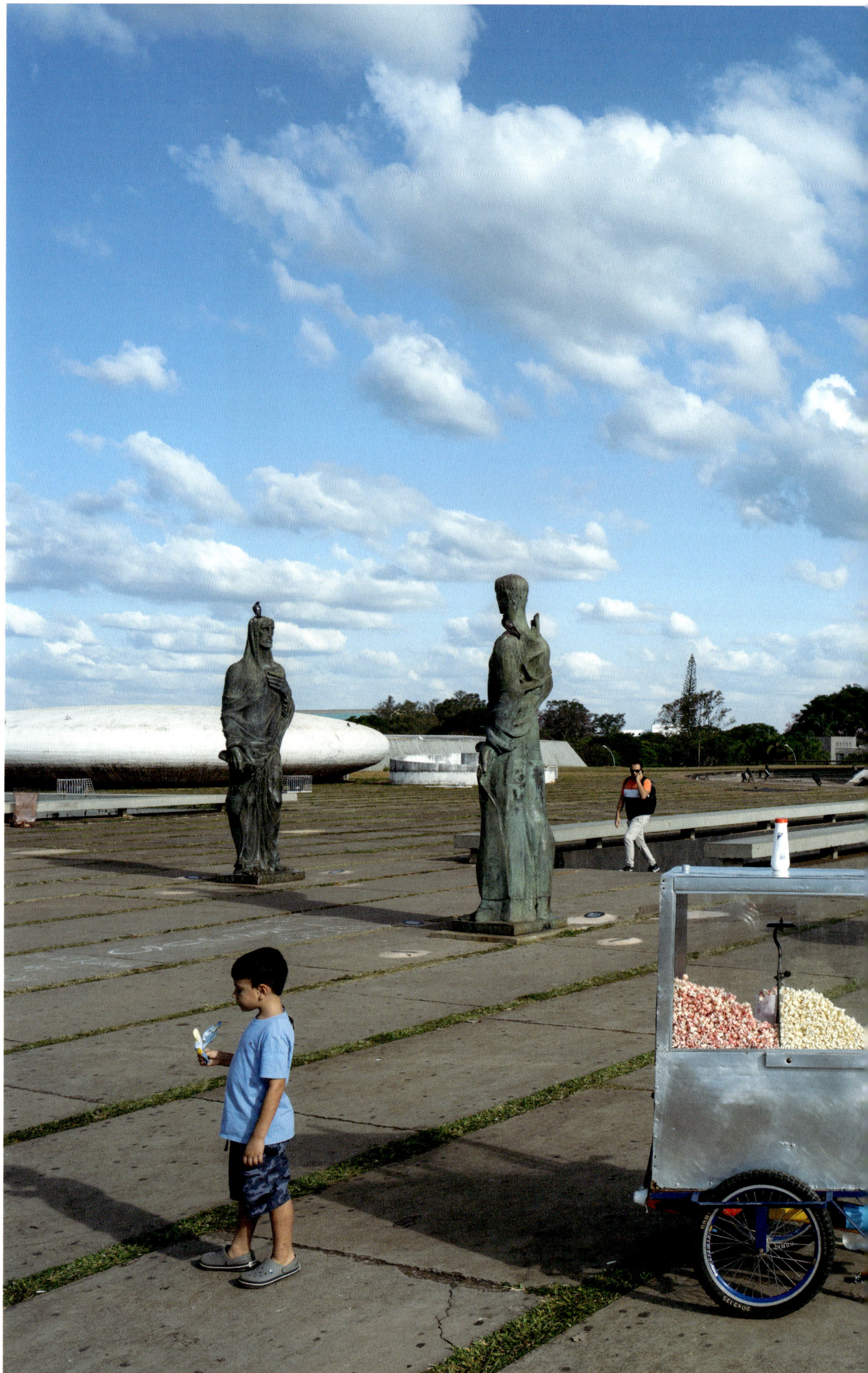

Metropolitan Cathedral of Brasília, designed by Oscar Niemeyer.

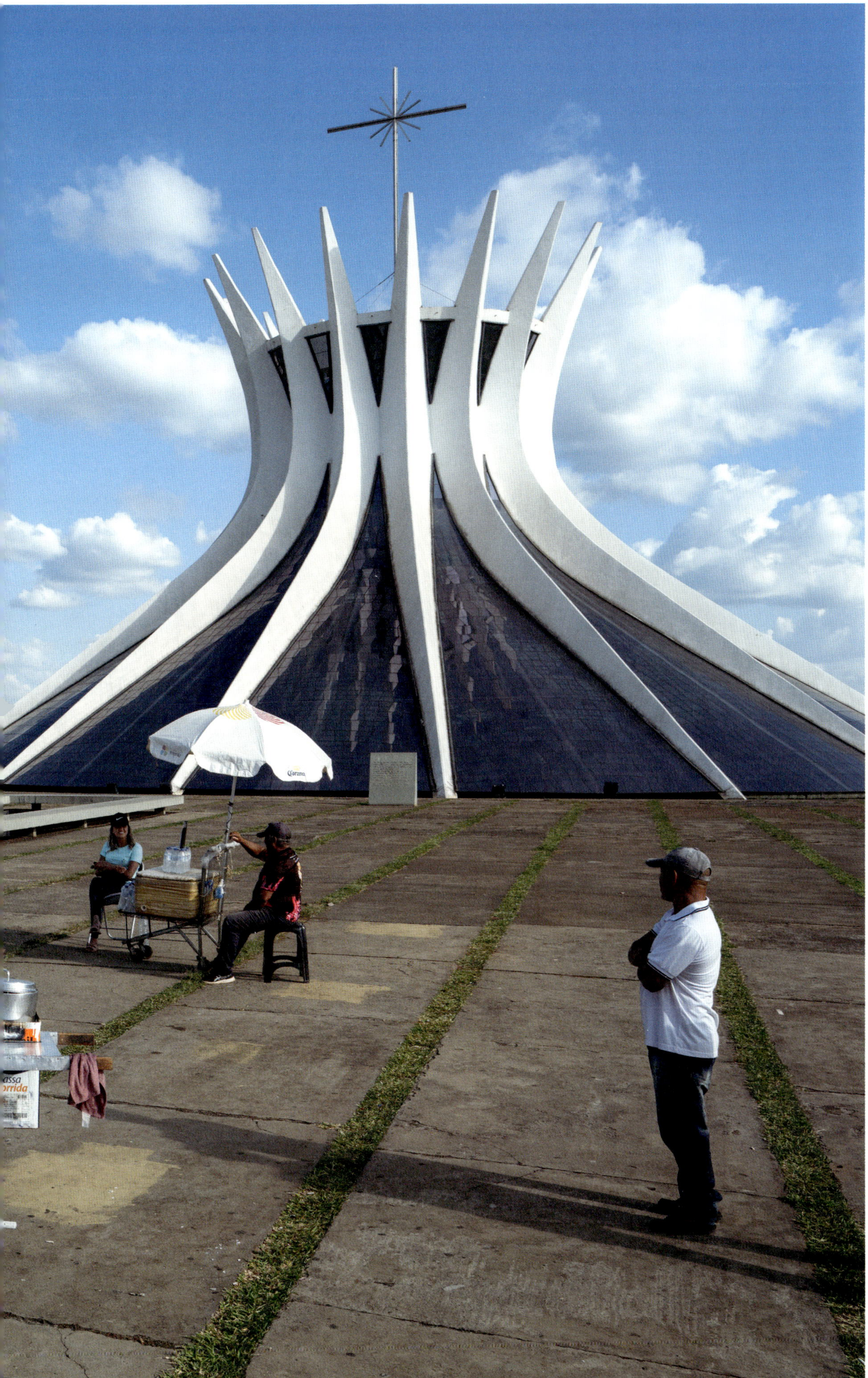

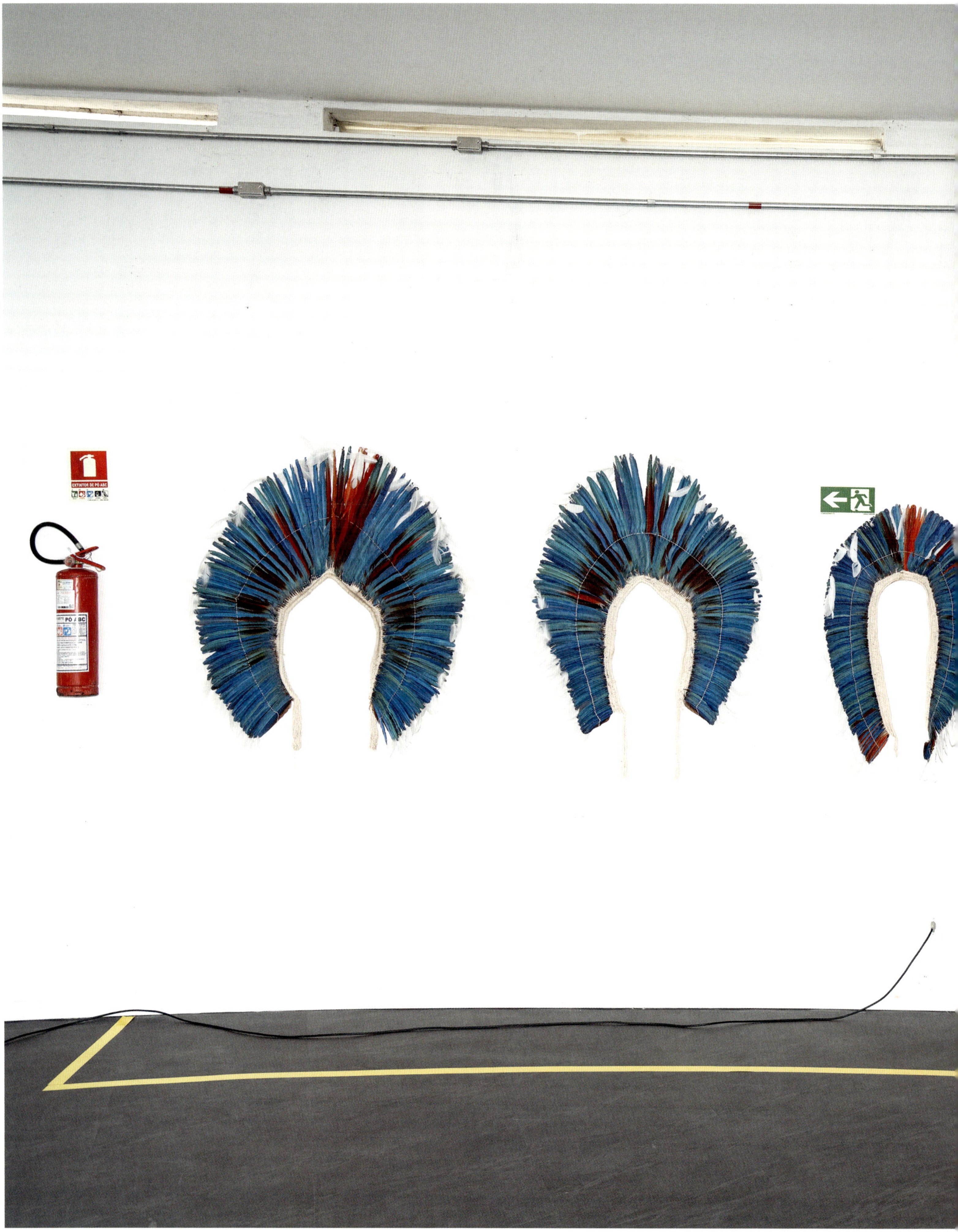
EXTINTOR DE PÓ ABC
PÓ ABC

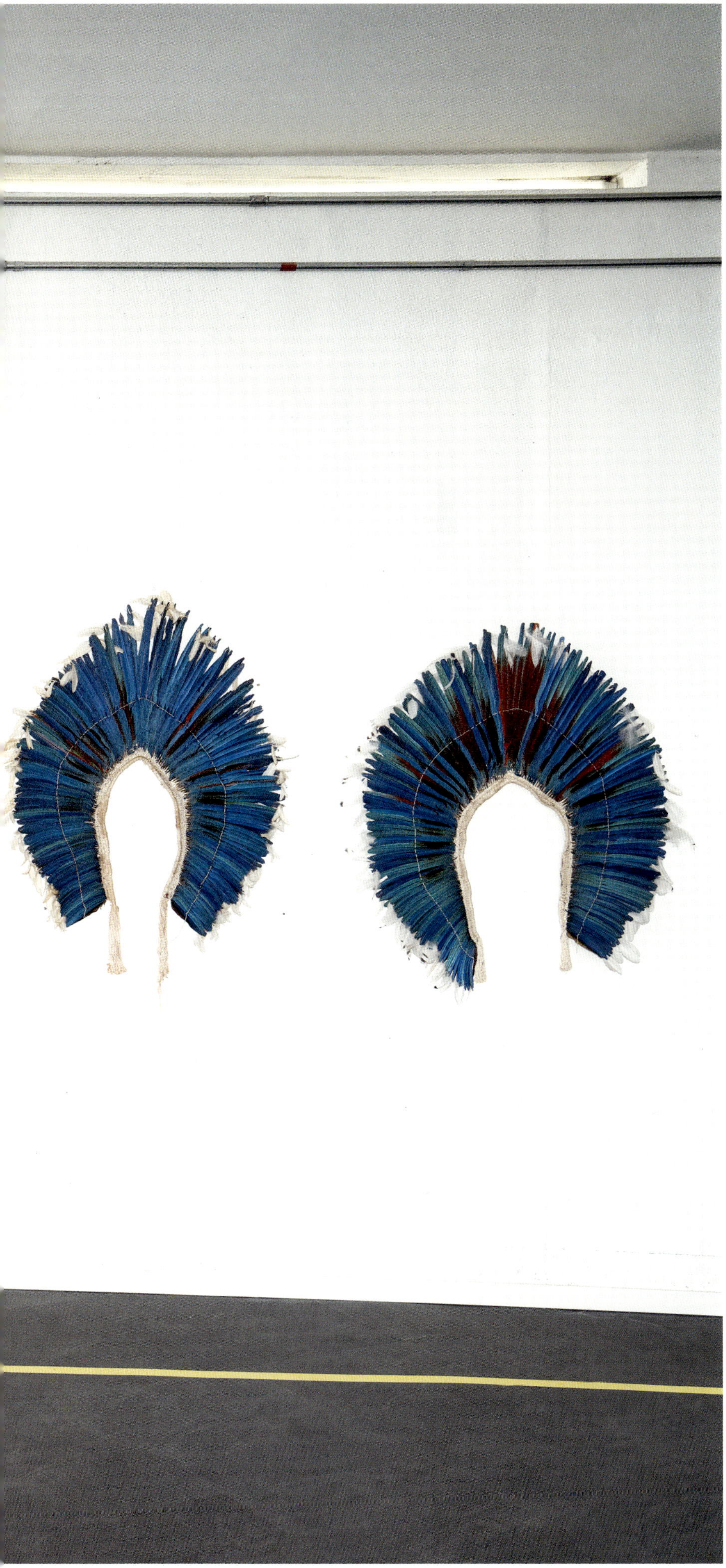

Feather headdresses at the Memorial of Indigenous Peoples.

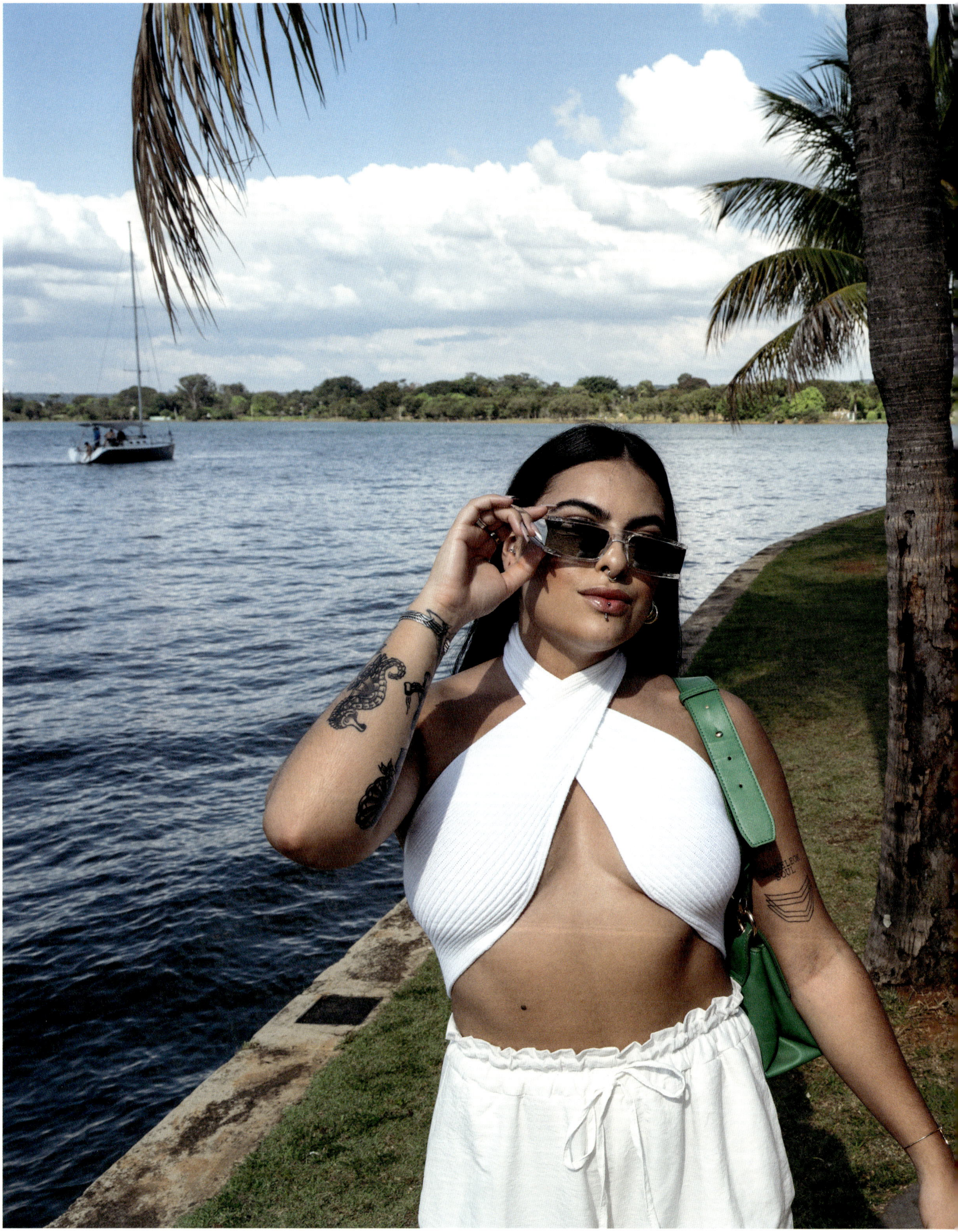

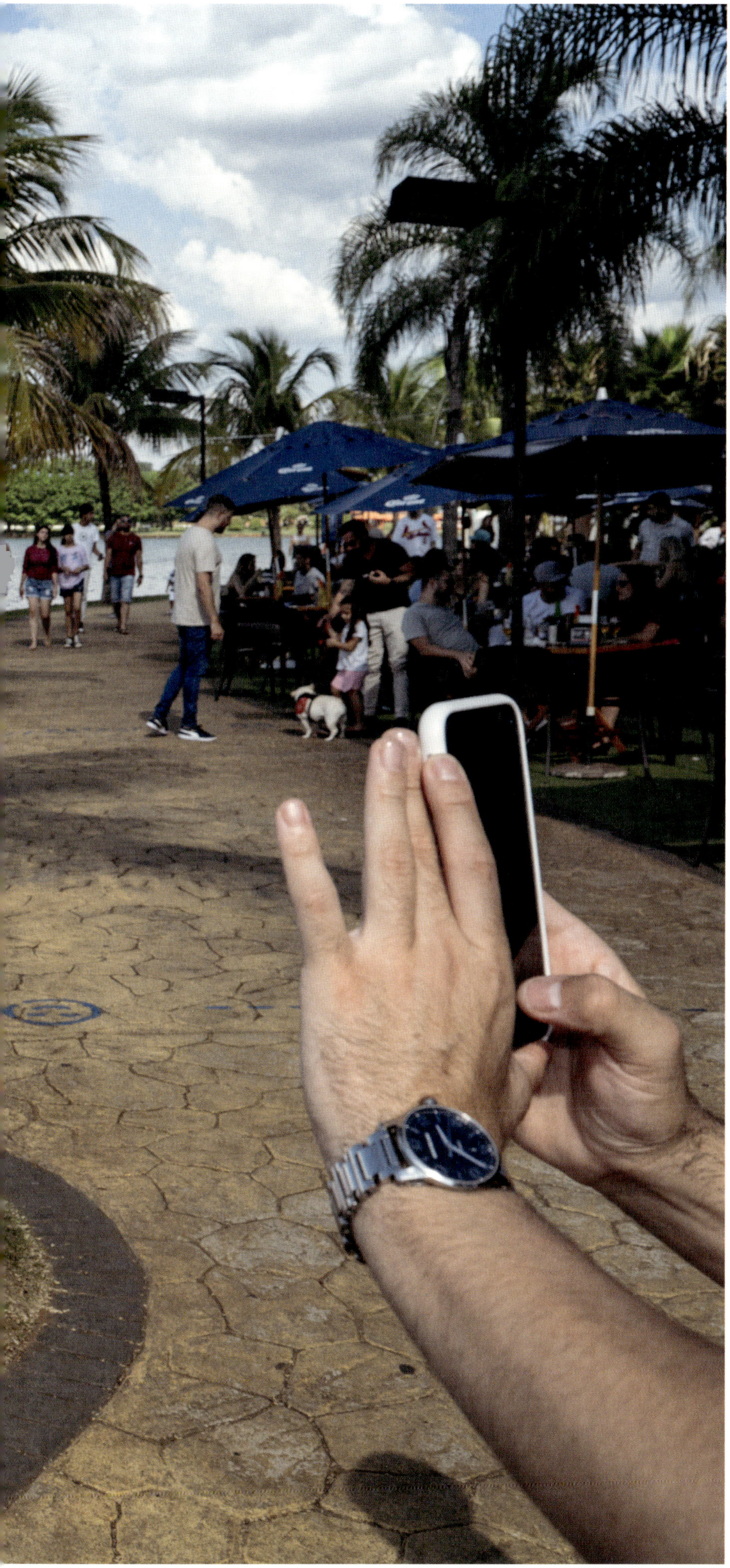

Pontão do Lago Sul leisure centre, Lake Paranoá.

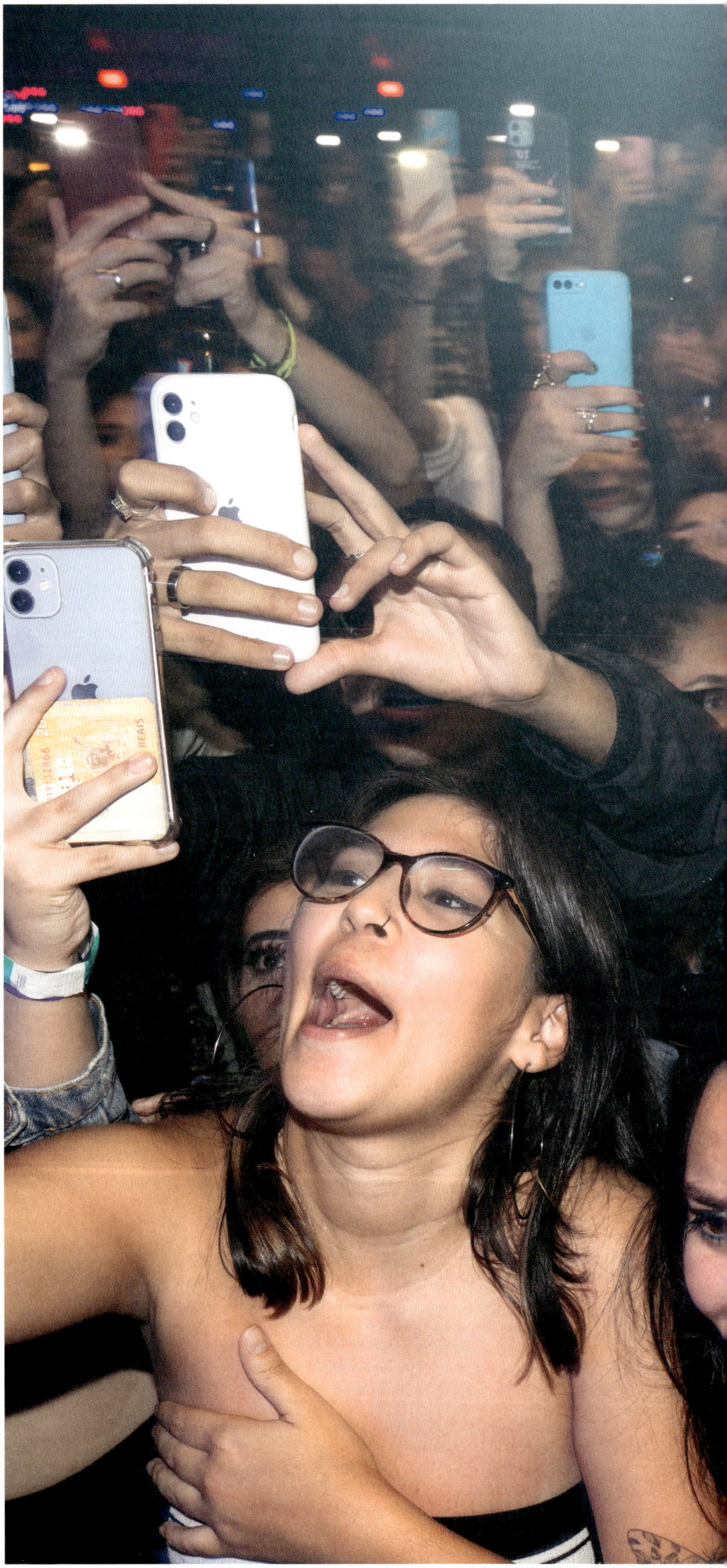

Concert by Brazilian rapper Delacruz
at Complexo Fora do Eixo.

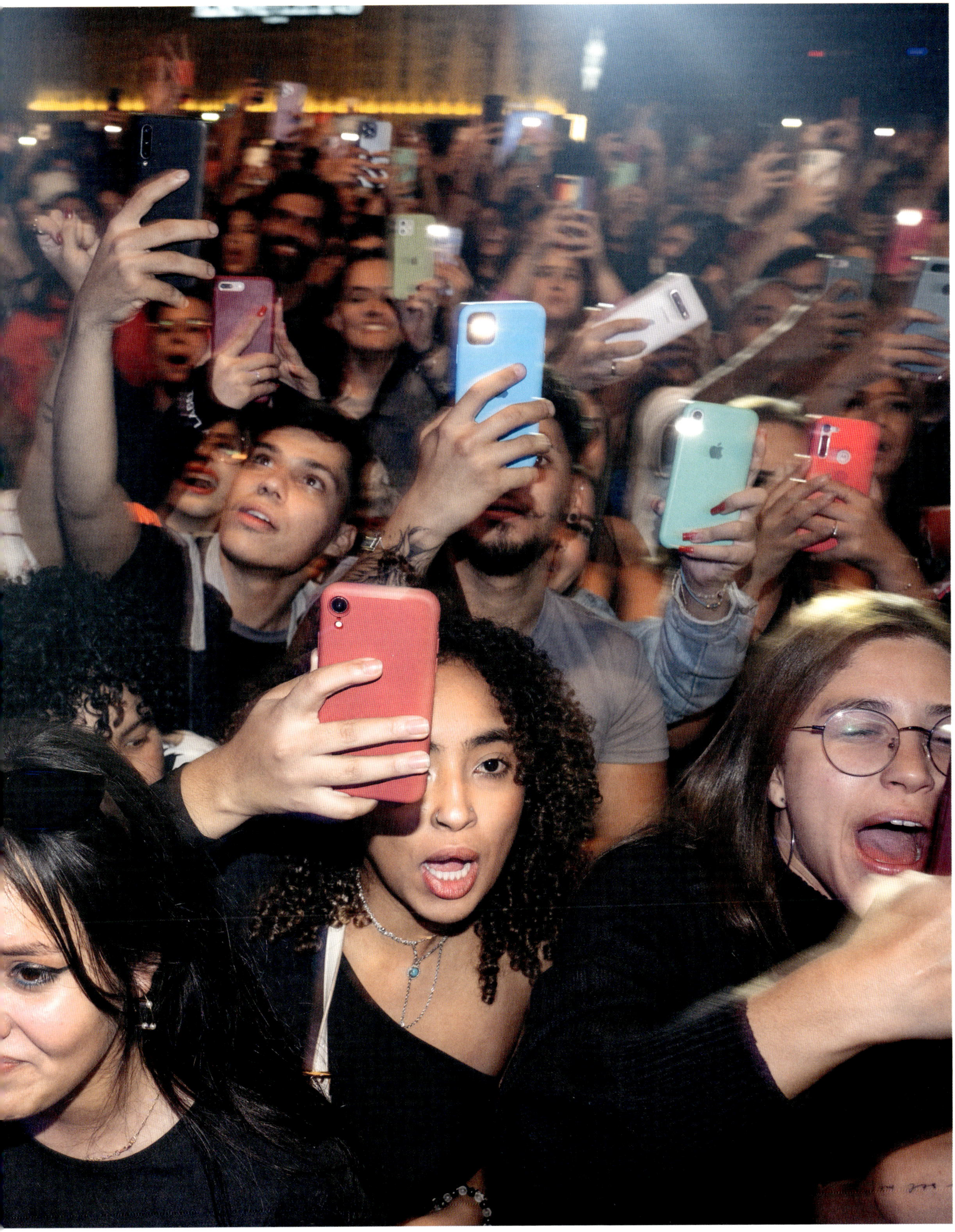

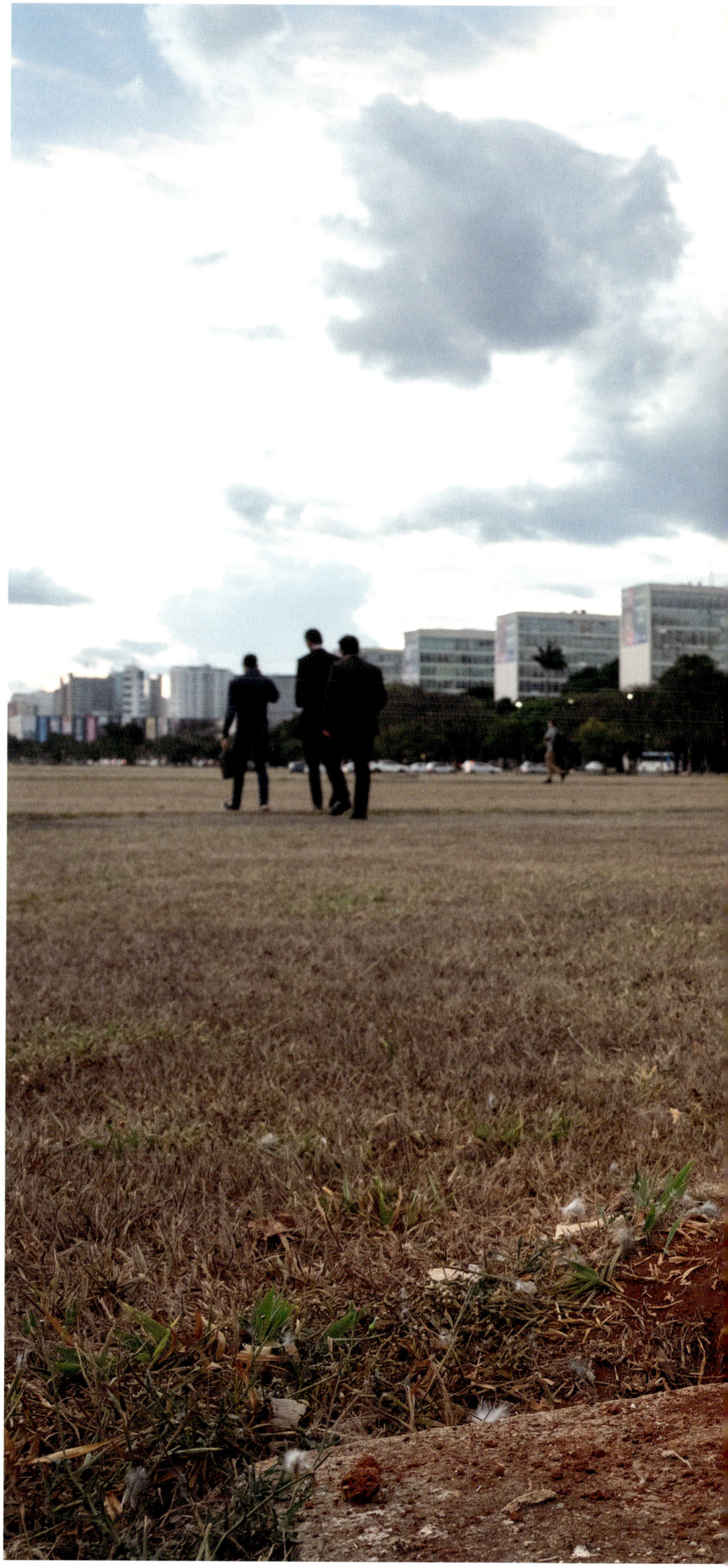

Burrowing owls nest on the Esplanade of the Ministries.

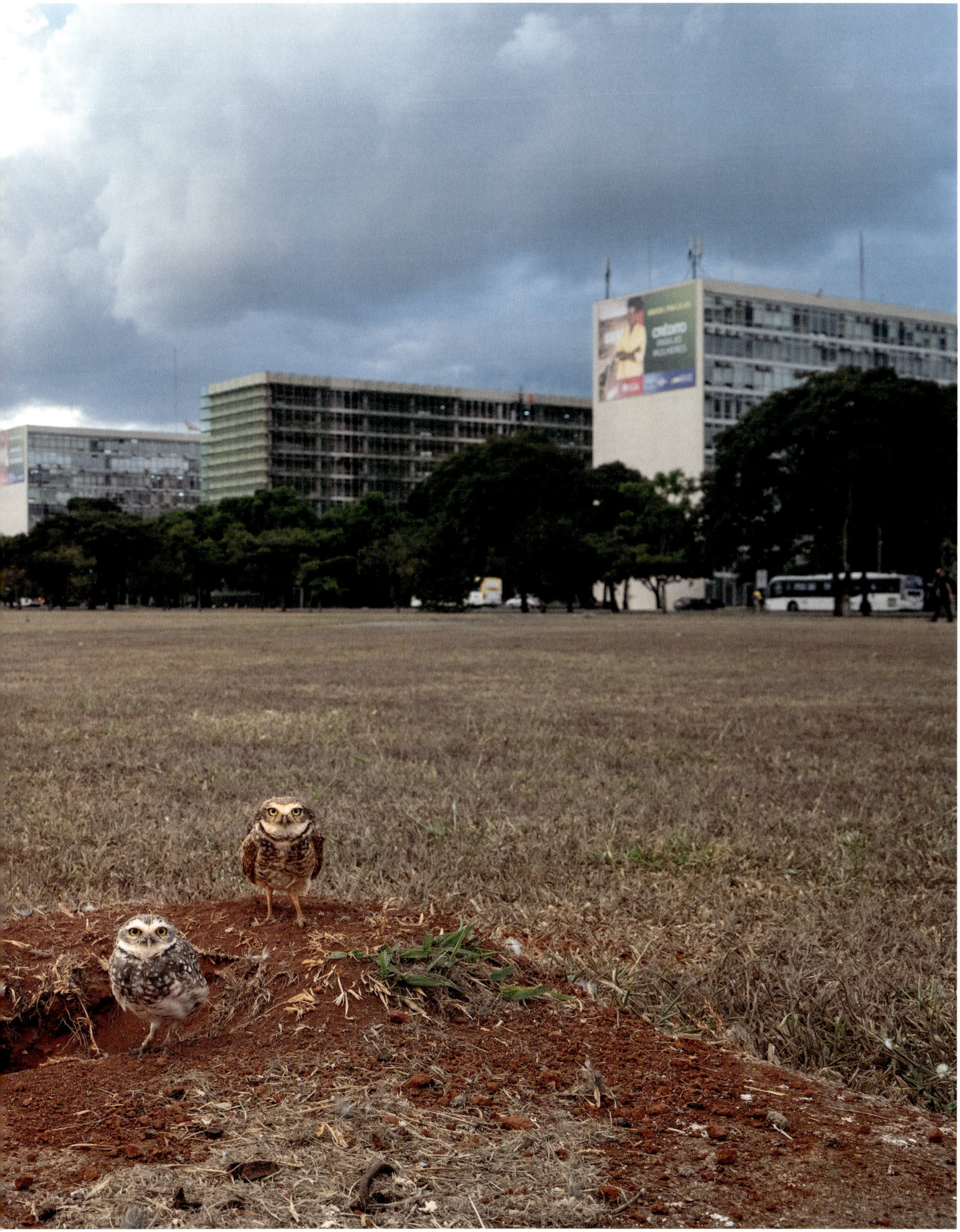

NIGERIA

ABUJA

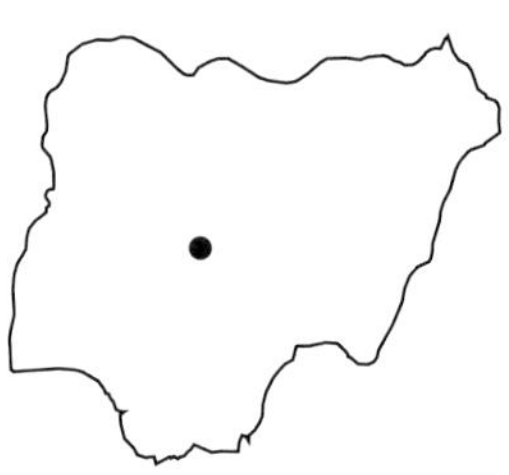

Start of construction: 1979
Inauguration date: 12 December 1991
Initiated by: General Murtala Muhammed
Master plan by: Thomas Todd — International Planning Associates; Kenzō Tange (Central Business District)
Urban agglomeration population in 2023: 3.8 million
Surface area: 1476 km^2
Former capital: Lagos

With 200 million inhabitants, Nigeria is Africa's most densely populated country. Roughly 10% of the population lives in the former capital, Lagos. To take the burden off it, a new city was built in the centre of the country in the 1980s. Abuja, officially inaugurated as the capital in 1991, was to become a leading and neutral city, strengthening unity within the ethnically and religiously divided country and spreading economic opportunities. In turn, Abuja became one of the fastest-growing cities in the world, with now almost 4 million inhabitants and a massive income gap.

Abuja is hard to capture in images. Despite its striking buildings, such as the Millennium Tower, the Abuja National Mosque and the National Ecumenical Centre, the city lacks a distinctive skyline. Abuja's planned urbanisation is a typical example of urban sprawl: a widespread urban area where motorways link the city's various neighbourhoods and facilities. Large open expanses give the city an unfinished appearance. In the Central Business District and even on the central reservation on the motorways, shepherds walk by with their herds of cattle. Just a stone's throw from the government district, farmers take over wasteland in order to grow crops.

Near Nnamdi Azikiwe International Airport, a new and prestigious city-within-a-city is being built, called Centenary City. 'Our model is Dubai,' explains property advisor Uchenna Aduba near the model of the complex. 'This will be the new heart of Abuja, with Africa's tallest tower, modern flats and luxury villas for celebrities, a five-star hotel, a golf course, an amusement park and a shopping centre. There will even be an urban safari park, but only with harmless animals such as antelopes and kangaroos. An art bazaar will sell crafts. This way, we can promote our culture without visitors having to go into the city. All of Centenary City will be a tax-free zone and will be completely walled in. Safety above all else. Only those who live or work here will get in. And tourists, of course.'

The security problem in Nigeria is real. Jihadists and criminals have developed a thriving business model based on kidnapping and extortion. Those who can afford it therefore live in one of the many luxurious estates, private residential areas that are sealed off from the chaos of the outside world, gated, with rolls of razor wire and manned checkpoints. They are safe havens, where lawns are neatly manicured and SUVs are parked in the driveways. A friendly man invites me into his garden. His pool is half filled with dirty green water. 'Well, after a while you get tired of a pool like that too.'

In Moscow Underground, one of Abuja's most famous clubs, a pint costs €11. Beer, however, is rarely drunk here. It is mostly bottles of whisky and champagne that are festively lit and brought out by sexy hostesses, so everyone can see where the money is. Clubbing is a status symbol.

Nigeria is not a poor country. Its wealth of natural resources and oil made it Africa's third-largest economy. And yet you cannot avoid poverty. In the entertainment districts and at the junctions in central Abuja, hawkers scrape together their daily income by selling chewing gum or windscreen wipers. An all-terrain vehicle with tinted windows skims past a crippled beggar sitting on a board fitted on a roller skate.

On the construction site for a new residential development, a builder whispers his salary to me: 3,000 naira a day, or €4. In town, recruitment posters for workers are put up here and there. They state the salary: 1,500 naira (€2) a day or 10,000 naira (€15) a week. This immediately explains the large number of staff in the hotel and hospitality sector. According to a 2022 United Nations report, 40% of Nigerians are living on less than US$1 a day.

What this means becomes clear during a visit to Mpape. Abuja's largest slum consists of a labyrinth of dusty alleys with open sewers, mud houses with corrugated iron roofs and rubbish dumps on the side. Residents fetch water from the collective pump. Many houses have a red cross painted on the wall, a sign that the property is unlawful and will be torn down.

The extreme poverty and inequality are due not to a lack of resources, but to the misuse of said resources. The political and economic elite has lost all touch with the daily lives of ordinary Nigerians. Corruption and bribery are rife in all walks of life. In the meantime, skyrocketing inflation is pushing even more people into the abyss.

More than once, photography sessions on the streets of Abuja lead to animosity. At such times, the usefulness of a fixer becomes obvious. When I take a picture of the World Trade Center towers, a female soldier pounces on me out of nowhere. She grabs my camera strap and does not let go. A group of bystanders looks on, resigned. The woman rambles on, tempers flaring. My fixer Majesty tries in vain to calm her down. She gestures for us to come with her to her tent. Once there, she offers us a chair and suddenly changes her tune. Majesty slips her some money. We are allowed to go. 'This is Nigeria,' he sighs. 'If you refuse to pay, you won't get anything done. On the contrary, your life will be made miserable.'

April 2023

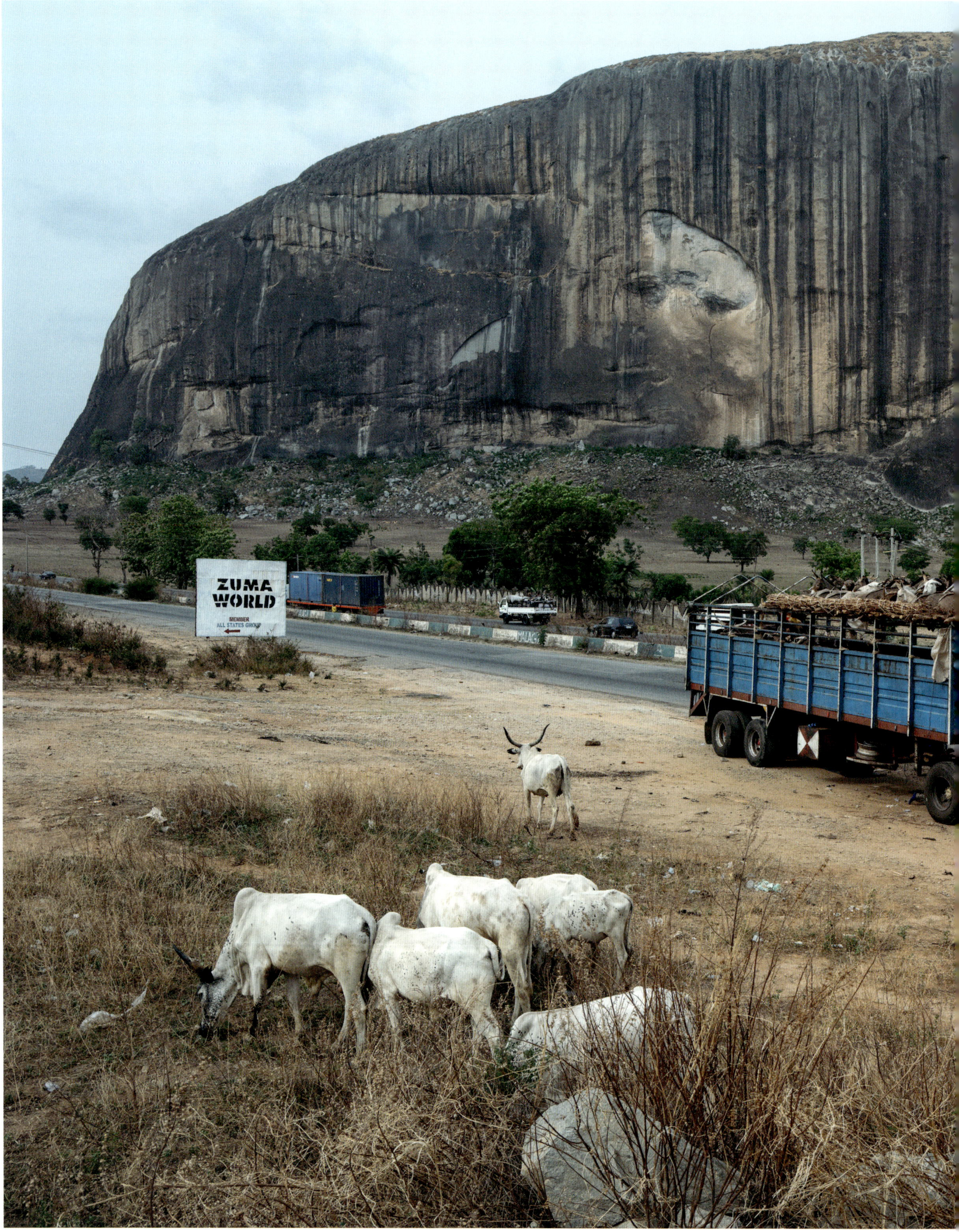
ZUMA
WORLD
MEMBER
ALL STATES GROUP

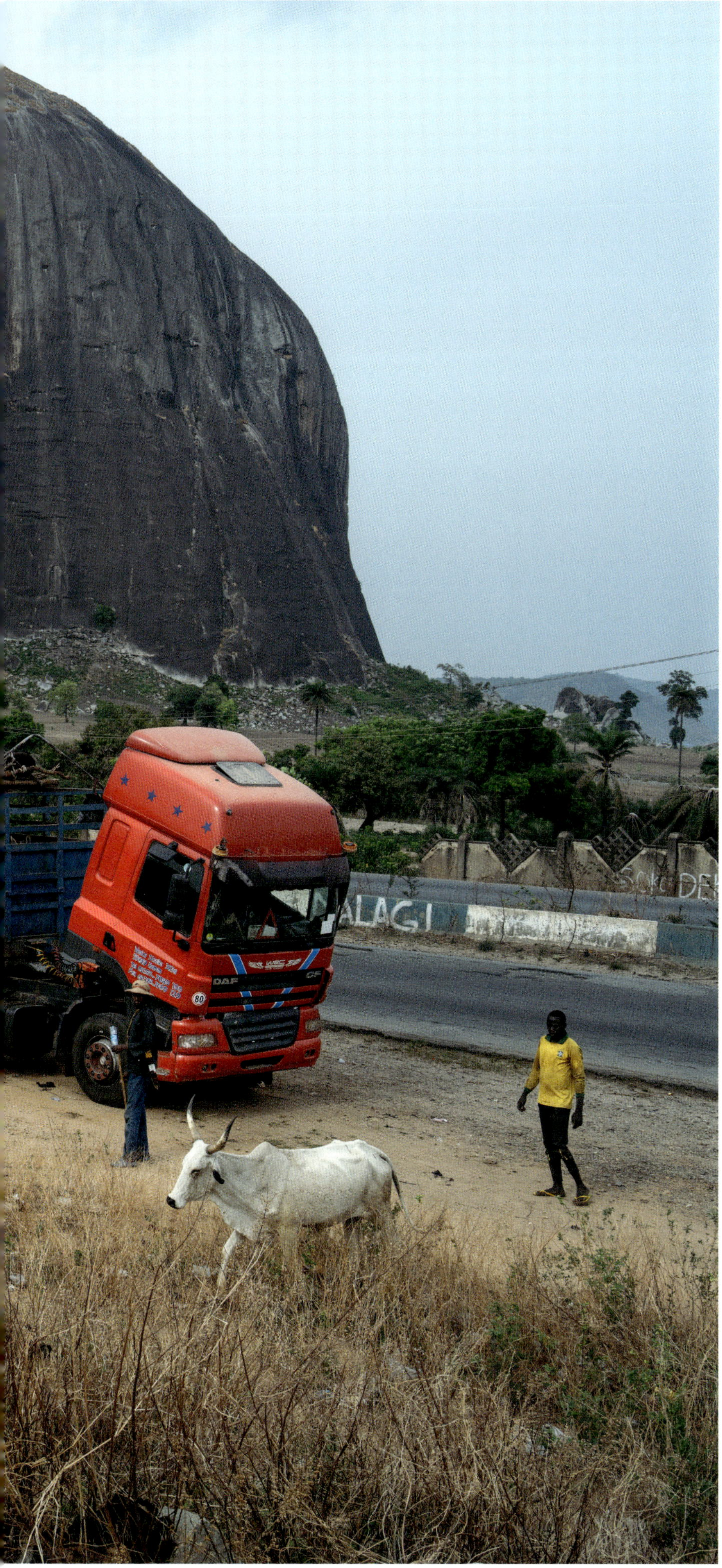

Zuma Rock, a 300-metre-high monolith
west of Abuja, has become a national symbol.

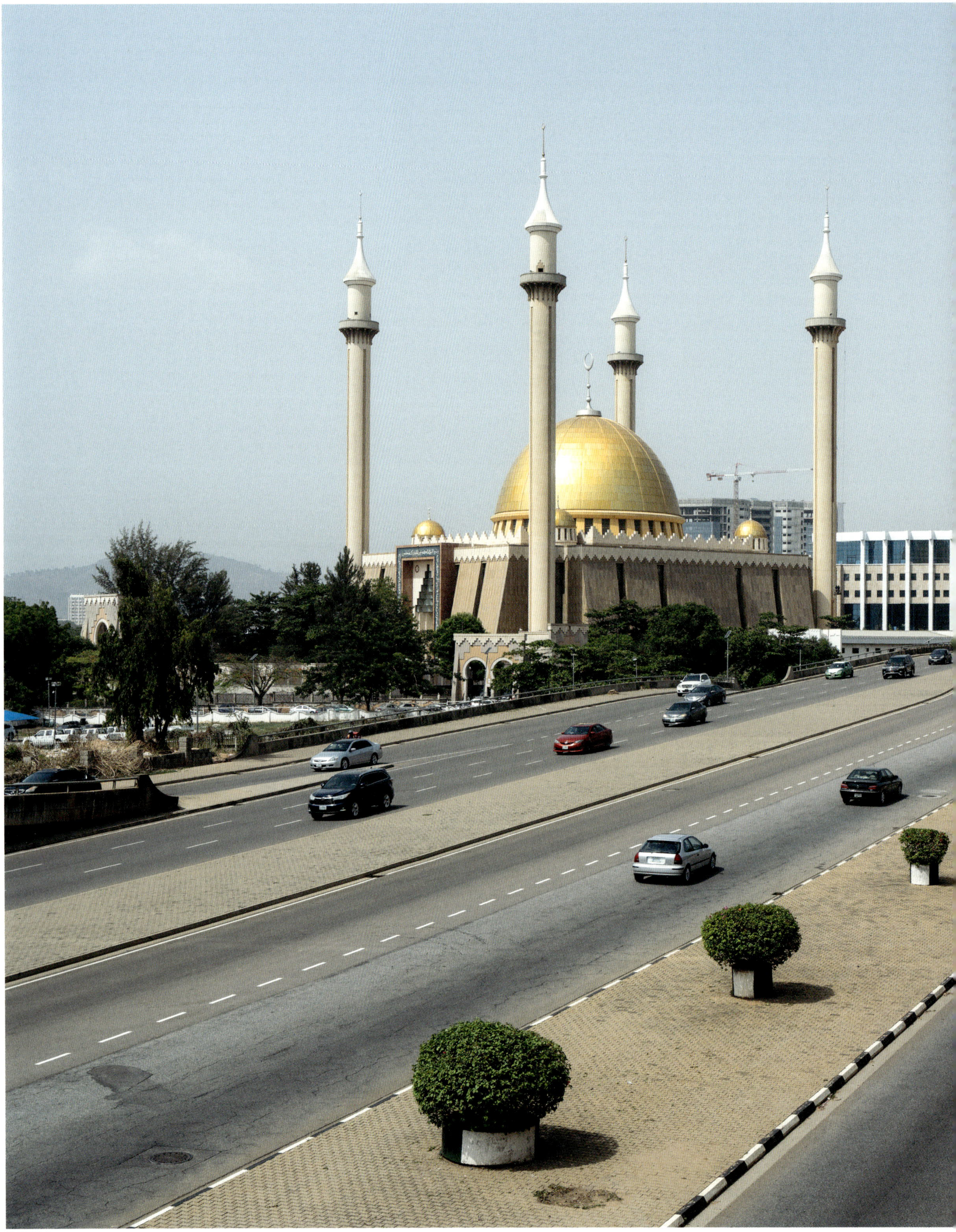

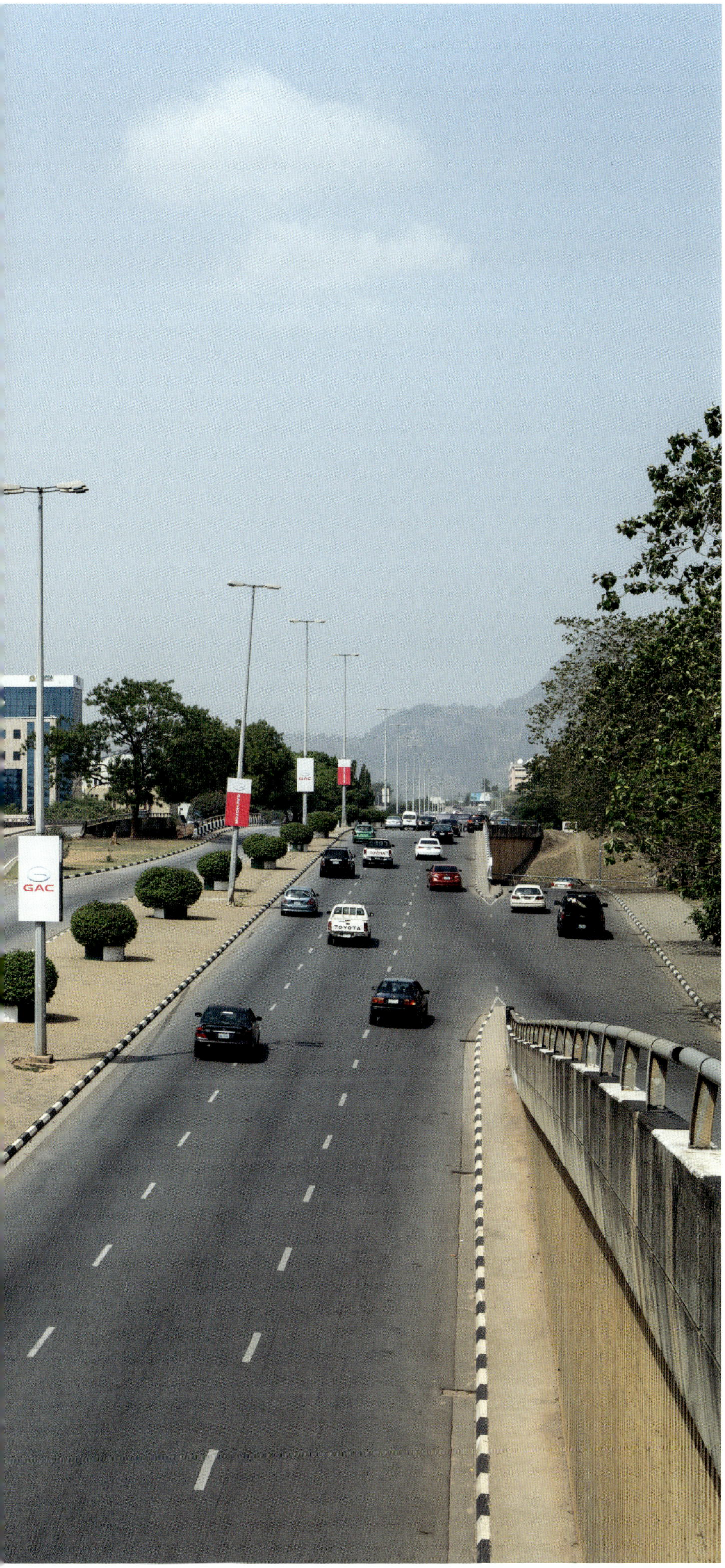

Abuja National Mosque on Independence Avenue.

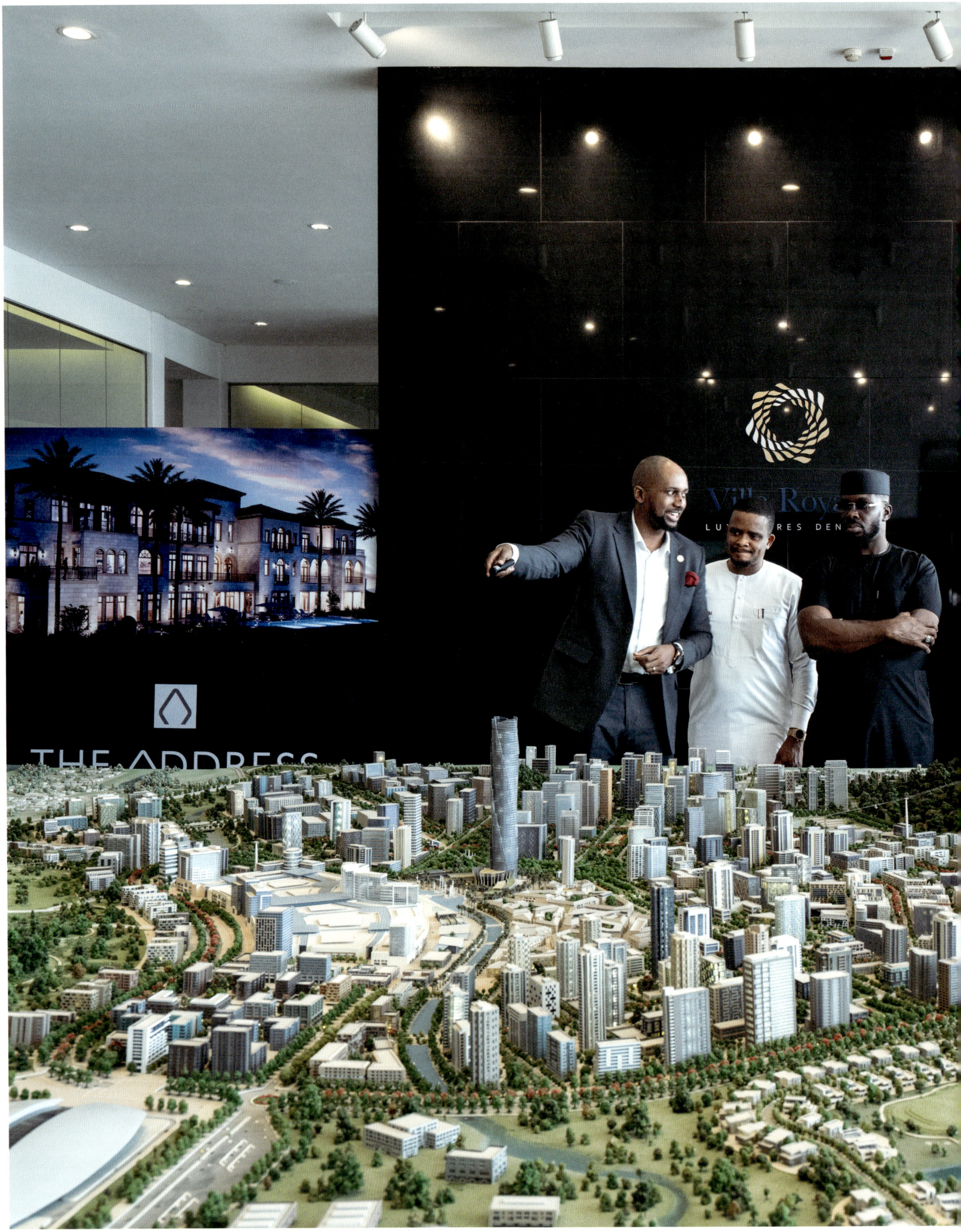

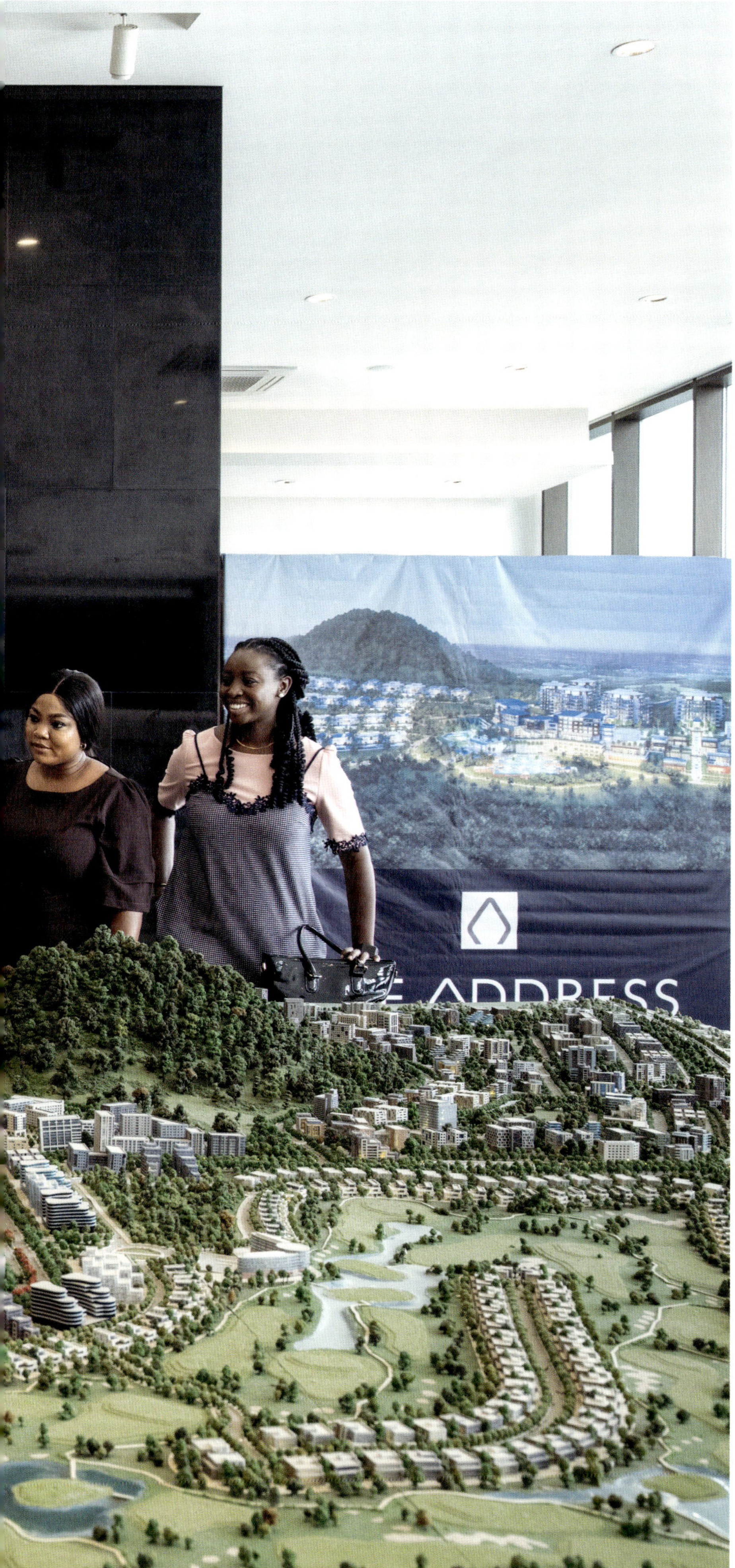

Sales office at Centenary City, a planned gated city-within-a-city near the international airport.

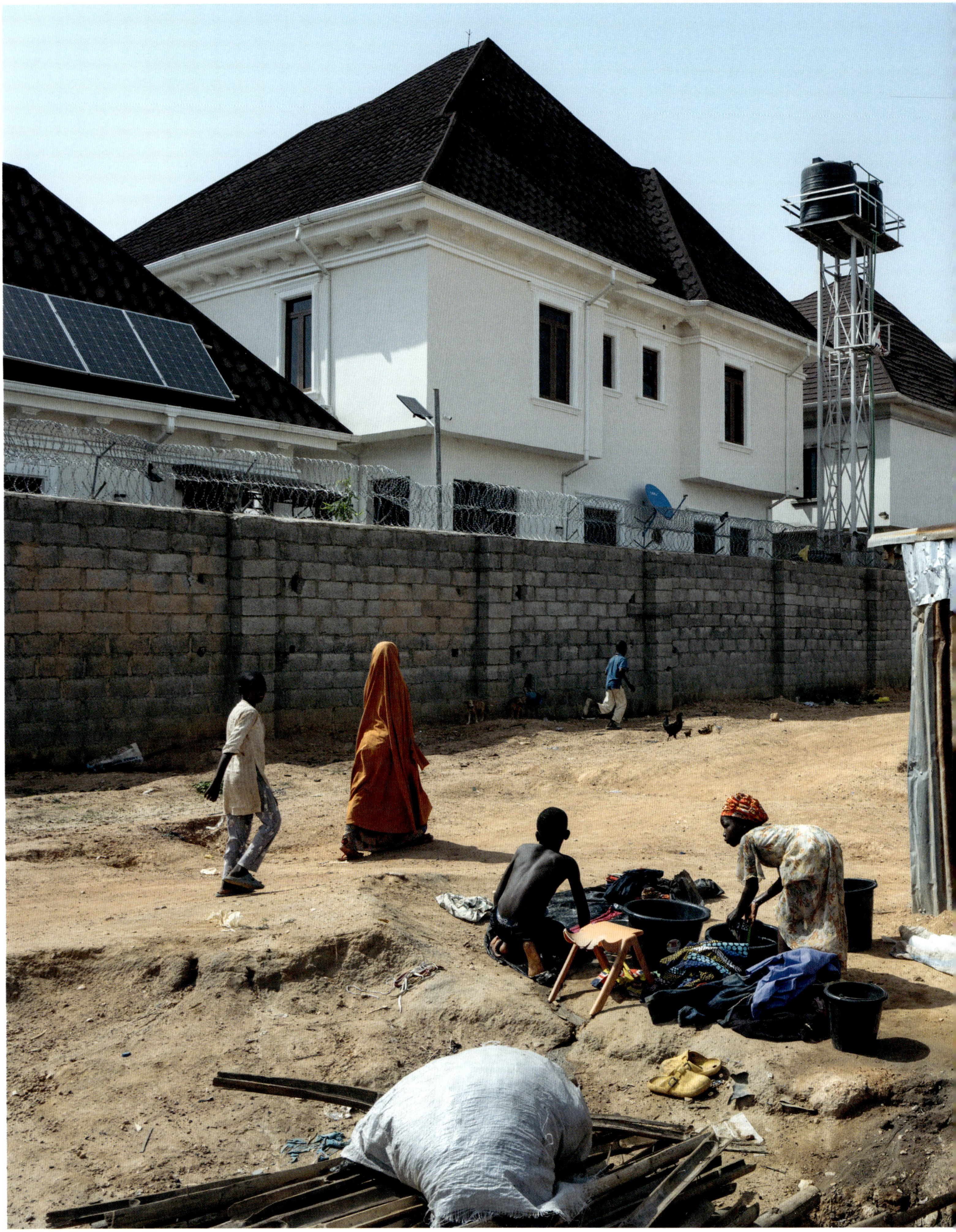

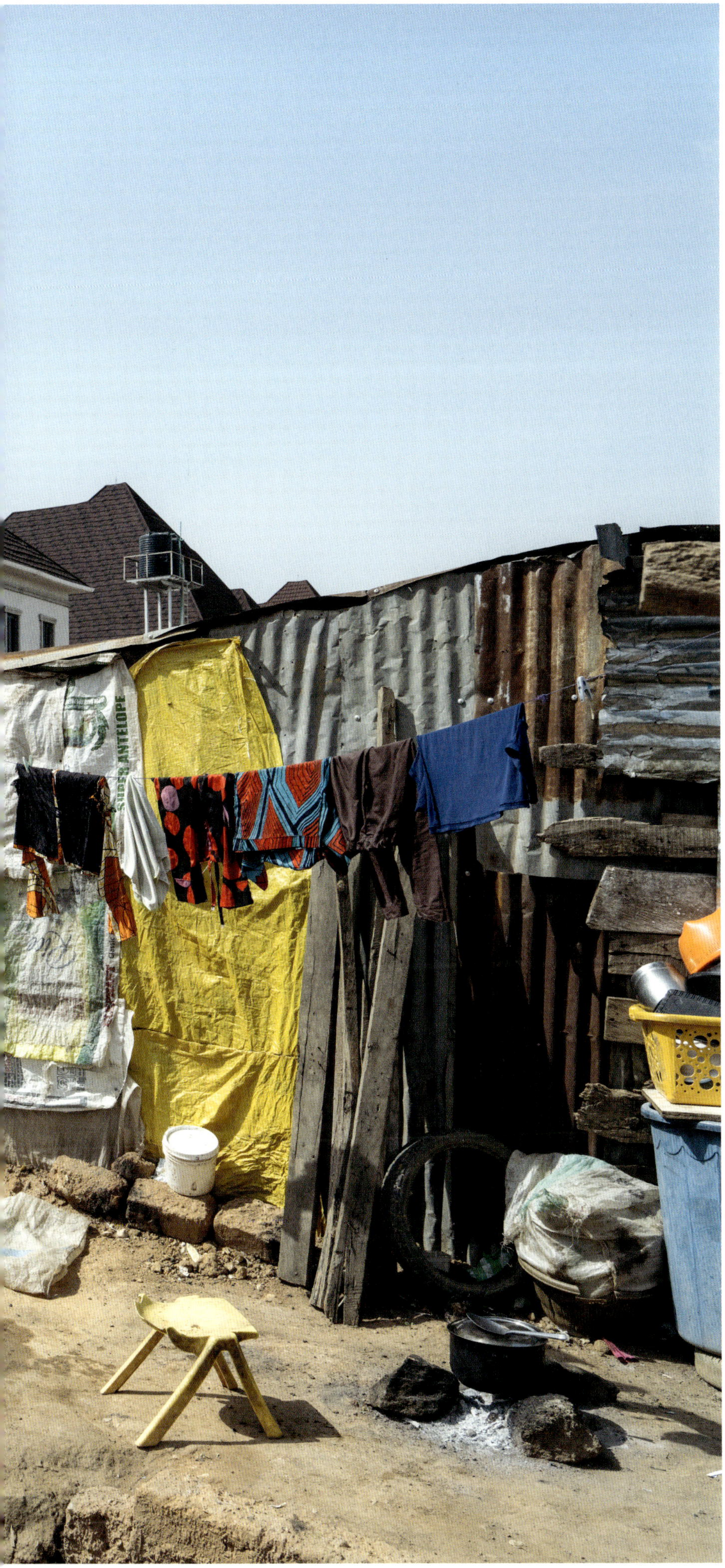

Slum outside MAB Global Estate, Gwarinpa district.

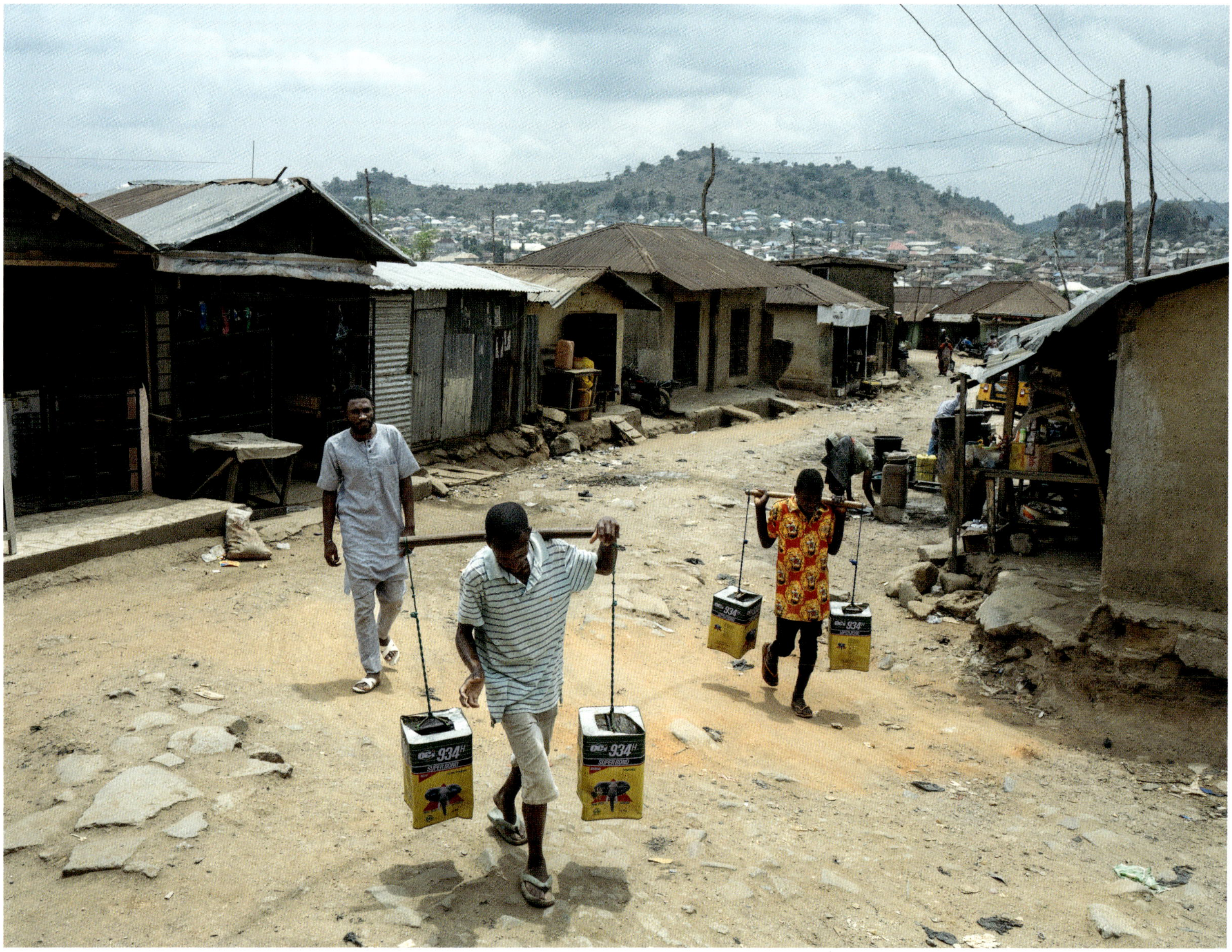

Mpape slum.

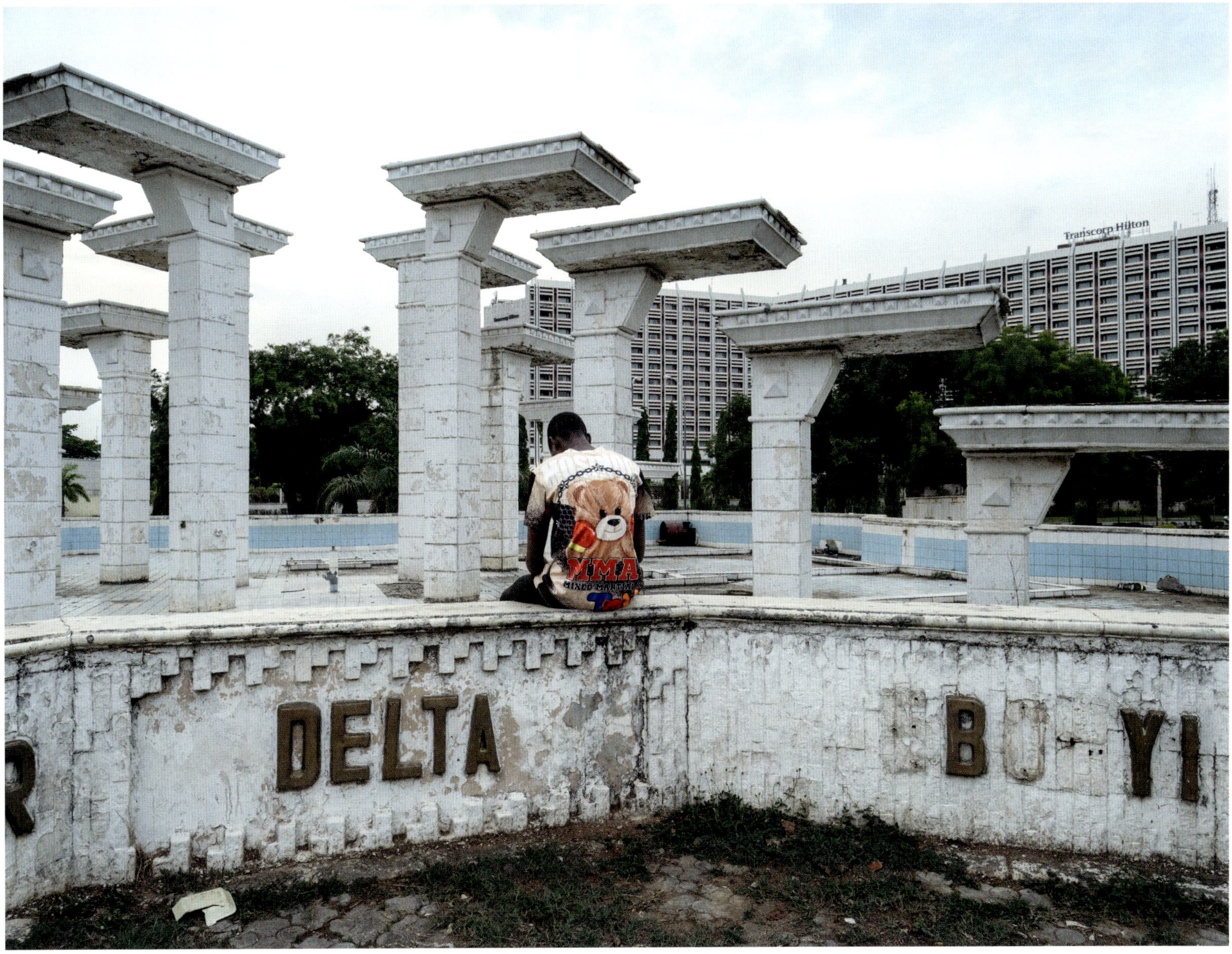

Unity Fountain, a symbol of the country's unity, near five-star Transcorp Hilton Abuja.

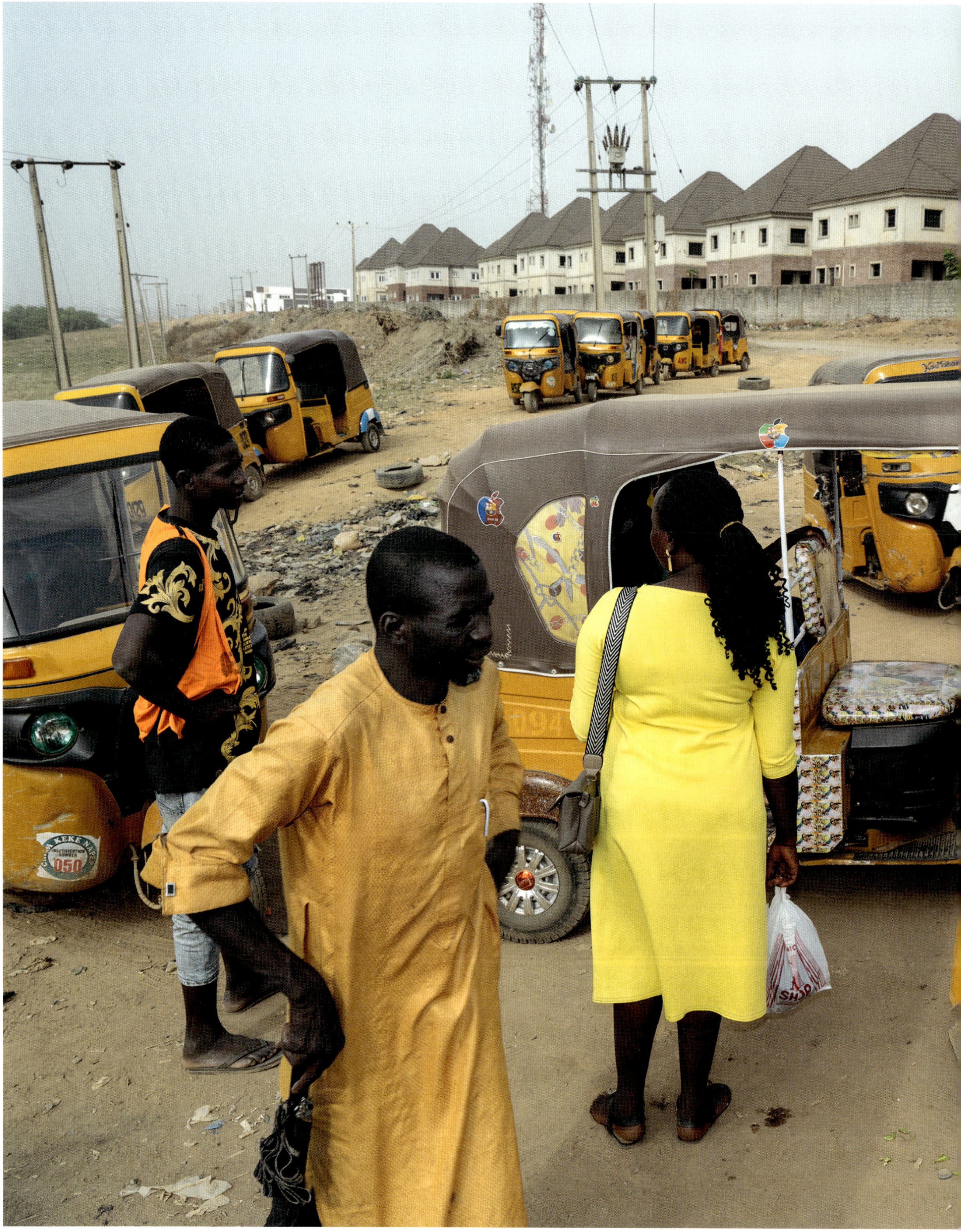
050

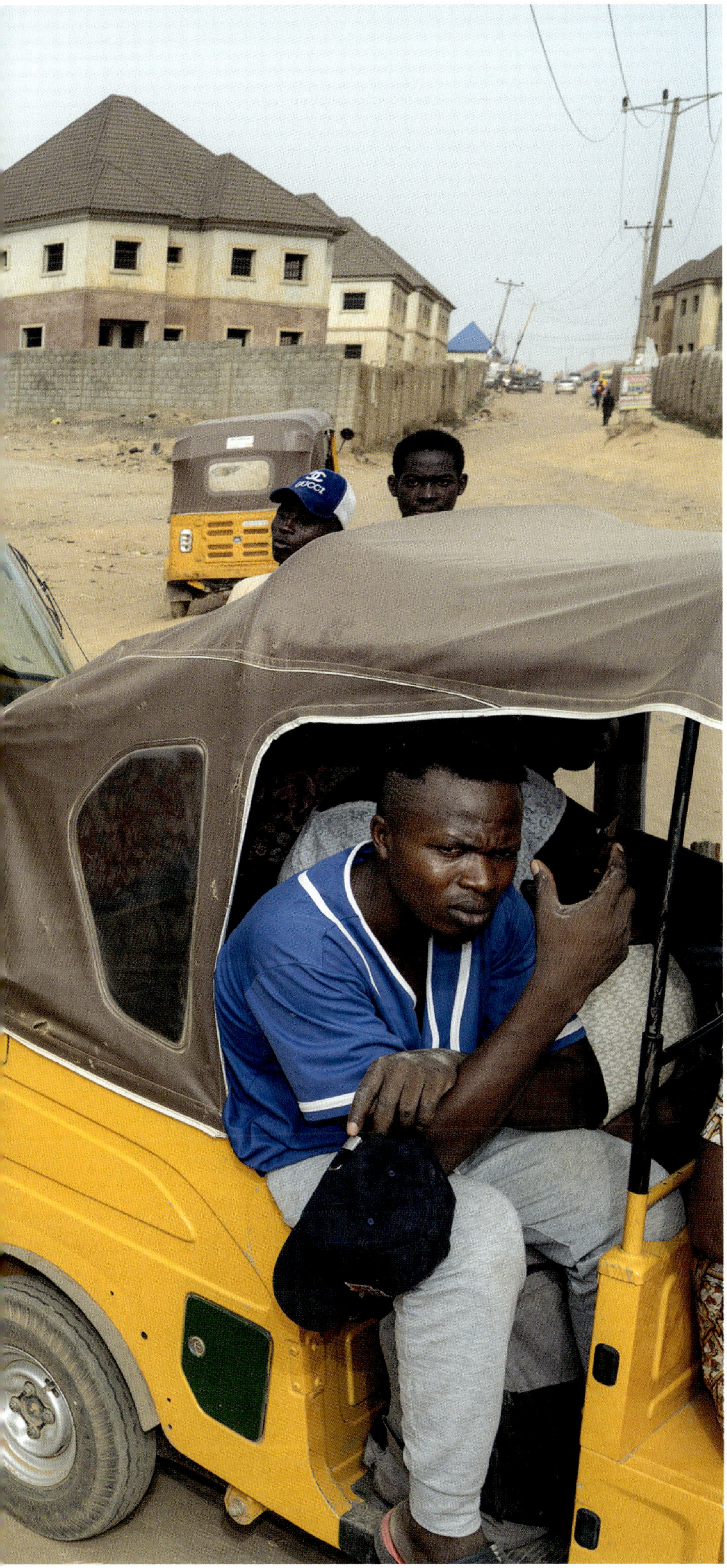

Taxi tricycle stand along Airport Road.

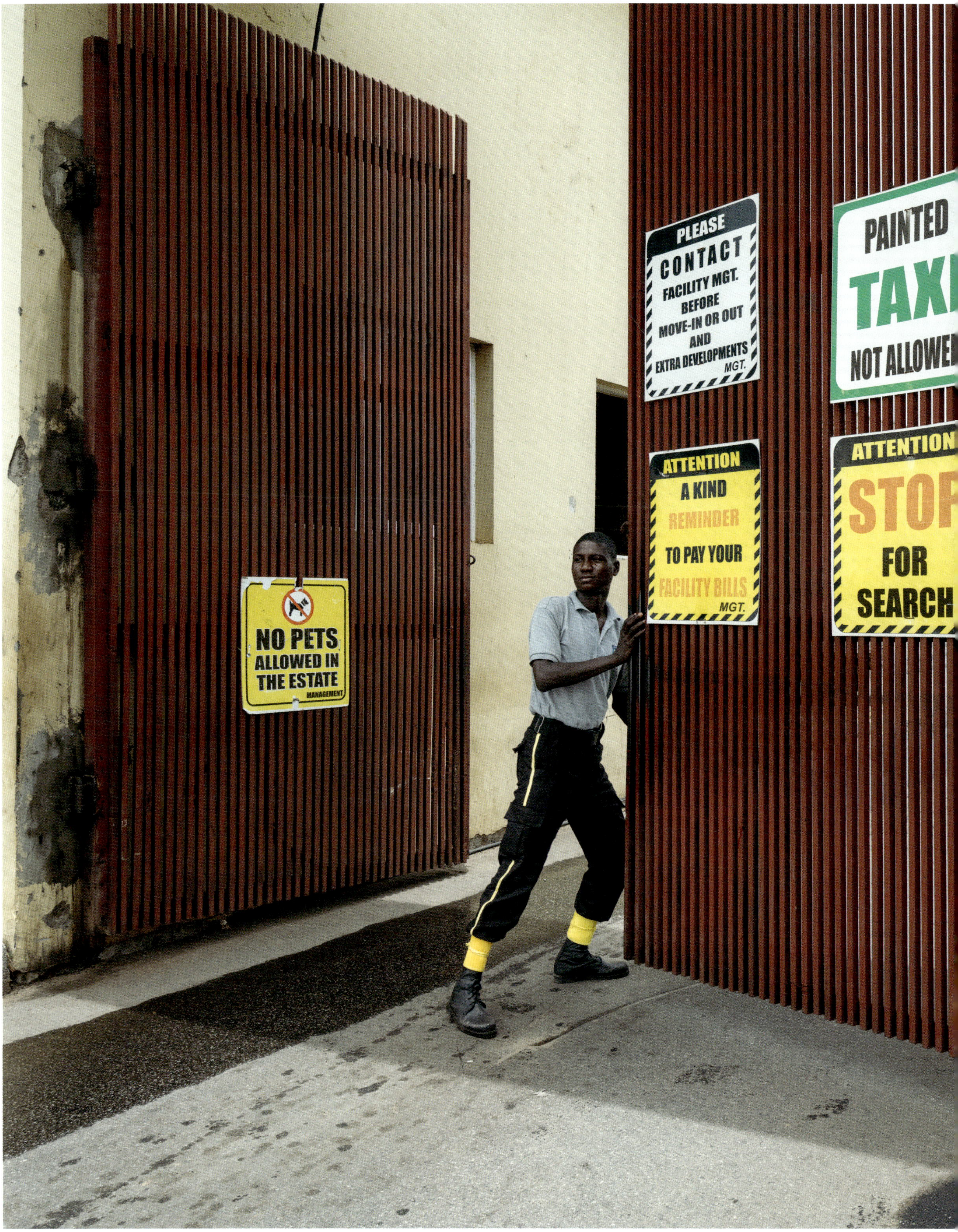
NO PETS
ALLOWED IN
THE ESTATE
MANAGEMENT
PLEASE
CONTACT
FACILITY MGT.
BEFORE
MOVE-IN OR OUT
AND
EXTRA DEVELOPMENTS
MGT.
ATTENTION
A KIND
REMINDER
TO PAY YOUR
FACILITY BILLS
MGT.
PAINTED
NOT ALLOWE
ATTENTION
FOR
SEARCH

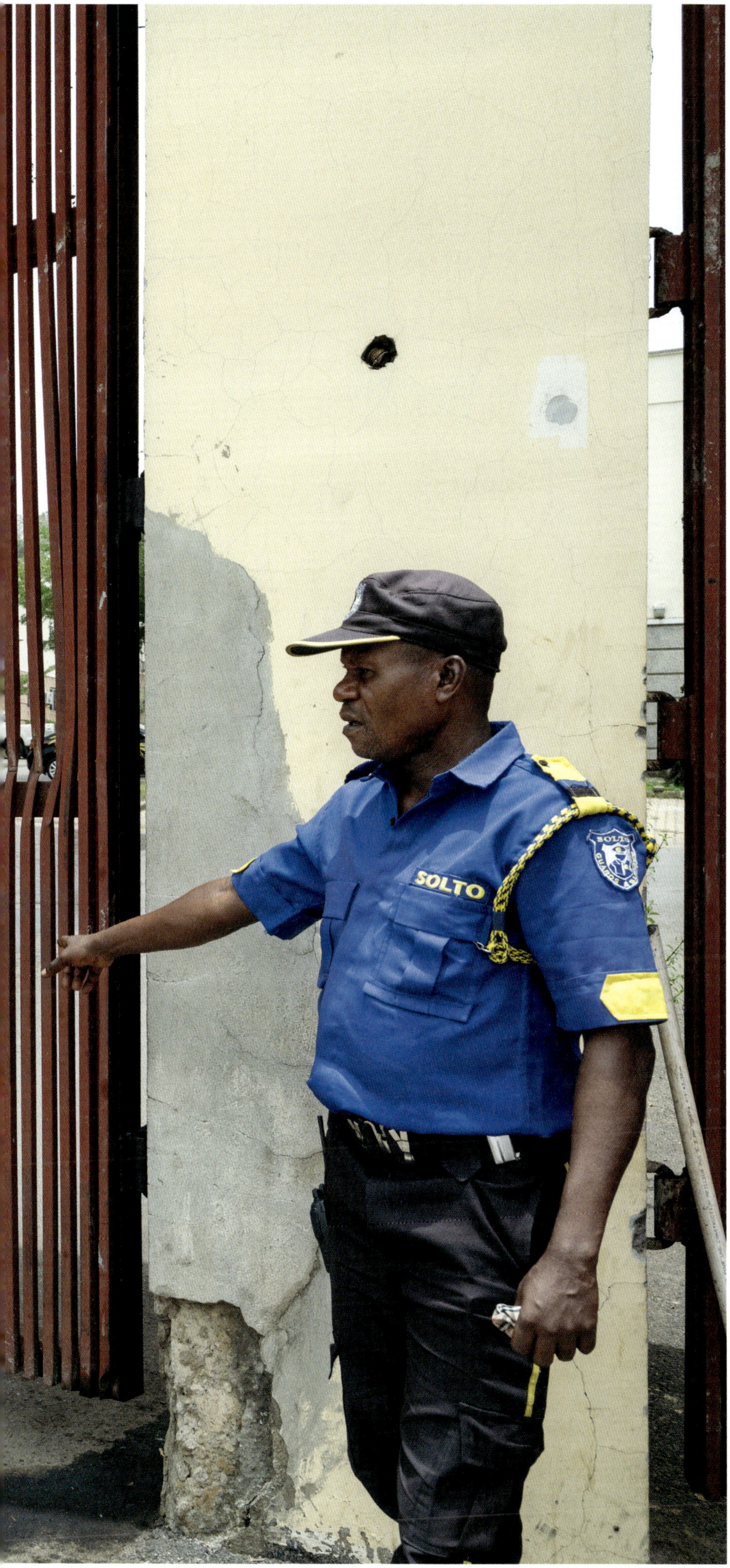

Entrance gate to Brains & Hammers City Estate, Life Camp district.

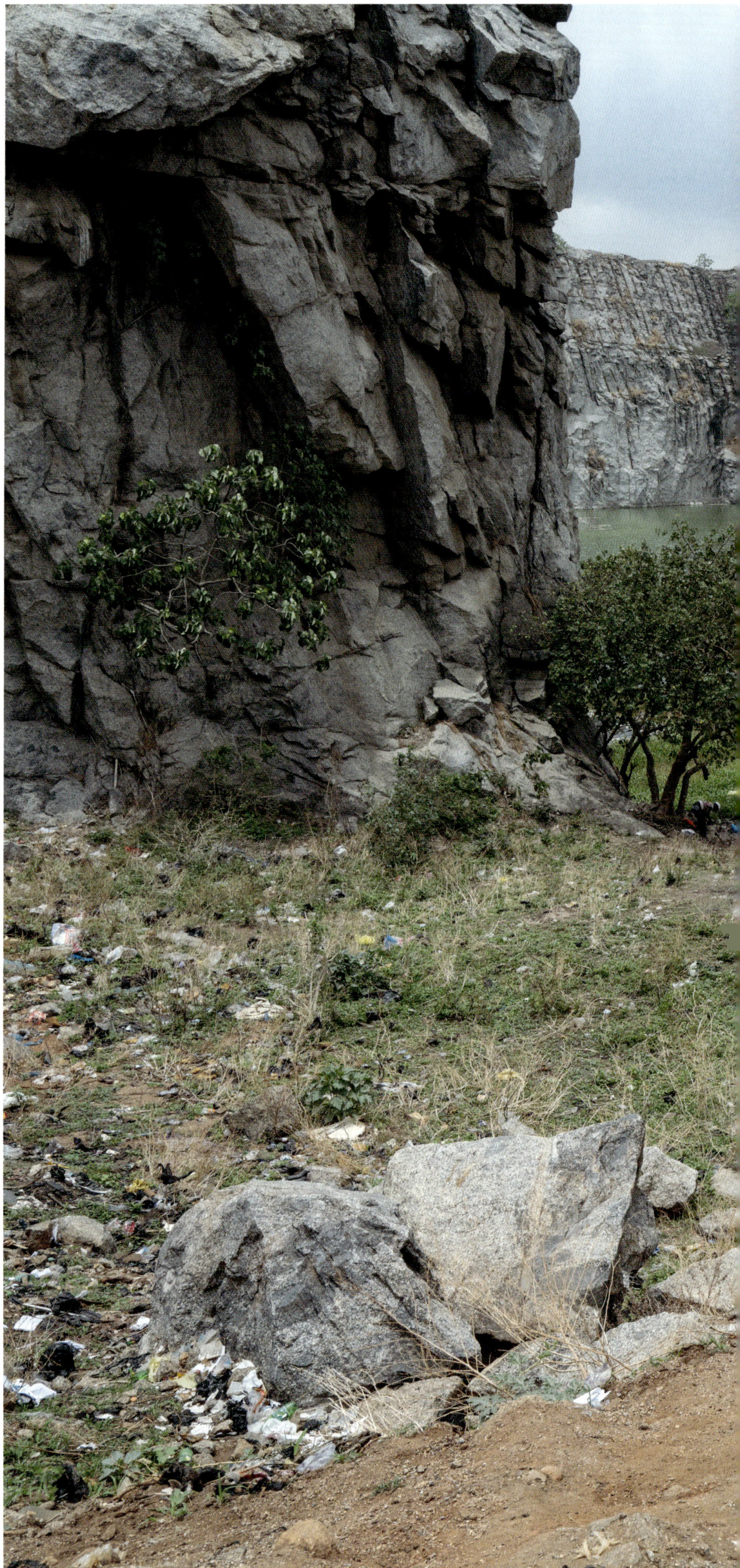

The abandoned quarry of crushed rock in Mpape supplied much of the stone used to build Abuja.

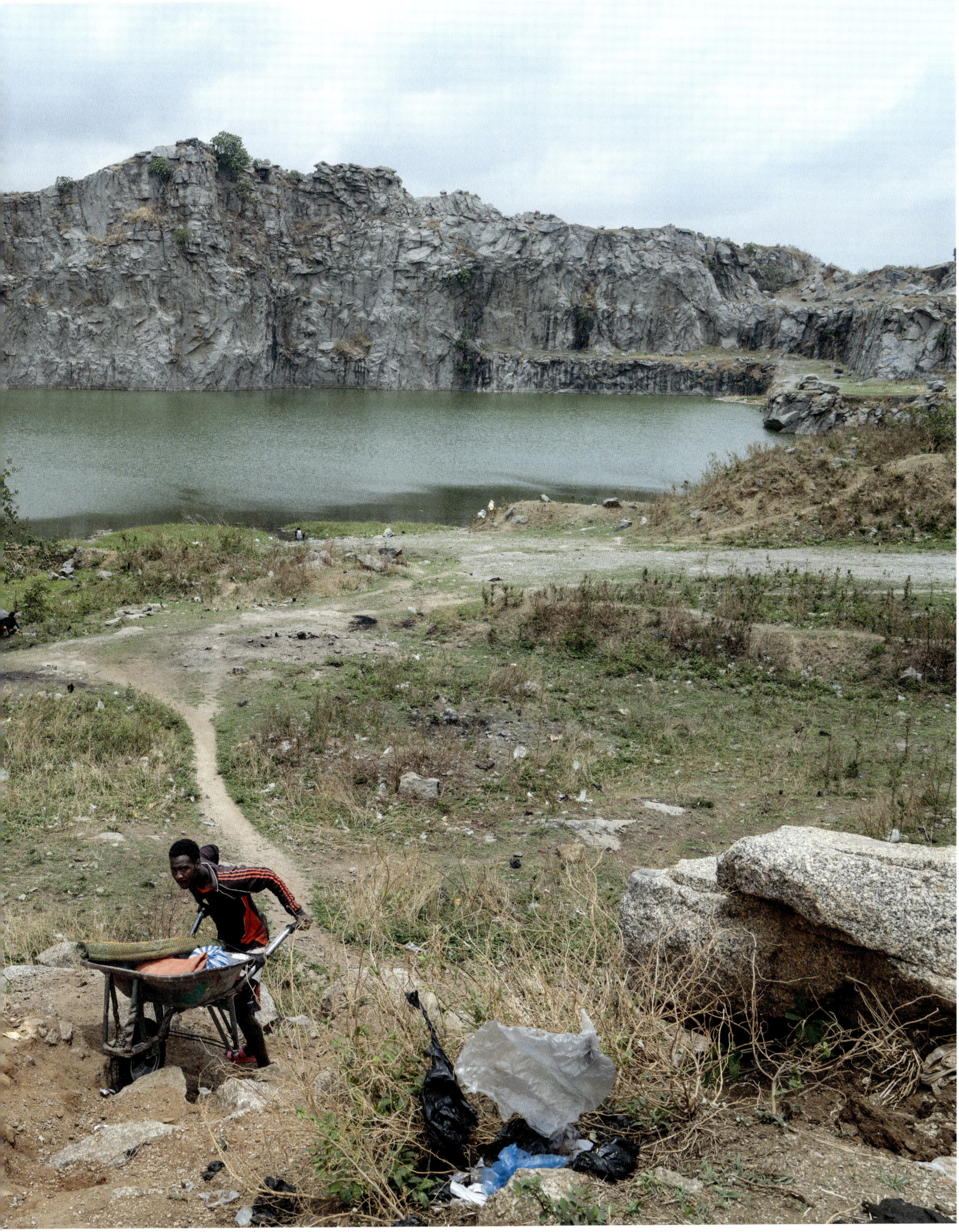

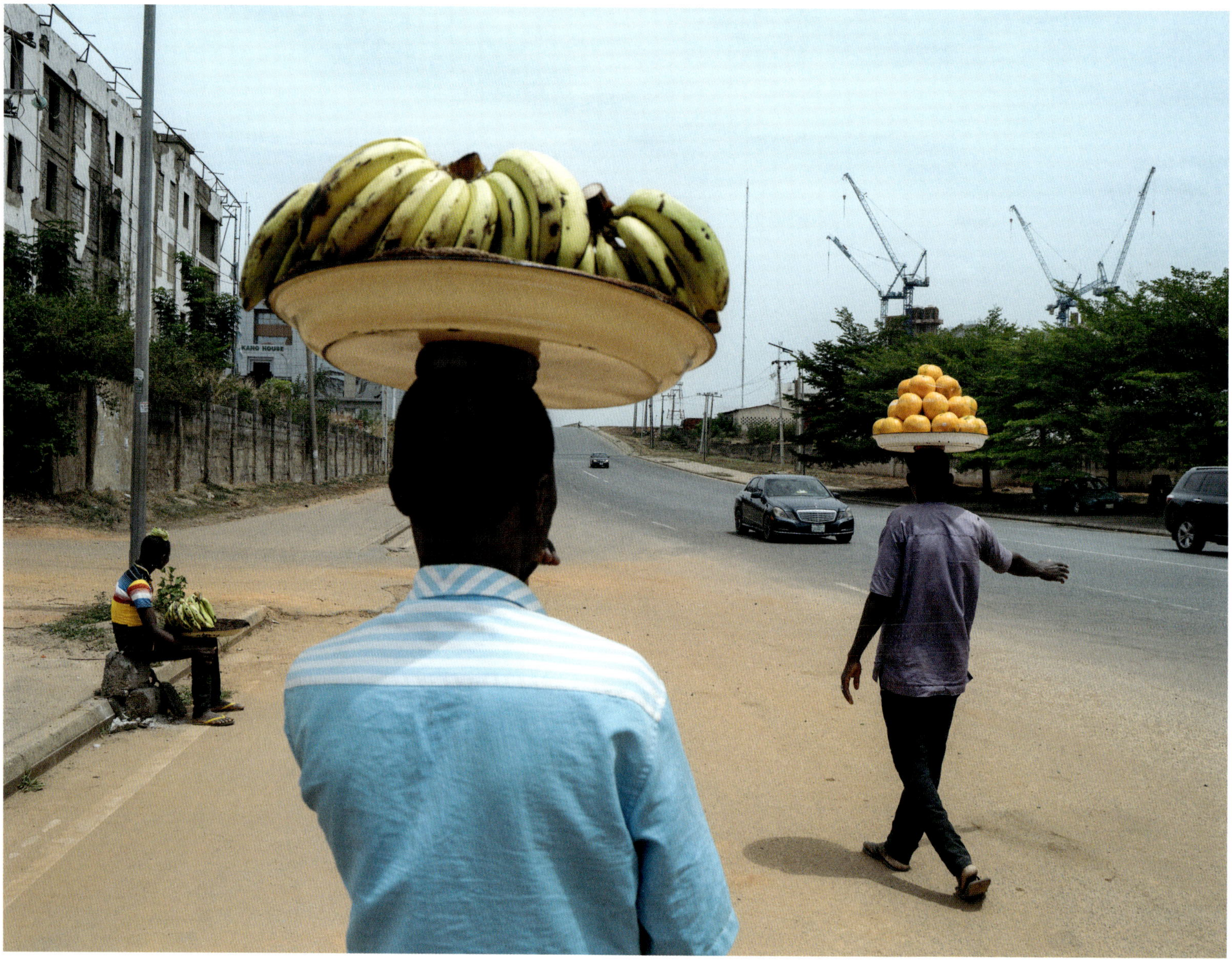

Fruit vendors near the National Ecumenical Centre.

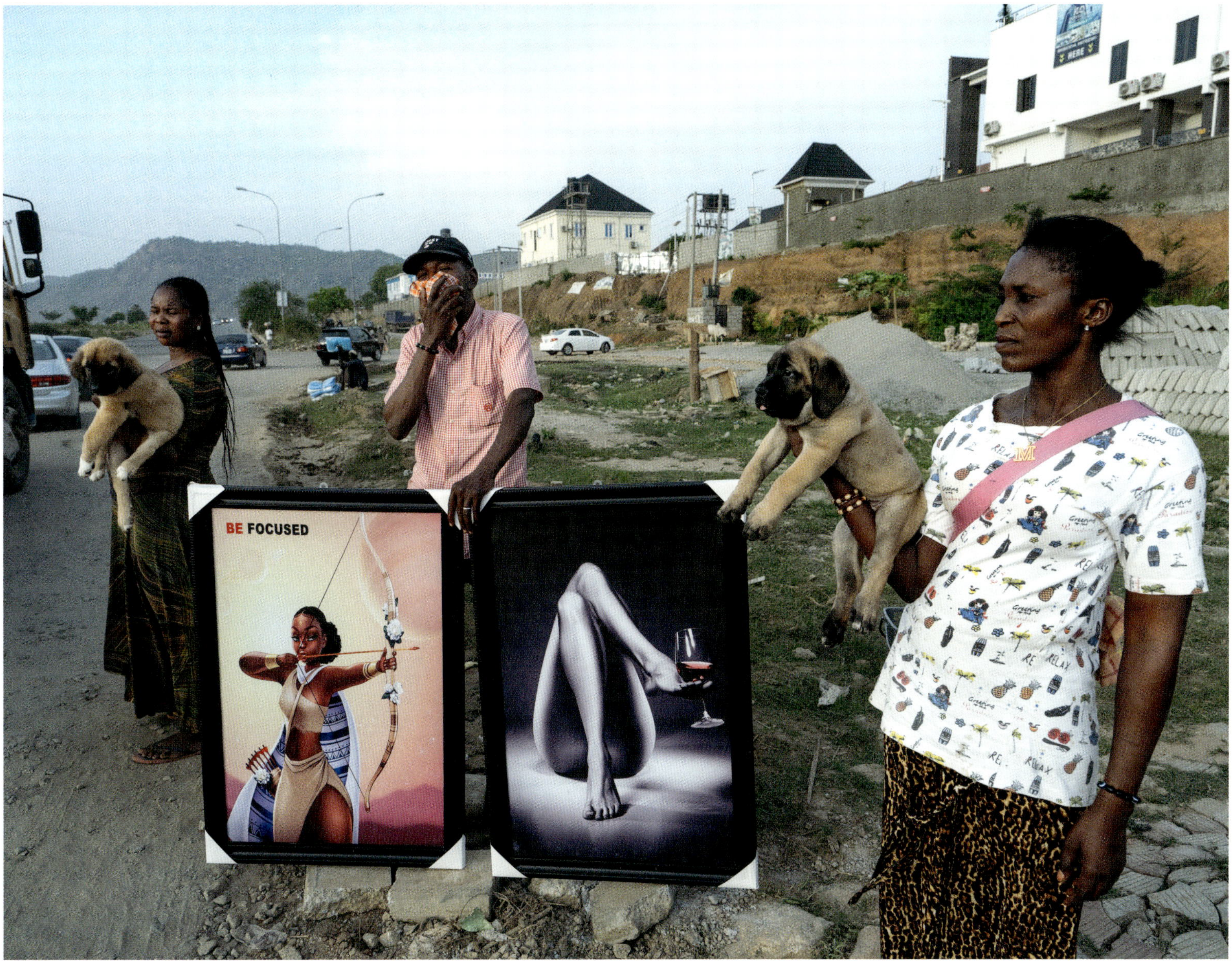

Street vendors in the Gwarinpa district.

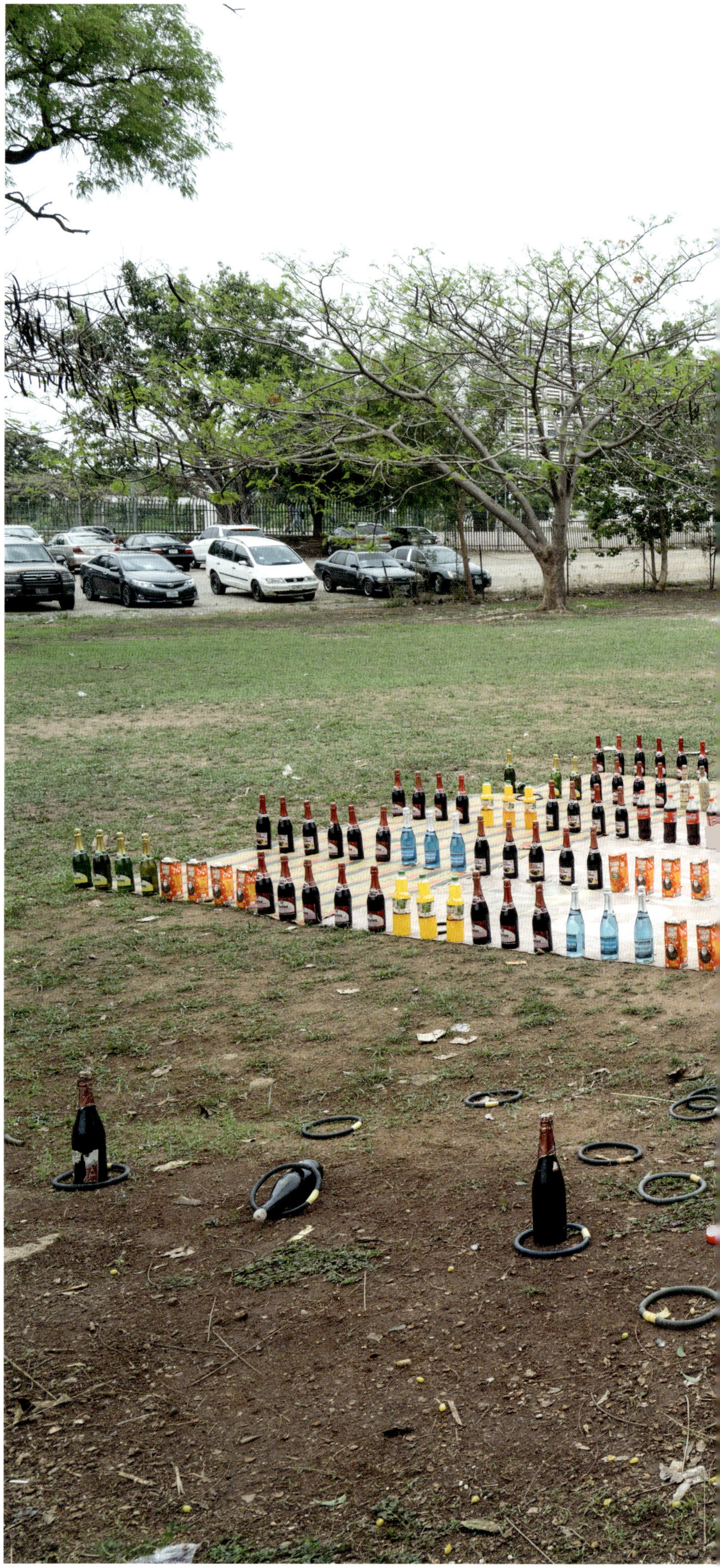

Millennium Park, Maitama district.

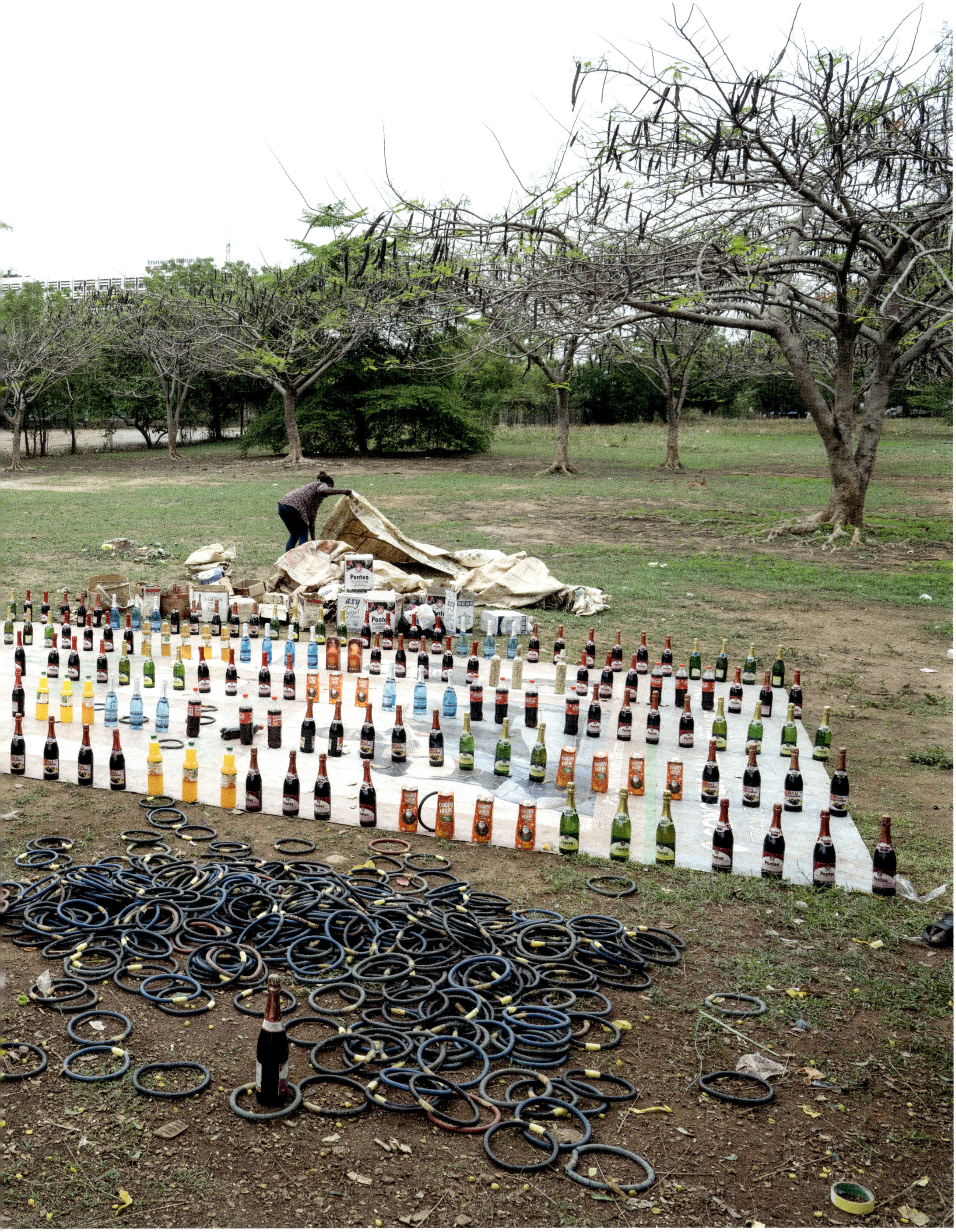
Ponteo

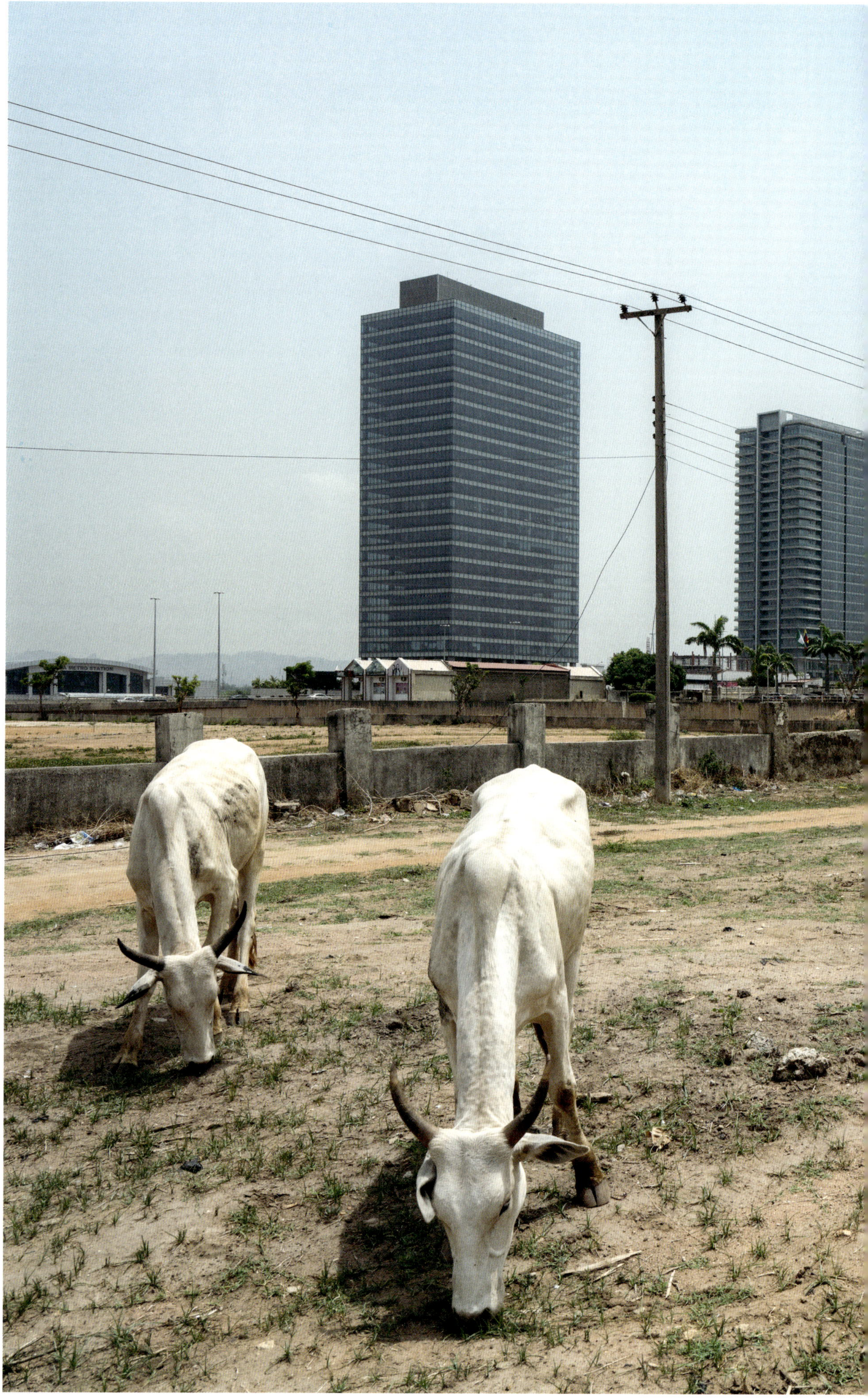

World Trade Center Abuja.

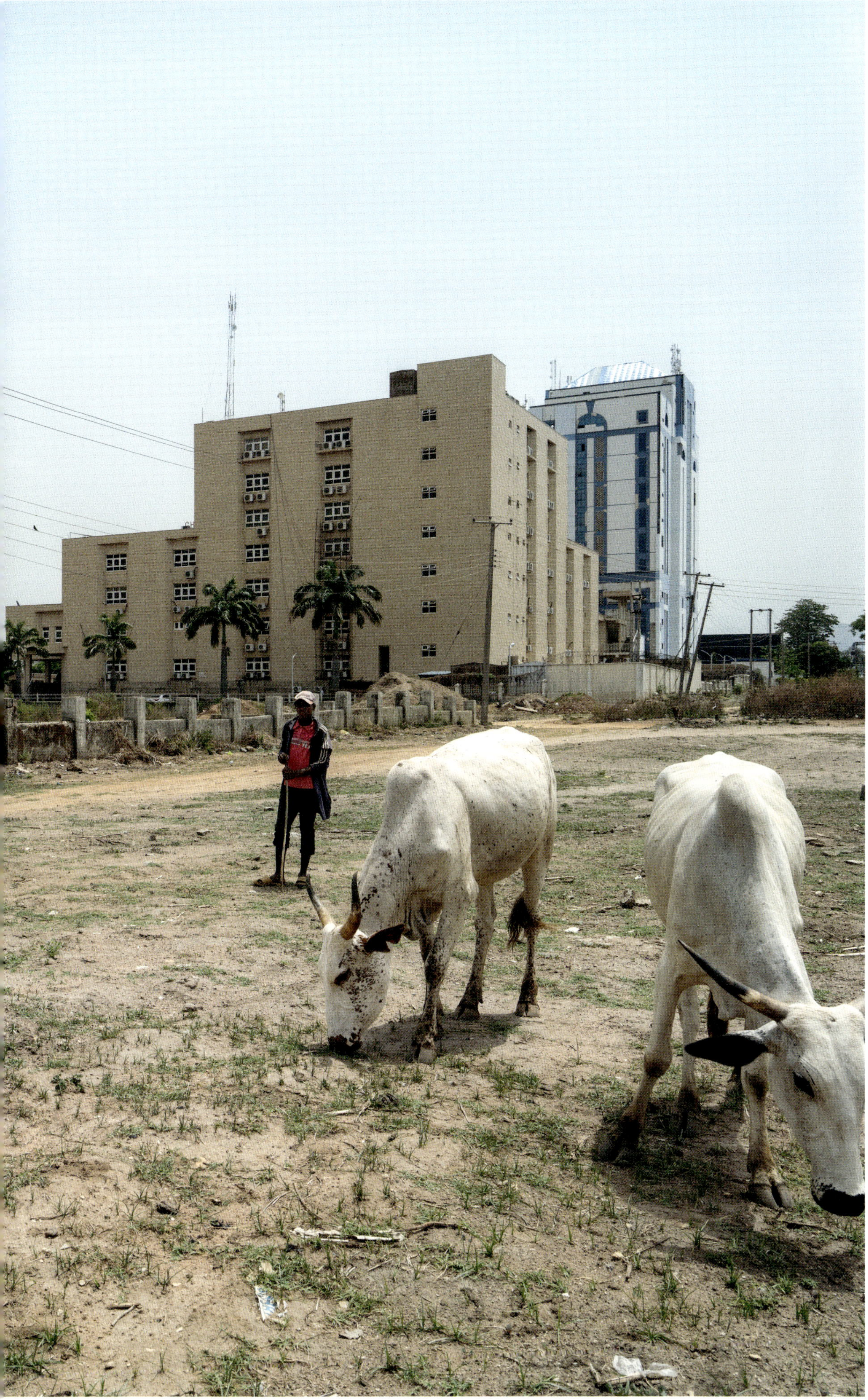

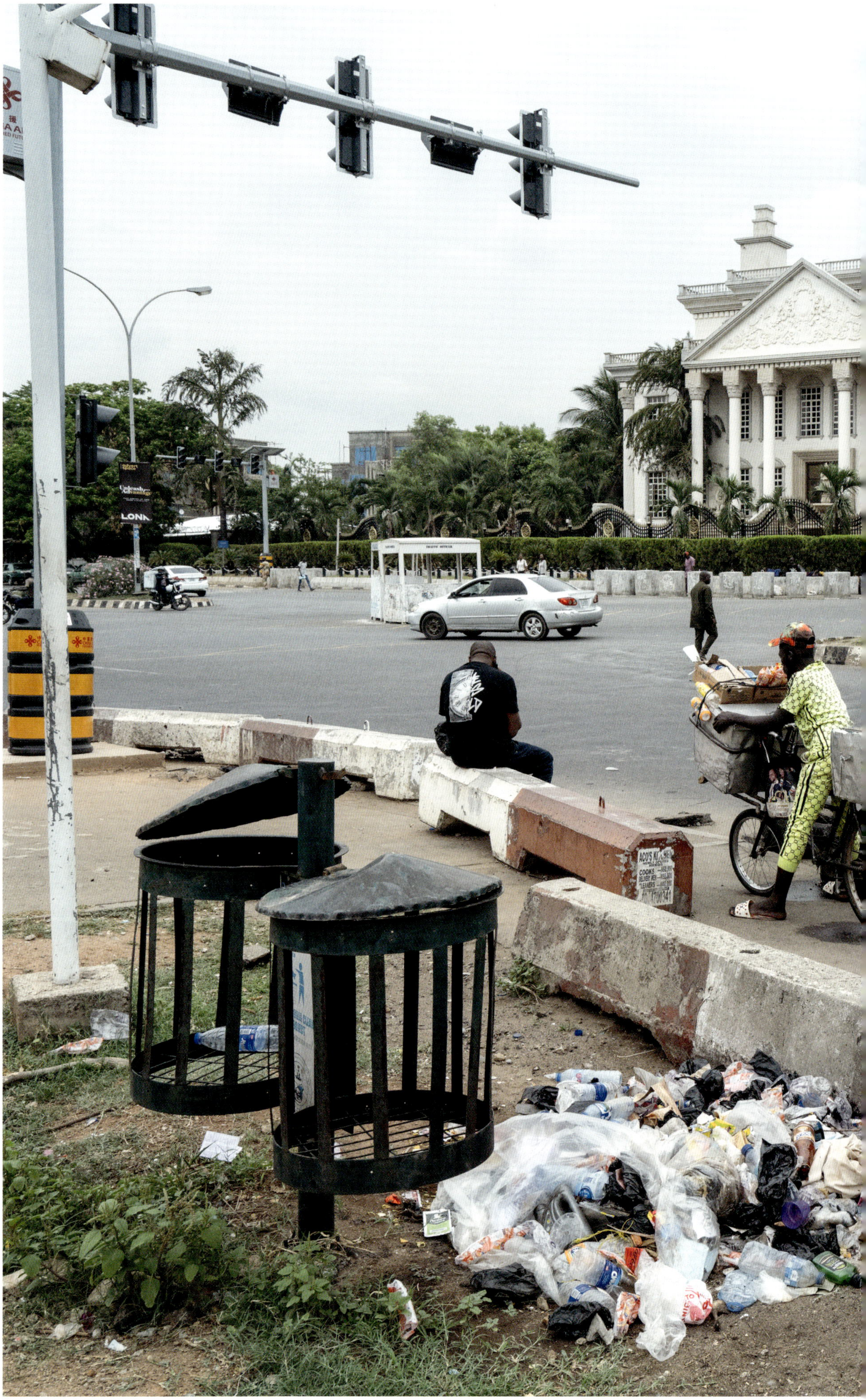

Villa of Alhaji Aliyu Abubakar, chairman of AA Oil Limited, in Maitama district.

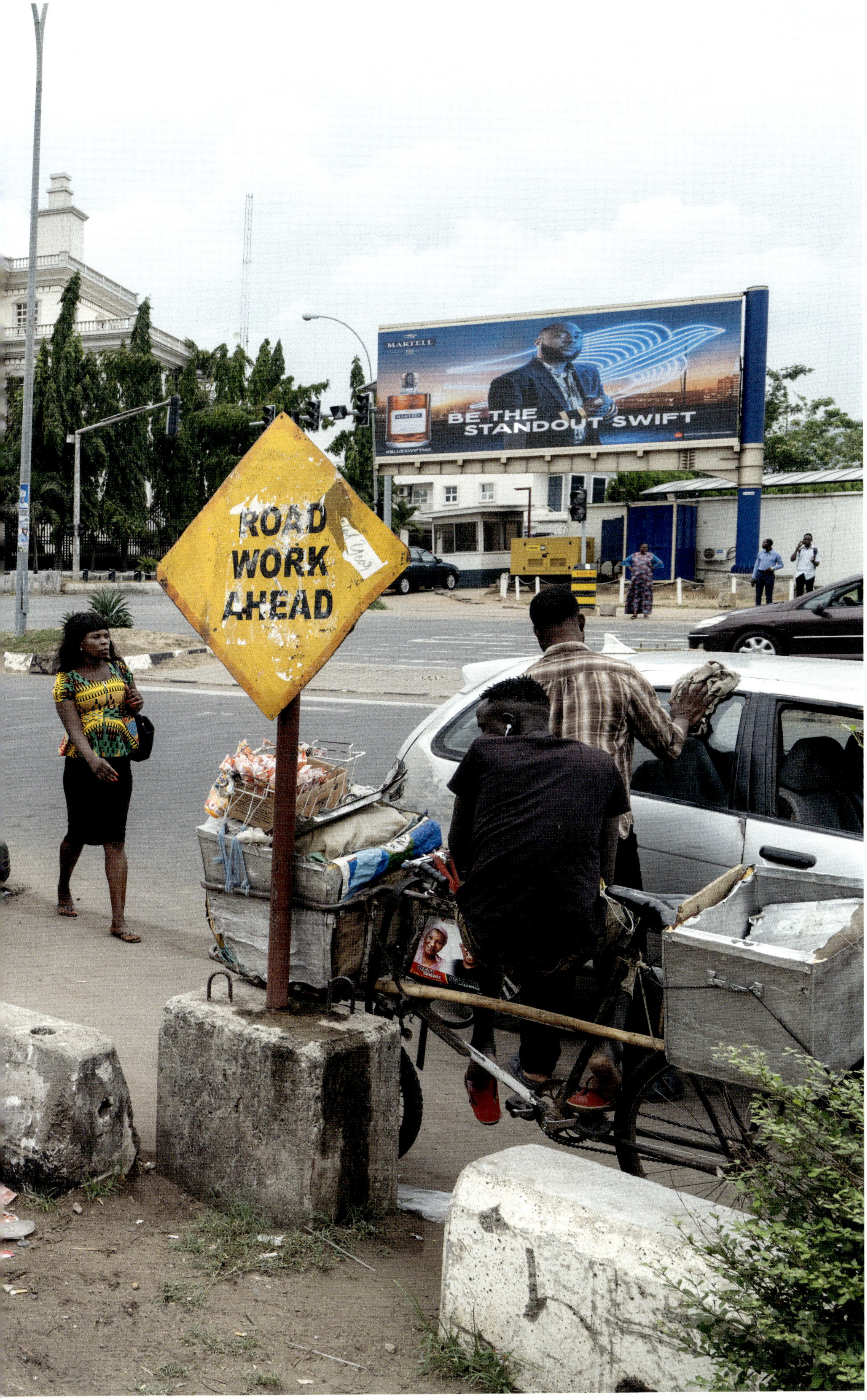
MARTELL
BE THE
STANDOUT SWIFT
ROAD
WORK
AHEAD

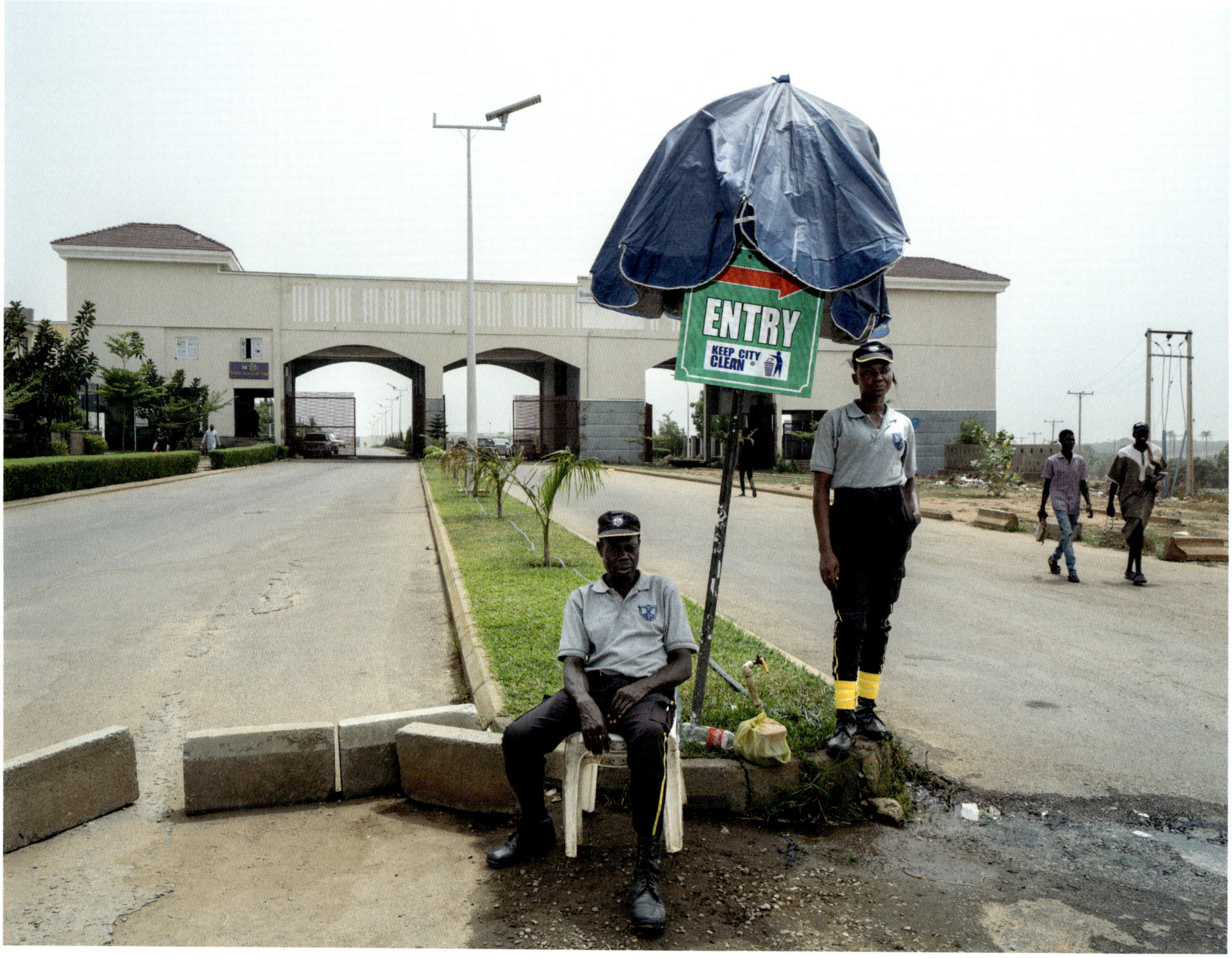

Entrance gate to Brains & Hammers City Estate, Life Camp district.

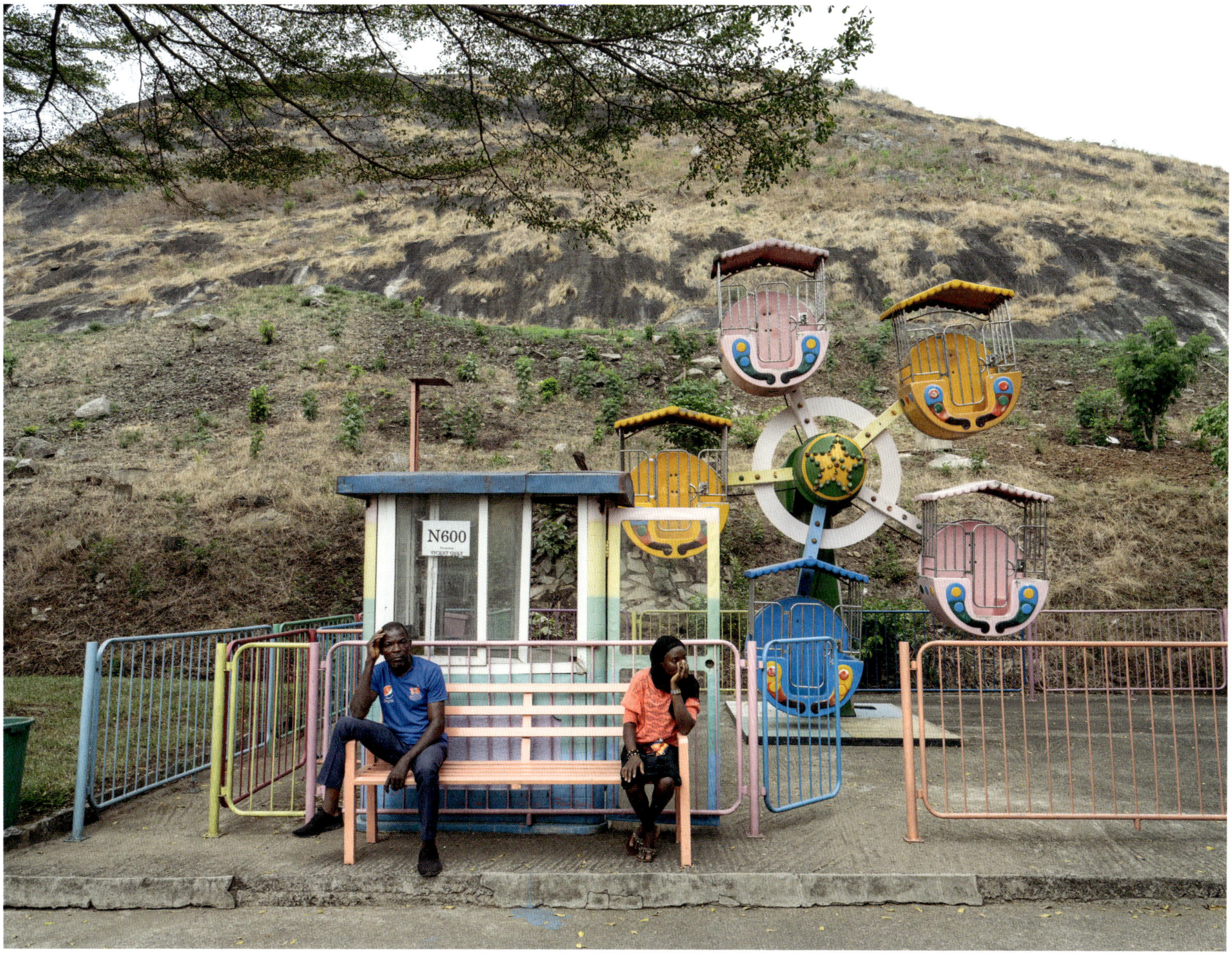

Magicland amusement park.

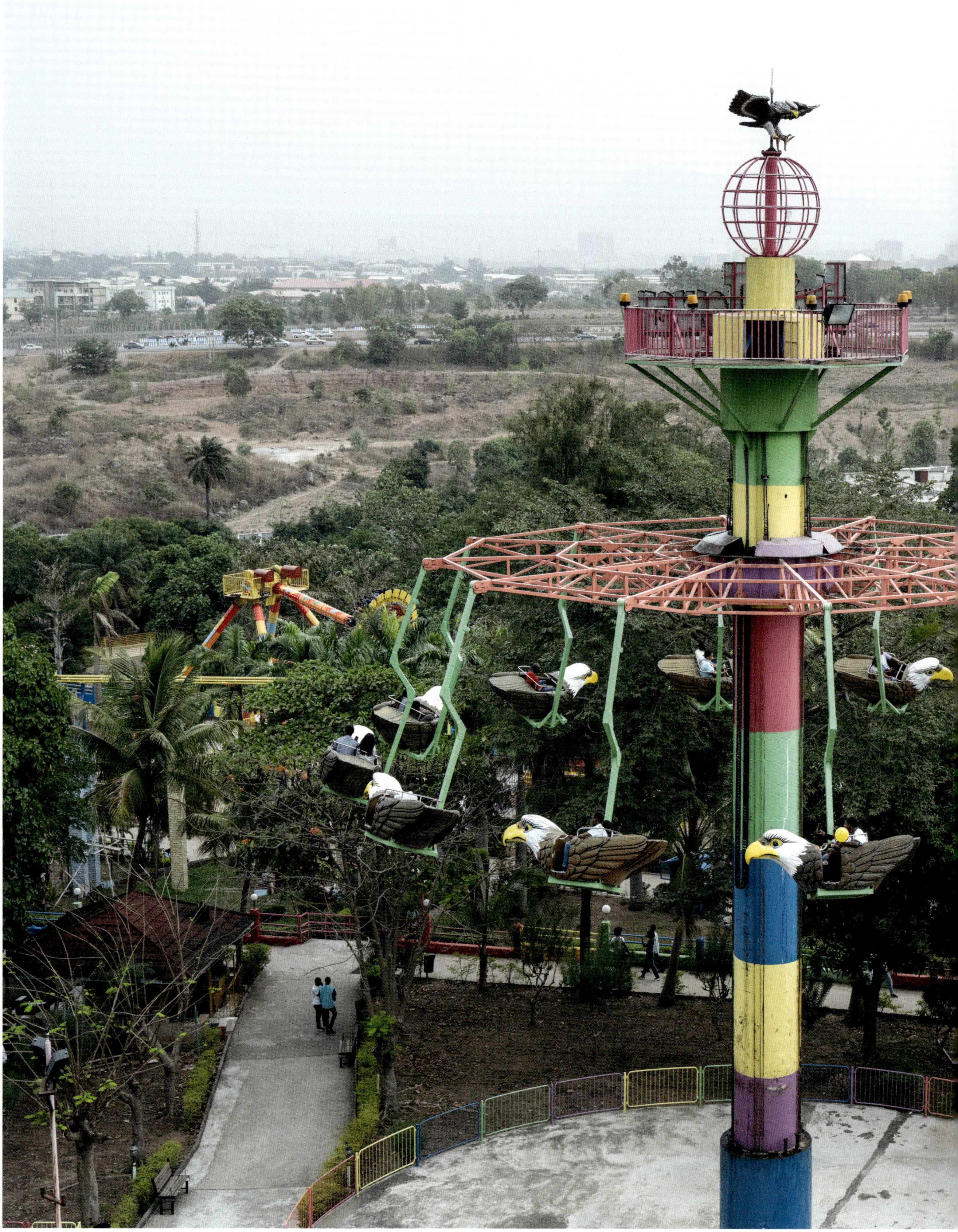

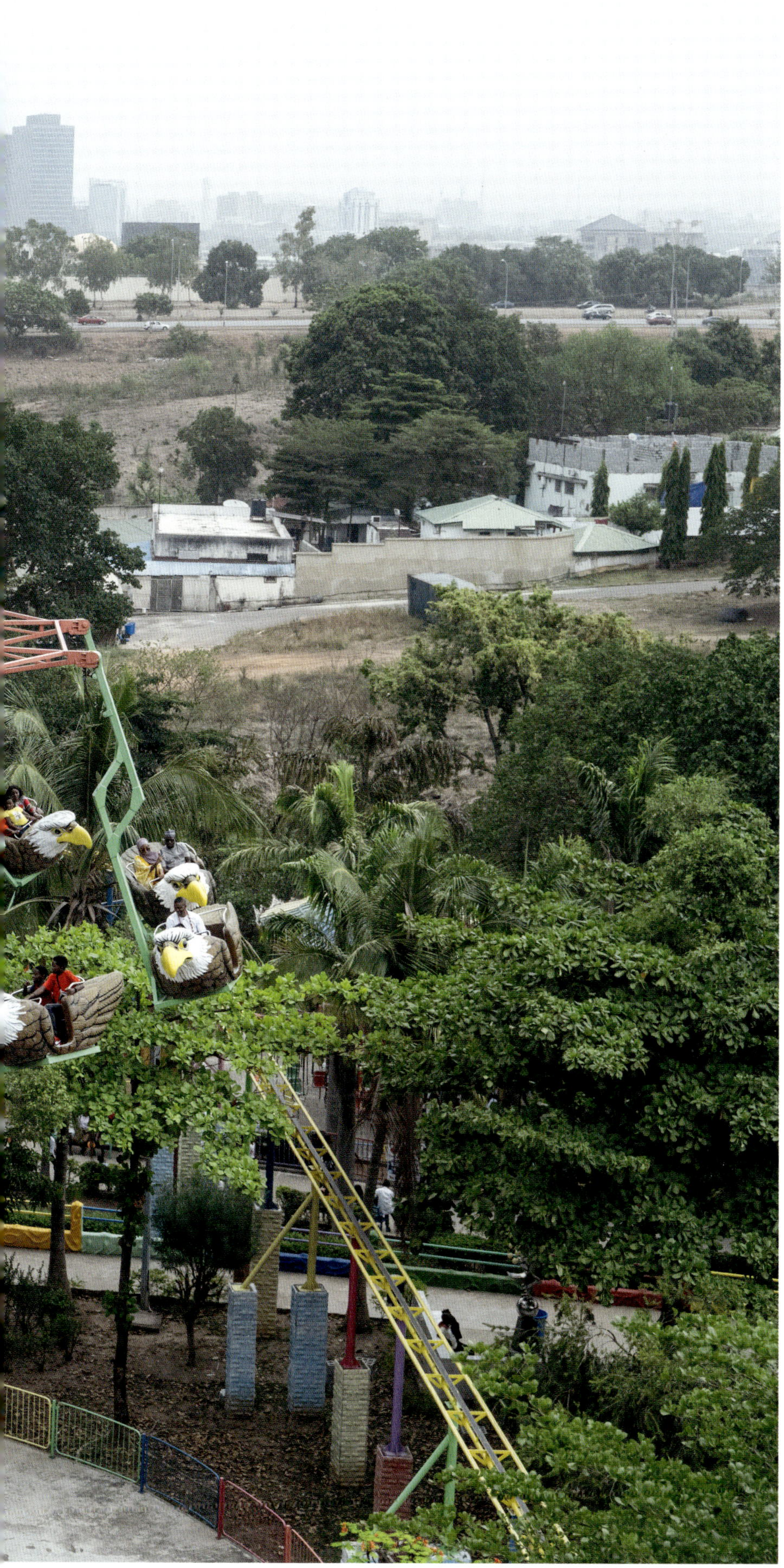

Magicland amusement park.

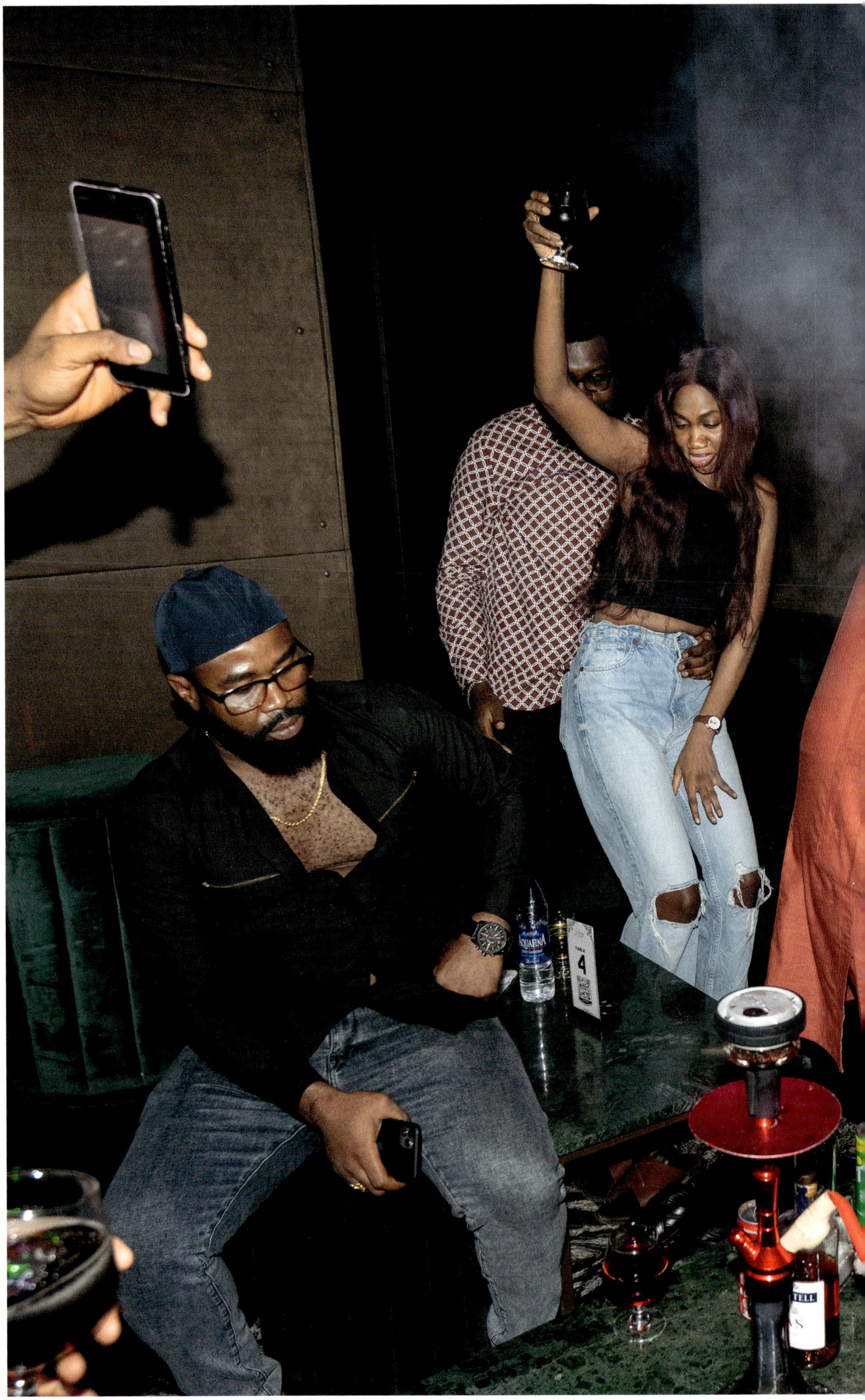
AQUAFINA

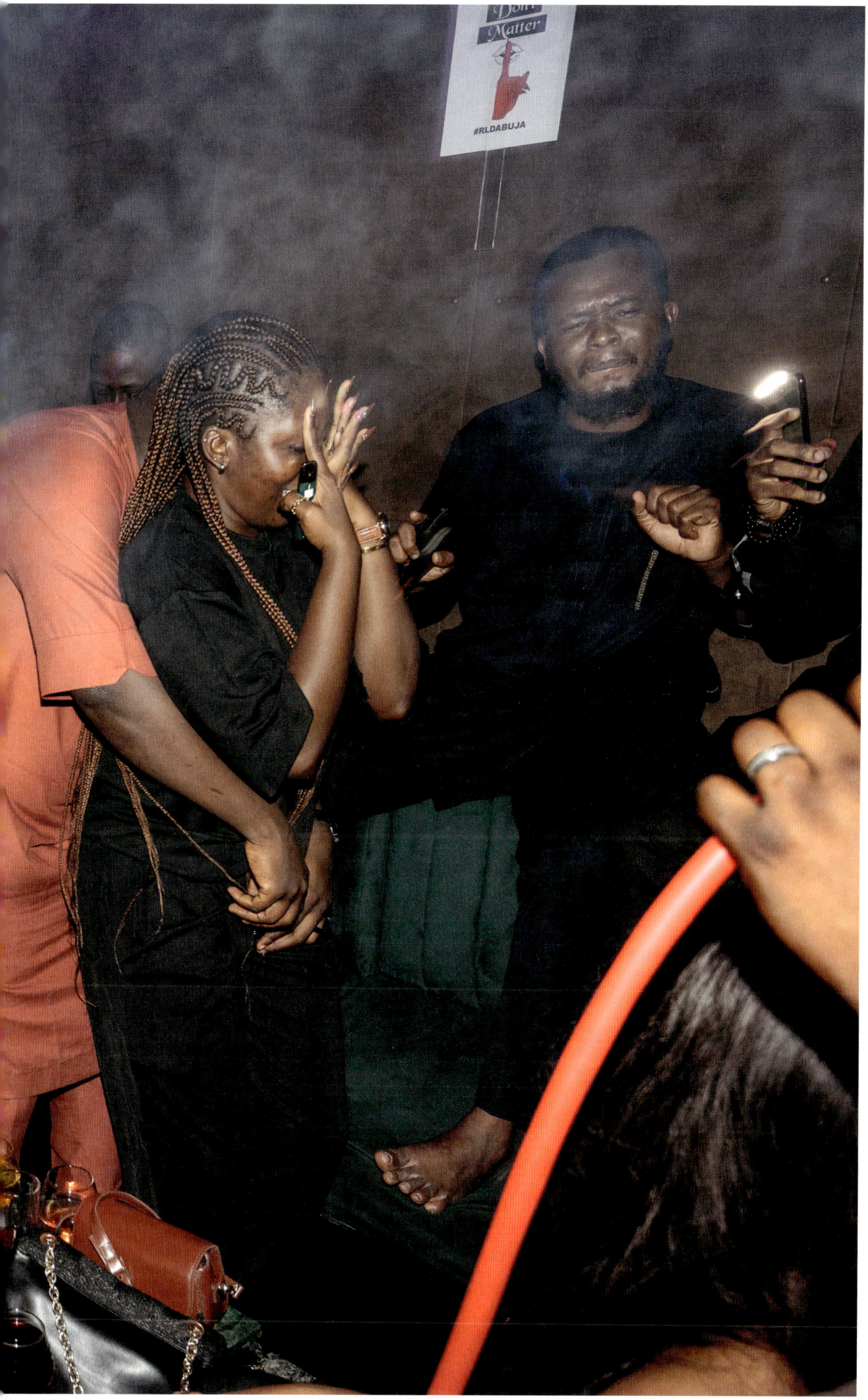

Whisky Mistress
nightclub, Wuse 2.

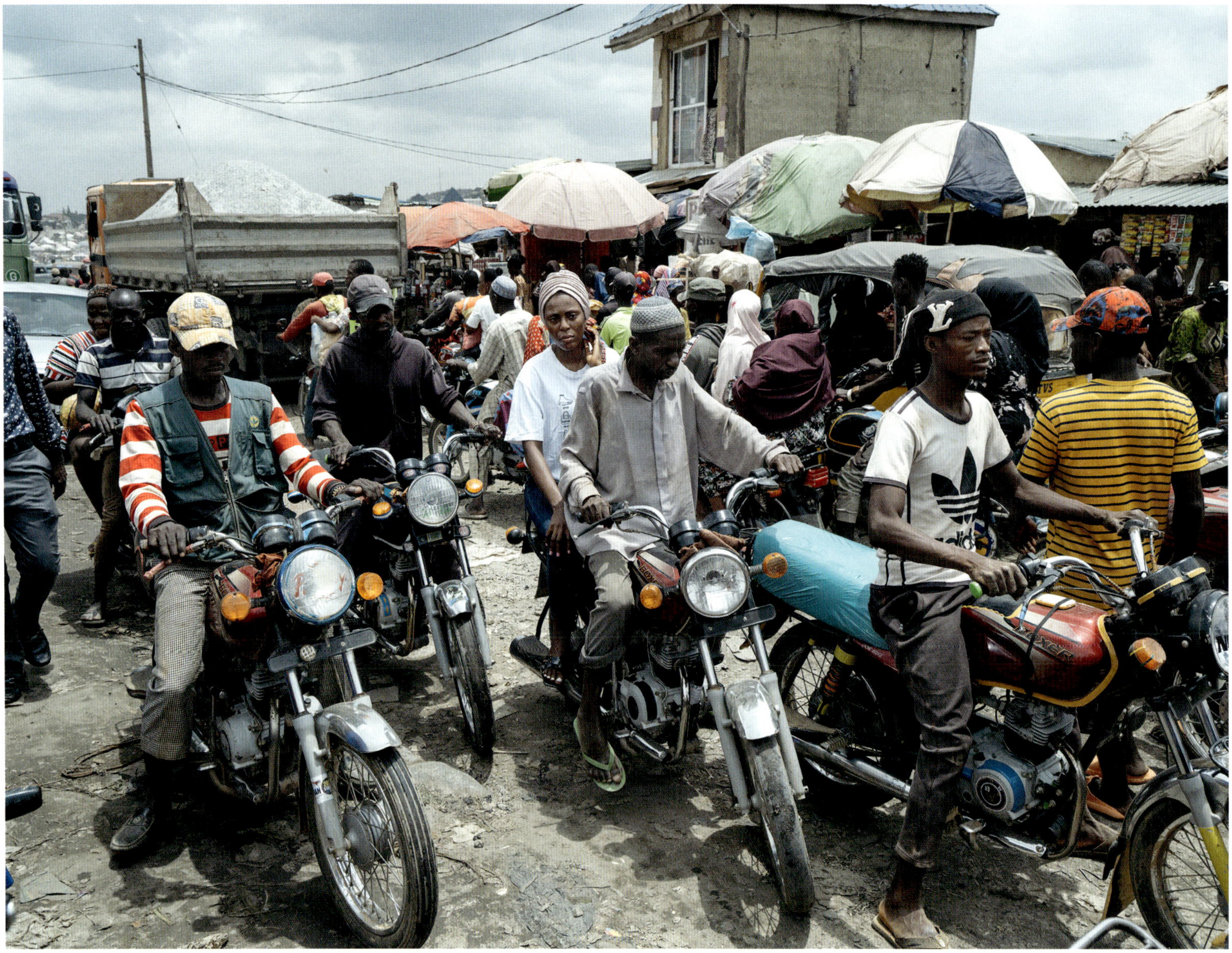

Mpape slum.

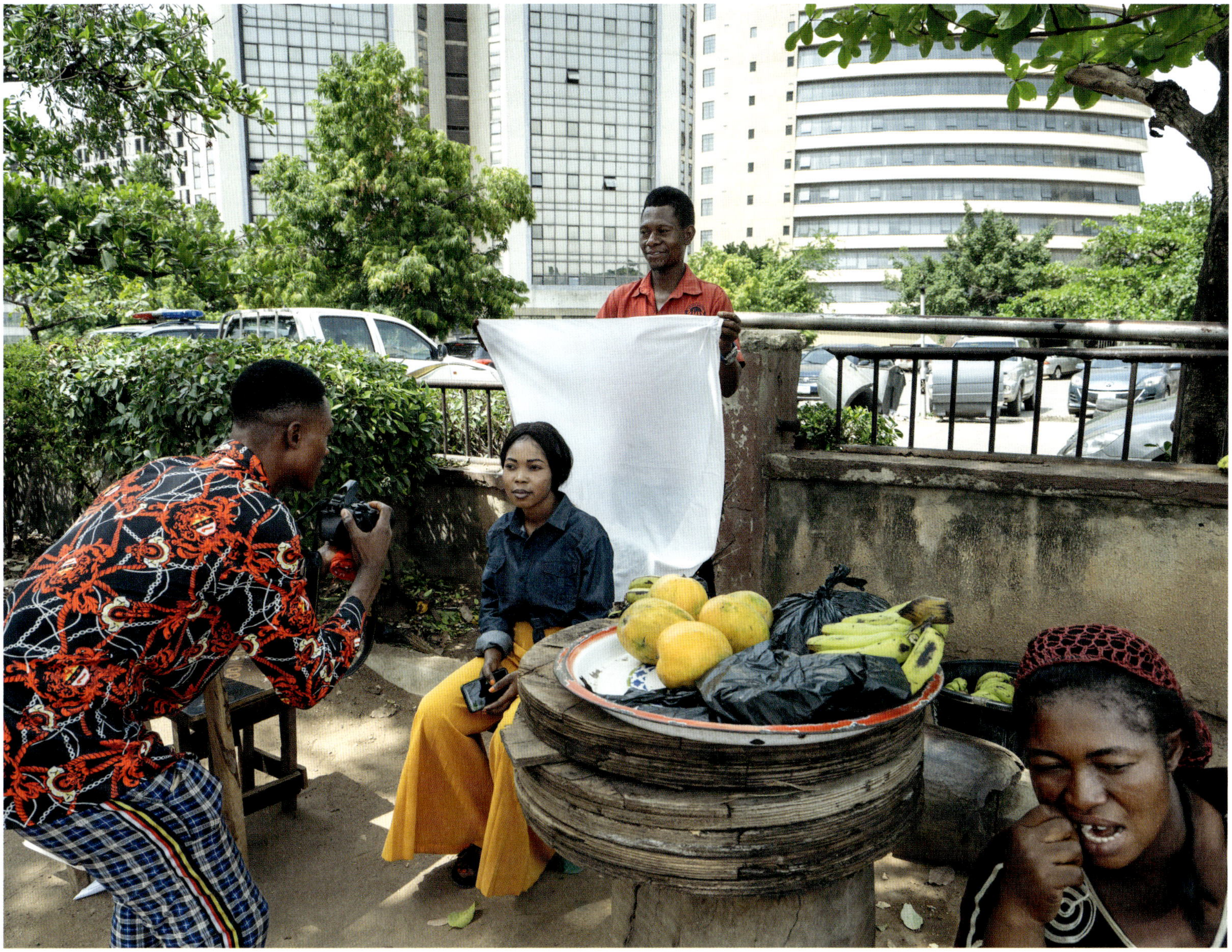

Central Business District.

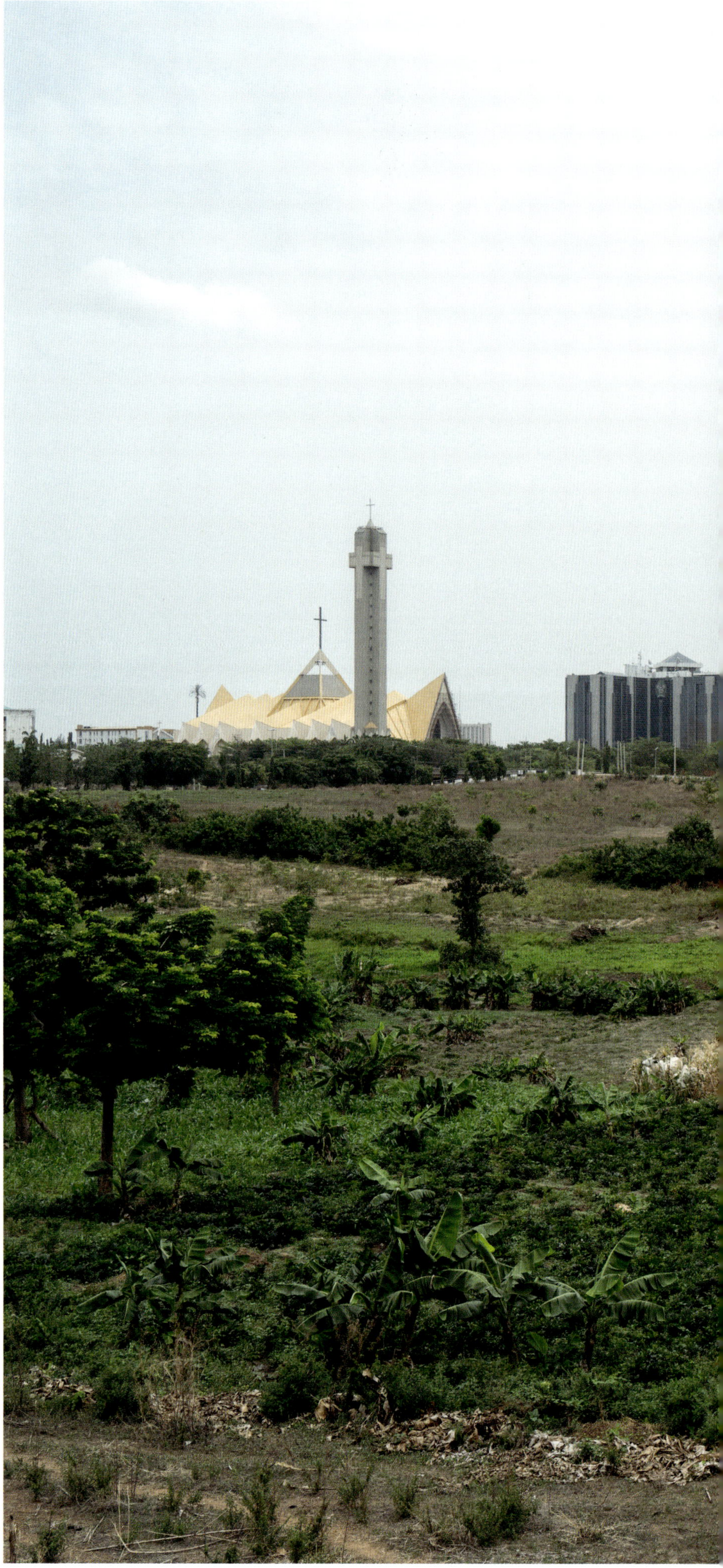

The Abuja skyline, featuring the National Ecumenical Centre, the Central Bank and the unfinished Millennium Tower.

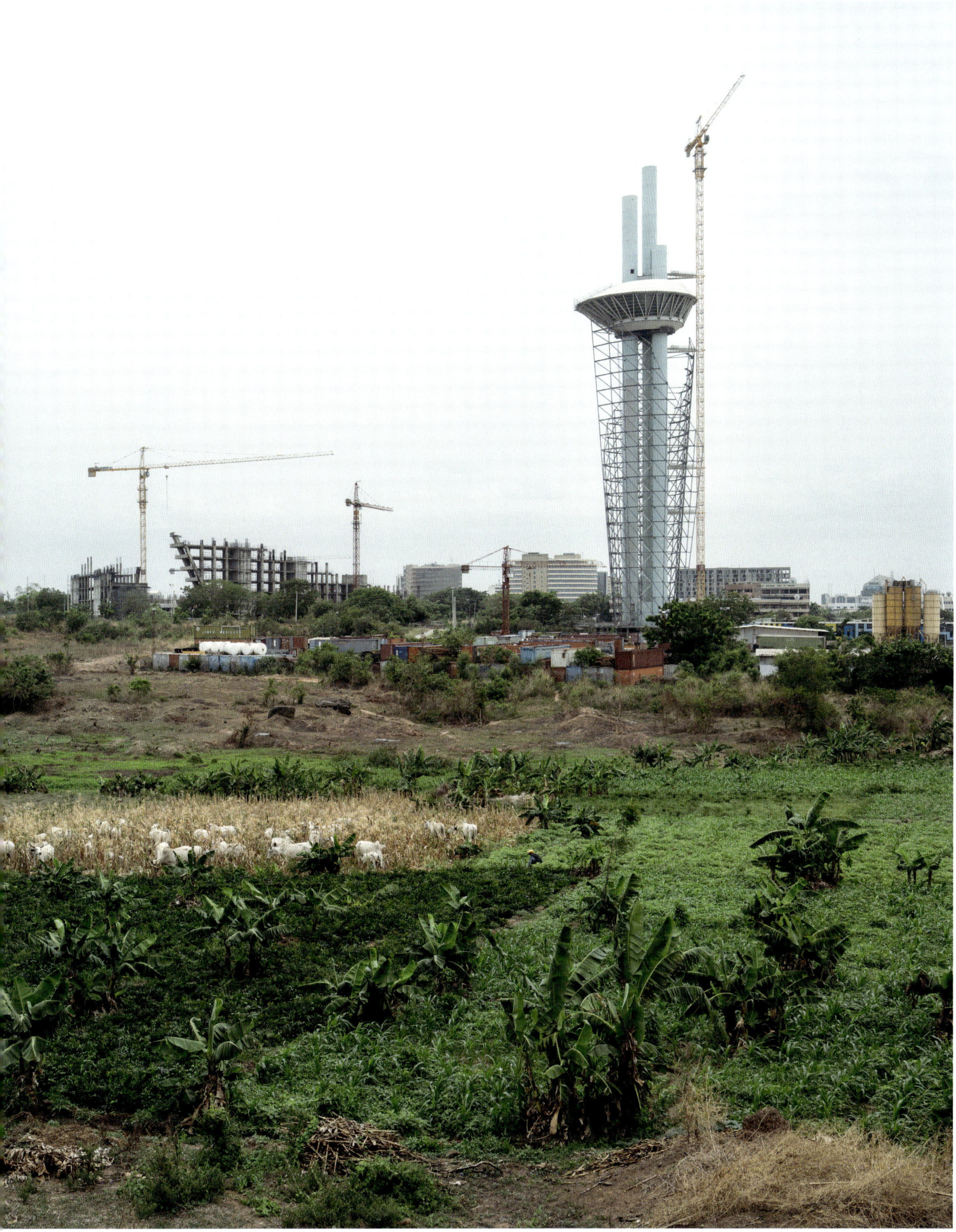

KAZAKHSTAN

ASTANA

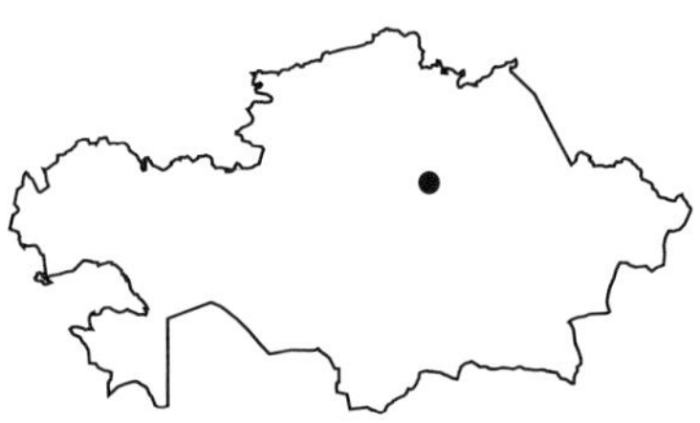

Start of construction: Russian military outpost since 1824
Inauguration date: 10 June 1998
Initiated by: President Nursultan Nazarbayev
Master plan by: Kisho Kurokawa
Urban agglomeration population in 2023: 1.3 million
Surface area: 800 km^2
Former capital: Almaty

The coronavirus is on its way out. The world is reopening cautiously. I am the only guest at the Sky Luxe Hotel in the Kazakh capital, Astana. The light in the lobby is dimmed; the tables in the restaurant are not laid. I hear no slamming doors in the corridor, just the monotonous hum of the minibar. I have breakfast in the room as I zap through the TV lineup, seven stations in languages I do not speak. A portly man in shorts and a vest knocks on the door. He says he is an osteopath and points to a well-worn massage table in the dark corridor.

The hotel is located on Nurzhol Boulevard, a three-kilometre-long promenade connecting the Ak Orda Presidential Palace with the marquee-shaped Khan Shatyr shopping and entertainment complex, designed by Norman Foster. The pedestrian zone between the two landmarks is a monumental showcase of architectural extravaganza, founded on prestige and nationalist symbolism. The eye-catcher is Bayterek, an iconic observation tower in the shape of a tree of life carrying a golden egg, within it the gilded handprint of former president Nursultan Nazarbayev. Visitors queue up there in droves to press their palms against the presidential hand while making a wish and taking a selfie.

Astana's urban planning metamorphosis is inextricably linked to the figure of Nazarbayev, who lets himself be called *Elbasy*, 'Leader of the Nation'. For 30 years, he has kept a tight hold on the reins of power. In 1997, he decided to move the capital from mountainous Almaty to Aqmola, 1,000 kilometres to the north. The steppe city was to become the spearhead of post-Soviet nation-building thanks to oil and gas revenues. A new city rose on the southern bank of the Ishim River according to the master plan by Japanese architect Kisho Kurokawa. Renamed Astana, in no time at all Aqmola emerged as a global city of more than 1 million inhabitants.

It is not by accident that the inauguration of the new capital coincided with the presidential anniversary. Nazarbayev's portrait can be found on numerous monuments, often in the company of historical Kazakh heroes or *batyrs*. Nazarbayev has his own museum, and the airport and university also bear his name. But the ultimate honour came after his resignation in March 2019. From then on, the capital would be called Nur-Sultan, 'Sultan of Light'. The majority of residents I speak to, however, stubbornly continue to call their city Astana.

The name change proved short-lived. In January 2022, street protests against high petrol prices got out of control. The protesters' anger was aimed at the power of the Nazarbayev clan. In clashes with law enforcement, 230 people lost their lives. To calm things down, in September 2022, President Kassym-Jomart Tokayev decided to revert to the name Astana.

Astana is a playground for architects and property developers, inevitably reminiscent of Dubai. Luxurious residential compounds are being built on the outskirts, protected by barriers and security posts. Shopping centres such as Mega Silk Way and Asia Park make small shops obsolete. Near the airport, Central Asia's largest mosque, with space for 18,000 worshippers, is nearing completion. The height record is held by Abu Dhabi Plaza, a 320-metre skyscraper paid for with oil money from the Emirates.

Fortunately, the city also boasts a number of sprawling parks and squares where the Kazakh national character is more in the forefront with street musicians, fairground stalls and ice cream carts. A drunkard is sleeping off his drunken stupor in a public garden.

In the endless steppe, city planners saw no reason to sparingly deal with open spaces. With its wide boulevards and extensive parking options, Astana was designed with the car in mind. A significant part of the fleet consists of Yandex taxis — the local Uber — which take on the role of public transport, leading to frantically tooting queues during rush hour.

Construction of an ambitious above-ground metro line began in 2011. However, this light rail transit (LRT) was never completed, because investor China Development Bank froze its credits due to financial mismanagement. Today, a string of 555 concrete support pillars meanders through the city. 'Our monument to corruption,' one passerby lets slip.

Corruption and nepotism are not unheard of in the former Soviet Union. It took very little effort to find a nightclub open as usual despite the strict Covid measures. No entry passes here, or face masks. A live band fills up the dance floor. 'Those with connections here can always find a loophole to get around the rules,' a lady confides in me.

Near the brand-new Nurly Zhol train station, hidden behind billboards for prestigious new construction projects, lie dilapidated residential areas from the days when Astana was still called Aqmola. The vibe is that of a sleepy Soviet village, with dusty streets, vegetable gardens, washing lines and barking dogs on chains. Shame and mistrust prevail. 'Nothing to see here,' a man gestures. 'Go photograph Bayterek!' Many houses have been abandoned or have already been torn down. At a public pump, the last residents come to fill up with drinking water. Where two worlds collide.

August 2021

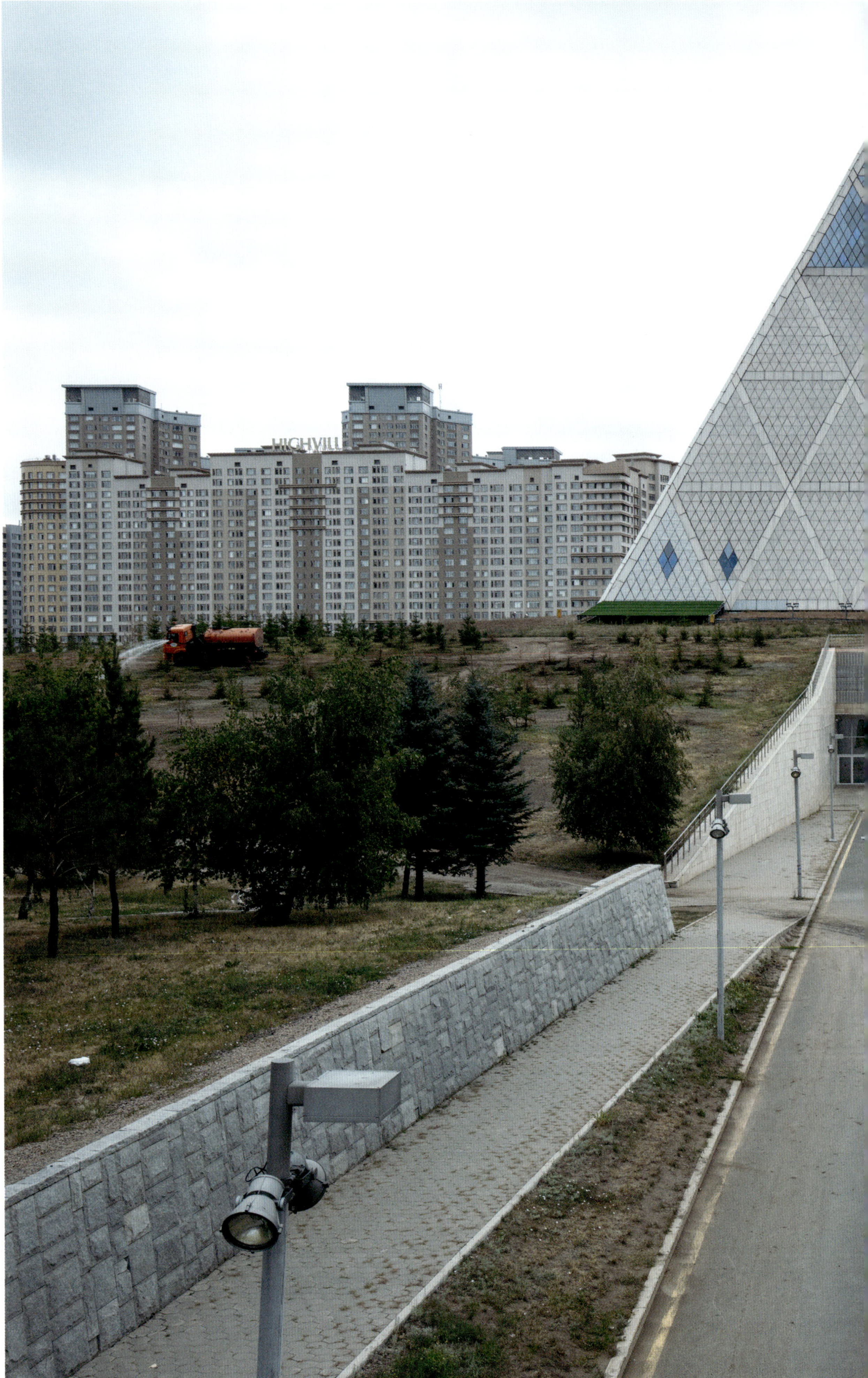

The Palace of Peace and Reconciliation, designed by Norman Foster.

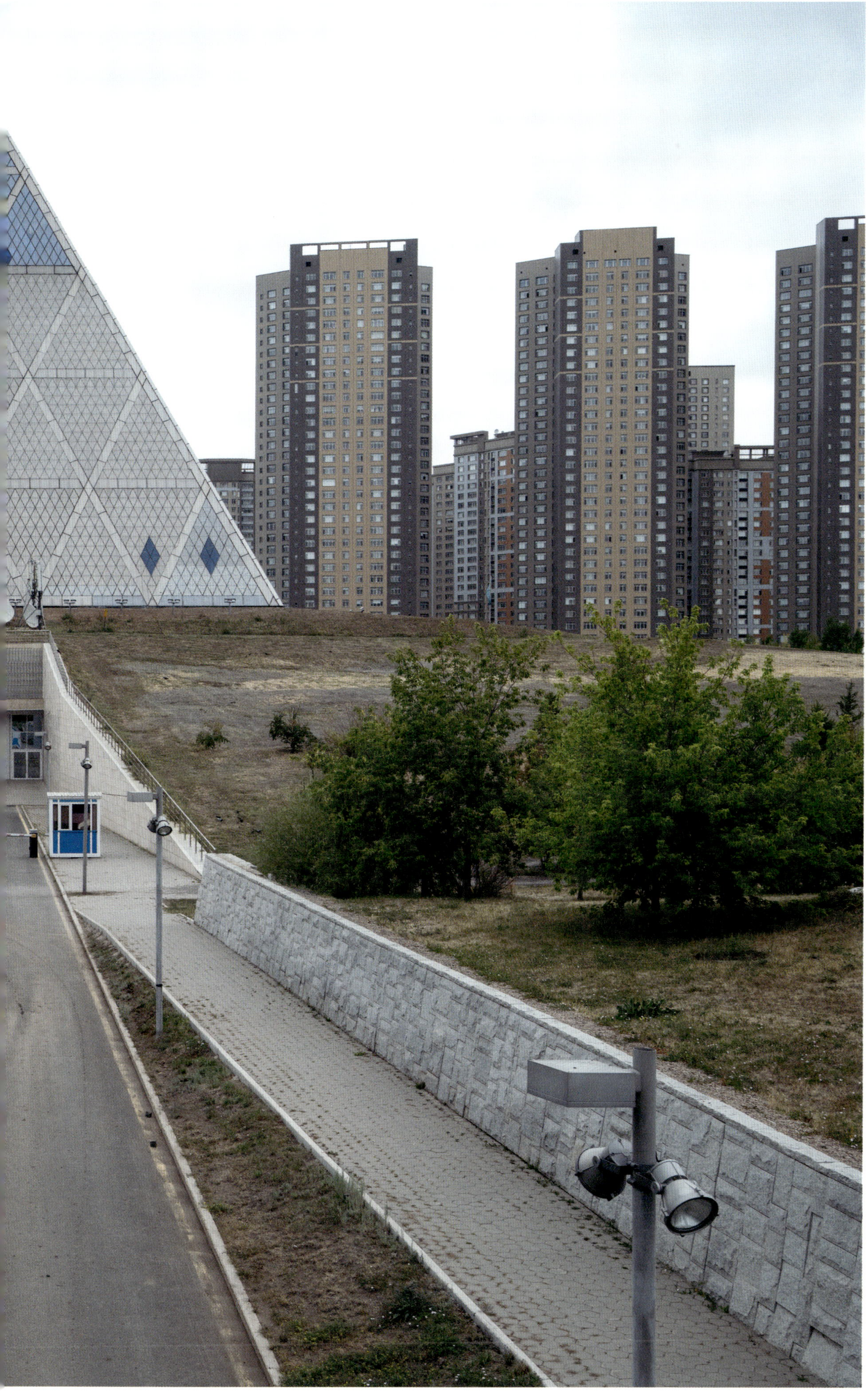

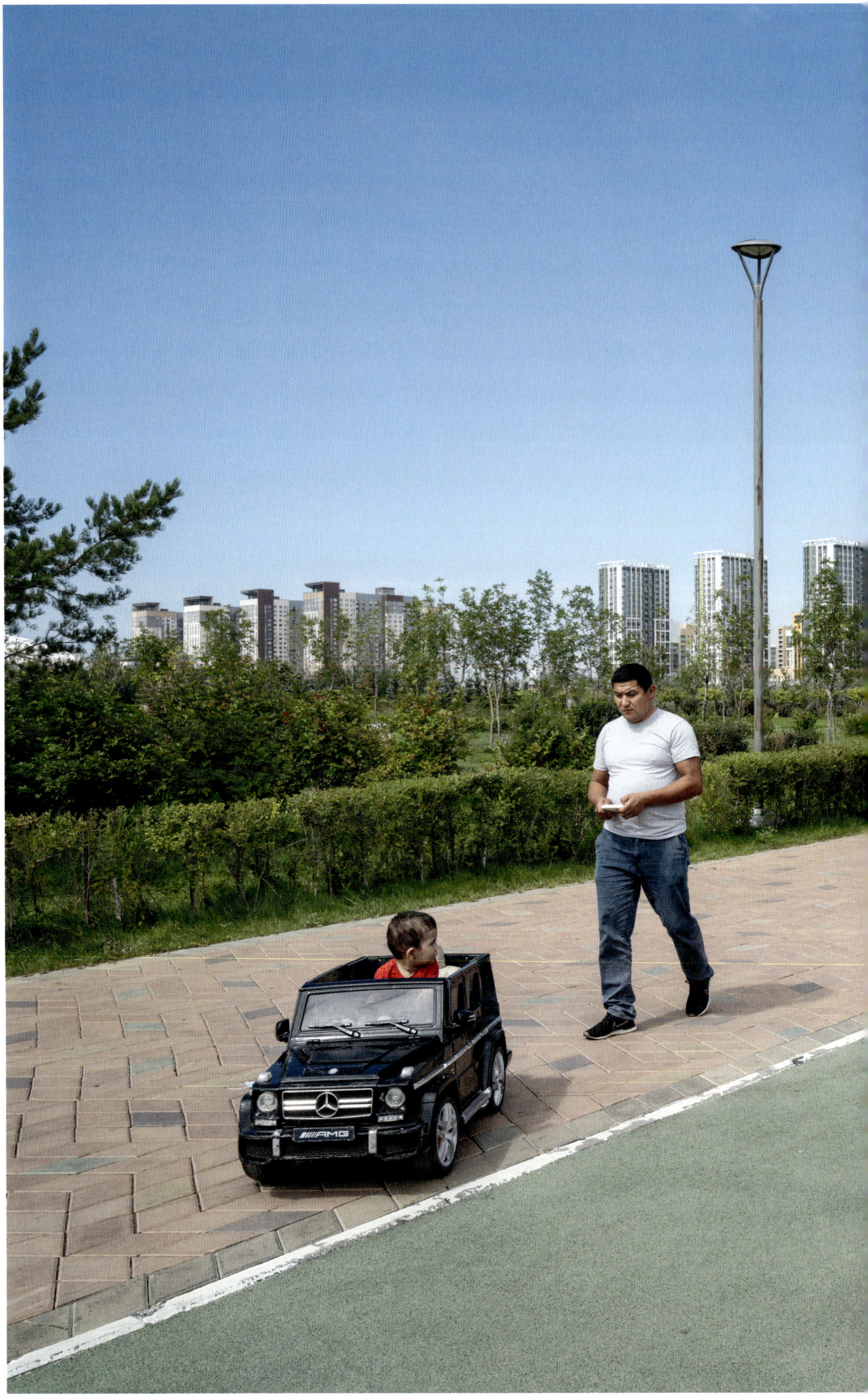

Astana Botanical Garden.

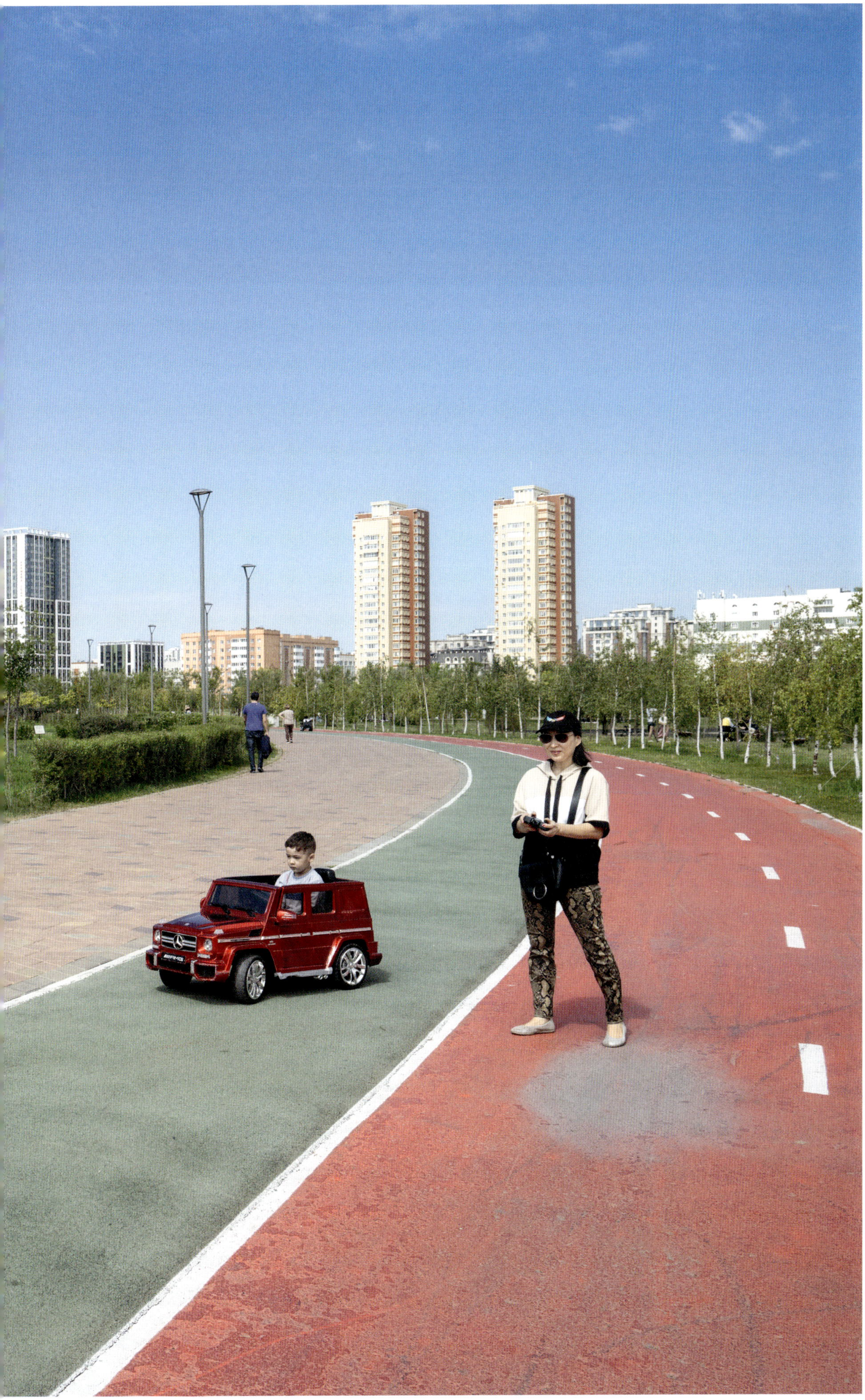

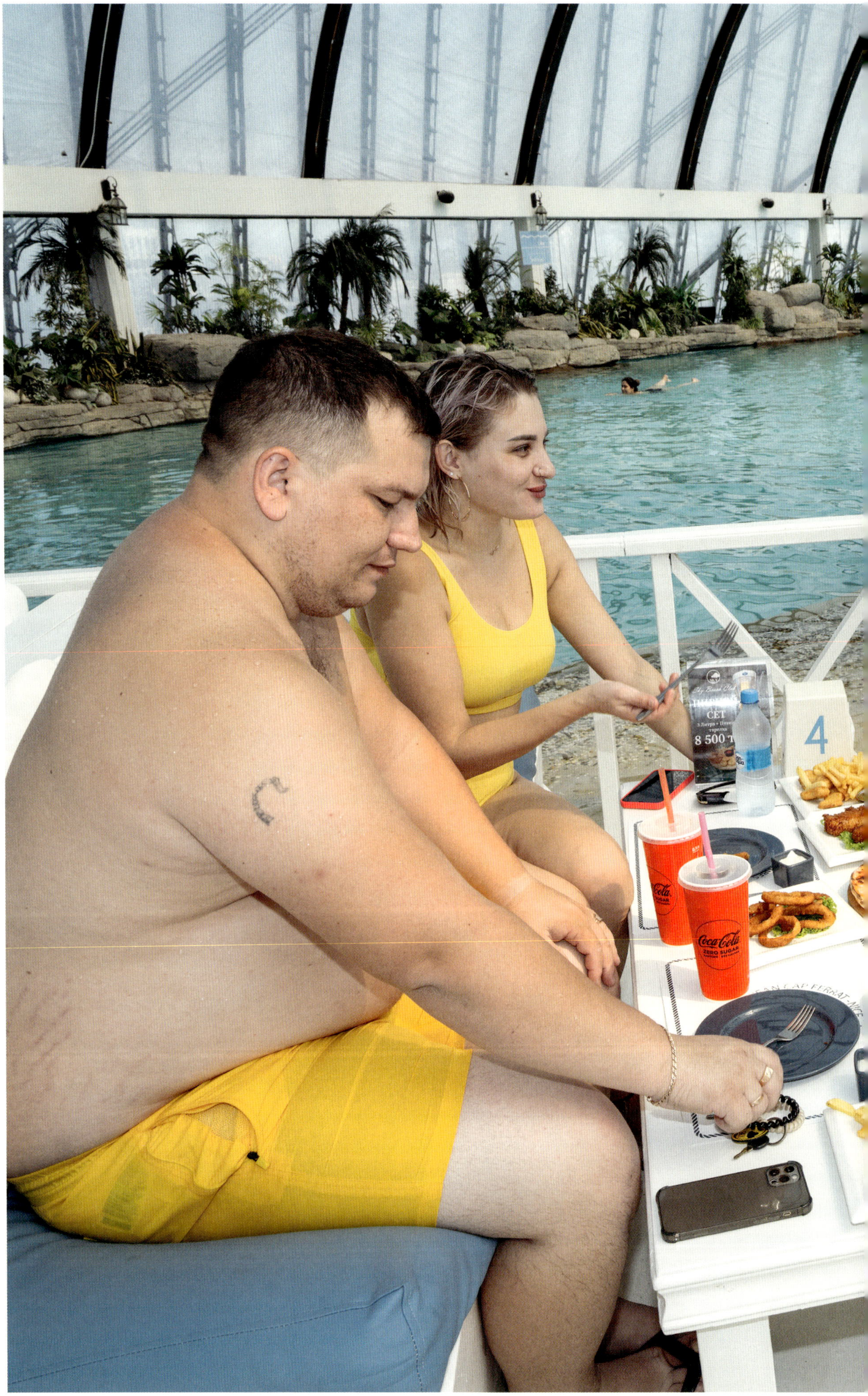

Sky Beach Club,
an indoor laguna in
Khan Shatyr shopping
and entertainment complex.

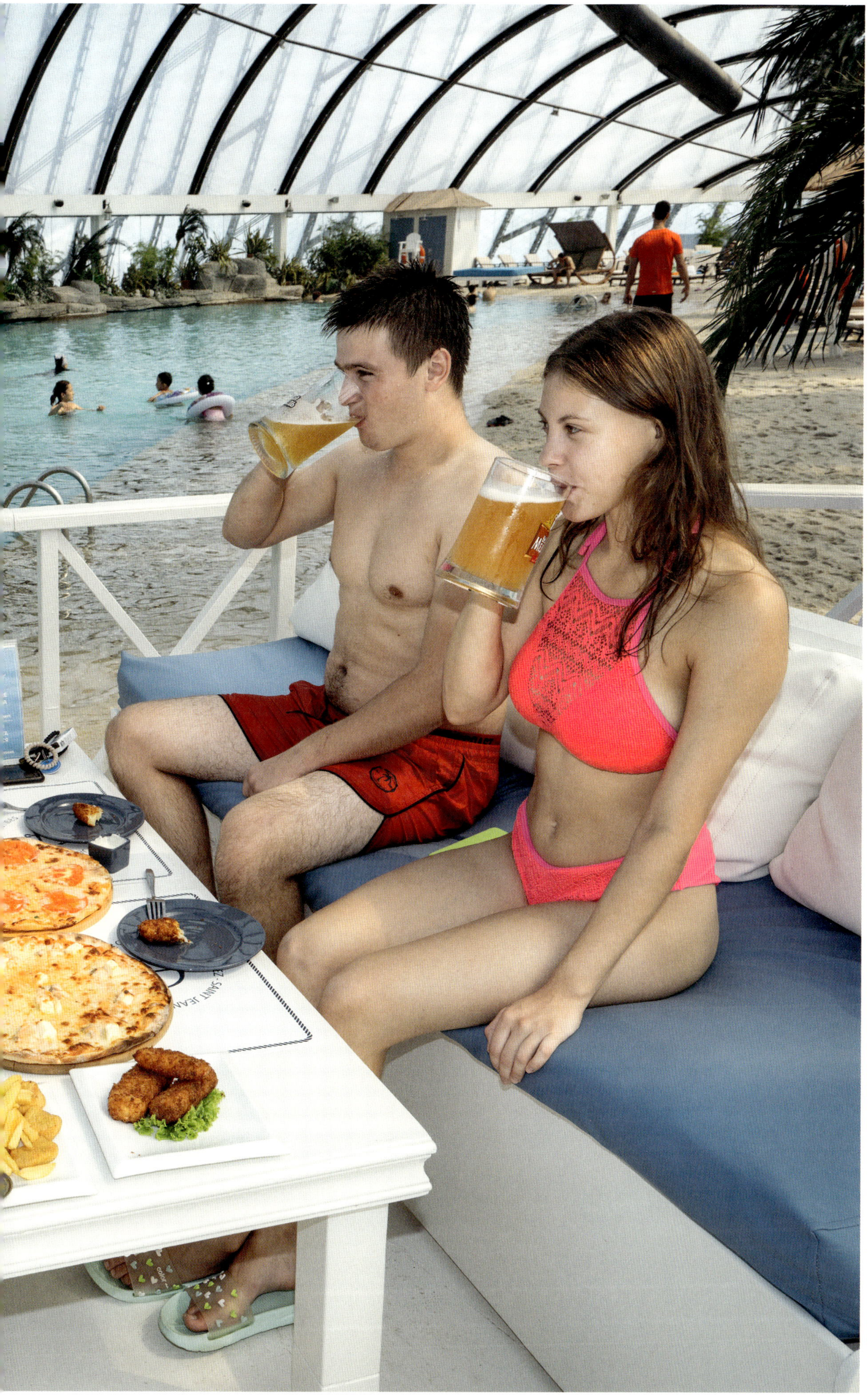

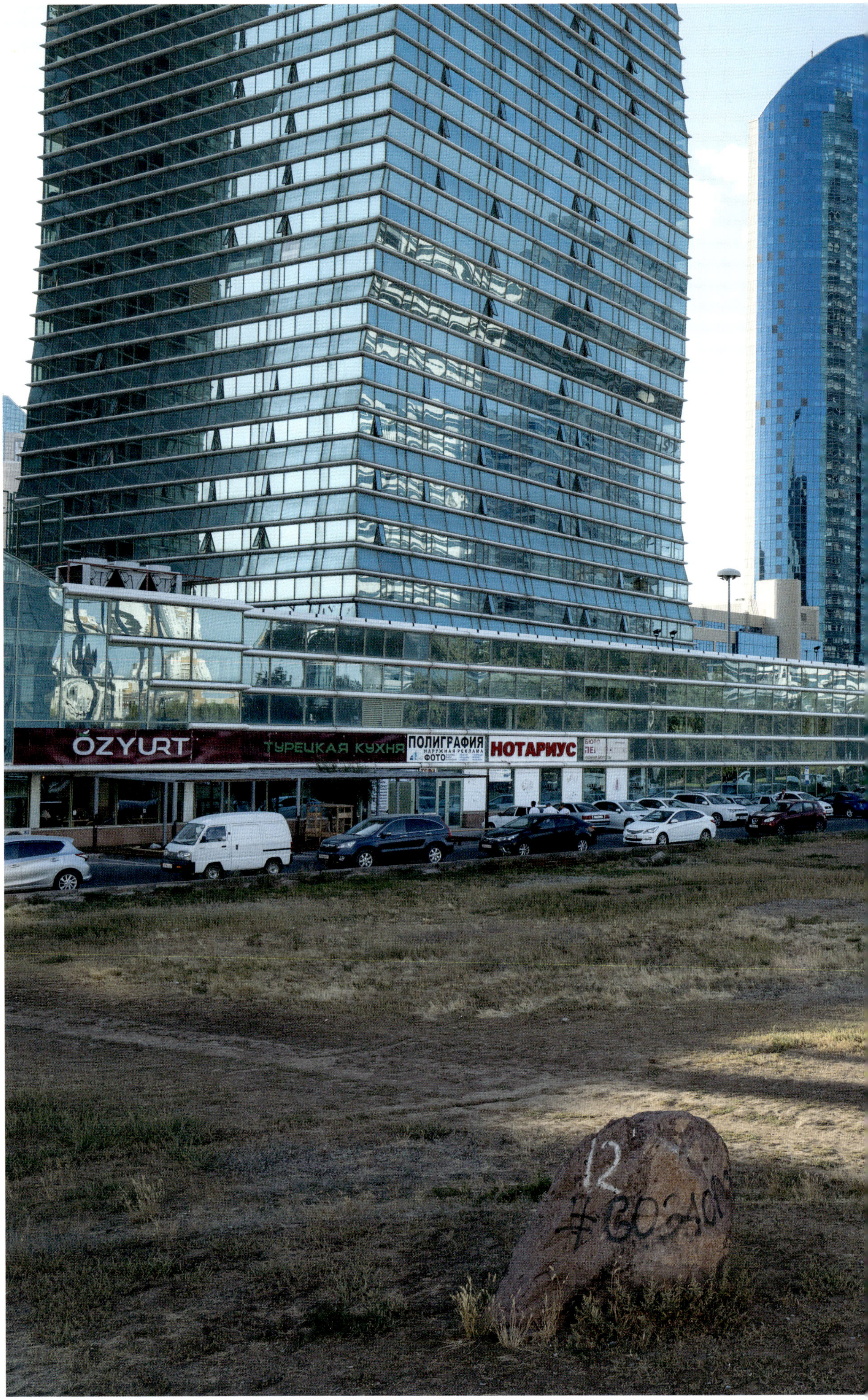

Northern Lights and Emerald Towers skyscrapers on Nurzhol Boulevard.

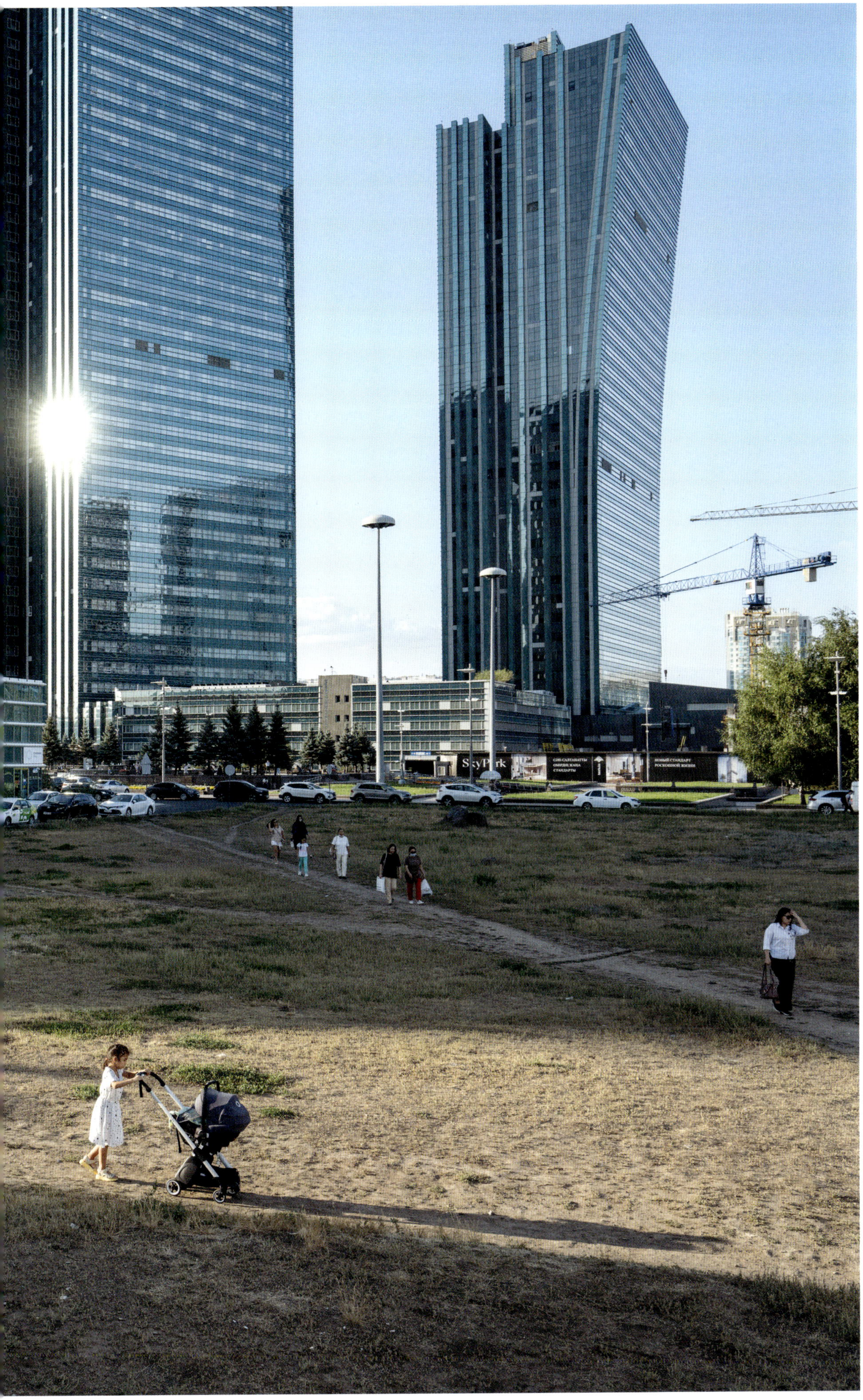
НОВЫЙ СТАНДАРТ
РОСКОШНОЙ ЖИЗНИ

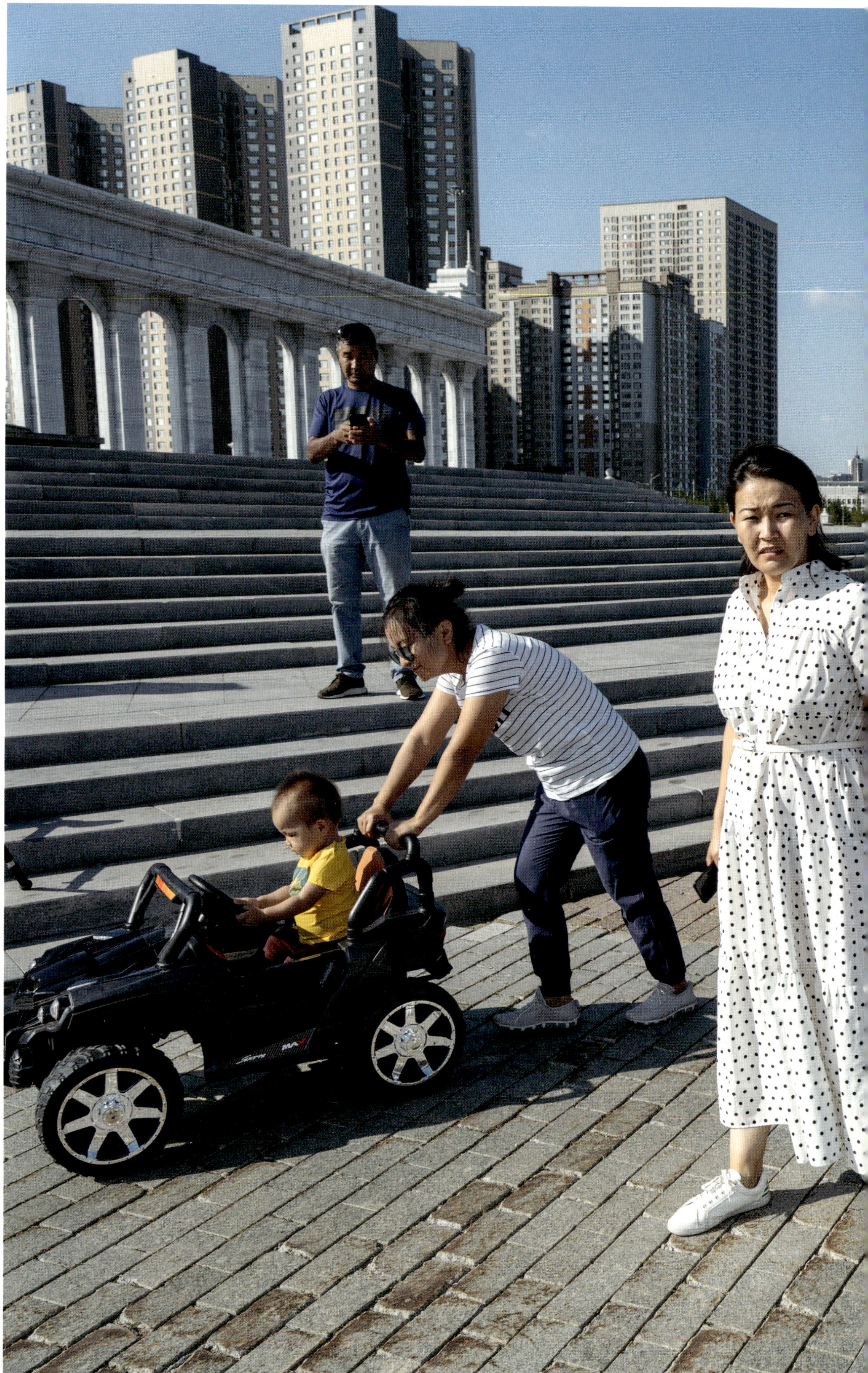

Independence Square
and Hazrat Sultan Mosque.

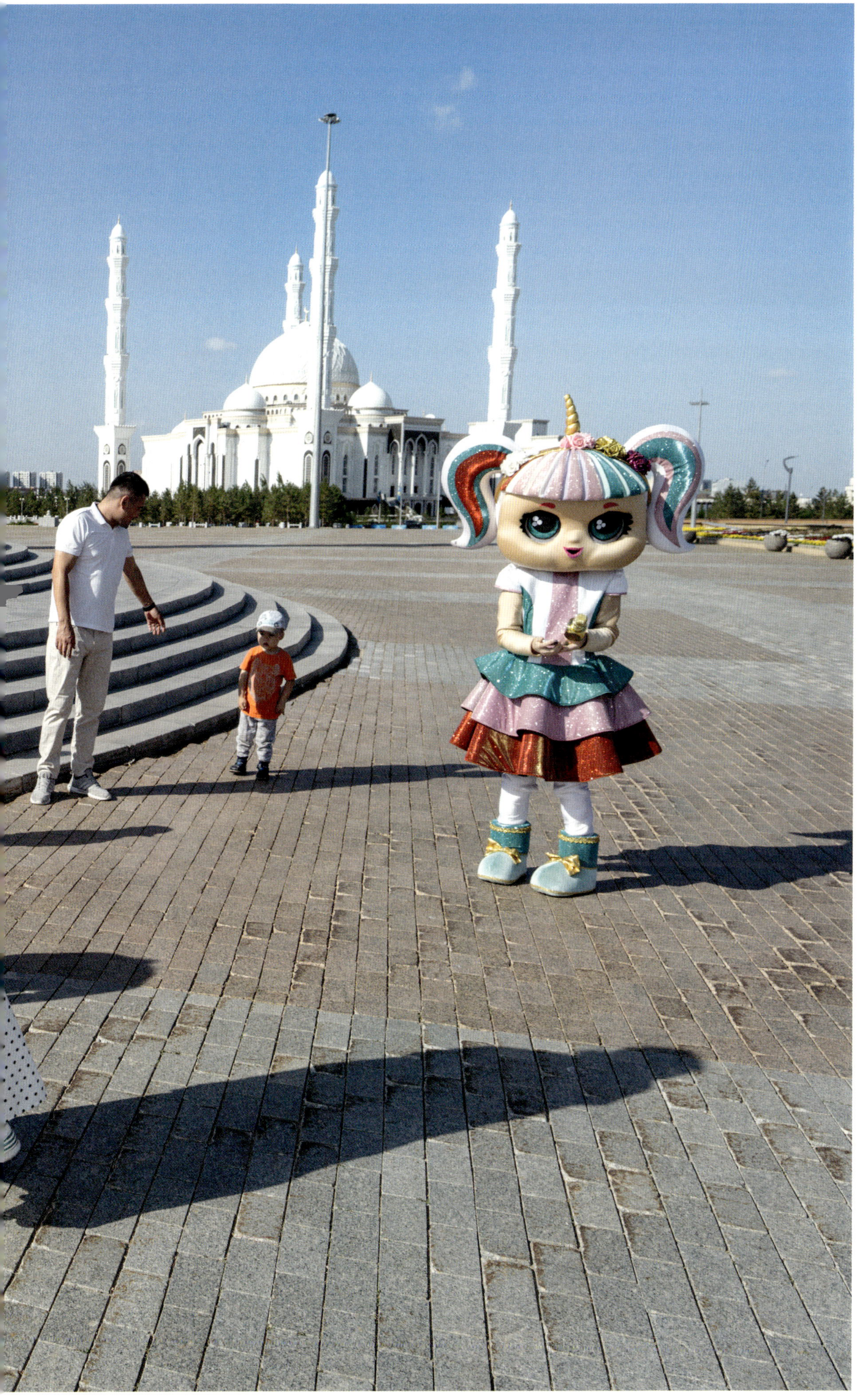

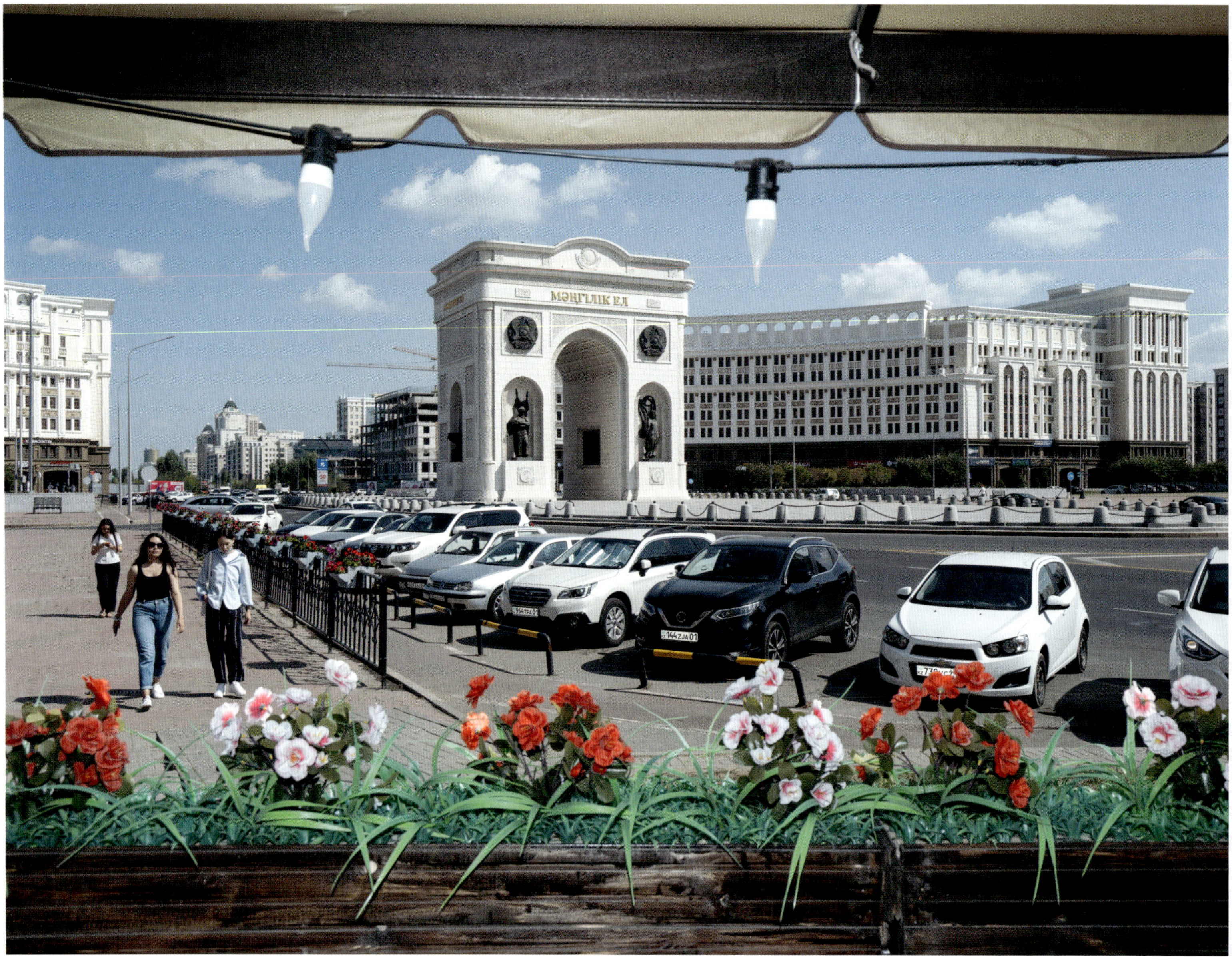

Eternal Nation Triumphal Arch.

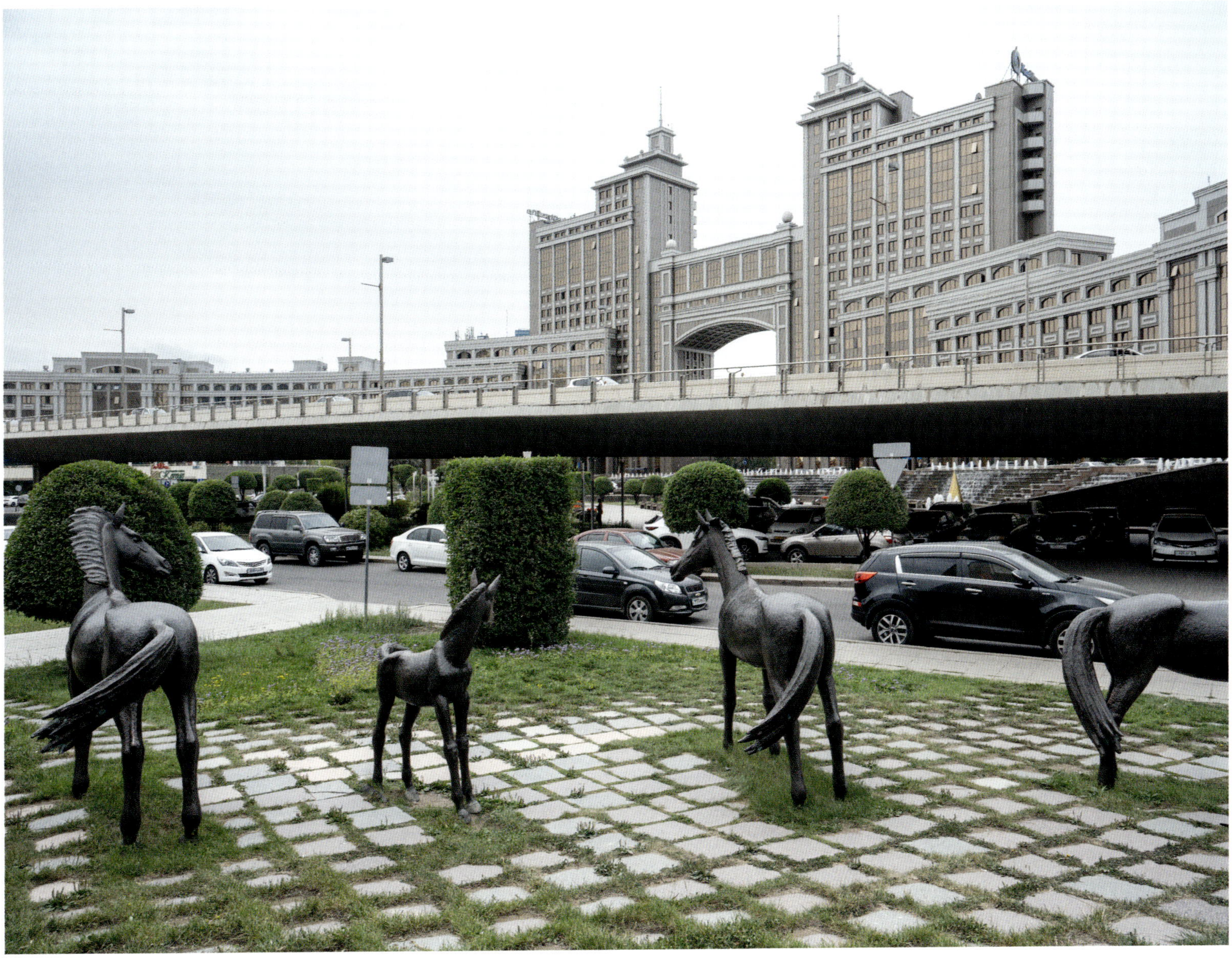

Headquarters of state-owned oil and gas company KazMunayGaz.

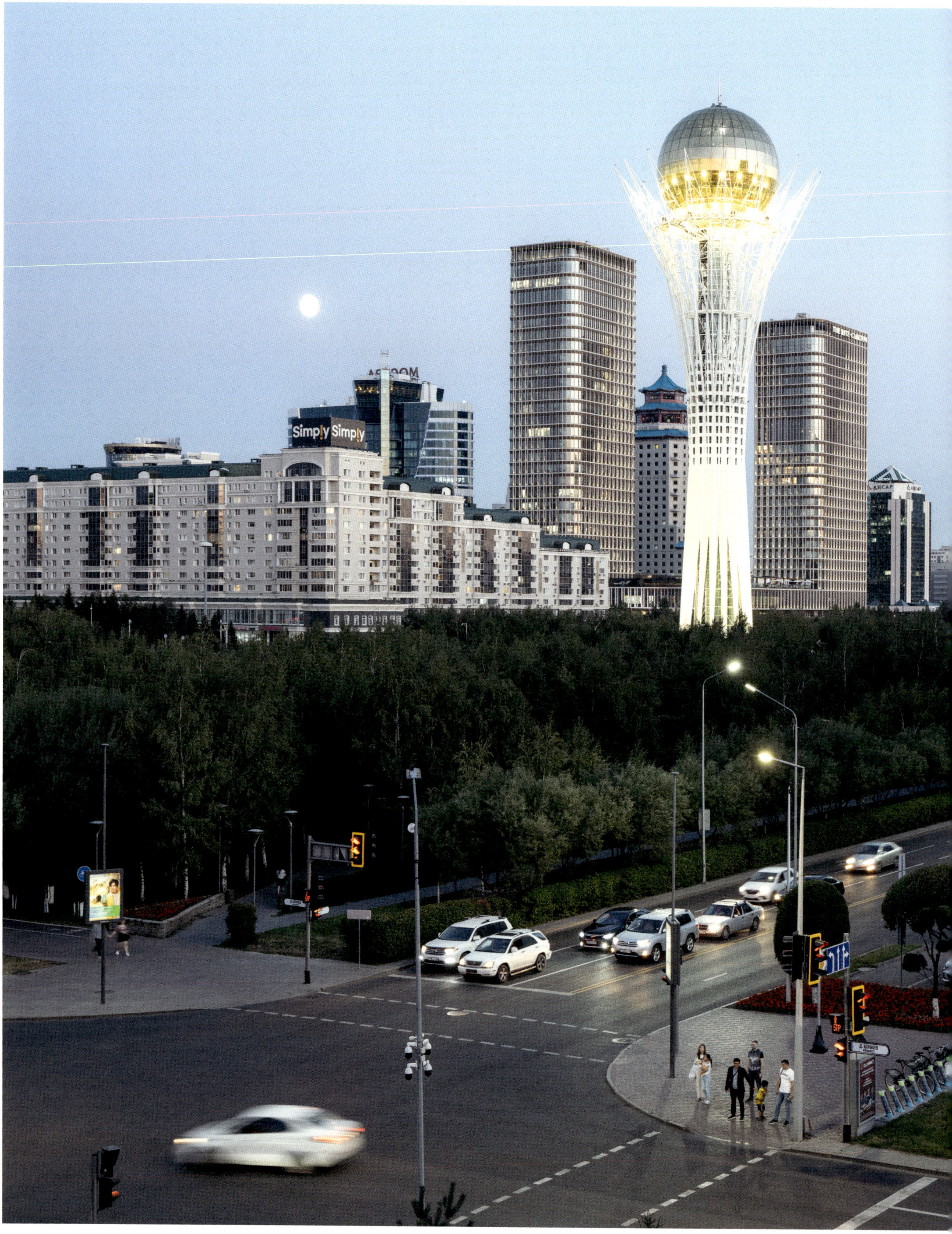
Simply Simply

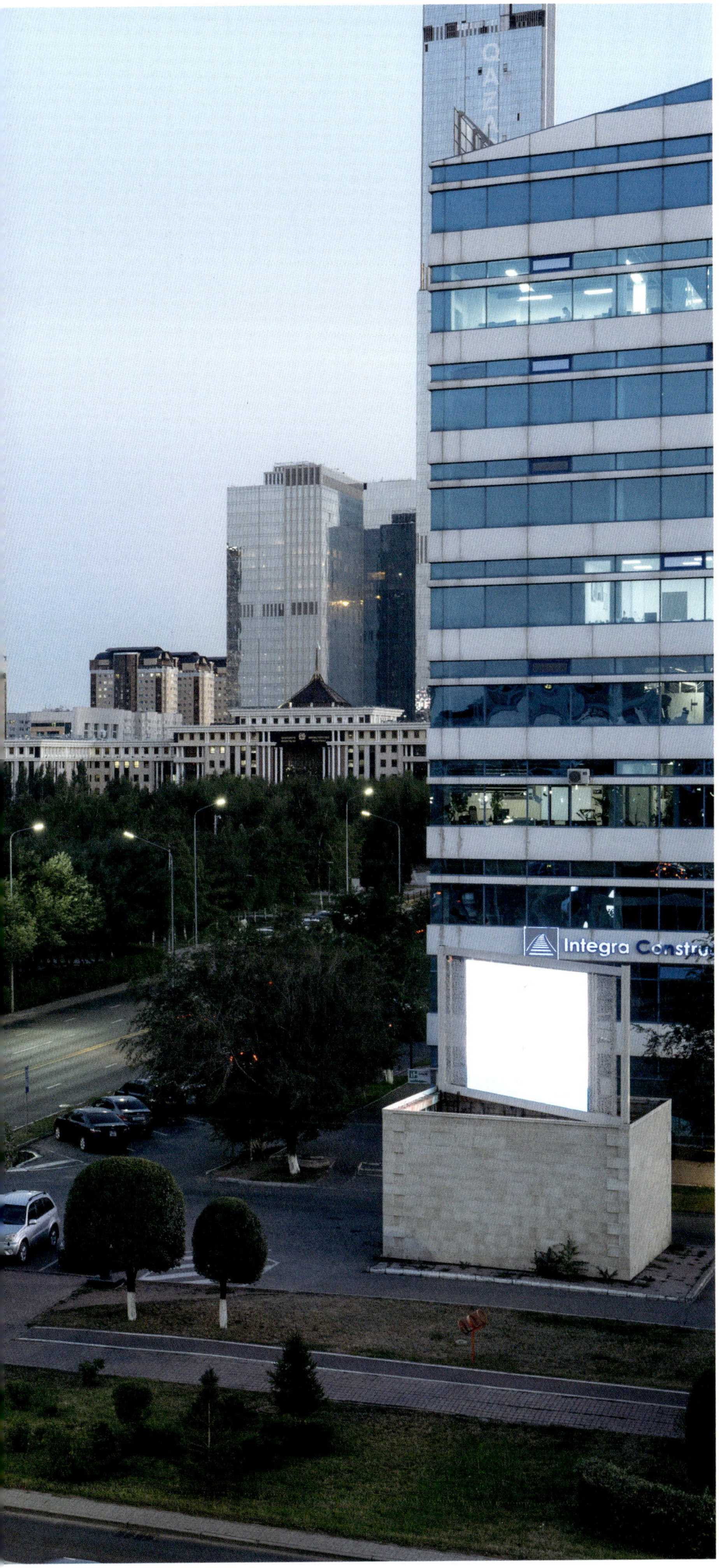

Bayterek Tower.

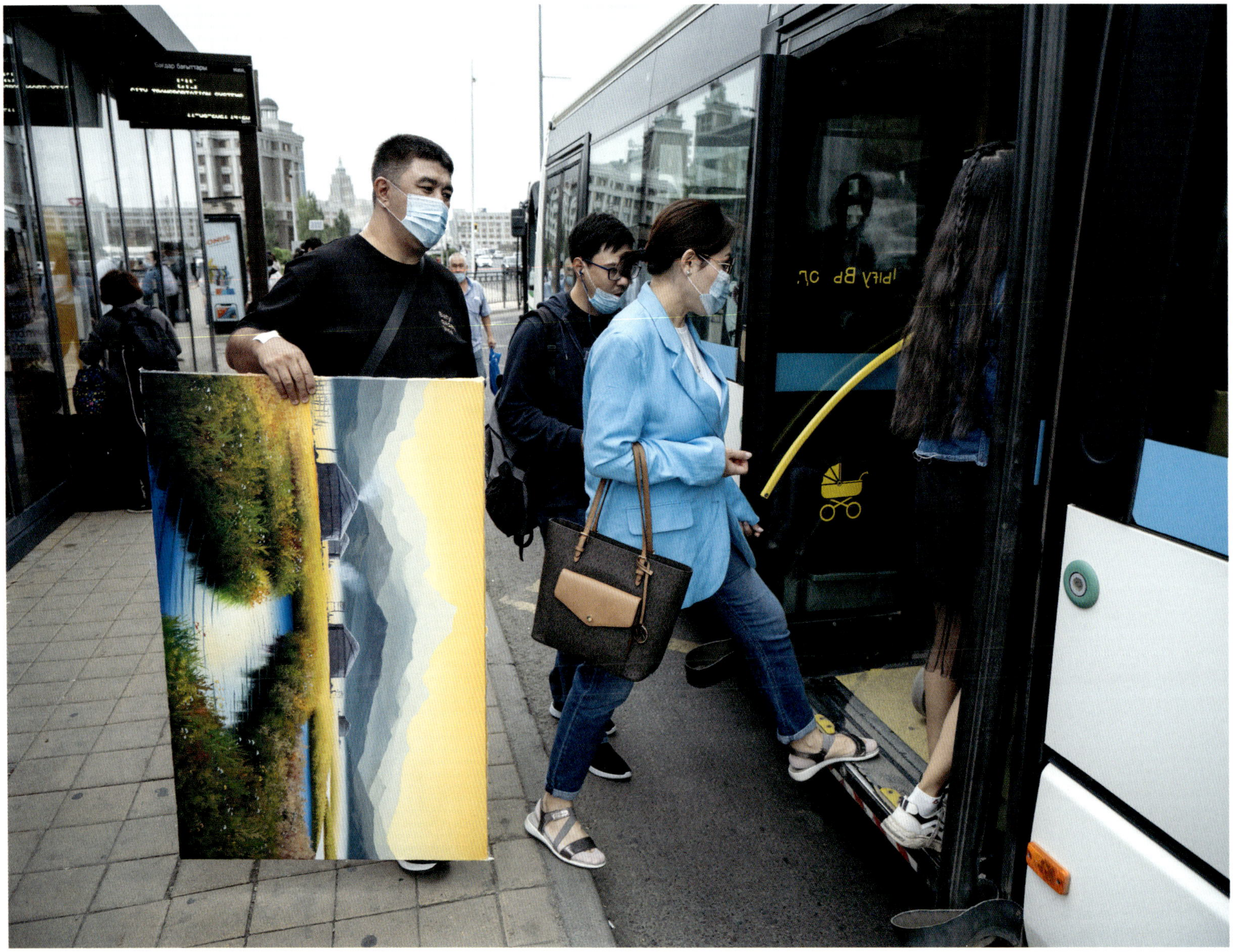

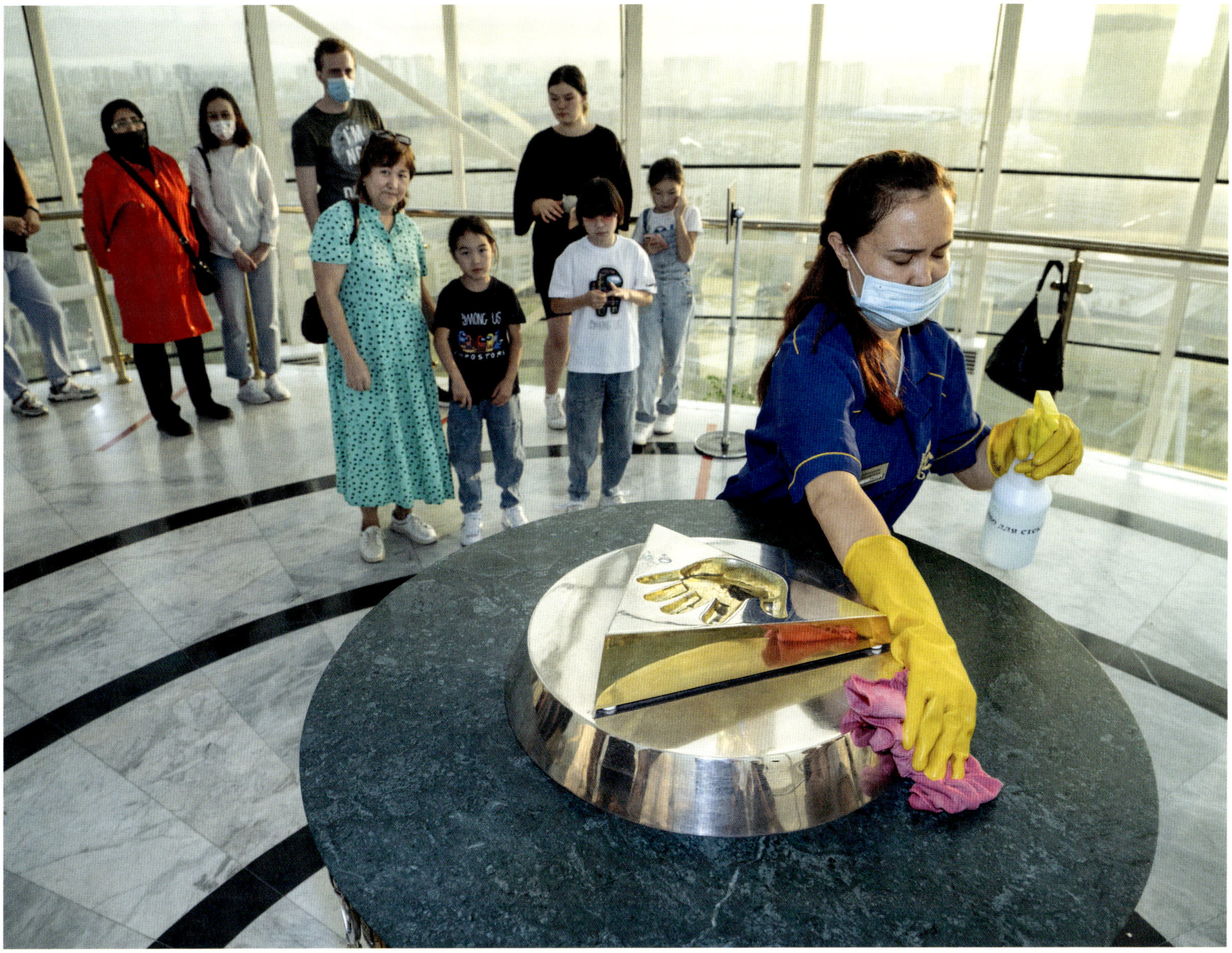

Golden cast of former president Nazarbayev's right hand at the top of Bayterek Tower.

Attendant at the top of Bayterek Tower.

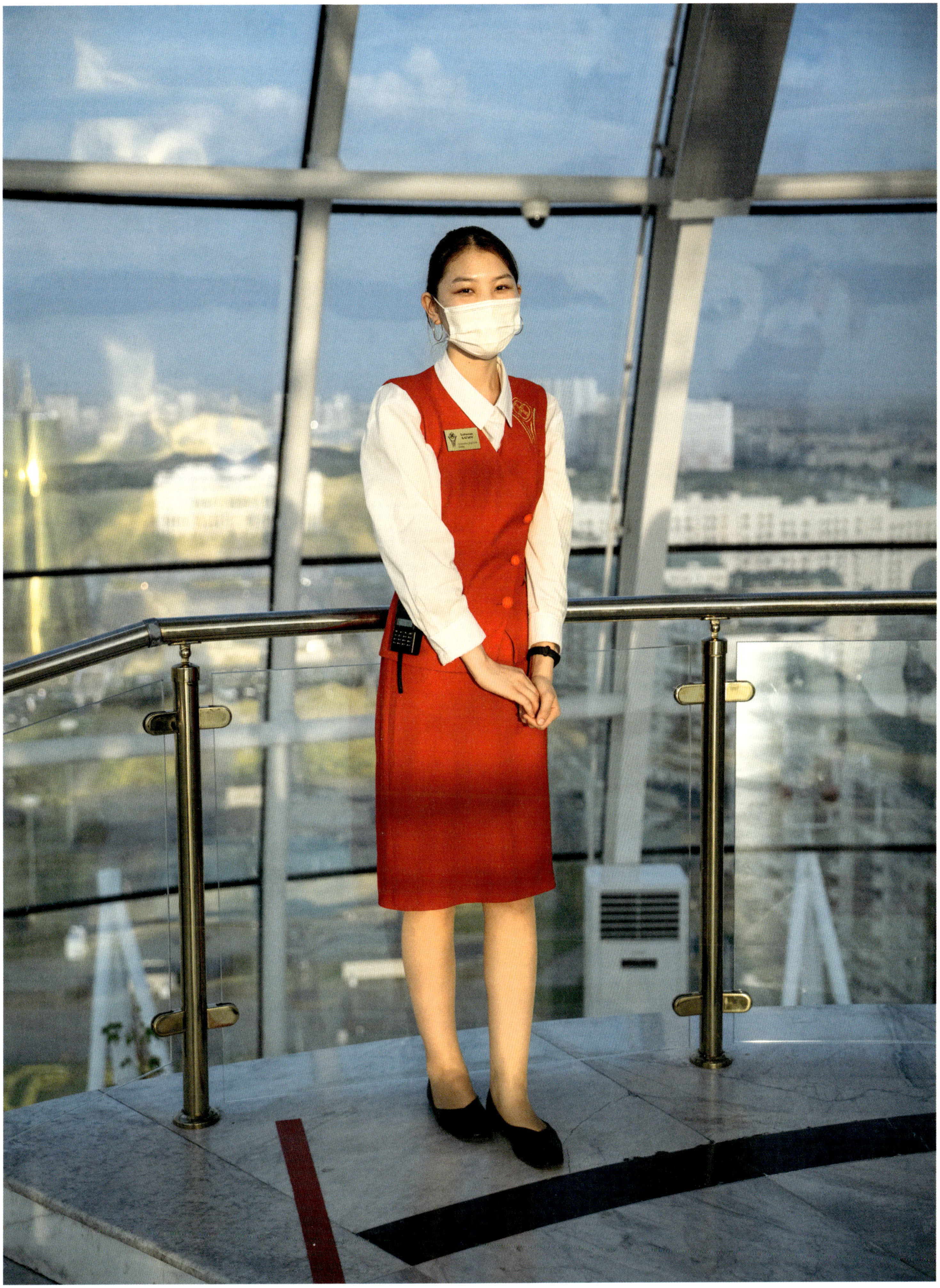

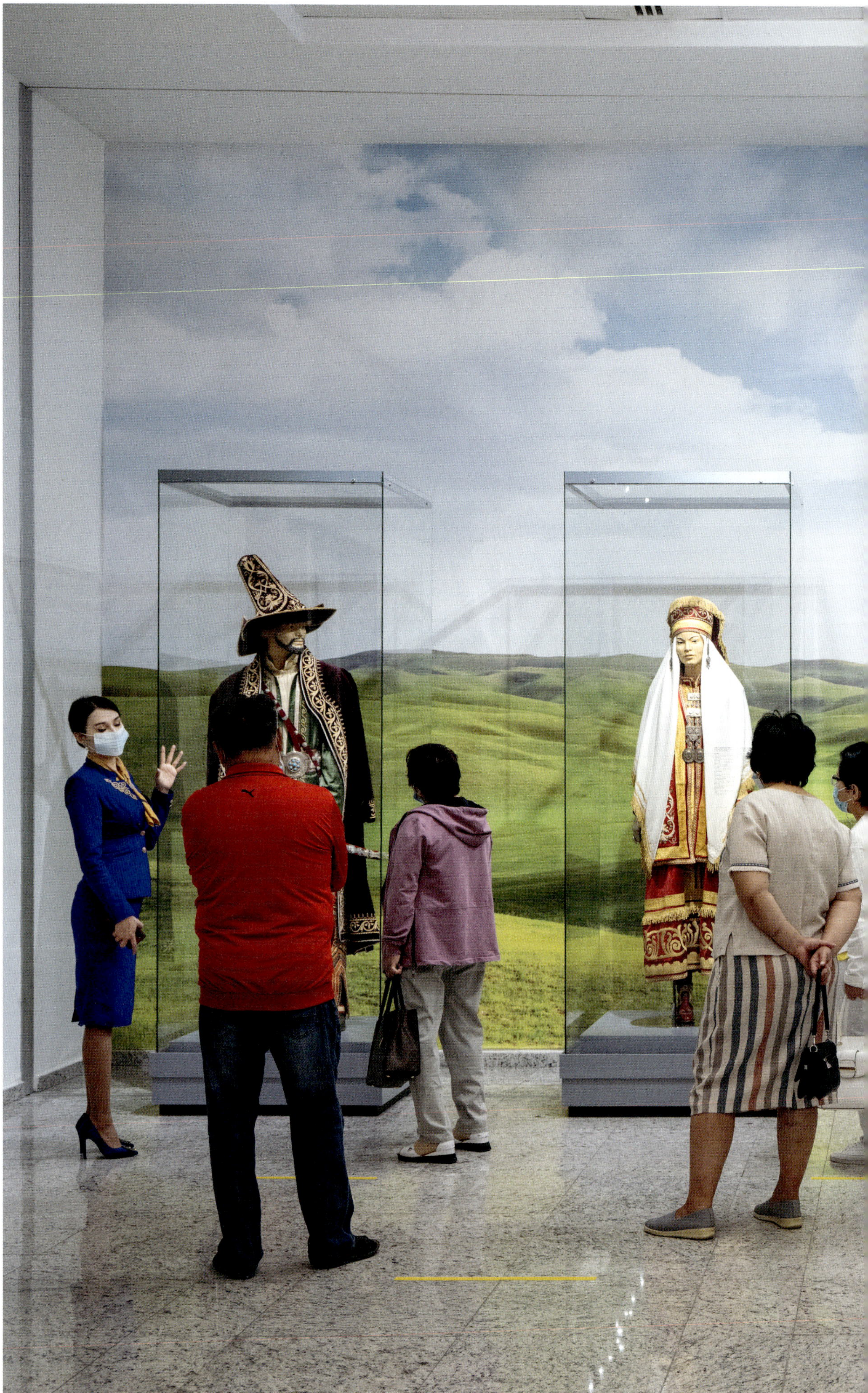

National Museum of
the Republic of Kazakhstan.

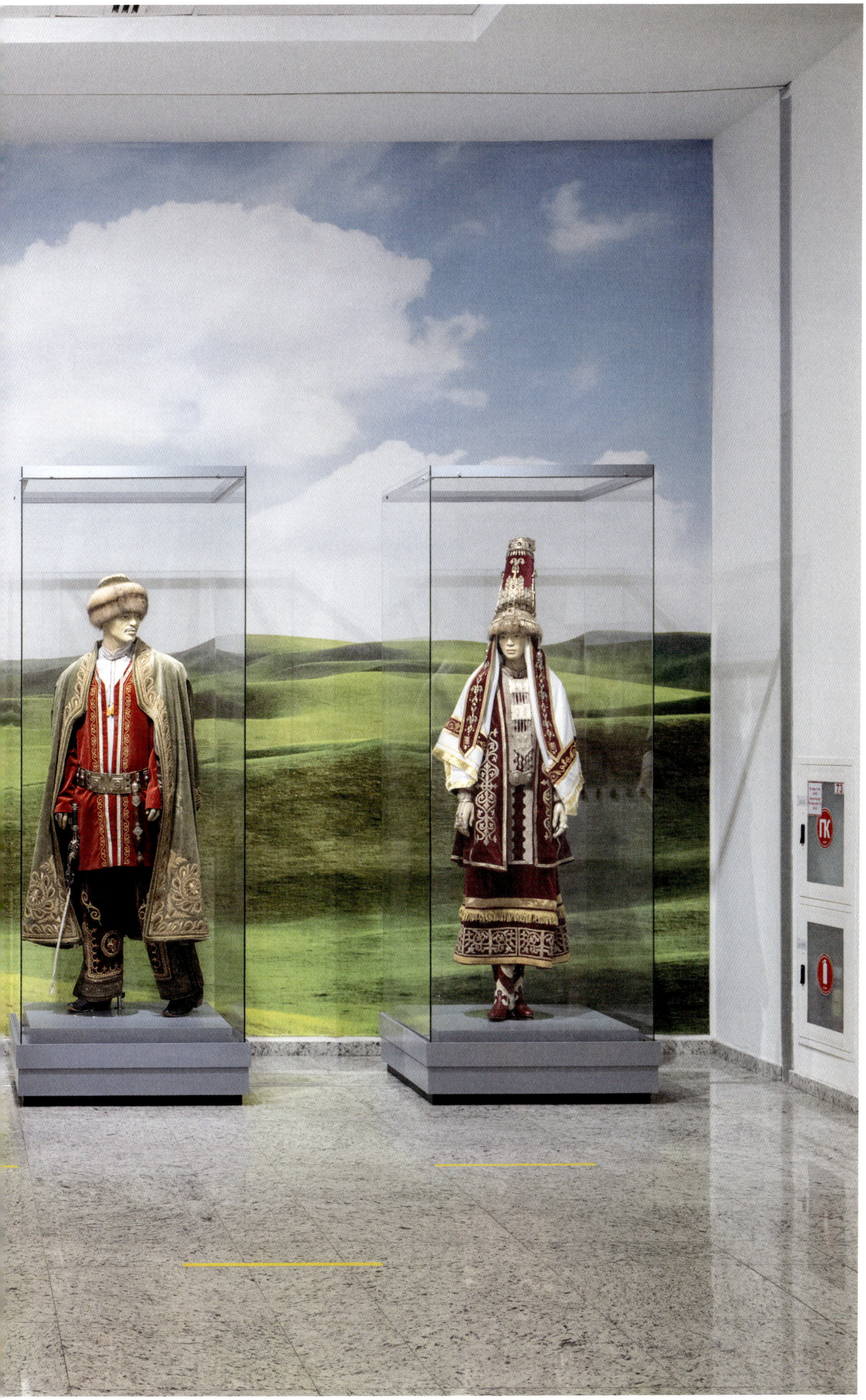
ПК

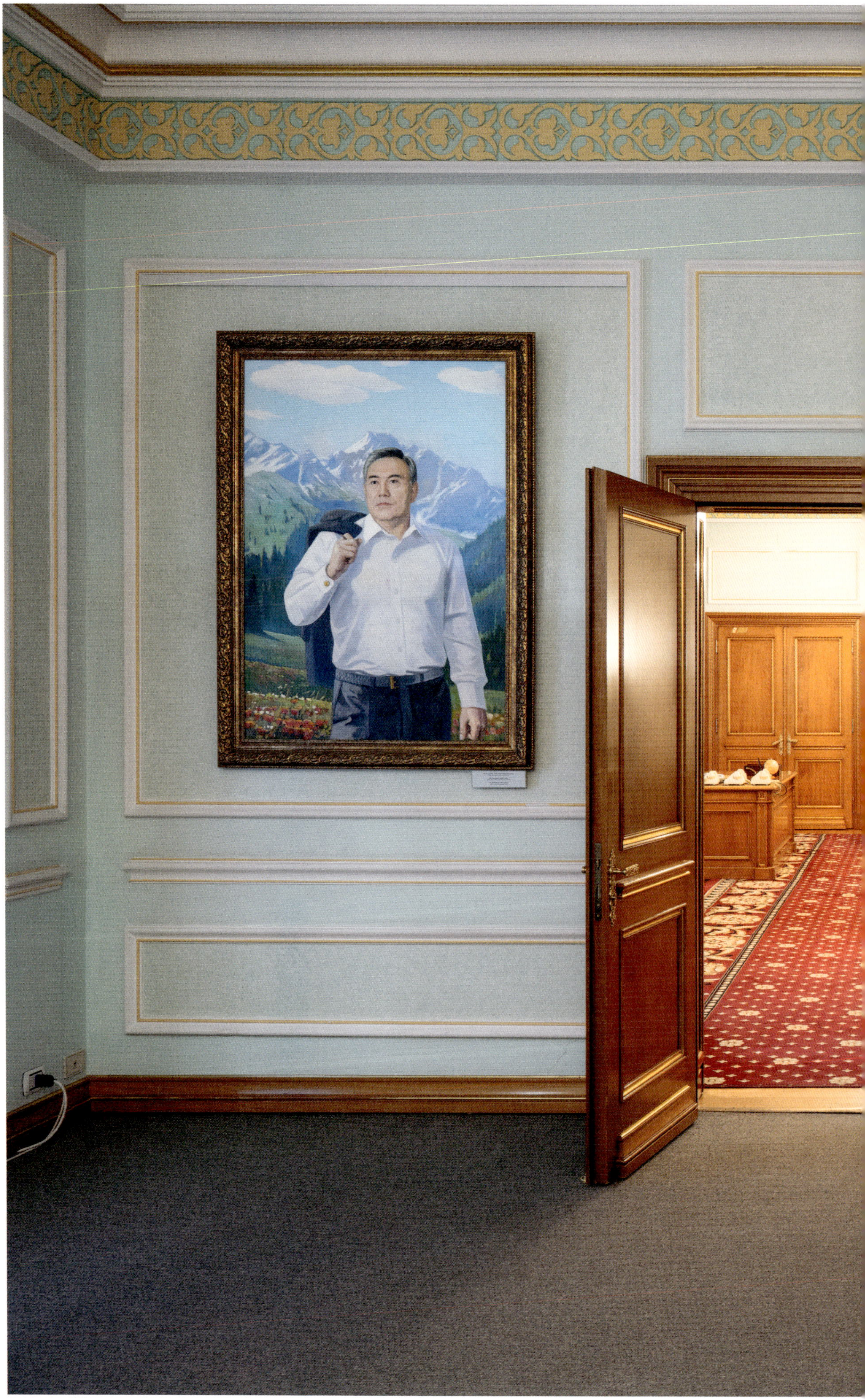

Portraits of former president Nazarbayev in the Museum of the First President of the Republic of Kazakhstan.

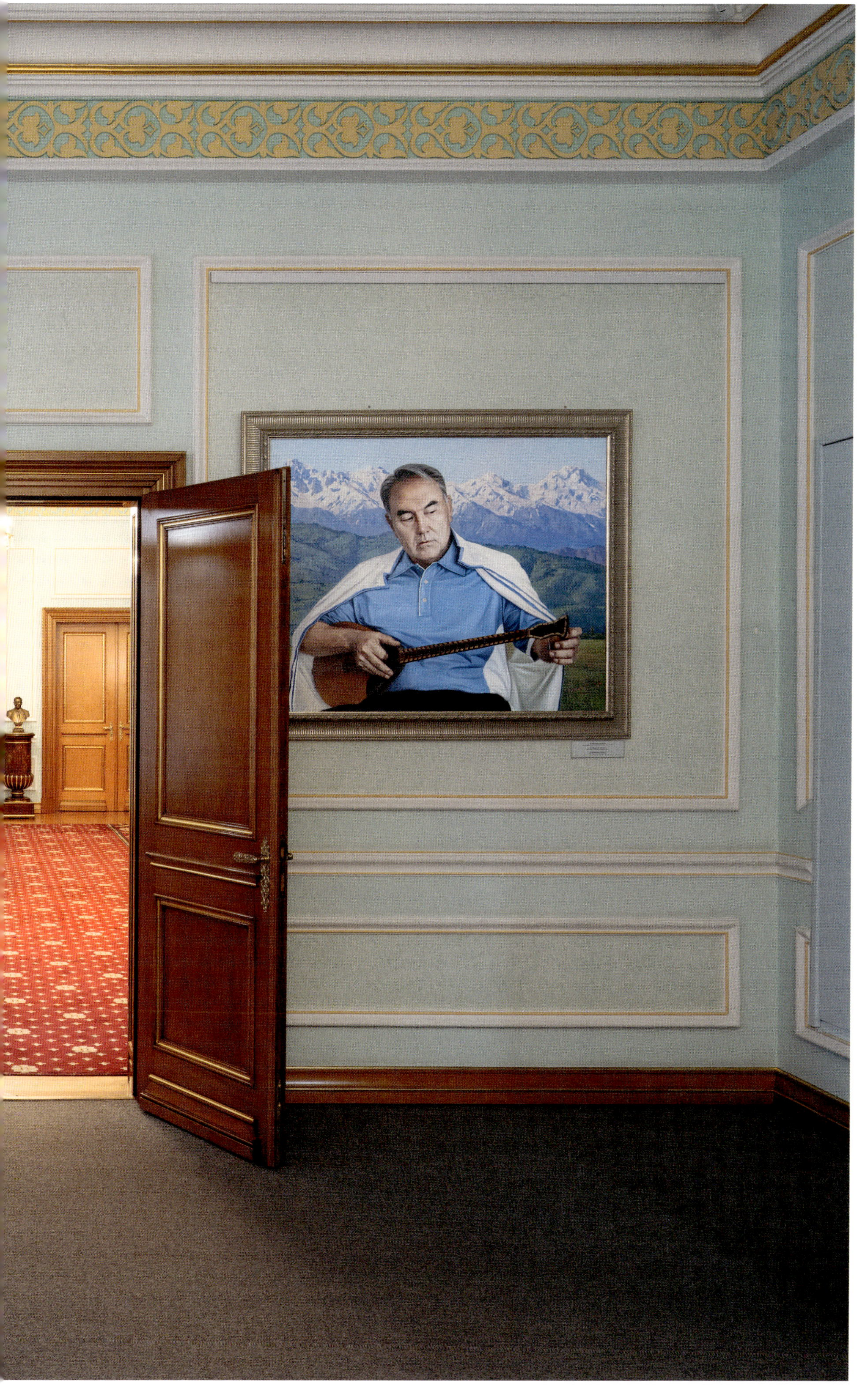

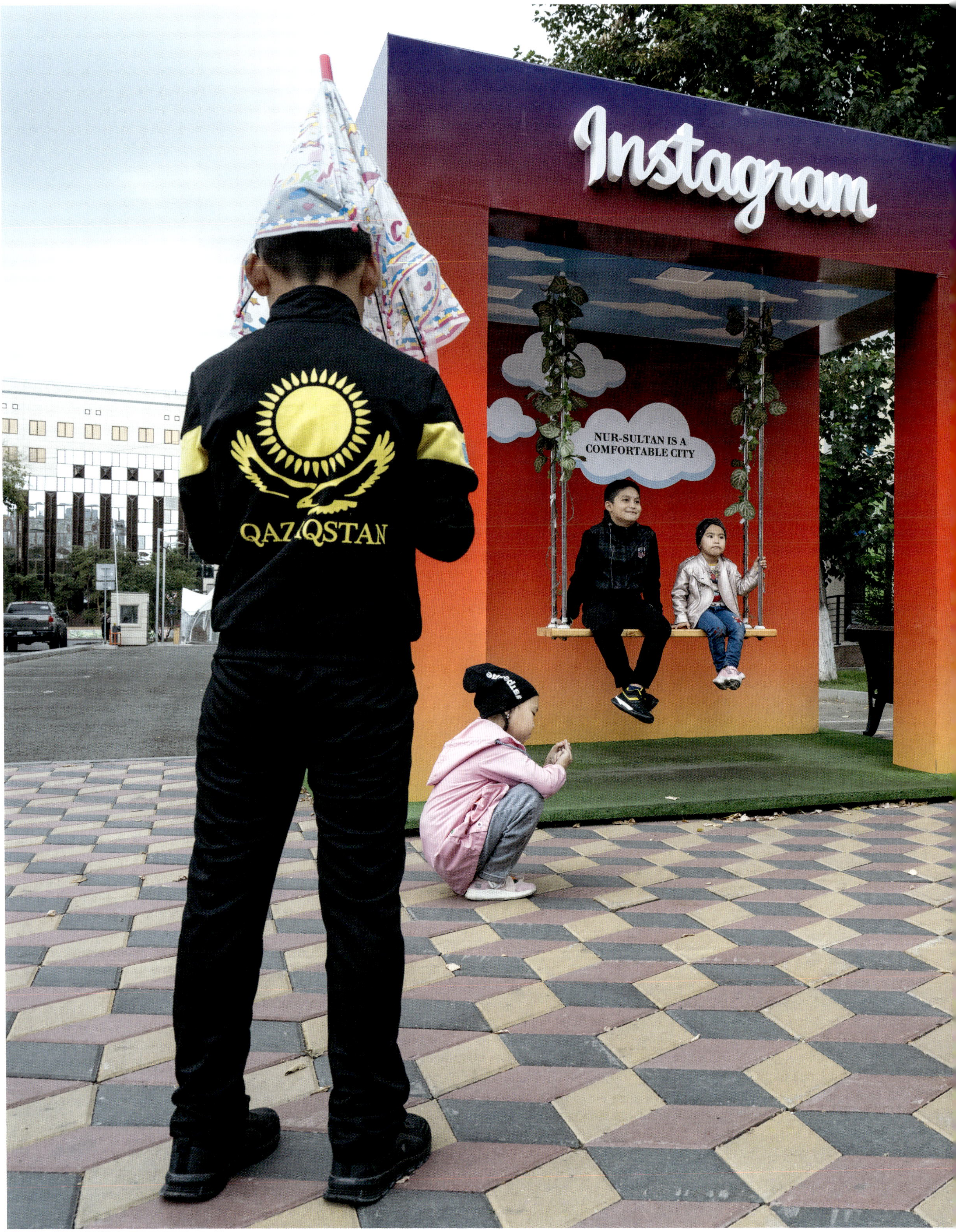
Instagram
NUR-SULTAN IS A
COMFORTABLE CITY

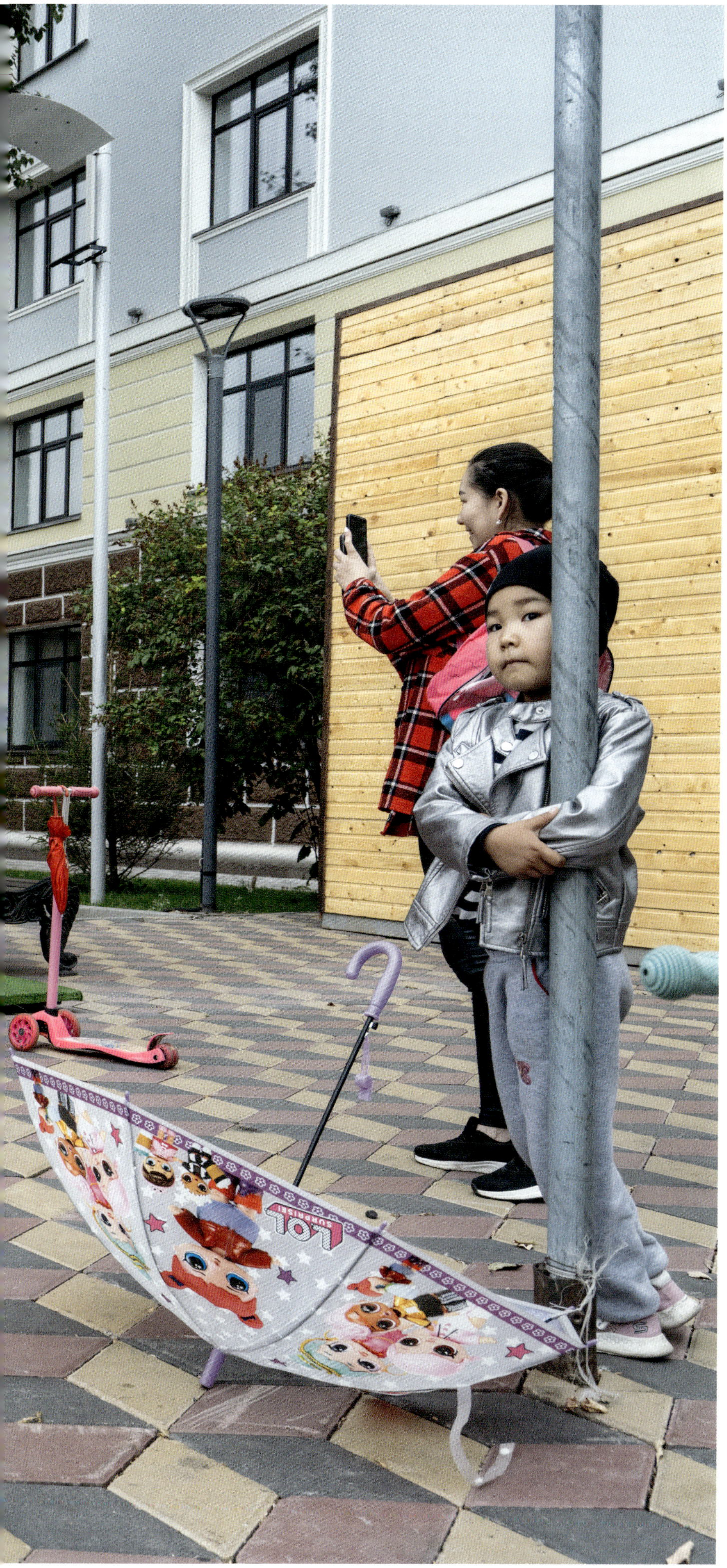

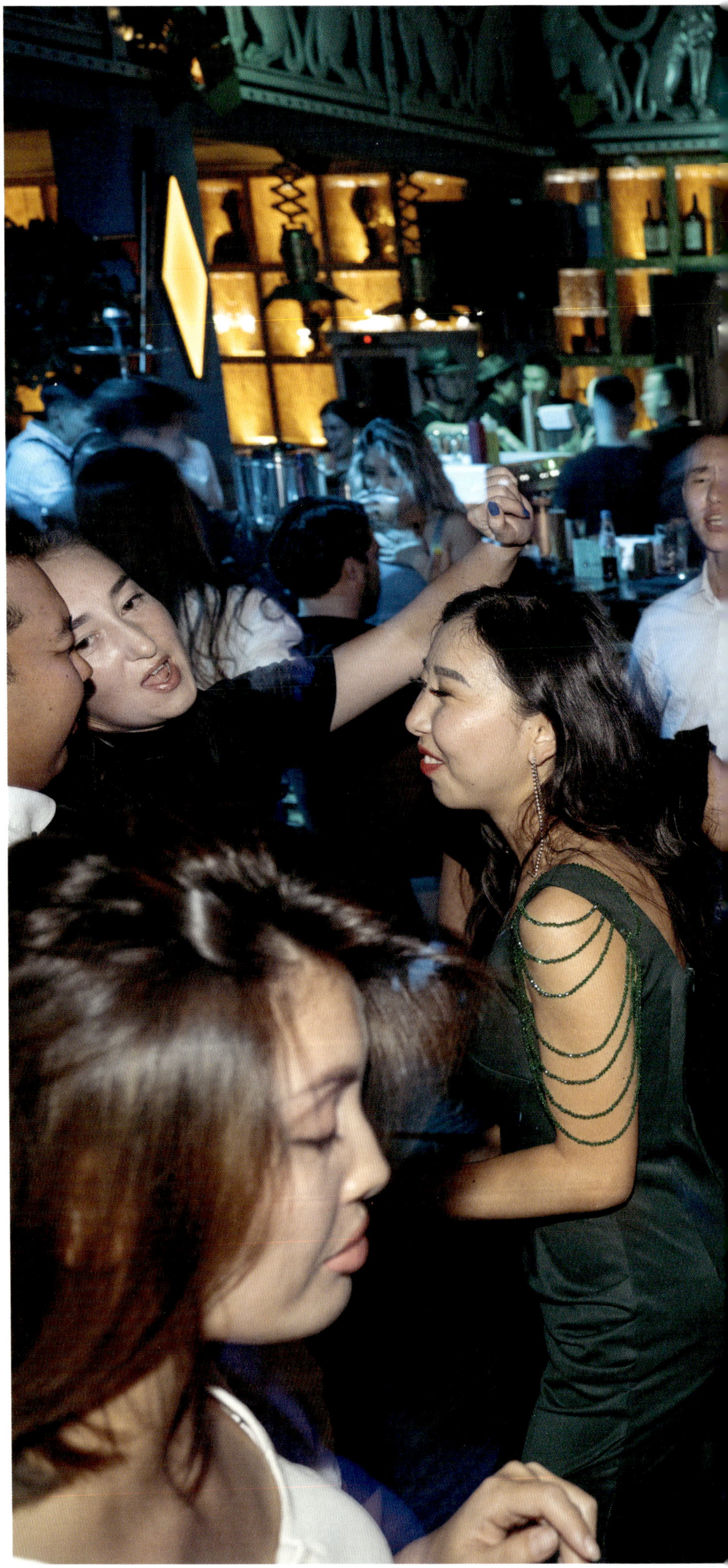

Zoloto nightclub.

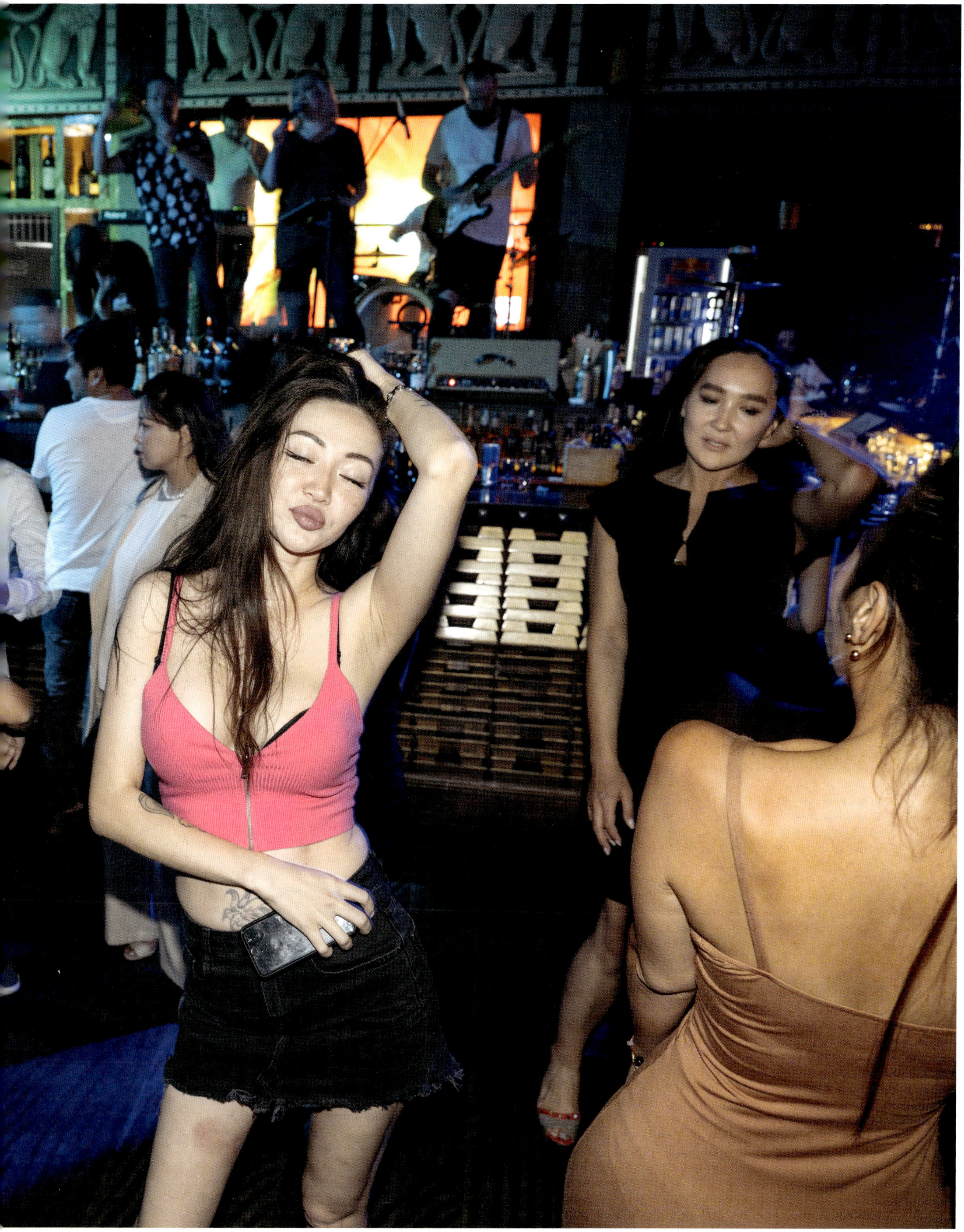

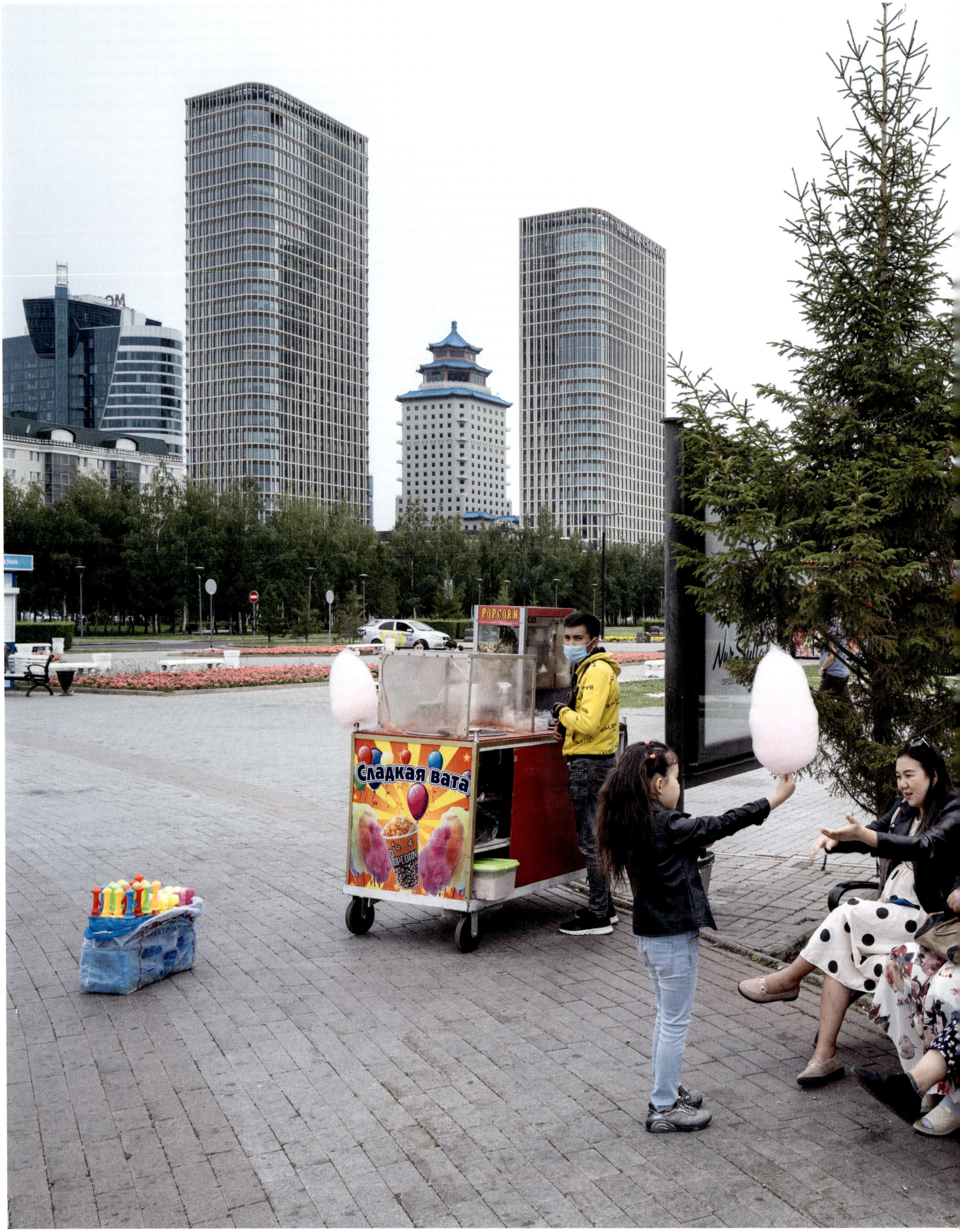
POPCORN
Сладкая вата
POPCORN

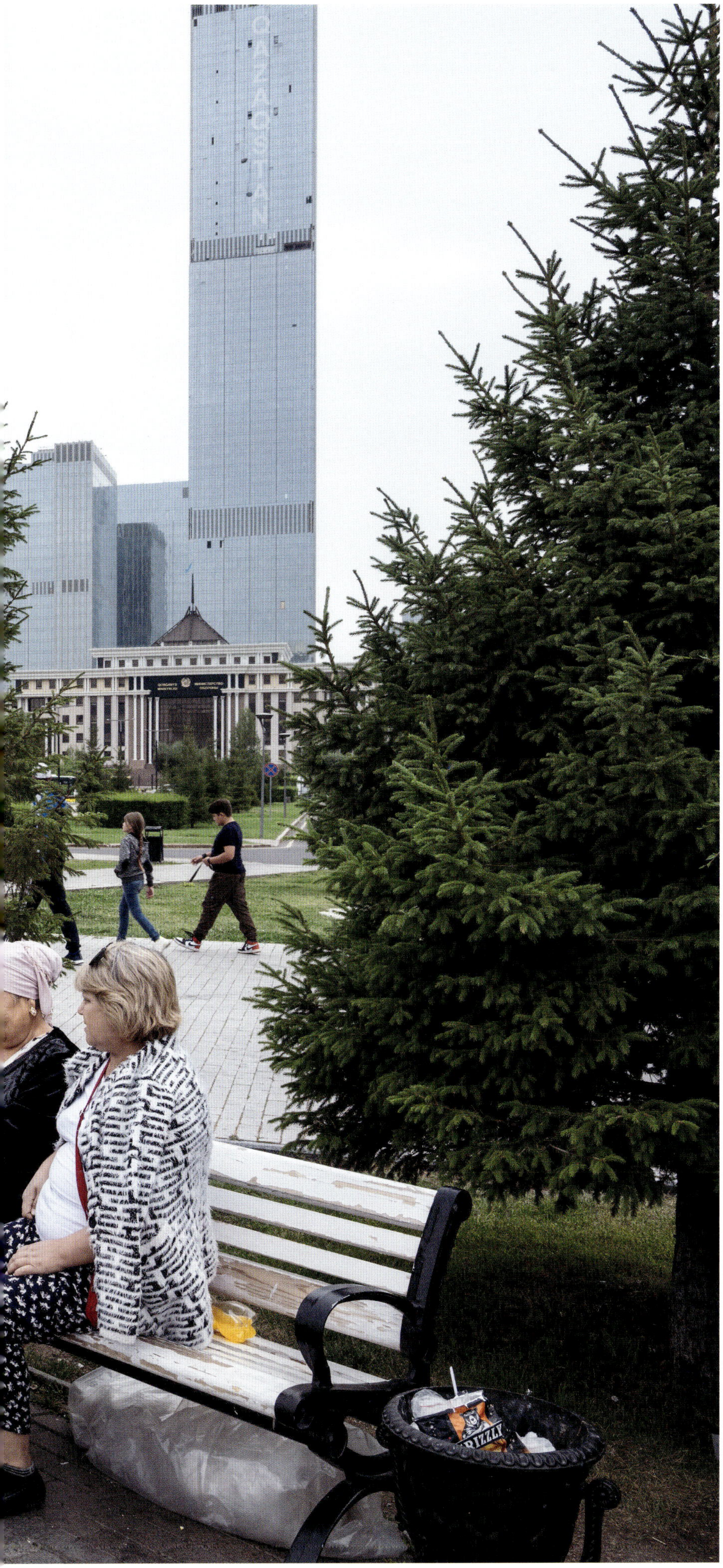

Bayterek Square.

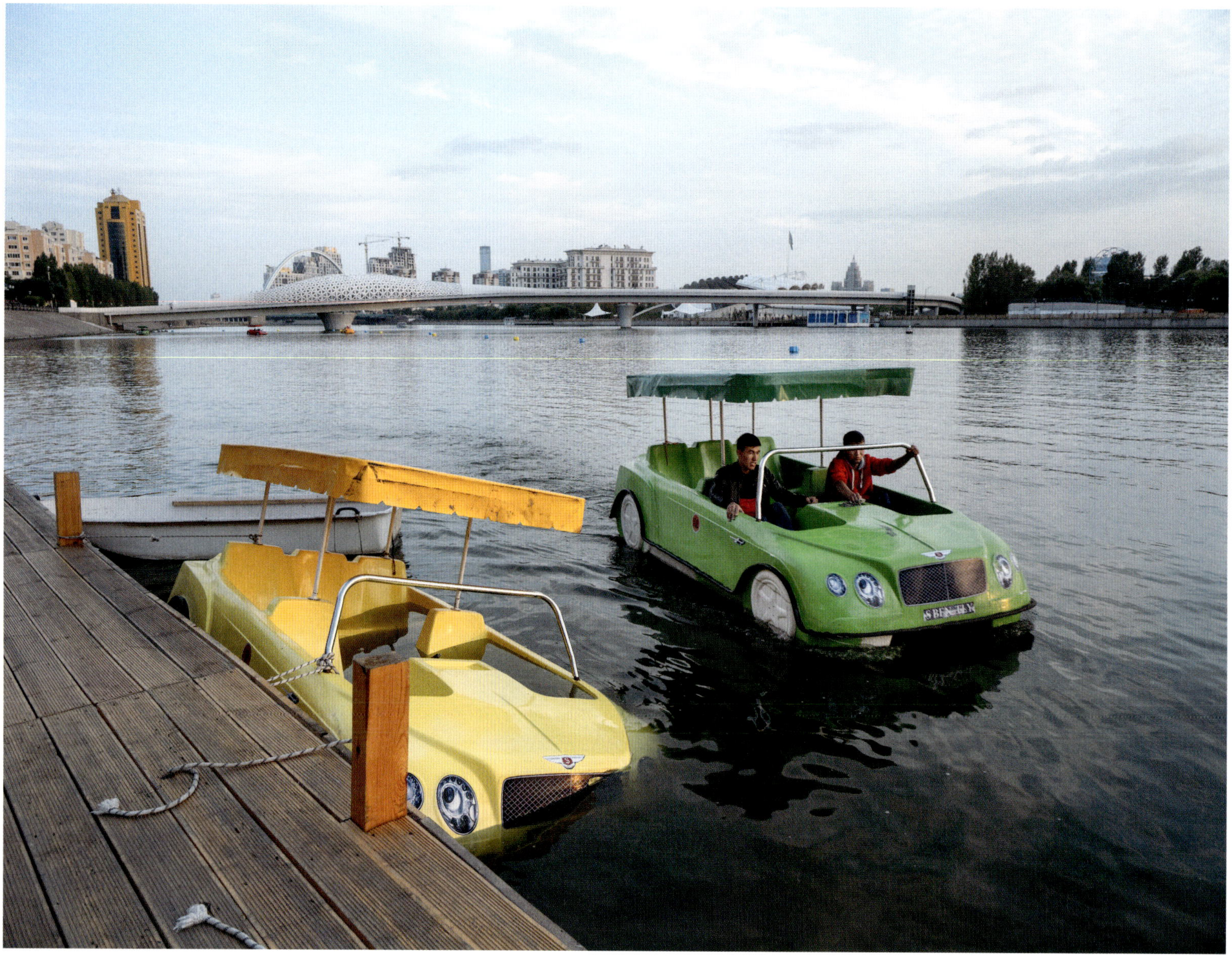

Ishim River.

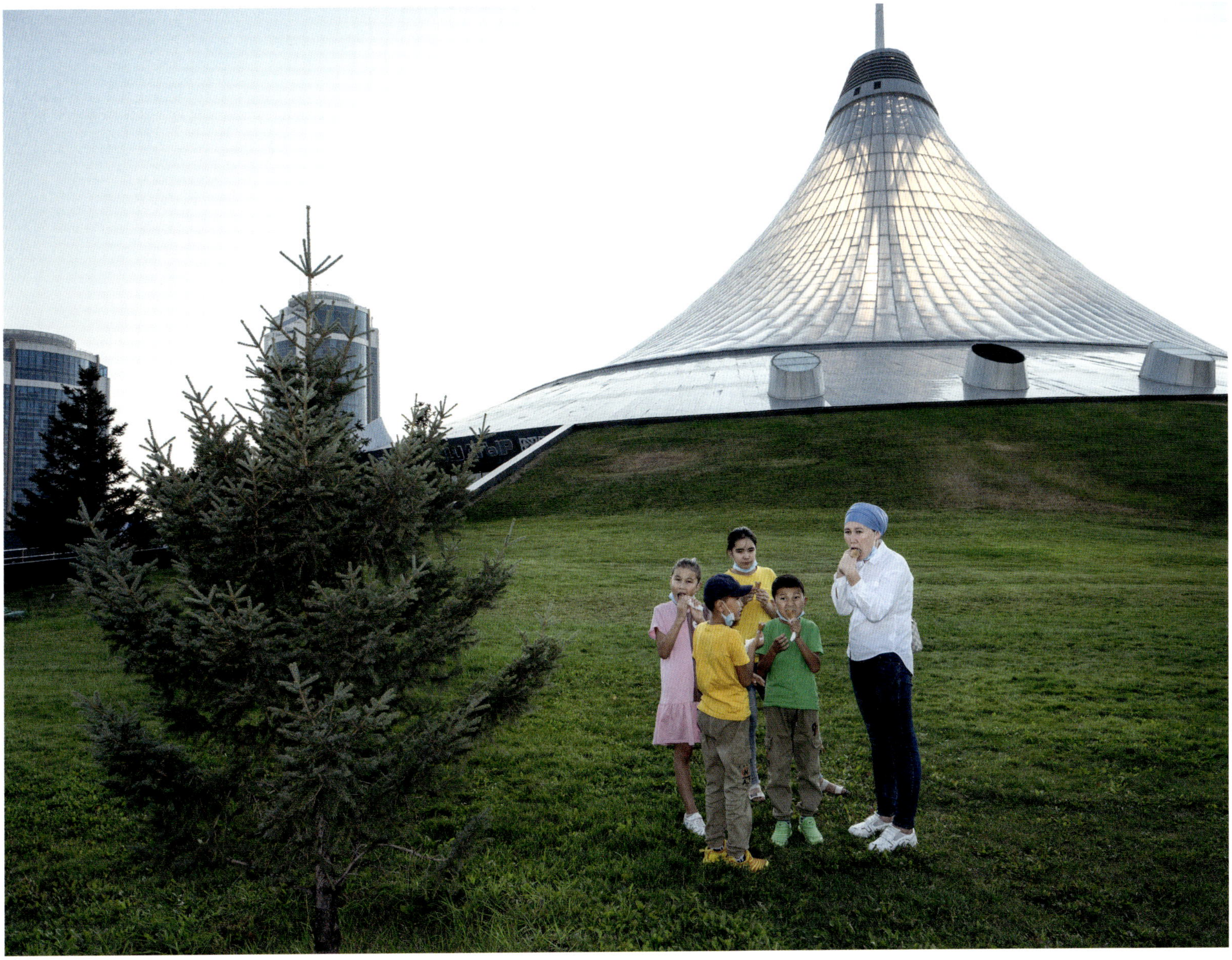

Khan Shatyr shopping and entertainment complex.

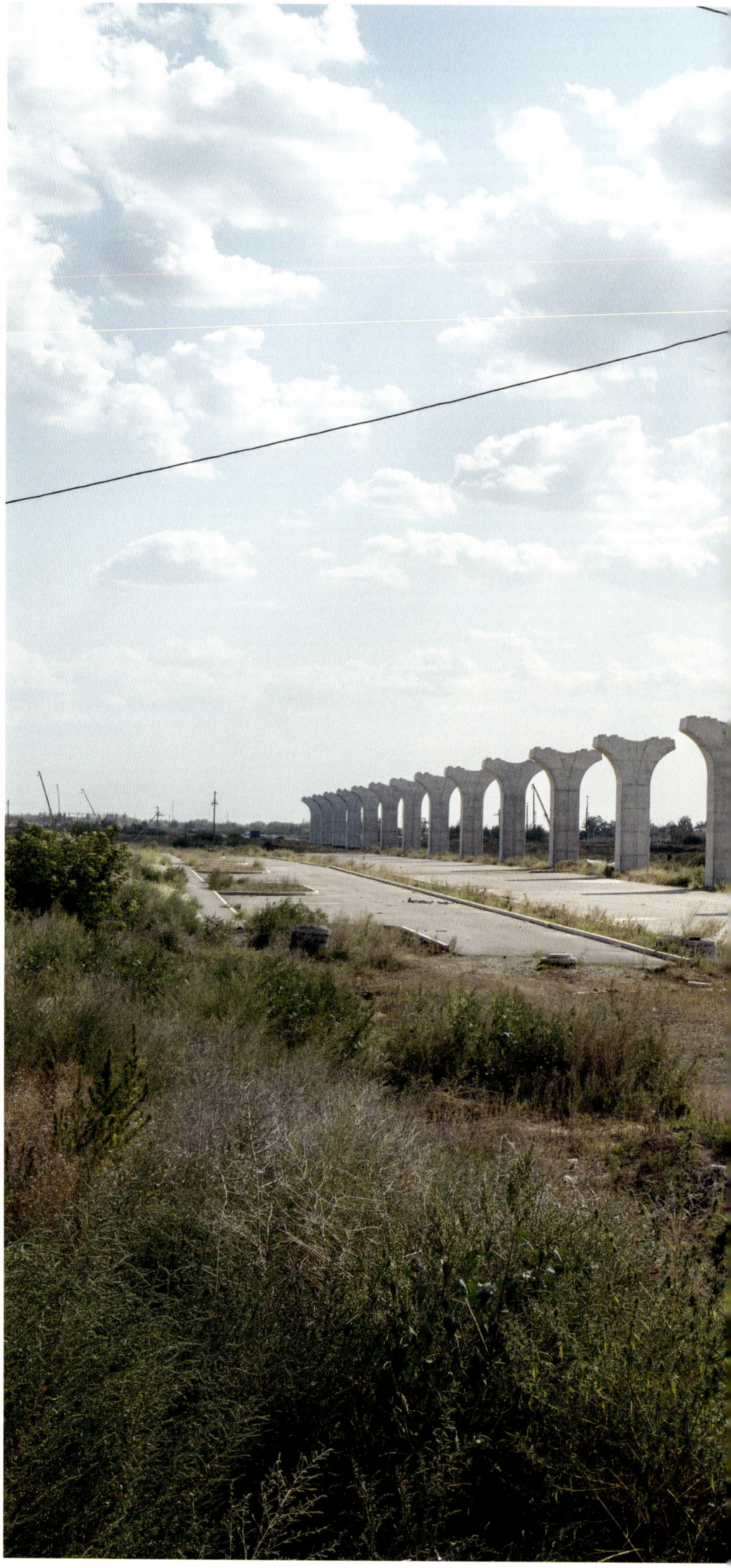

Unfinished construction site
of the light rail transit.

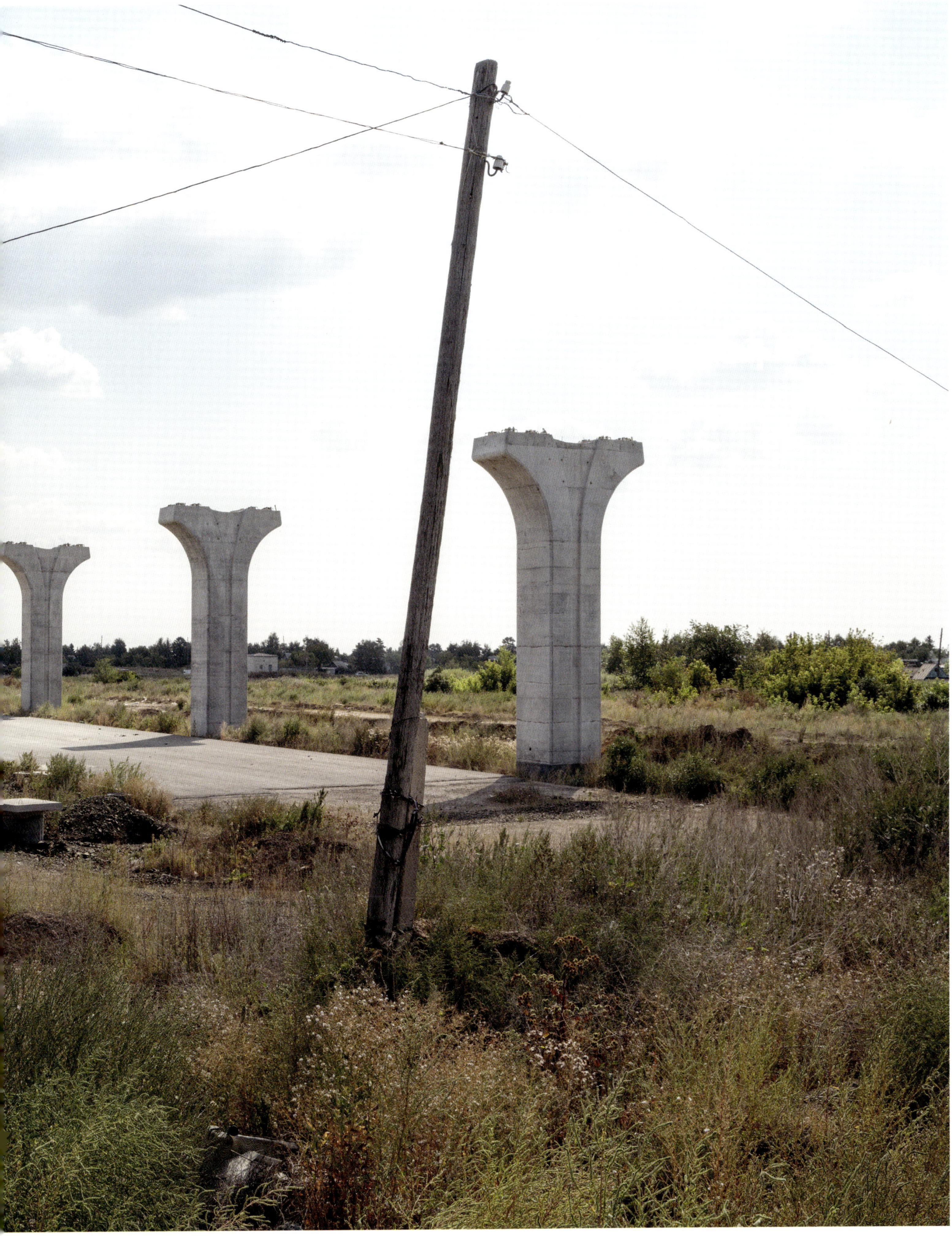

SOUTH KOREA

SEJONG

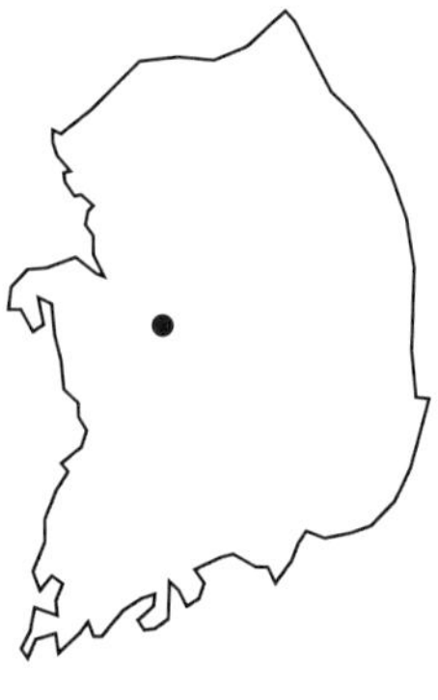

Start of construction: 2007
Inauguration date: 2 july 2012
Initiated by: President Roh Moo-hyun
Master plan by: Ahn Gun-hyuk (based on ideas of Andrés Perea Ortega and Jean-Pierre Dürig)
Population in 2023: 390,000
Surface area: 465 km²
Current capital: Seoul

It is a rainy Sunday evening in Sejong. The area around Sejong Convention Center, where my guesthouse is located, is deserted. No shop to be found in the wider area, no restaurant, nothing moves in the street. The loud croaking of bullfrogs can be heard from a draining gutter. I feel like I am on *The Truman Show*, after everyone has left the set.

Tomorrow, Monday, this neighbourhood will wake up again. Very briefly, during the morning rush hour, it will get busy. Then a queue will form near the Government Complex, an irregular string of 15 government buildings linked by pedestrian bridges. The 'Dragon', as this complex is also called, made it to the *Guinness Book of Records* for having the longest rooftop garden in the world. Guided botanical tours are conducted daily along the 3.5-kilometre-long walkway.

The Government Complex is at the heart of this burgeoning city. Sejong Special Self-Governing City, as it is officially called, is South Korea's de facto administrative capital. It is supposed to help spread investment and business opportunities and relieve the overcrowding of Seoul — located 125 kilometres to the north.

But according to Jinhee Park, professor of urbanism at Seoul National University, the creation of a new capital for half a million residents will not do much to help Seoul's congestion. 'Seoul city has a population of 10 million, the greater metropolitan area as many as 25 million. The new capital is mainly a political joust between the Democratic Party, which aims to extend its influence, and the right-wing conservatives of the Grand National Party, who filibuster.'

Until 2007 this was countryside. Today Sejong has 390,000 inhabitants, all housed in new blocks of flats that surround the centre. 'Housing in Sejong is more expensive than elsewhere in Korea,' says real estate agent Lee Min-ae, while she pours fresh coffee. 'The average price of an 80-square-metre flat is 700 million won, the equivalent of €493,000. Only Seoul is more expensive.'

For that price, you do live in a smart city, equipped with extensive information and communication technology infrastructure and a host of urban monitoring systems. Sejong is the city of digital info boards, touch screens, QR codes, CCTV cameras and sensors. Air quality, weather conditions, traffic congestion and safety are constantly monitored. Defibrillators, lifebuoys and public emergency buttons are available to those who need help. Waste is disposed of from every block of flats through an underground pipe system. Even the toilet in my hotel room is smart.

To keep streets and roadsides clear, cars are parked underground to the extent possible. Separate bus lanes take express buses through the city without delays. Experiments are being conducted with self-driving vehicles, delivery robots and drones.

Sejong also promotes itself as green and sustainable. Sejong Lake Park, a huge green space along a man-made water feature, is located in the middle of the city. With manicured lawns, an artificial beach, an observation tower, play areas, sports grounds and an arboretum, the purpose is recreational rather than ecological.

From a distance, it looks dystopian, but at the base of the many residential towers, a microcosm of social life unfolds. 'Until the 1960s, tower blocks were considered accommodations for the less well off,' Jinhee Park explains. 'The first high-rises for the middle class proved to be a success. A flat is easy: fees and maintenance are shared; it is more social and energy-efficient. Gradually there was a change in mentality. Today, tower blocks are mainly for the upper middle class.'

In fact, Sejong looks prosperous. Nowhere do I see poverty. Not once does anyone come begging for money. No crime, no litter, no smell of urine. The public domain is tidy; society operates efficiently. Sejong is a 'world-class model city where everyone wants to live', I read in the promo brochure from the National Agency for Administrative City Construction.

No, not everyone. Quite a few civil servants refuse to give up bustling Seoul as their place of residence and prefer to commute to their workplace in Sejong. I, too, after two weeks of wandering around this generic and conformist 'happy city', yearn for the unpredictability and diversity of the metropolis. In Seoul, I salute the statue of 15th-century King Sejong the Great, after whom the new capital was named. I give Sejong some more credit. All beginnings are difficult. It takes time for a city to mature.

May 2023

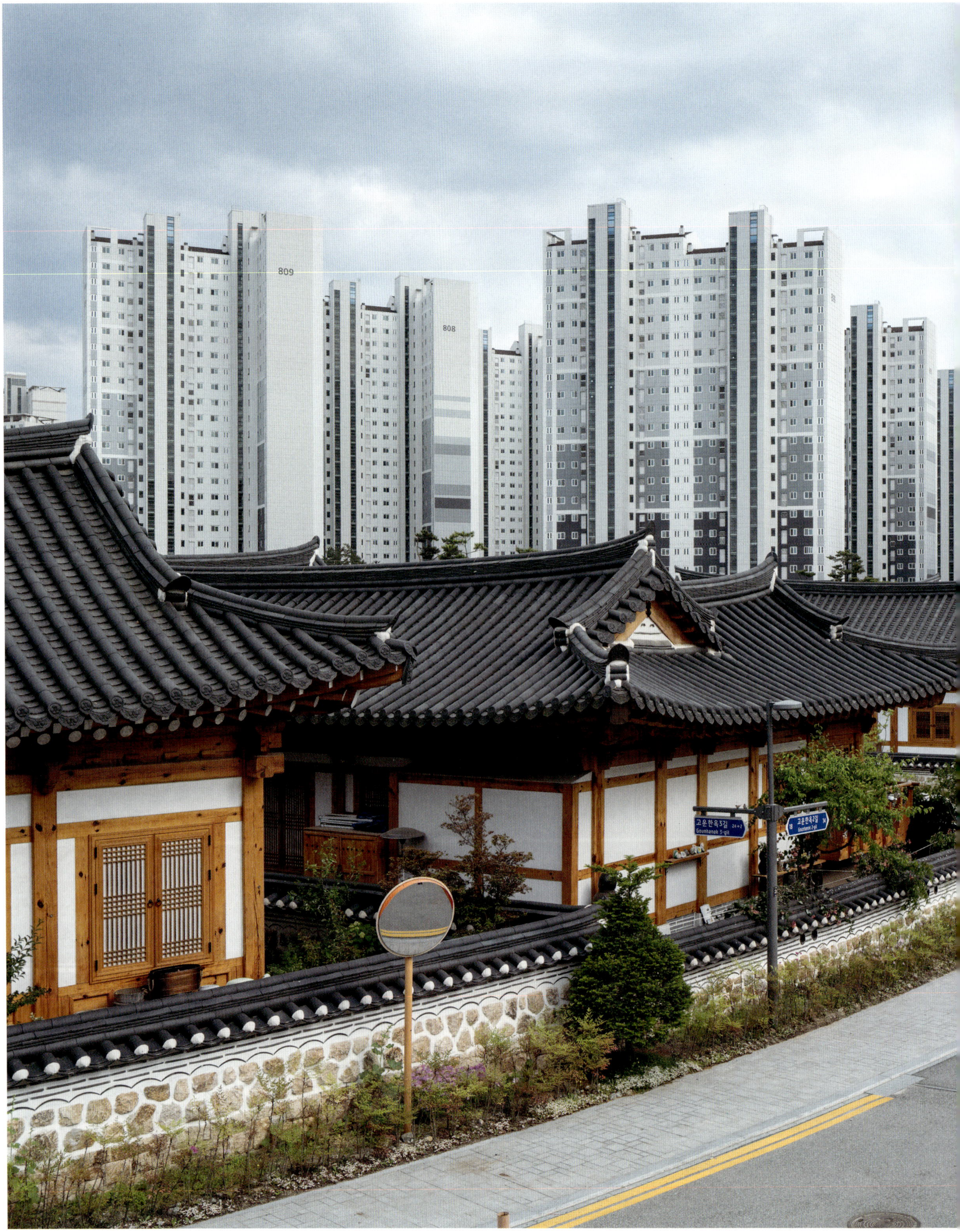
809
808
고운한옥3길 24→2
Gounhanok 3-gil
18 고운한옥2길 14
Gounhanok 2-gil

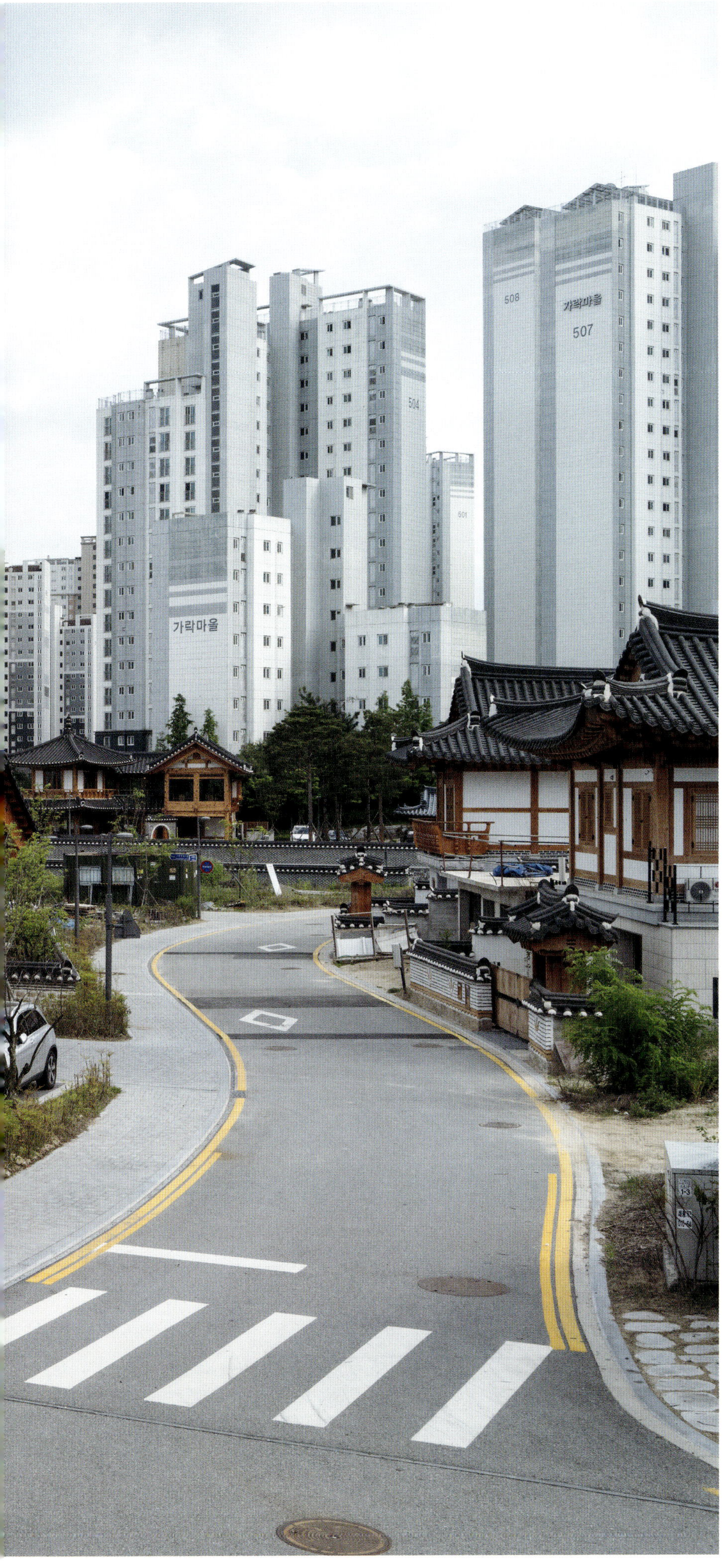

Hanok Village, a new residential quarter with luxury single houses in traditional Korean style.

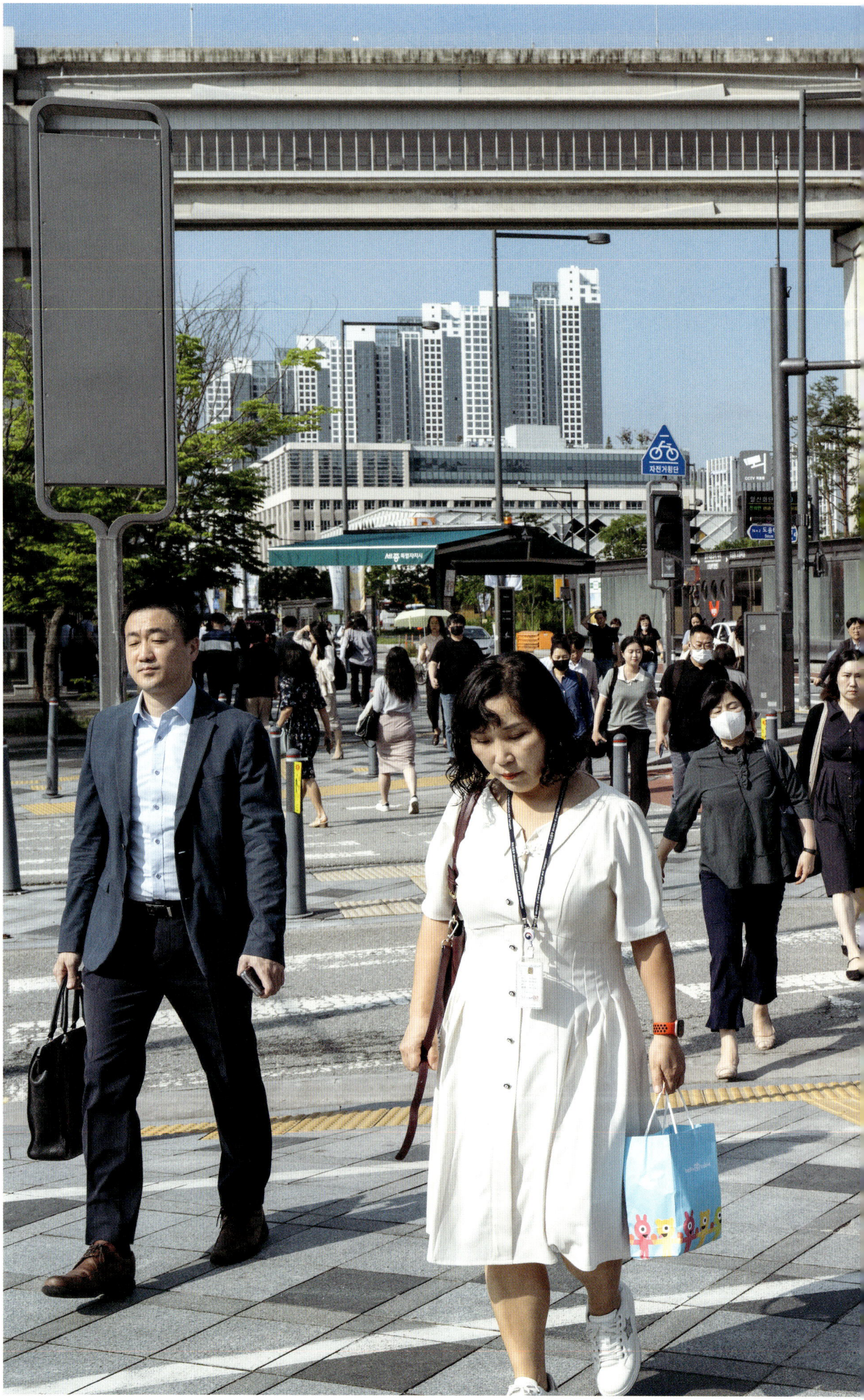
자전거횡단

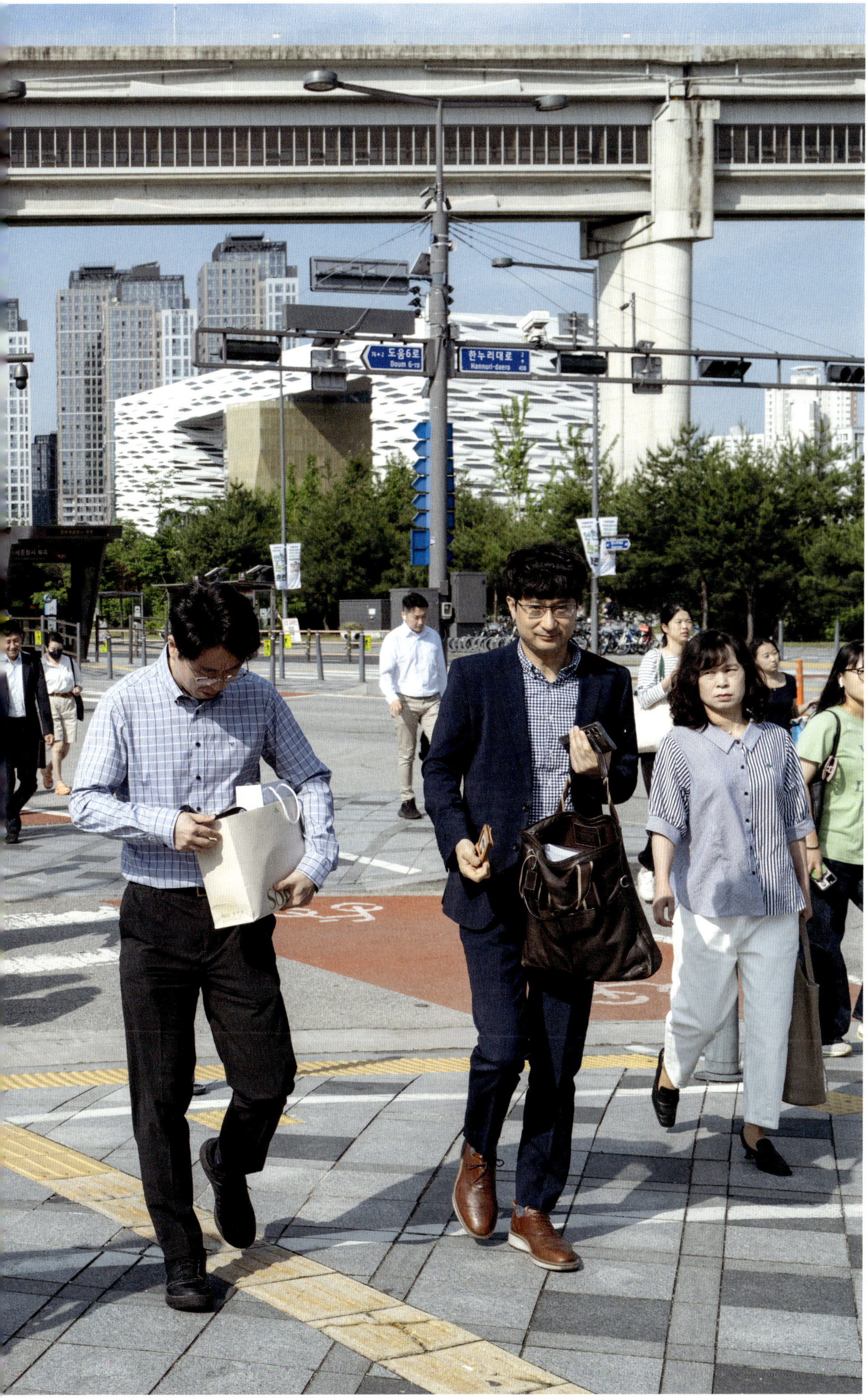

Morning rush hour near
the Government Complex.

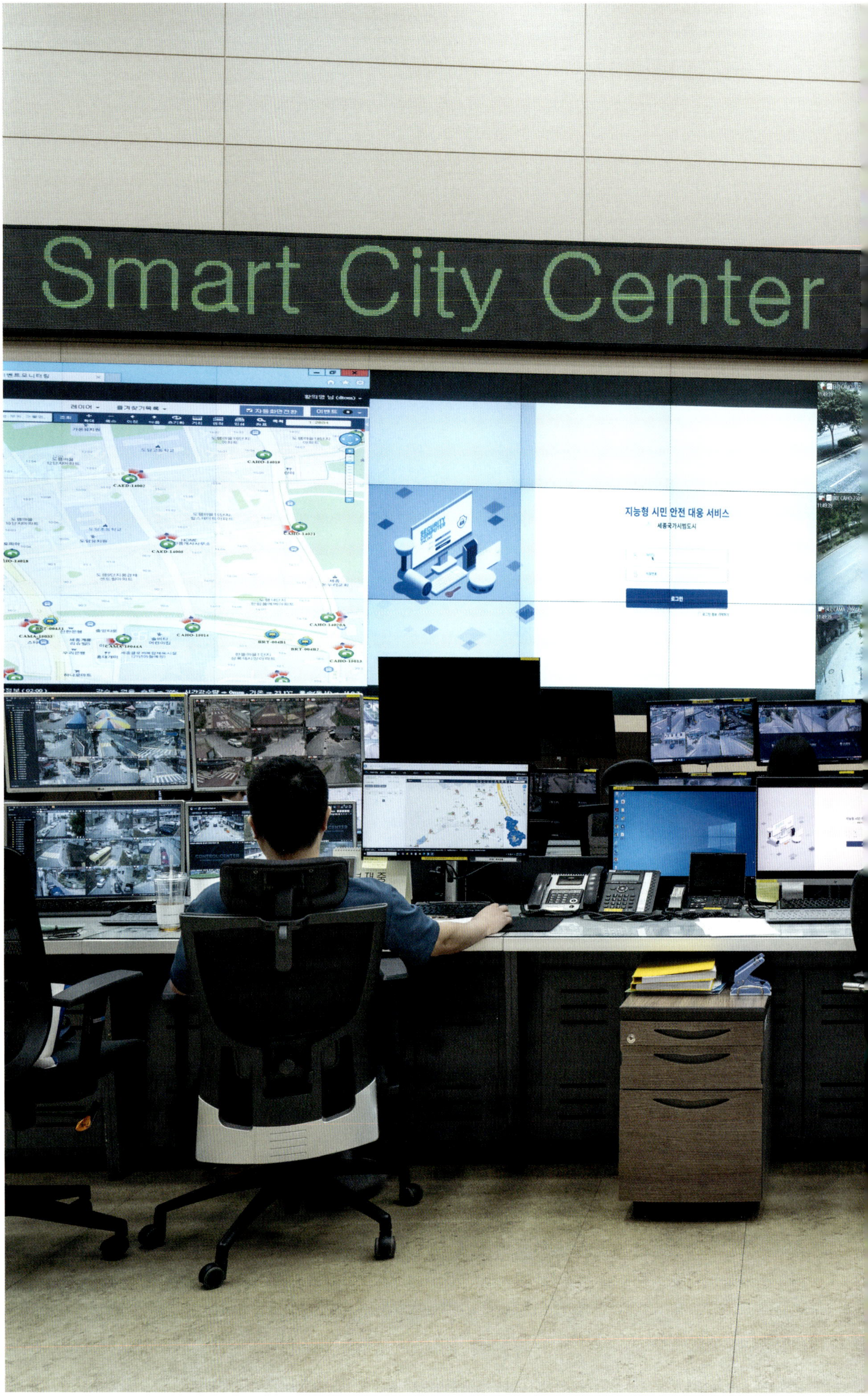
Smart City Center
지능형 시민 안전 대응 서비스
세종국가시범도시

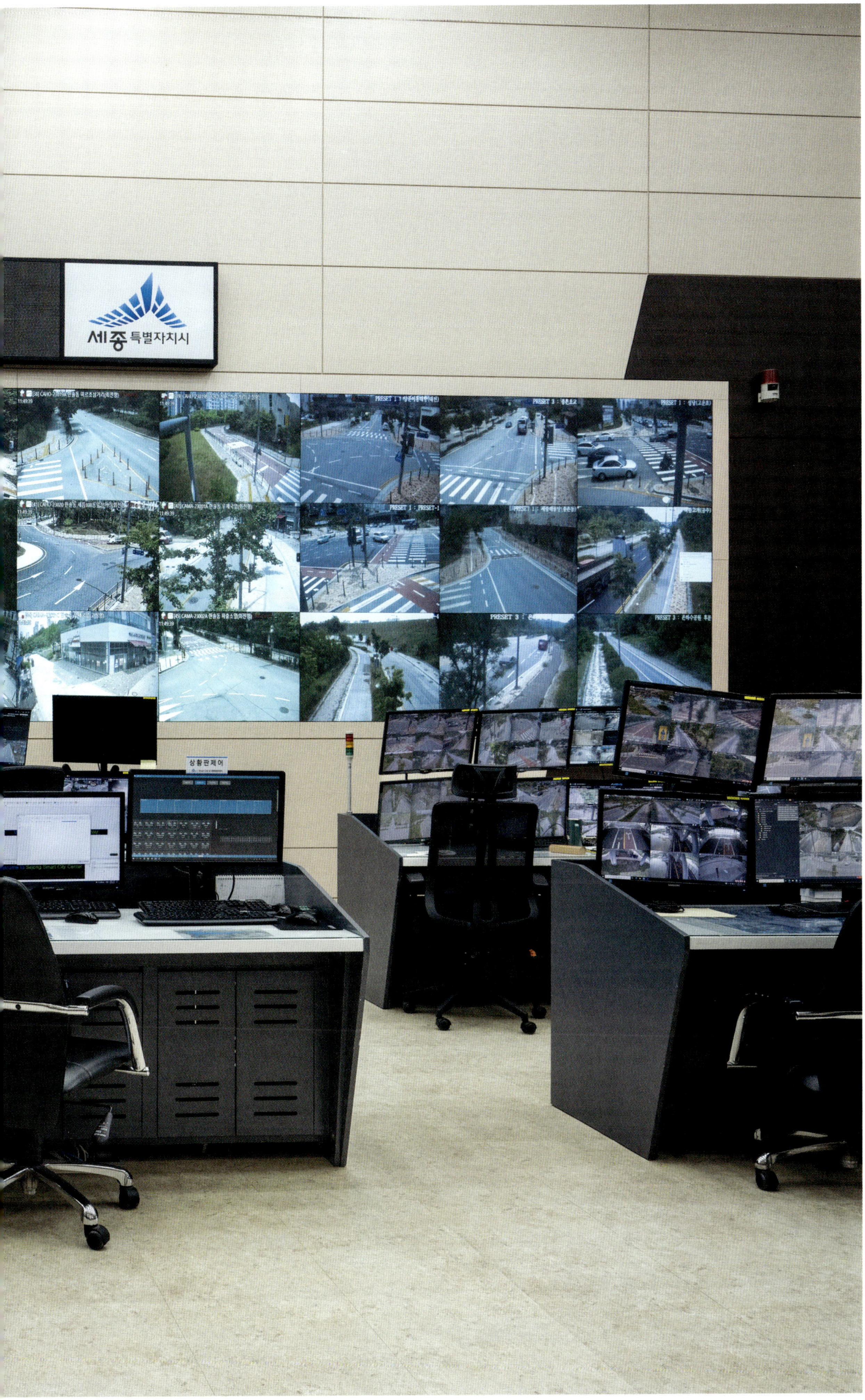

CCTV control room at the Urban Integration Information Center.

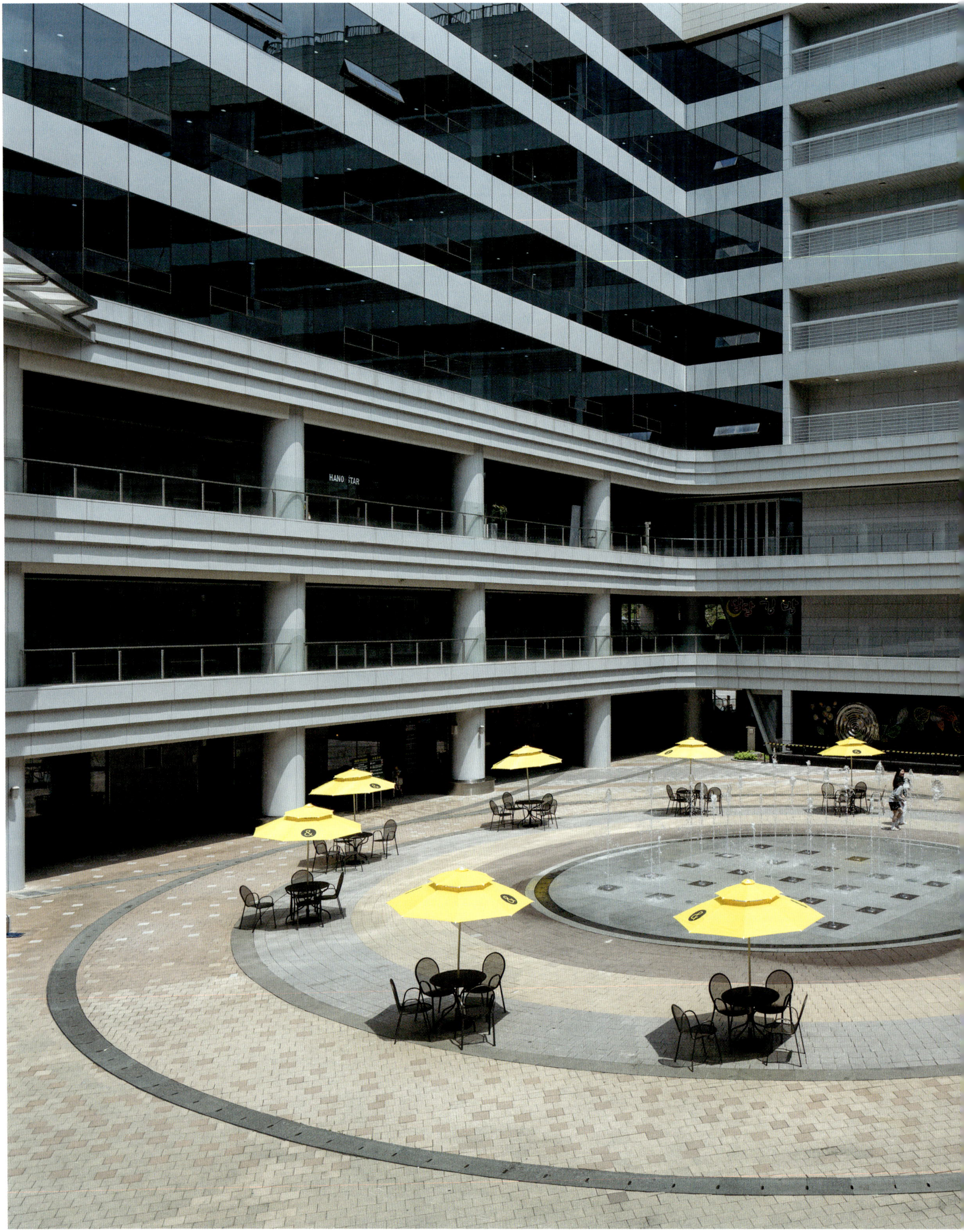

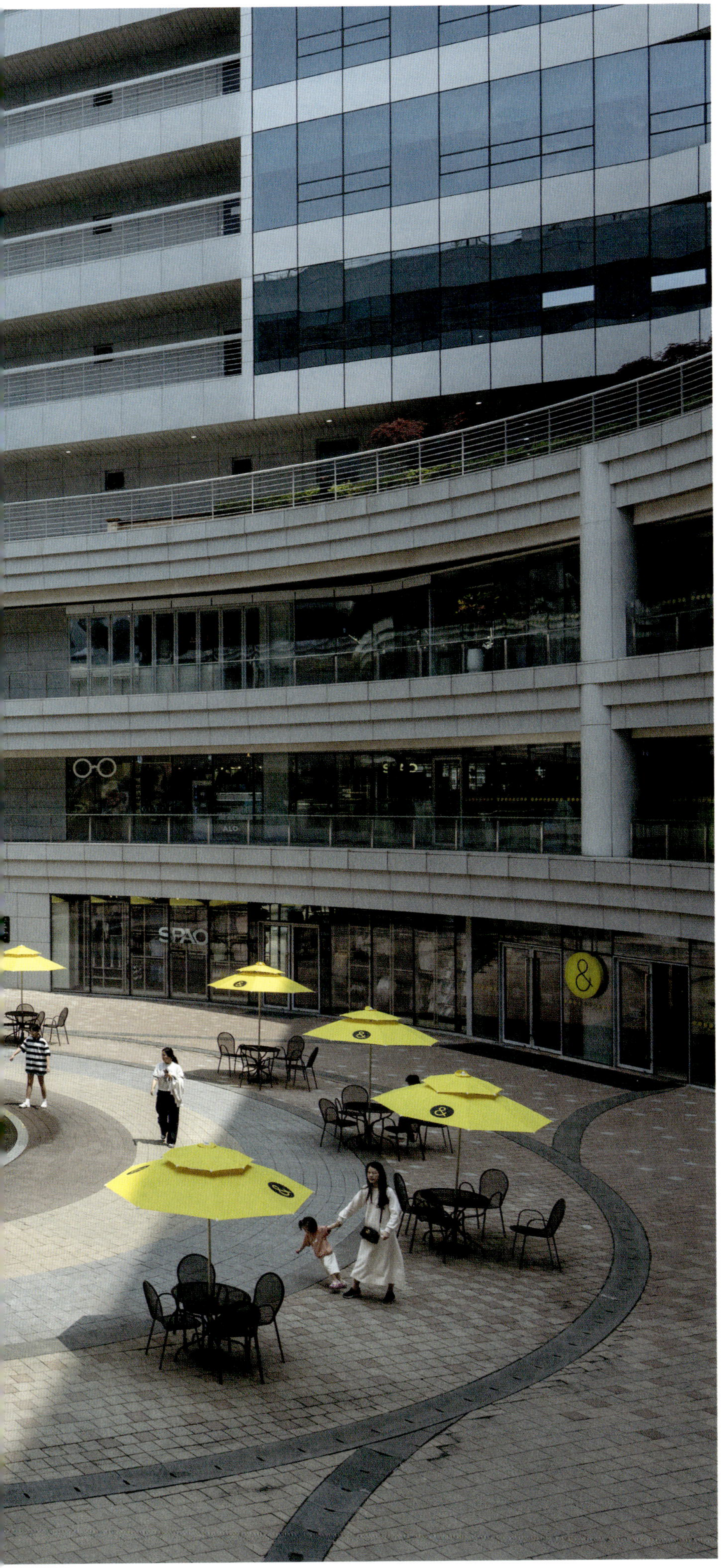

AK& shopping centre.

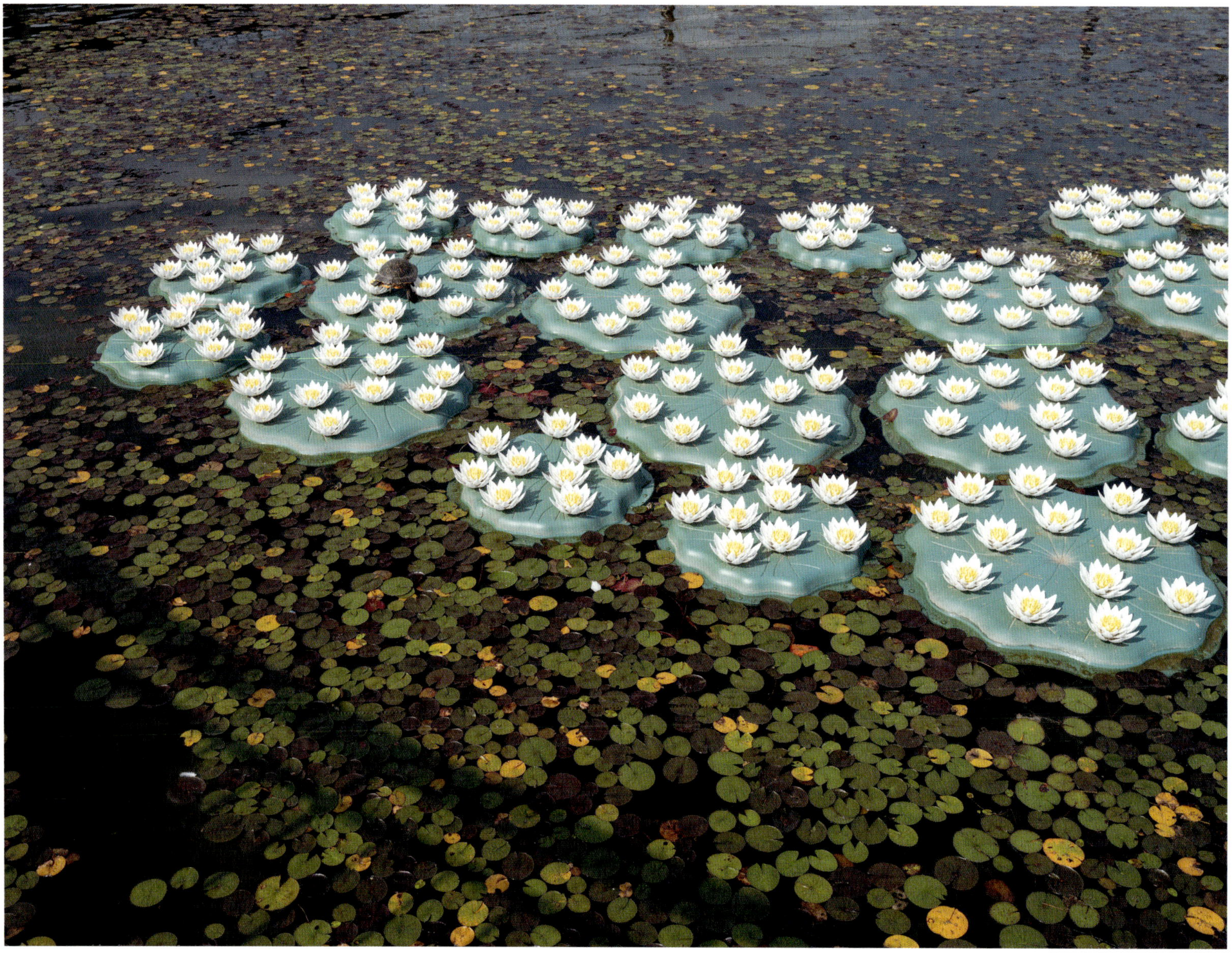

Sejong Lake Park.

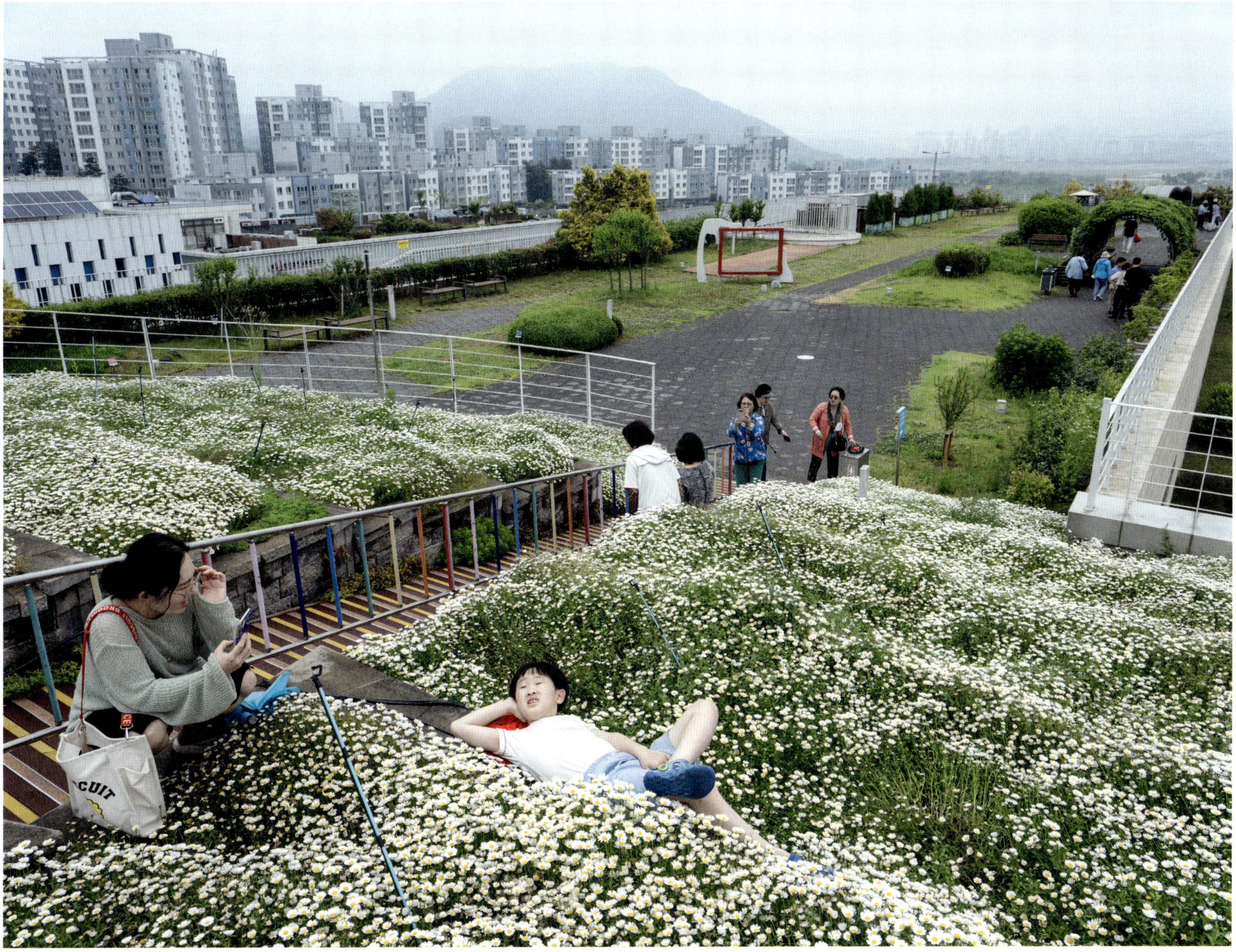

Rooftop garden in Sejong Government Complex.

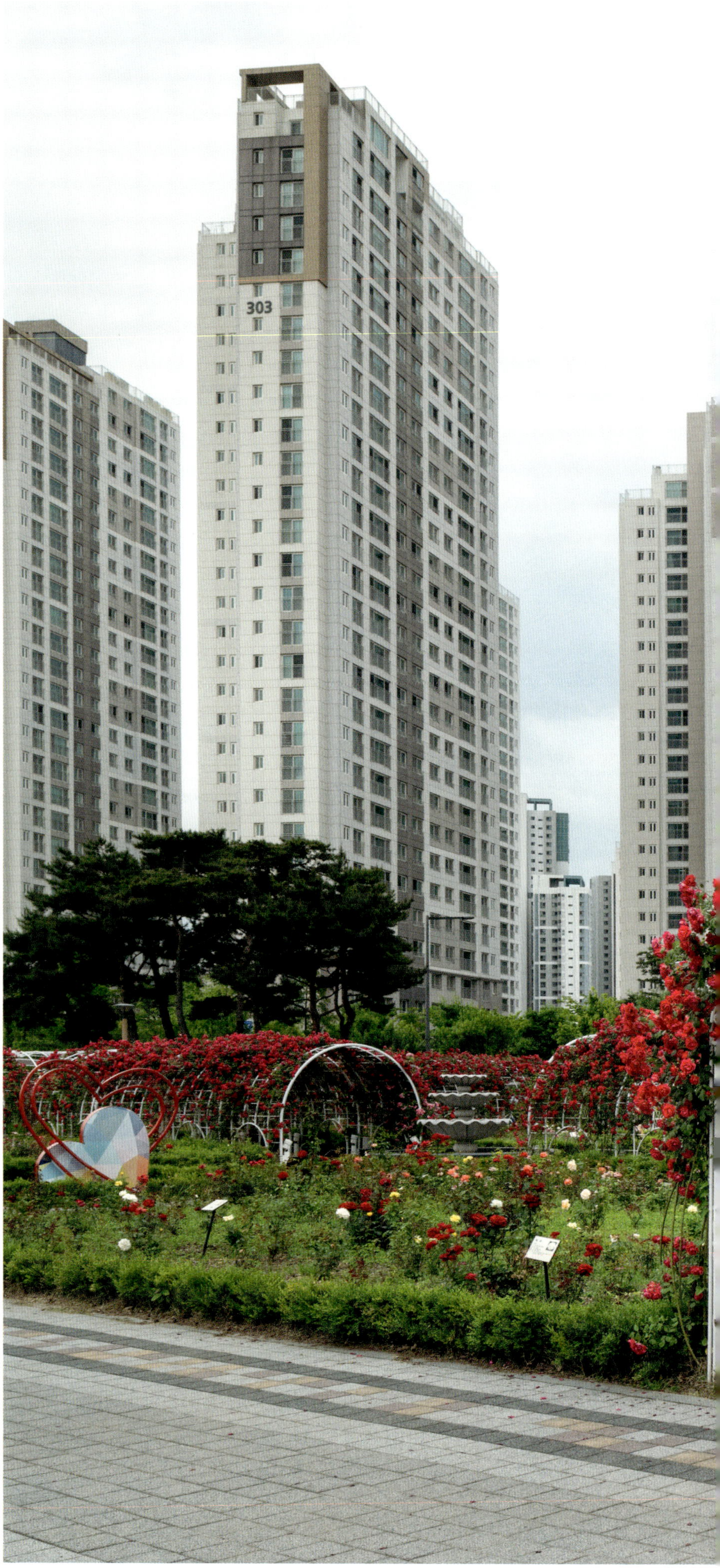

Sejong Supbaram Rose Garden.

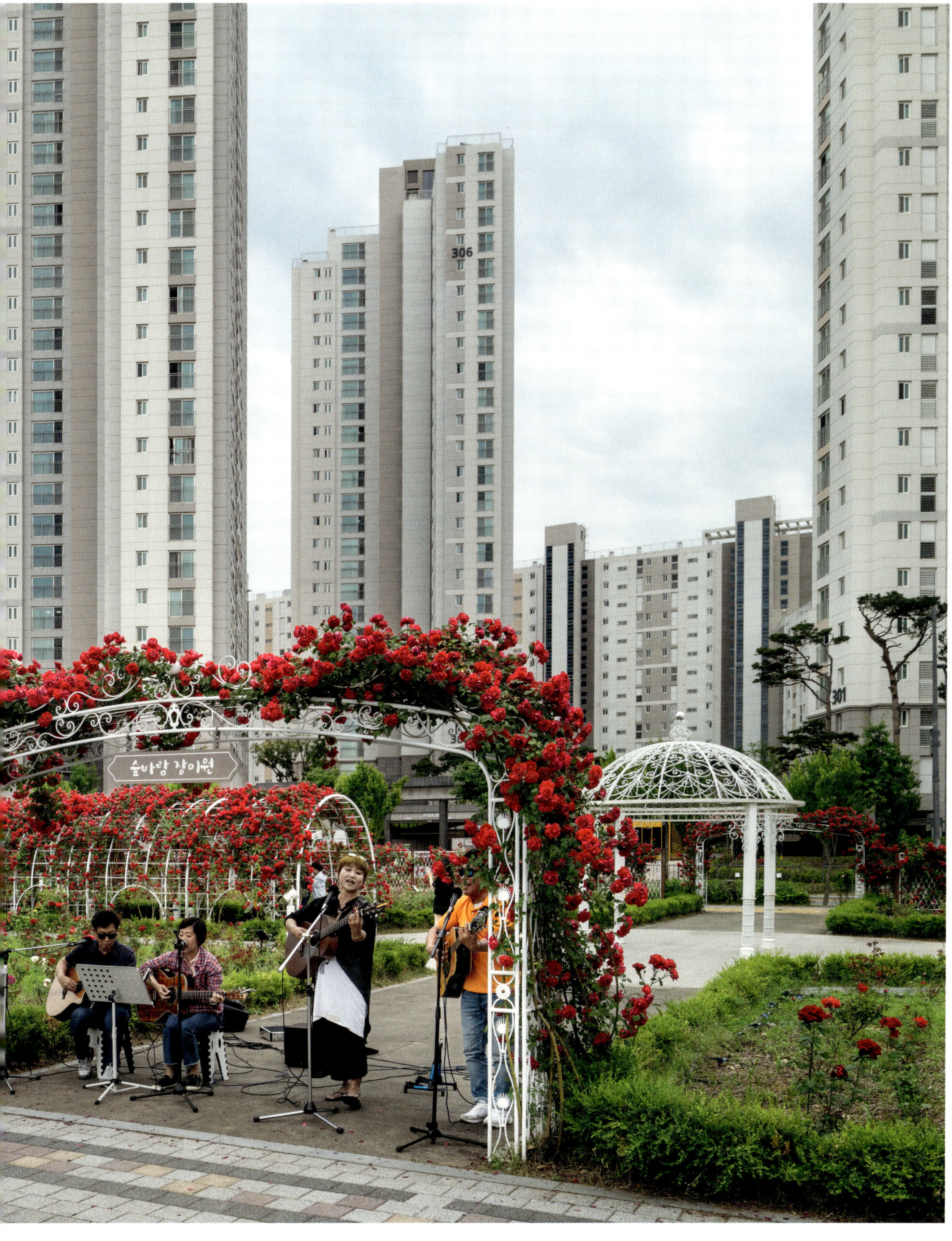
306
301
숲바람 장미원

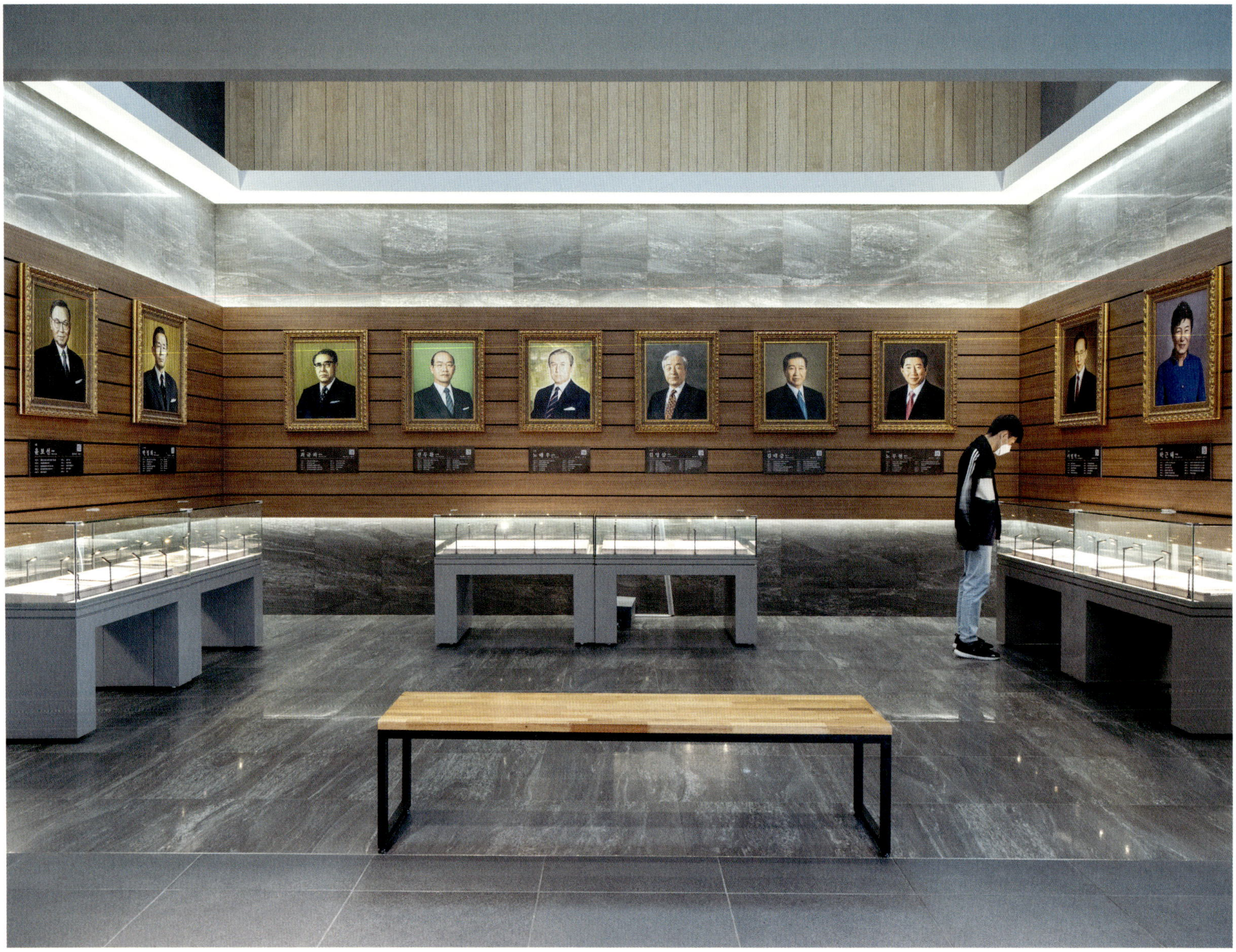

Portrait gallery of all Korean presidents in the Presidential Archives.

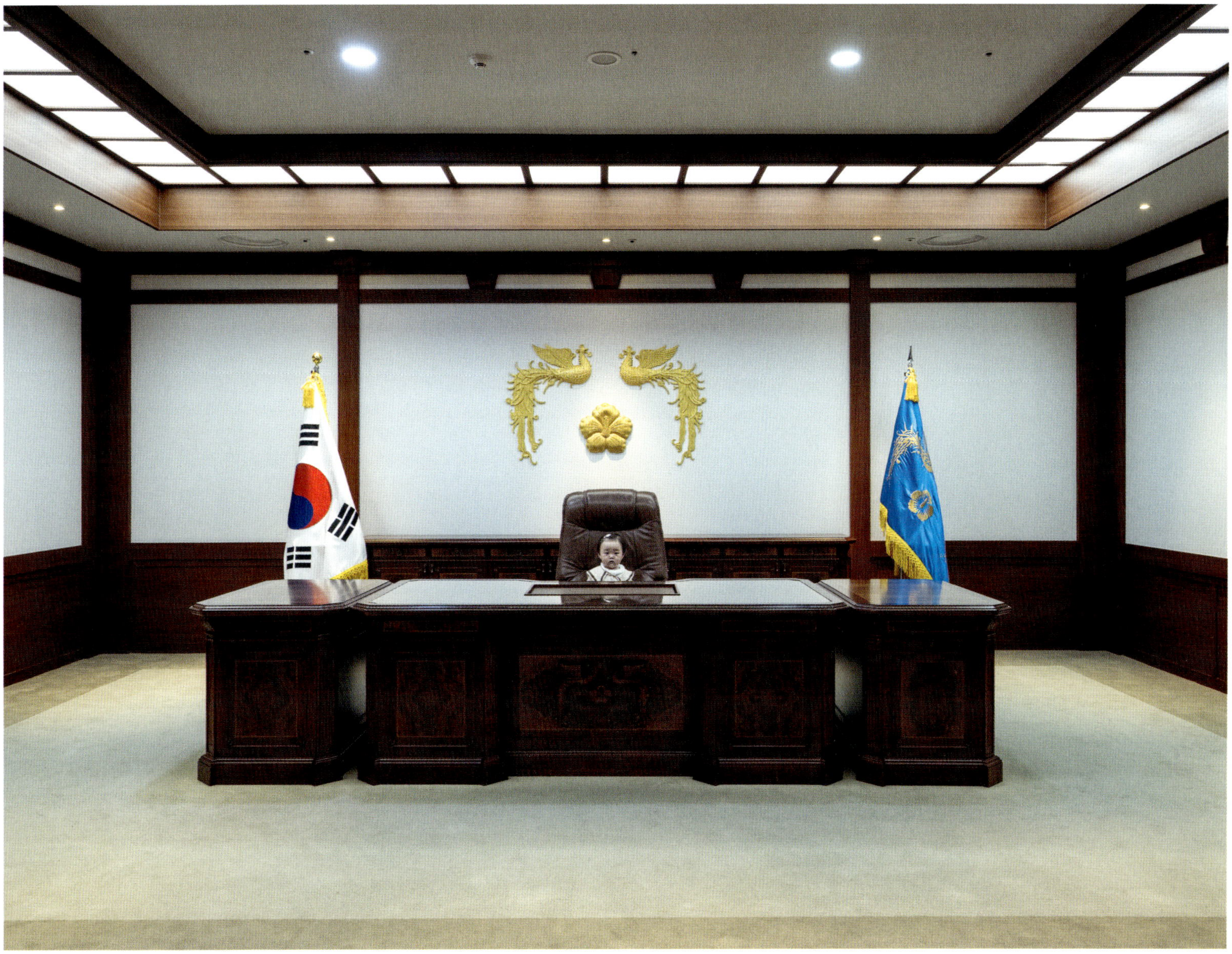

Set-up of the presidential office in the Presidential Archives.

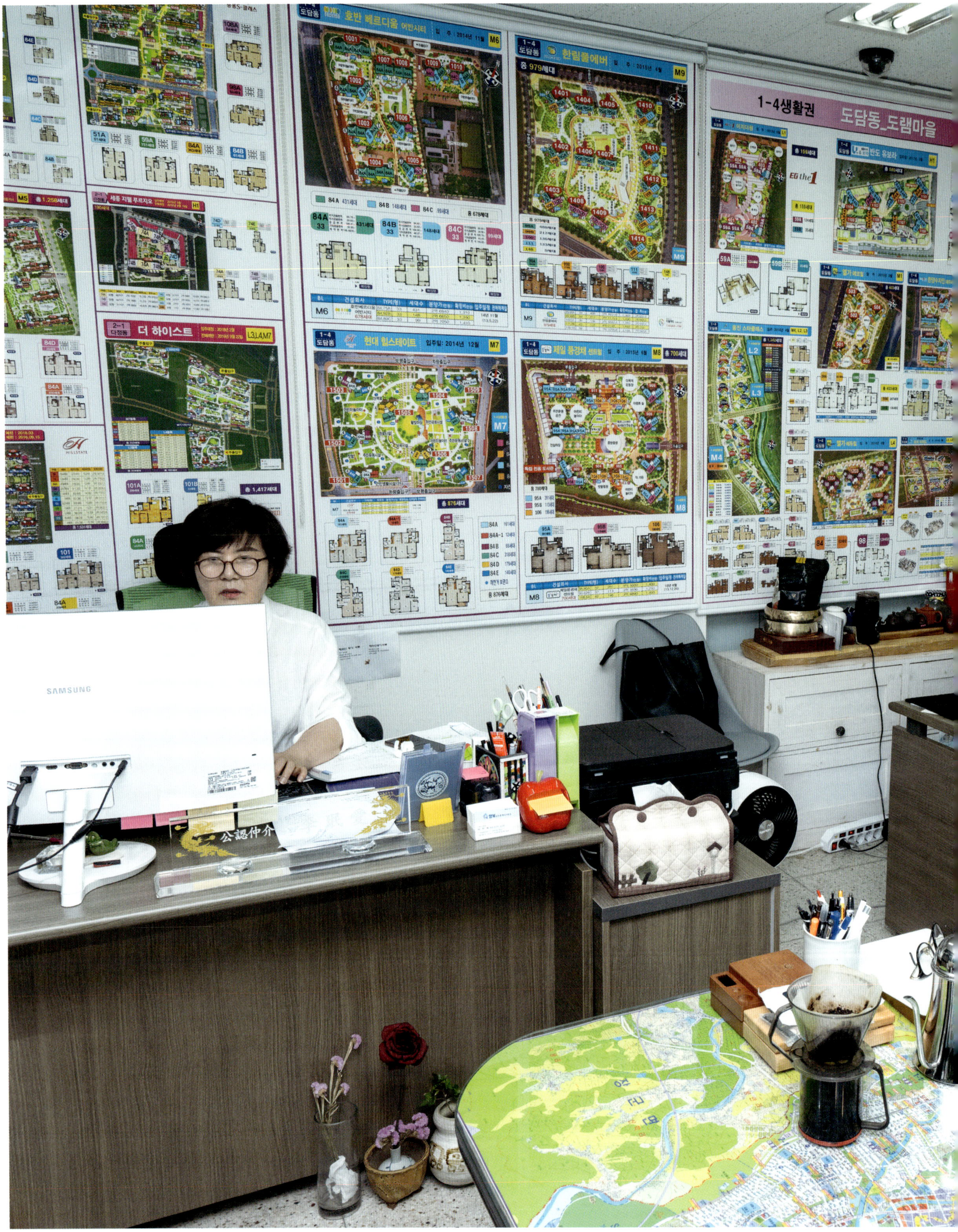

1-4생활권
도담동_도램마을
호반 베르디움 어반시티
한림풀에버
현대 힐스테이트
제일 풍경채
더 하이스트
SAMSUNG
公認仲介

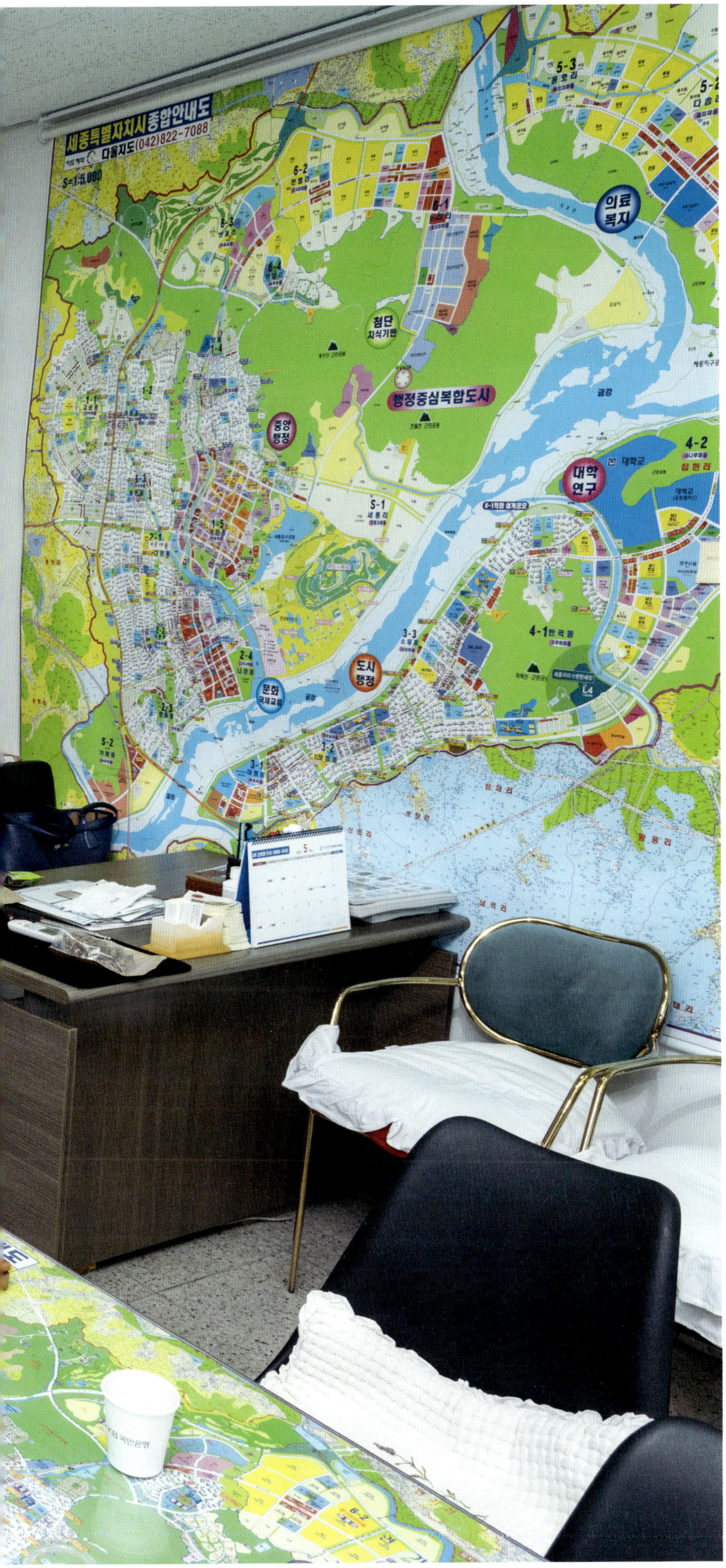

Lee Min-ae runs a real estate office selling flats in Sejong.

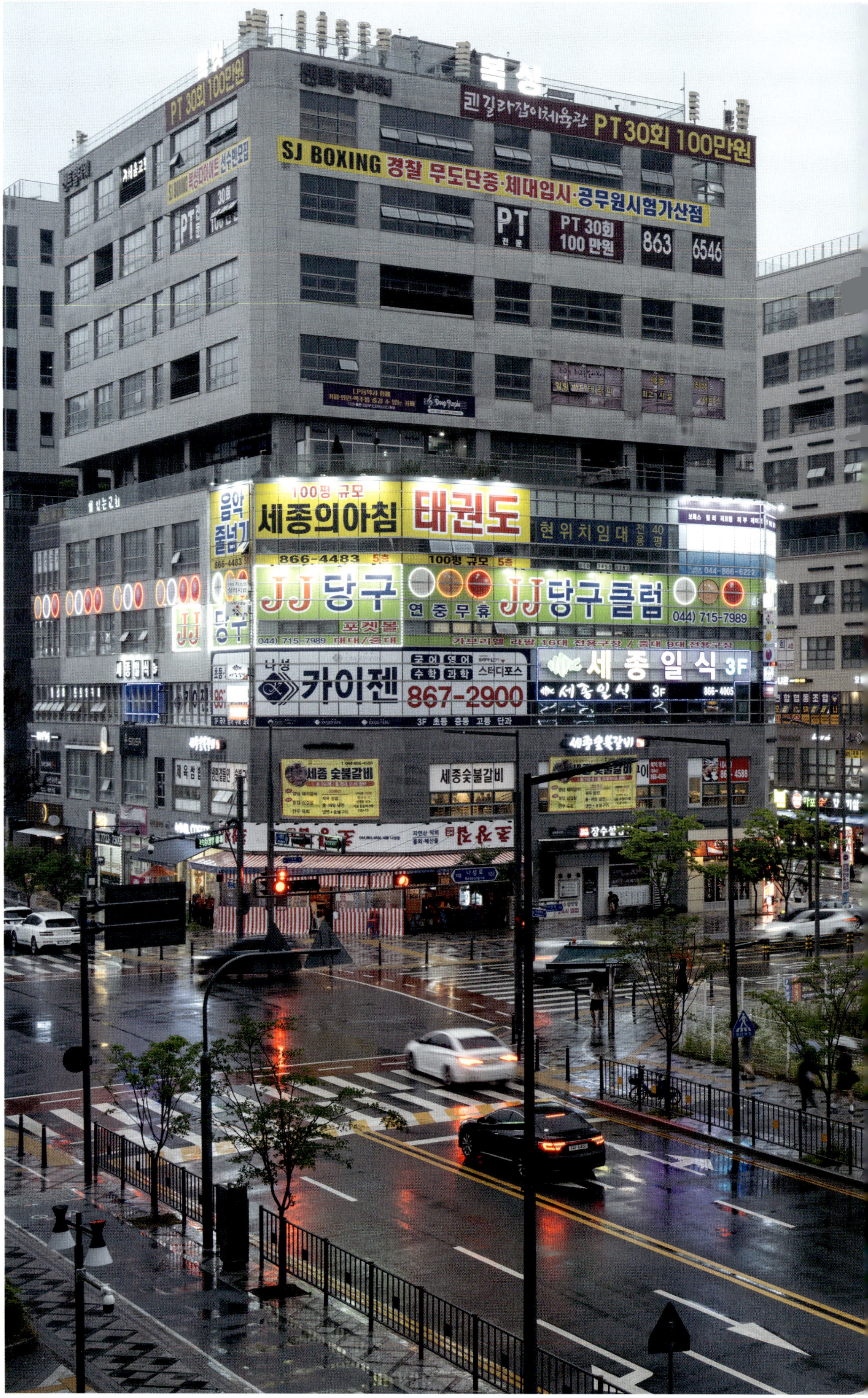
PT 30회 100만원
SJ BOXING 경찰 무도단증·체대입시·공무원시험가산점
PT30회 100만원
PT 전문
PT 30회 100 만원
863
6546
100평 규모
세종의아침
태권도
음악 줄넘기
866-4483
JJ당구
연중무휴
JJ당구클럽
044) 715-7989
포켓볼
나성
카이젠
국어 영어 수학 과학 스터디포스
867-2900
3F 초등 중등 고등 단과
세종일식 3F
세종숯불갈비

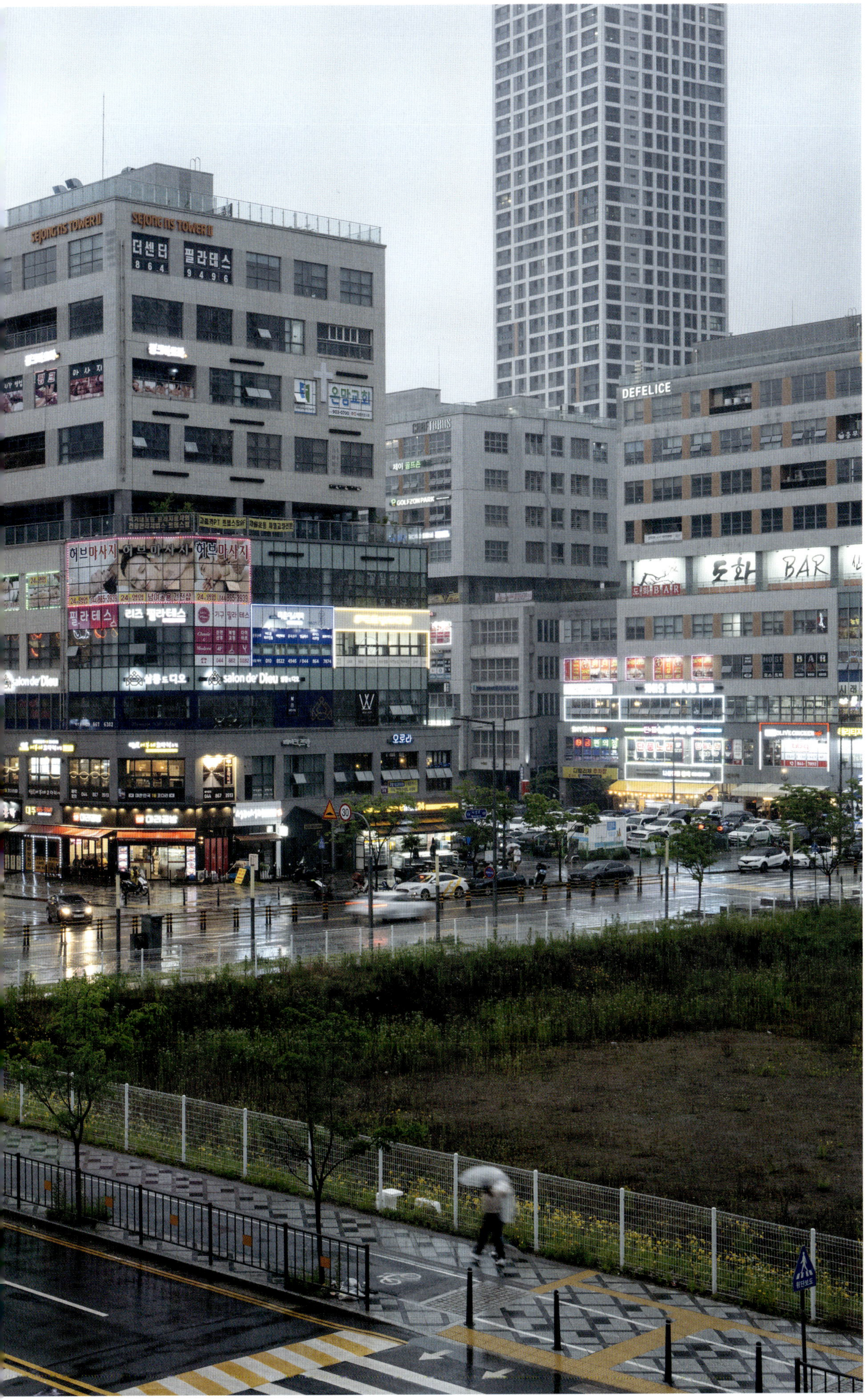

Naseong-ro,
Sejong's nightlife district.

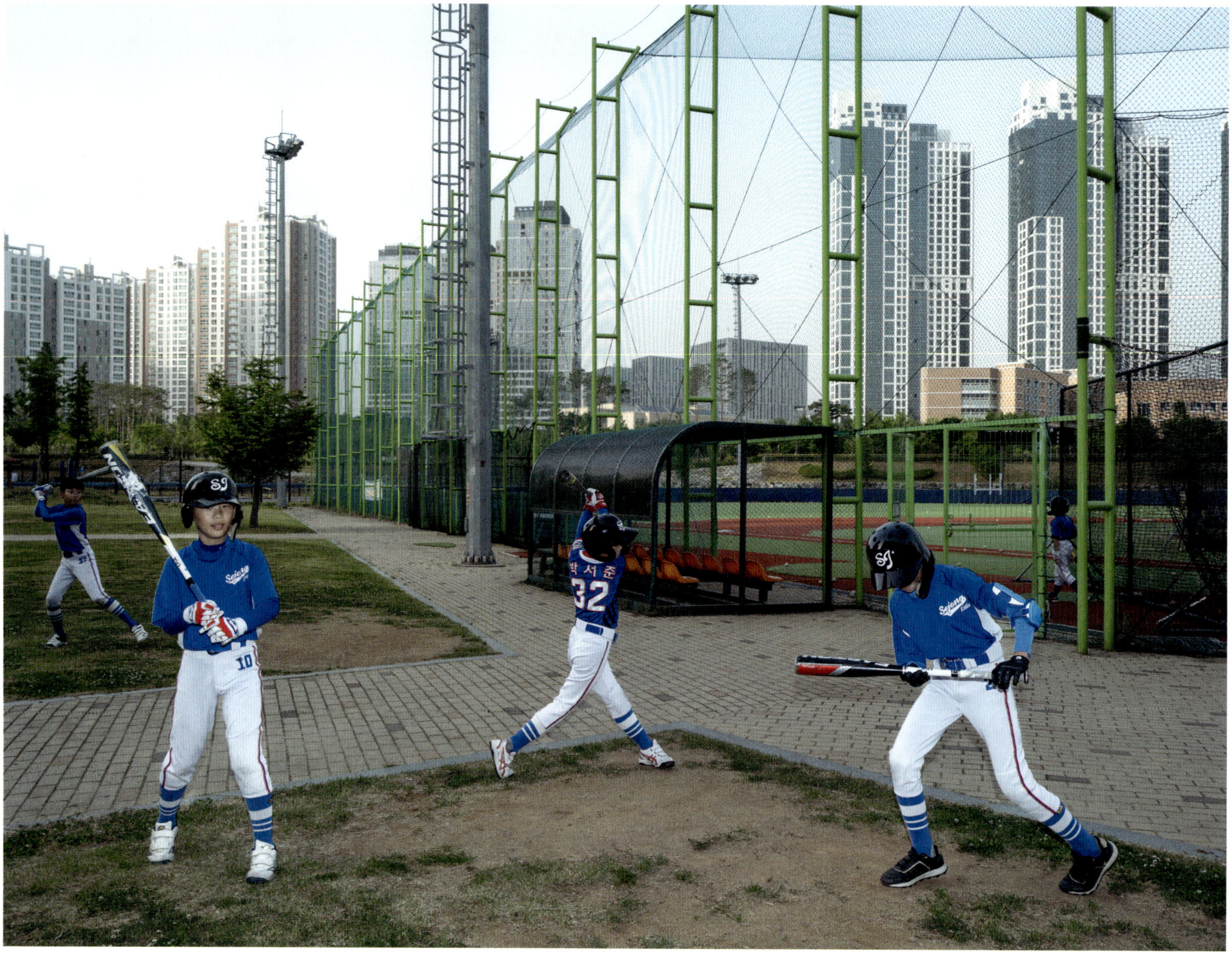

Dajeong-dong.

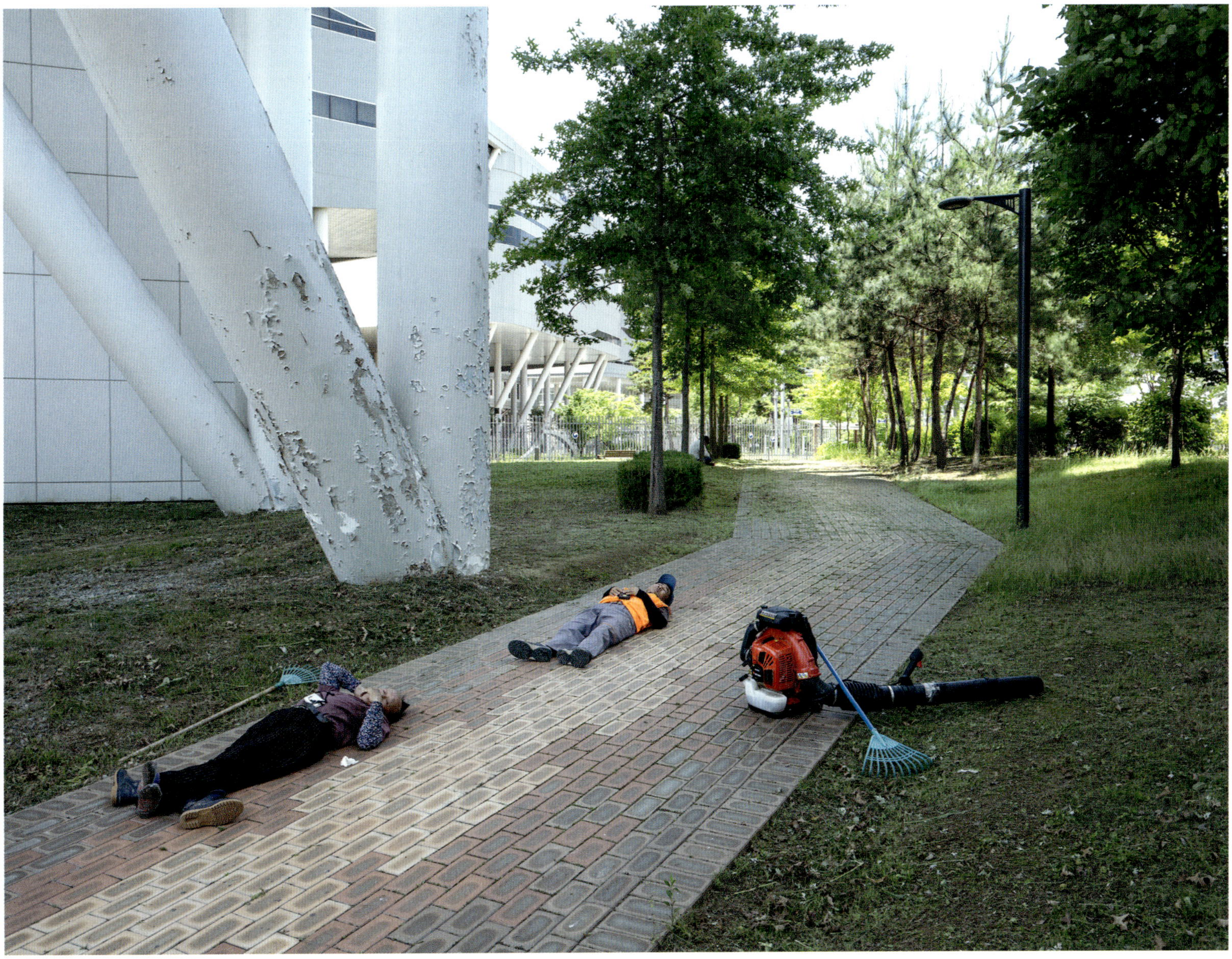

Sejong Government Complex.

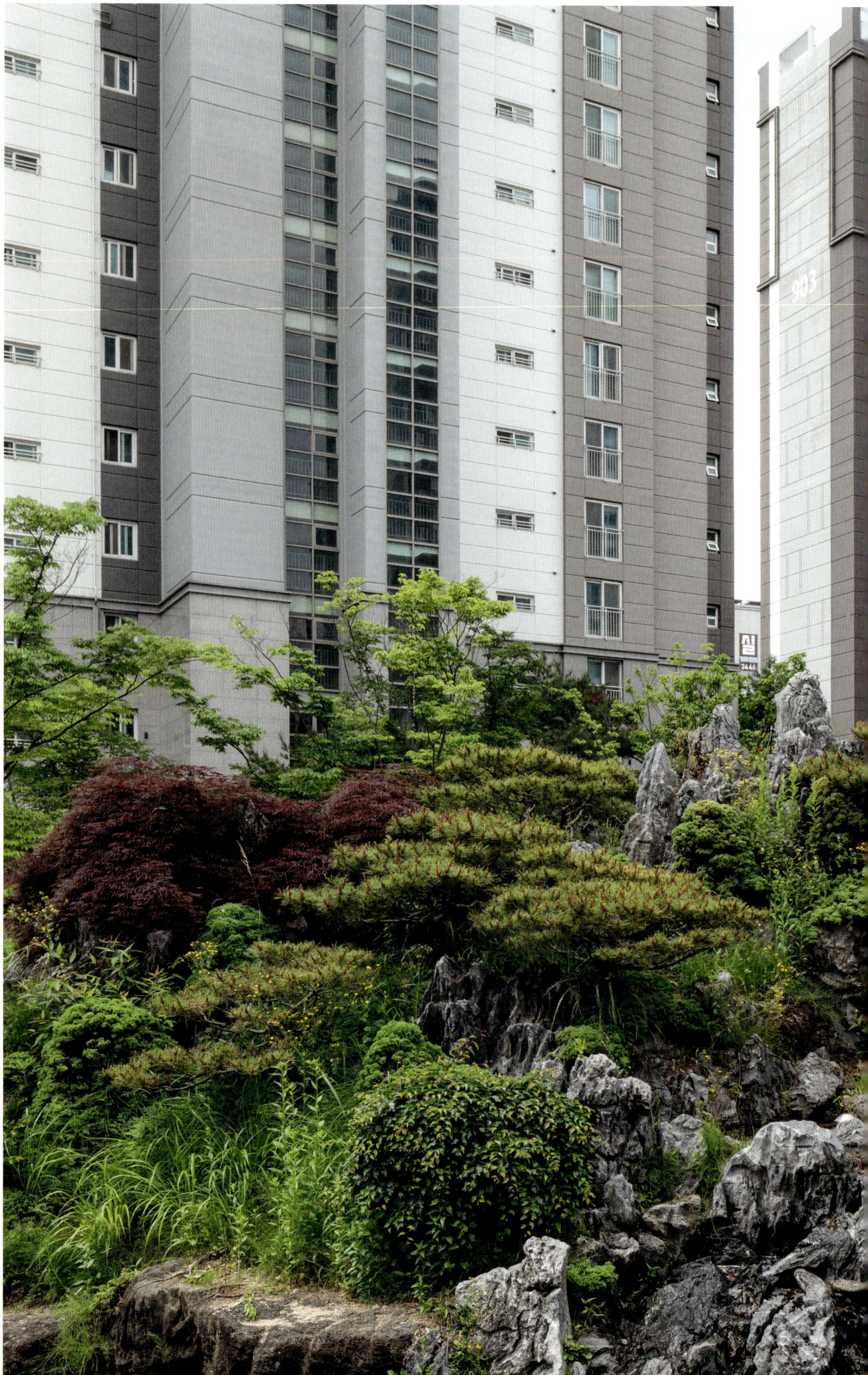

Dodam-dong residential neighbourhood.

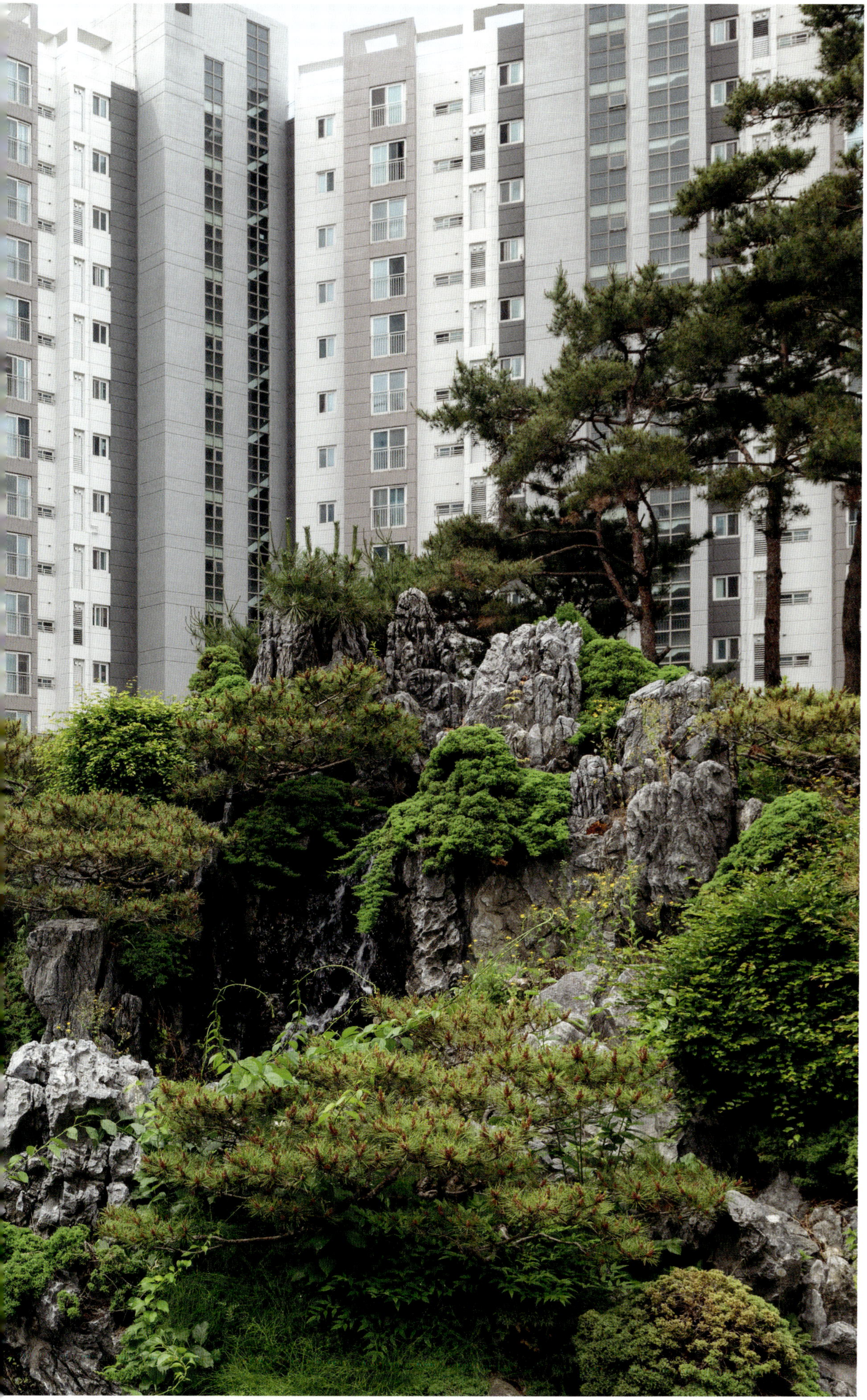

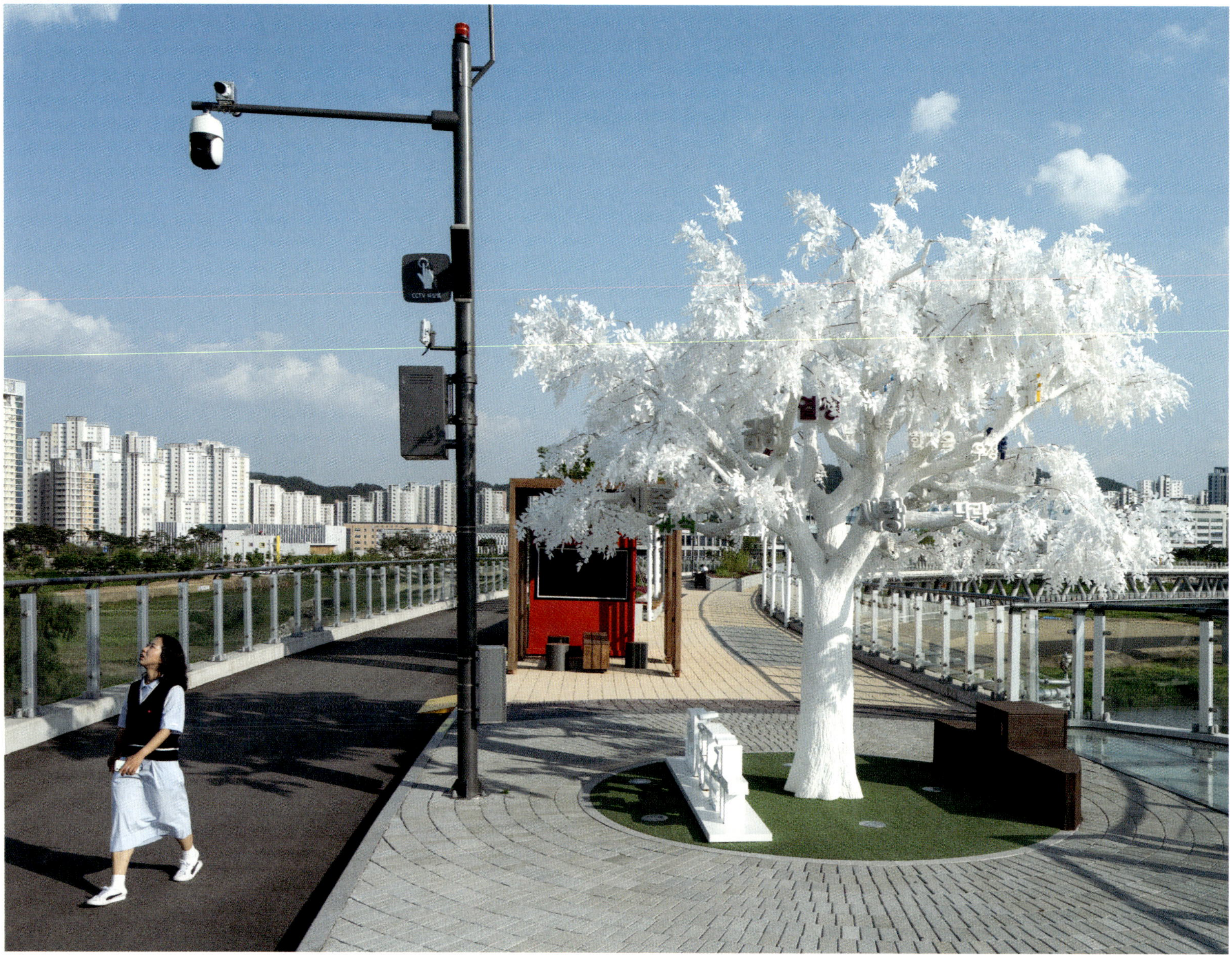

Geumgang Pedestrian Bridge.

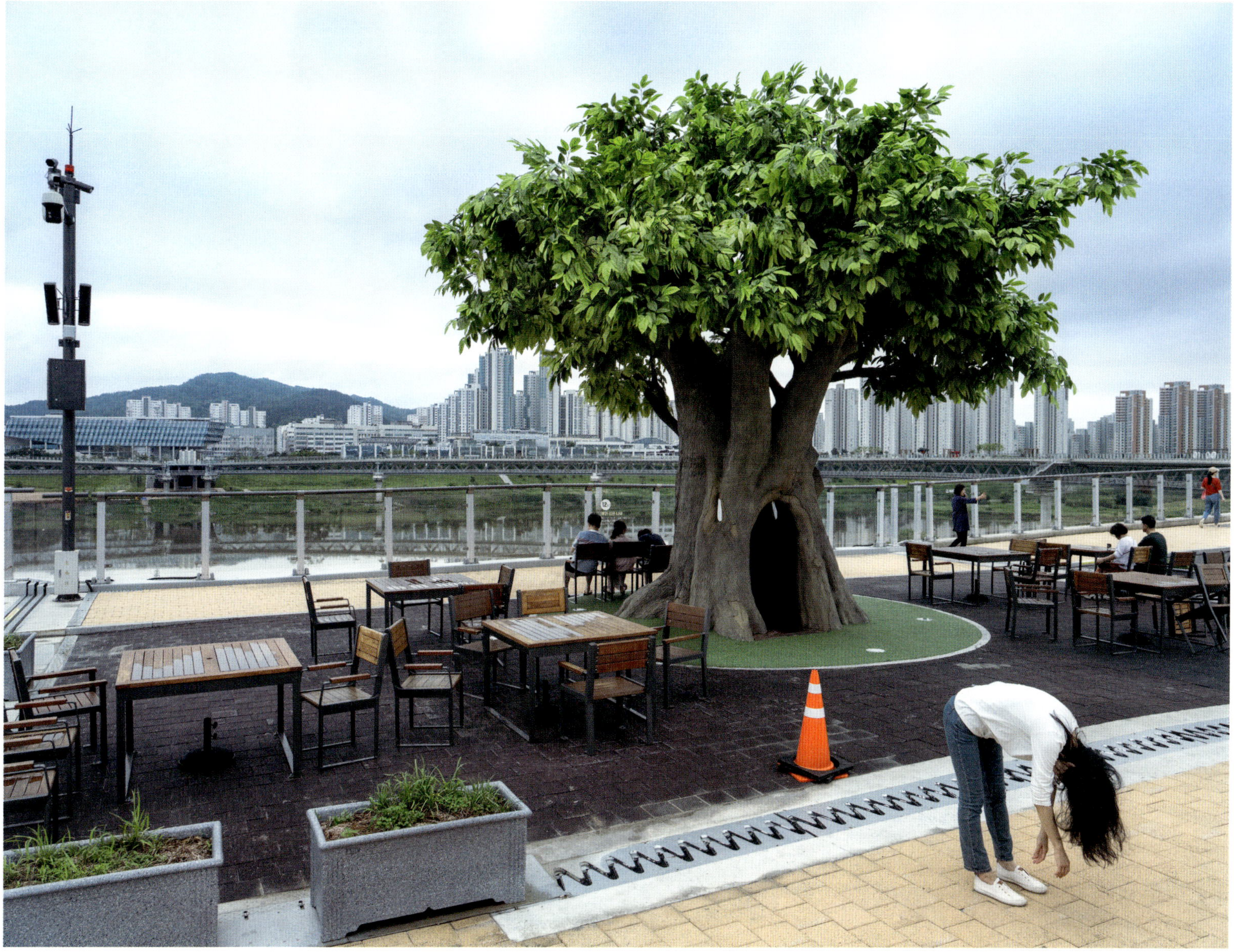

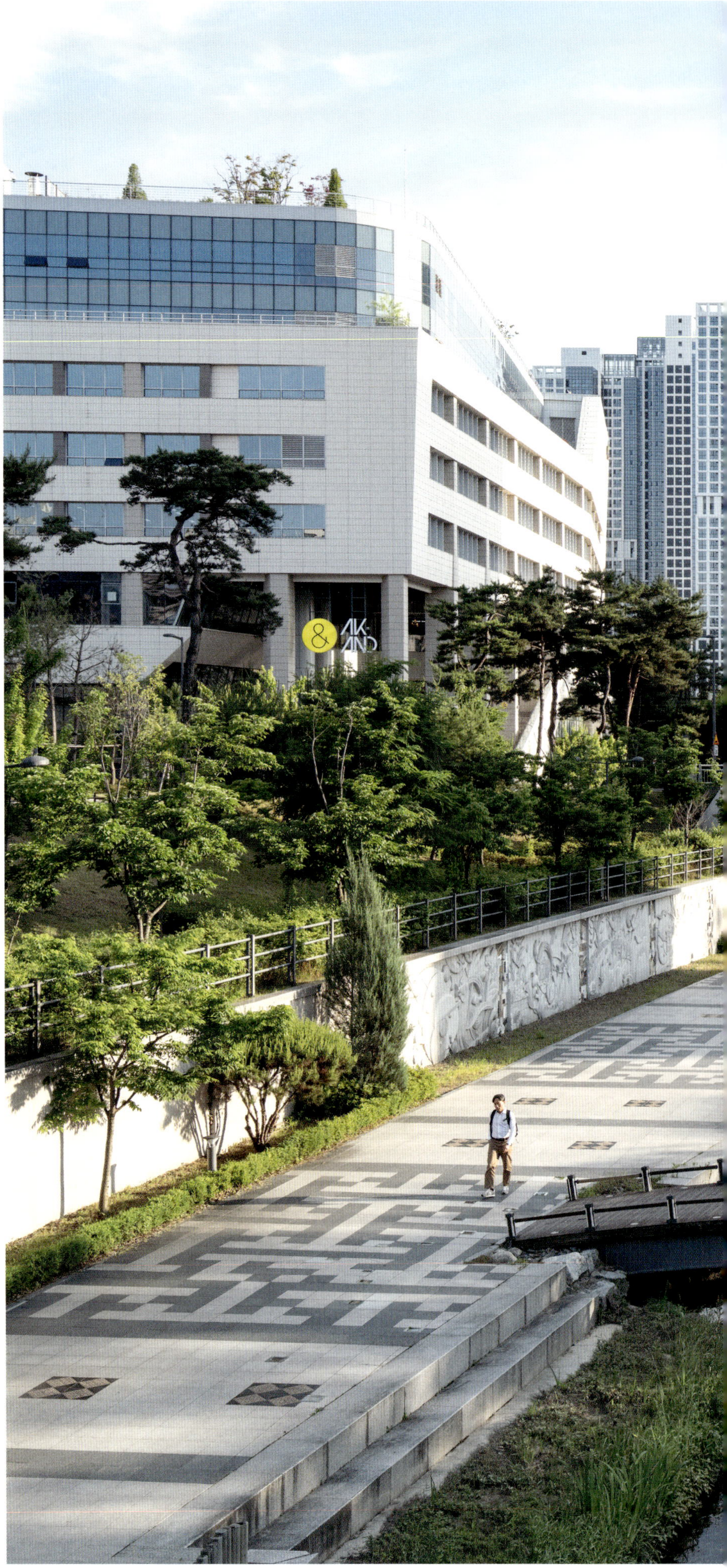

Bangchukcheon Riverside Park.

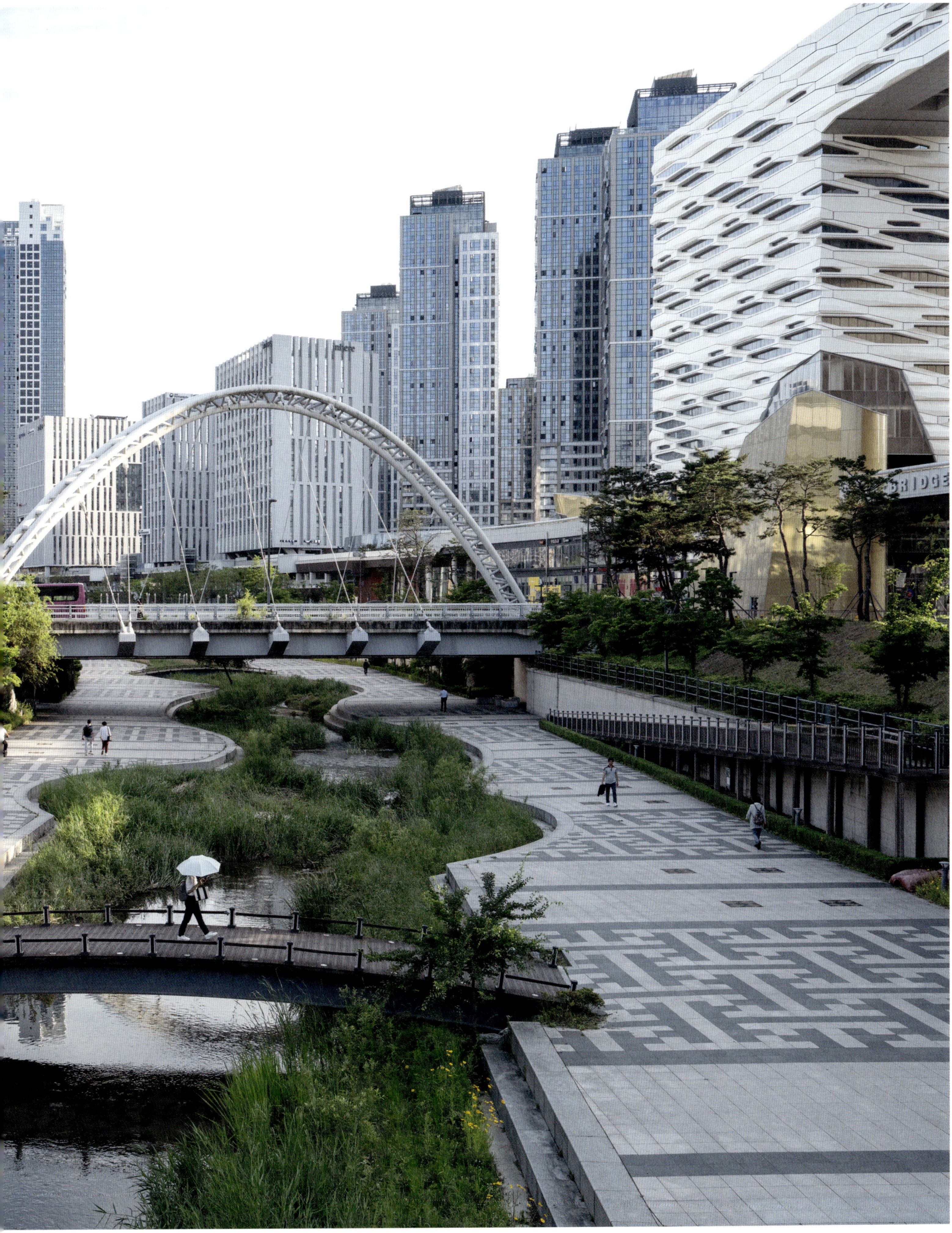

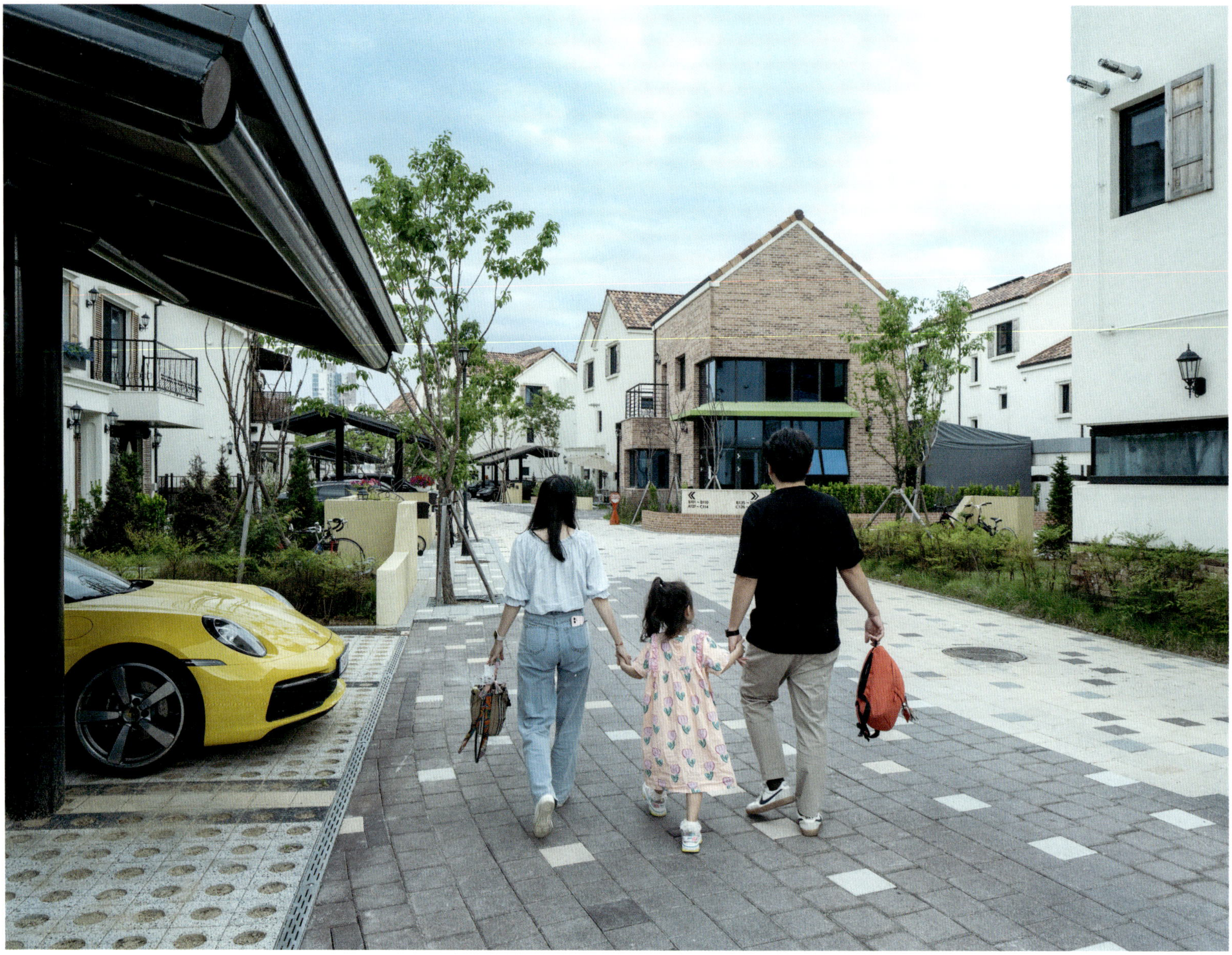

European Village, a gated compound featuring luxurious European-style homes.

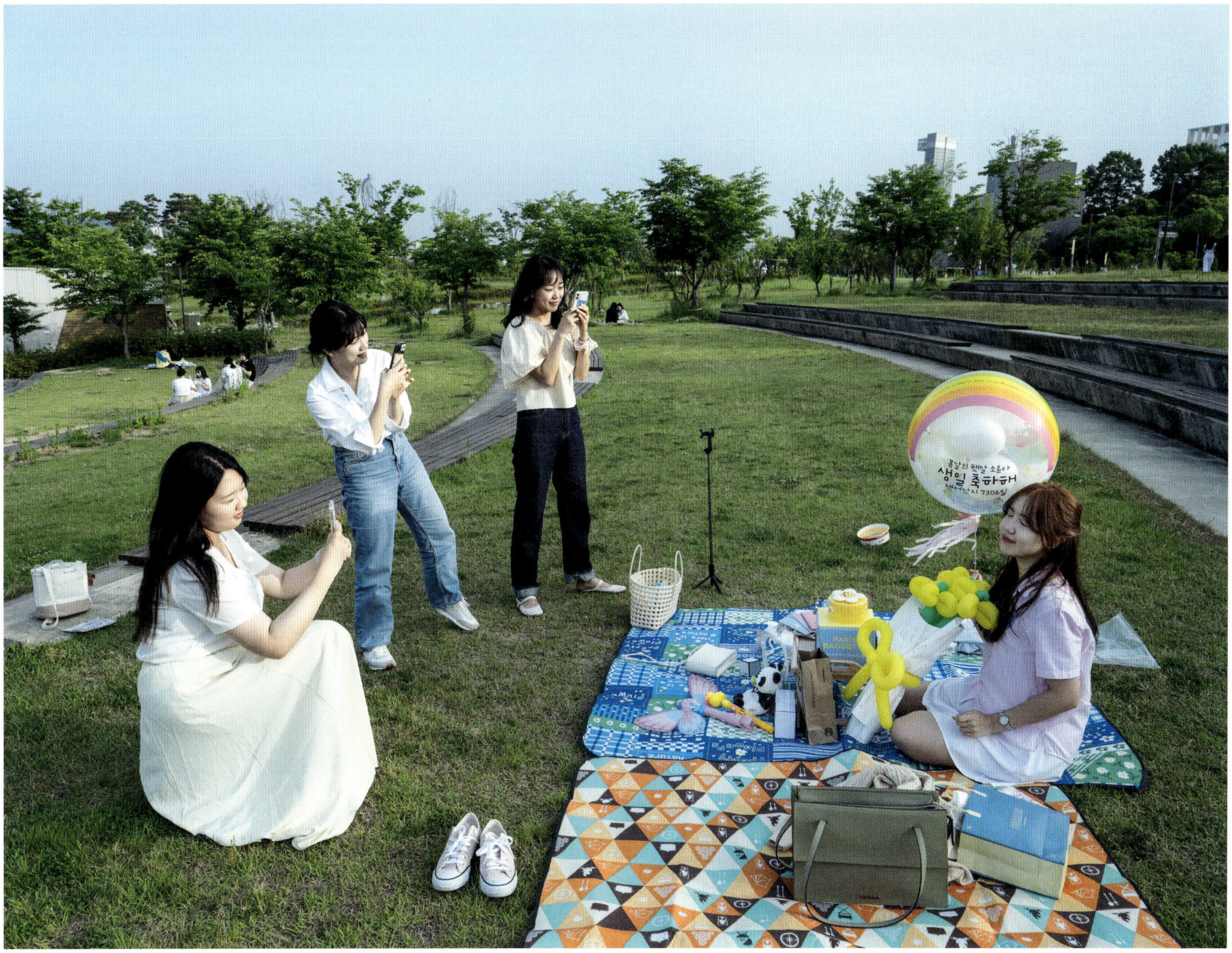

Birthday party in Sejong Lake Park.

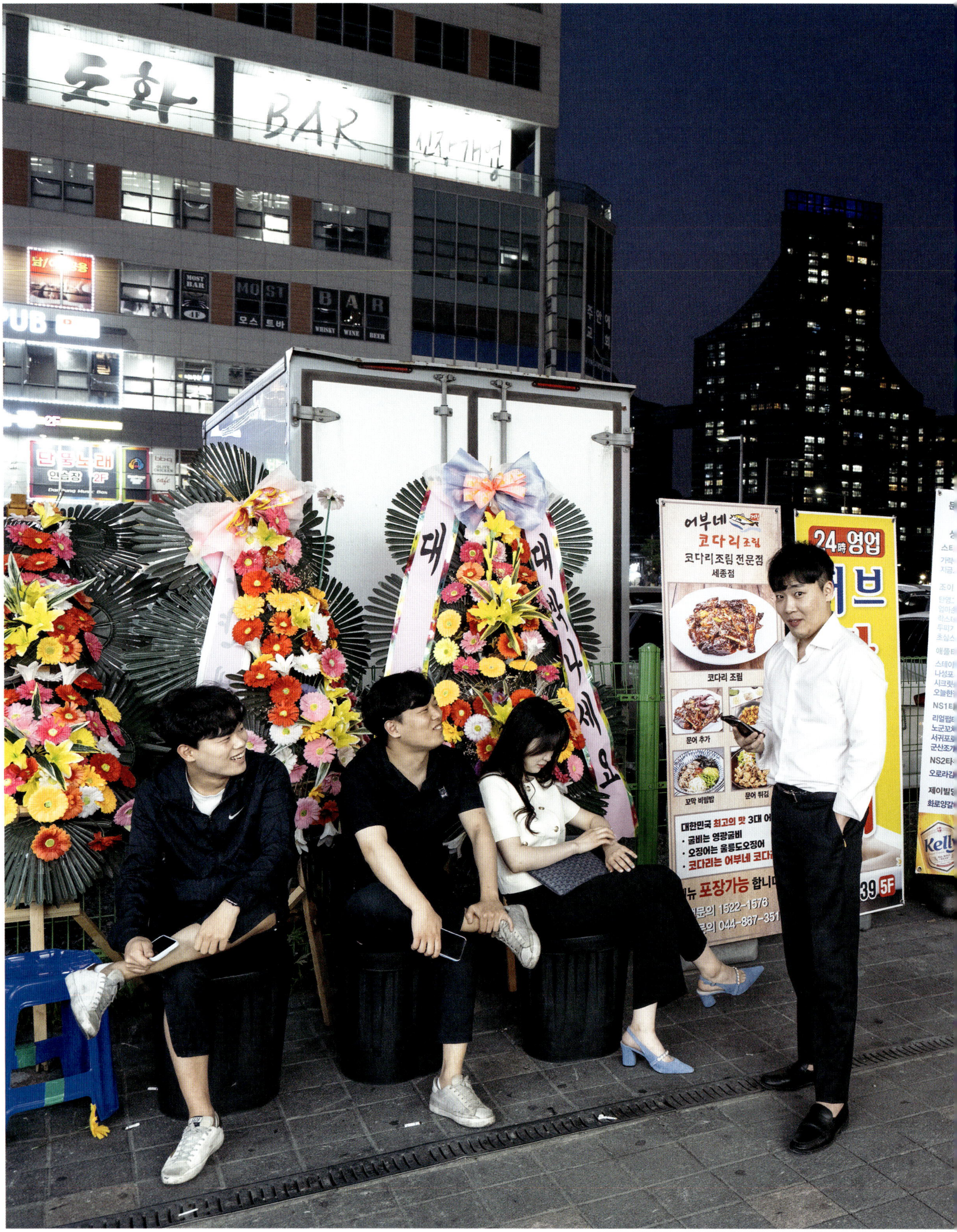
도화
BAR
신장개업
MOST BAR
WHISKY
WINE
BEER
어부네
코다리조림
코다리조림 전문점
세종점
코다리 조림
문어 추가
꼬막 비빔밥
문어 튀김
· 굴비는 영광굴비
· 오징어는 울릉도오징어
24時 영업

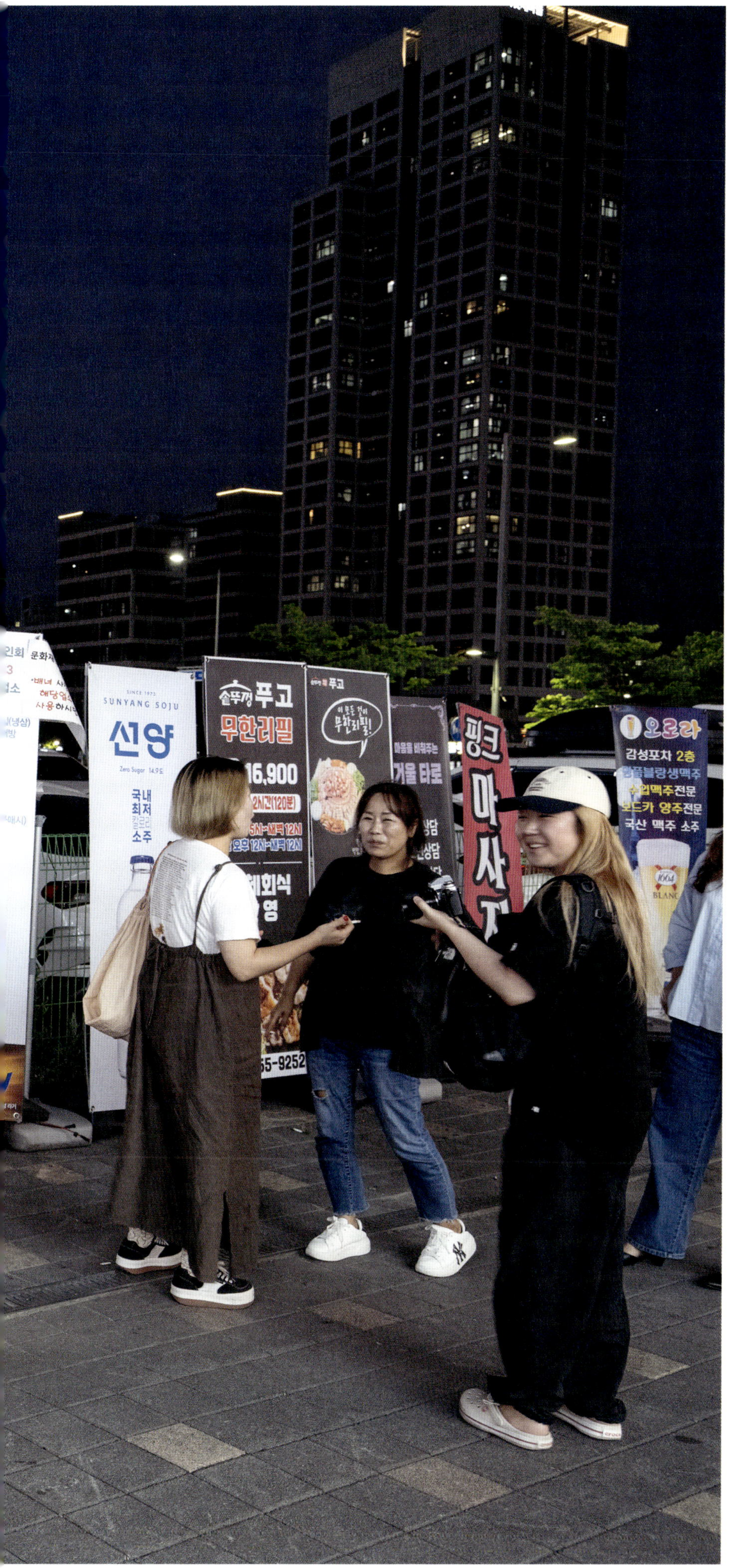

Sejong's nightlife district Naseong-ro.

EGYPT

NEW ADMINISTRATIVE CAPITAL

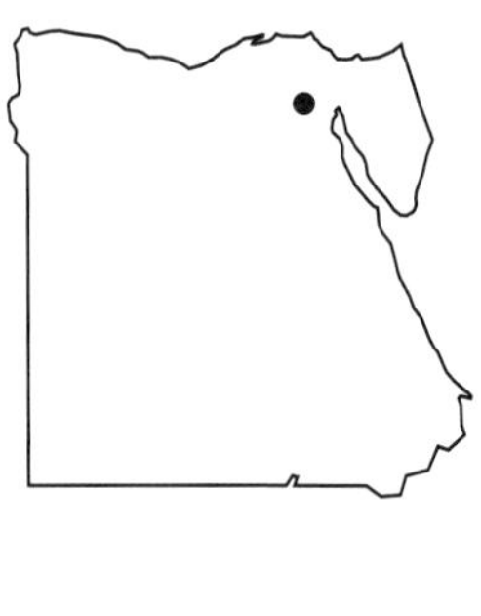

Start of construction: 2016
Inauguration date: —
Initiated by: President Abdel Fattah el-Sisi
Master plan by: Skidmore, Owings & Merrill
Expected population by 2050: 6.5 million
Surface area: 725 km²
Current capital: Cairo

After a complex and nerve-wracking application process, I finally get the green light to photograph Egypt's New Administrative Capital (NAC). The authorities, in this case the Ministry of Defense and the Ministry of Housing, Utilities & Urban Communities, grant me a measly four days to explore the new city-to-be. Improvising is out of the question. Only the locations mentioned on the permit are allowed. Staying after sunset is prohibited.

I enter Egypt's largest construction site, sprawling across 725 square kilometres of desert east of Cairo, through a gaudy gate with pharaonic flair. The scale is unreal. Long rows of analogous luxury flats loom on the horizon left and right. Black holes instead of windows. Streets and squares look unfinished and deserted. No one lives here yet. The only living souls I see are workers, supervisors, security personnel and police. They take their work extremely seriously. The sight of a foreign photographer sets off all kinds of alarm bells. In an empty city, it is hard to disappear into the crowd. The permit in my pocket prevents me from getting into too many predicaments.

'Dubai is our example,' says Khaled Al-Husseini, spokesman for the military-led government consortium Administrative Capital For Urban Development (ACUD), which coordinates the works. 'The new capital will become a safe and ultra-modern smart city. A central command centre will be able to monitor all infrastructure, facilities, traffic flows and air quality using sensors, drones and 6,000 cameras. The subsoil is full of fibre-optic cables to forward data. Residents will receive a smart card that they can use to make payments, park and gain access to their property. We are striving for a cashless society.'

'NAC will also be a green city. Whilst Cairo has less than one square metre of green space per inhabitant, in NAC that will increase to 15 square metres. There will be cycle paths, and 20% of energy will be renewable. Even the roof on the presidential palace will be fitted with solar panels.'

The Emirates also inspire in terms of urban design and architecture. In the Central Business District, an impressive cluster of high-rise buildings, the Chinese are building the Iconic Tower. With its 395 metres, this concrete and glass obelisk will be Africa's tallest tower. The nearly completed Grand Mosque and the Cathedral of the Nativity of Christ are the country's largest houses of worship. In the square in front of the presidential palace stands the world's longest flagpole, 190 metres high. Meanwhile, the Financial District, the Government District, Sports City and the City of Arts and Culture are also taking shape. Alongside all that architectural spectacle, a gigantic 30-kilometre-long city park with an artificial river is being built. Further away from the centre is the Ministry of Defence, called the 'Octagon', which far exceeds the US Pentagon in size.

'Egypt has more than 100 million inhabitants,' Al-Husseini explains. 'We have to constantly create accommodation to deal with population growth. Cairo city alone is home to 11 million people. The infrastructure cannot handle that. The new capital is part of the solution. Within 25 to 30 years, 6 million people will live there.'

To house them, some 20 residential compounds are rising from the desert sands. These islands of luxury and privacy are being built by workers who, like the vast majority of Egyptians, will never be able to afford to live here.

The relentless urban expansion has created a city of alarming scale. A huge excess of upper-middle-class housing has emerged in the satellite cities around Cairo. There are warnings around about this real estate bubble bursting.

The contrast with the overcrowded Old Cairo could not be greater. 69% of the people live in impoverished 'informal areas', illegally built dense neighbourhoods with unattractive blocks and little greenery. In addition to the permanent traffic jams and the matching smog, there are ongoing issues with safety, sewers, waste collection and energy supply. Critics view the construction of the new capital as another step in the ever-growing socio-economic gap between the hapless masses and the happy few. The residents of Old Cairo are left to their own devices. Whilst the state is emerging as a powerful property developer, the military is tightening its grip on society.

January 2022

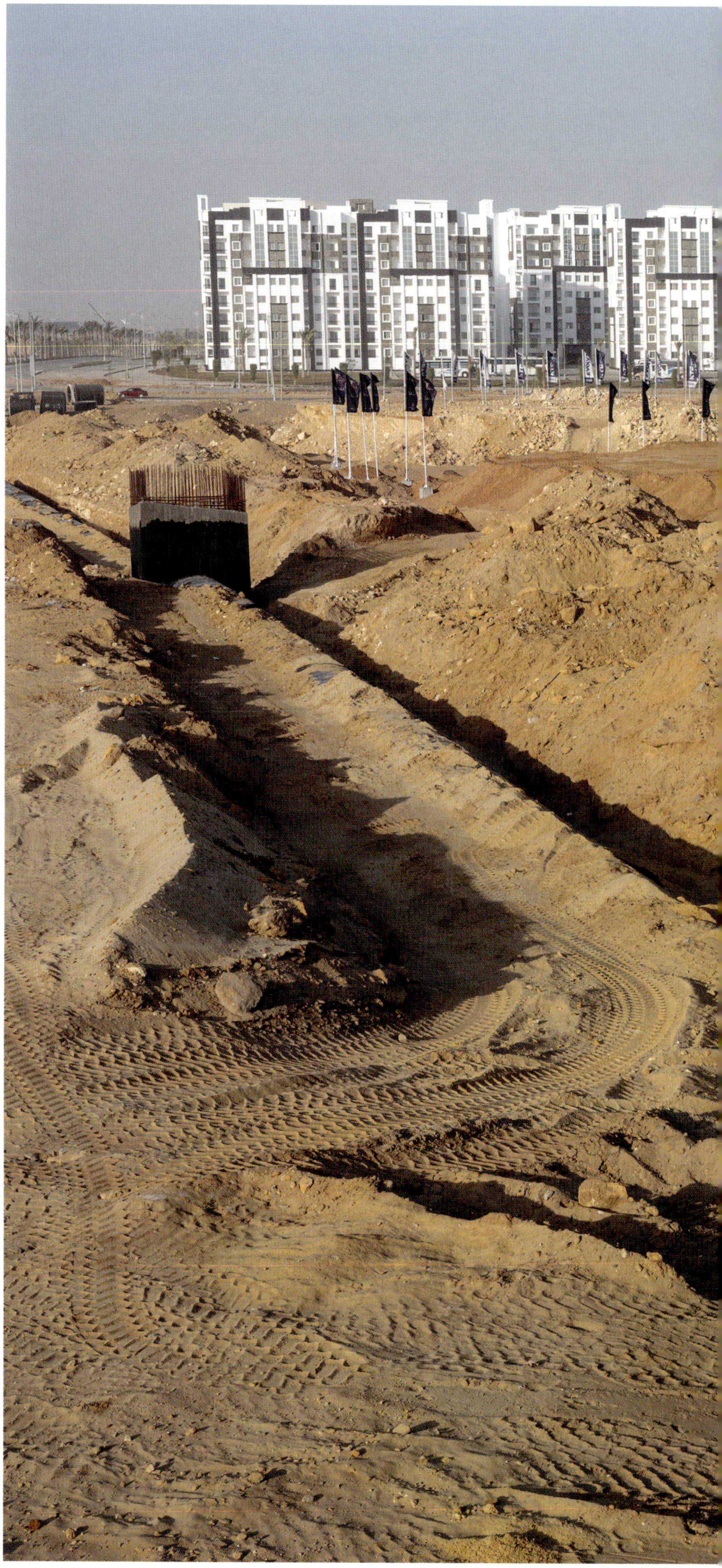

Third Residential Neighbourhood (R3).

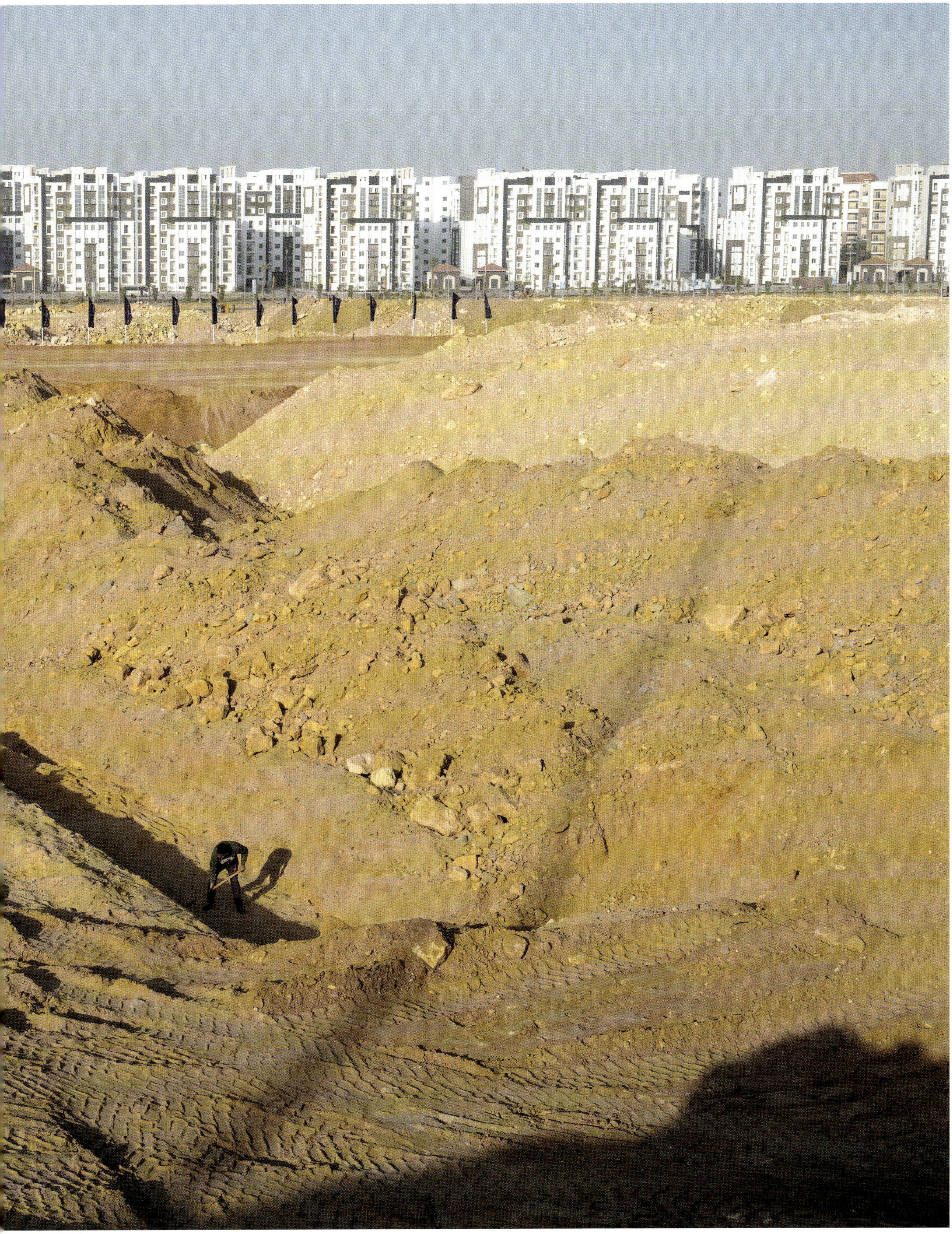

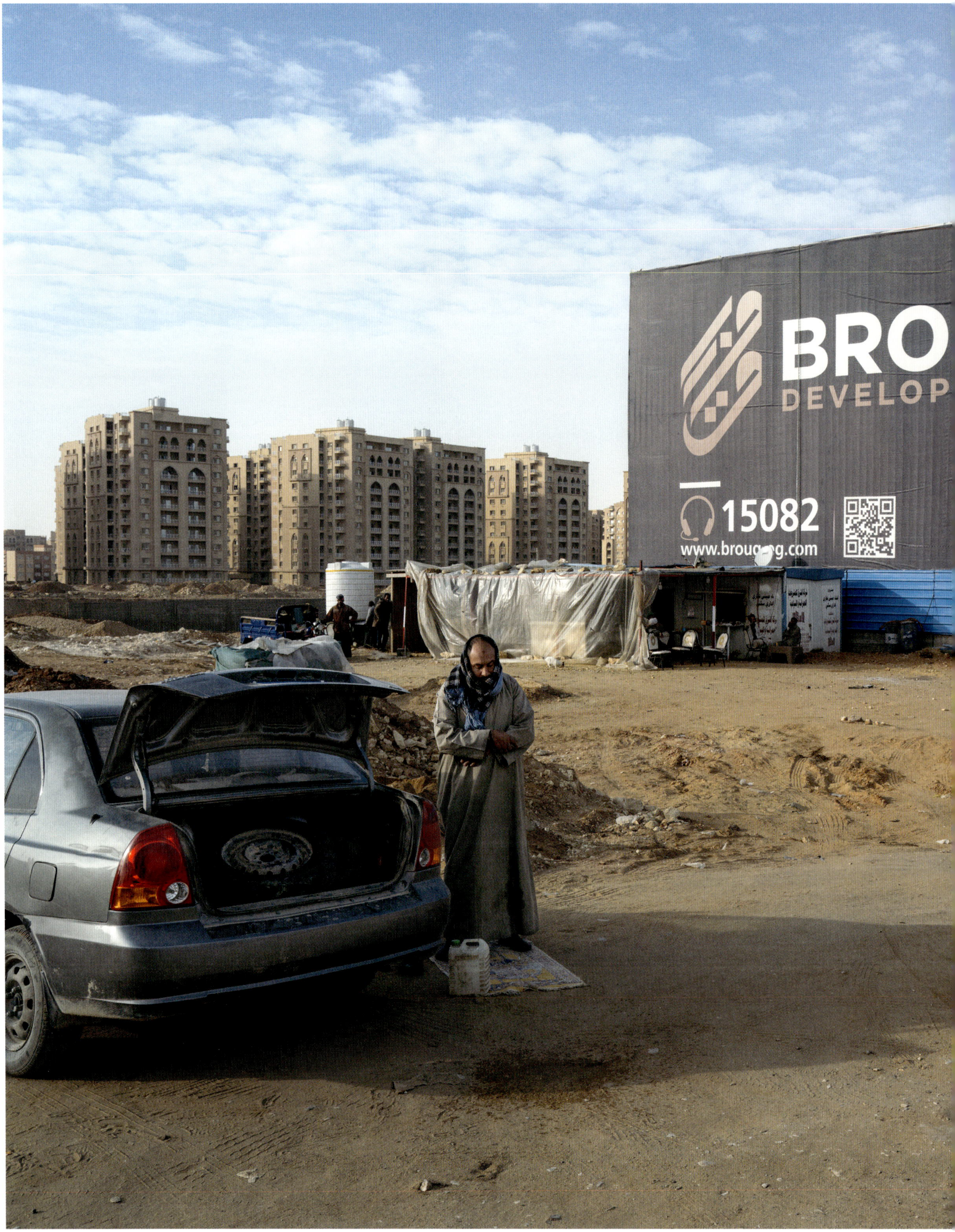
BRO
DEVELOP
15082

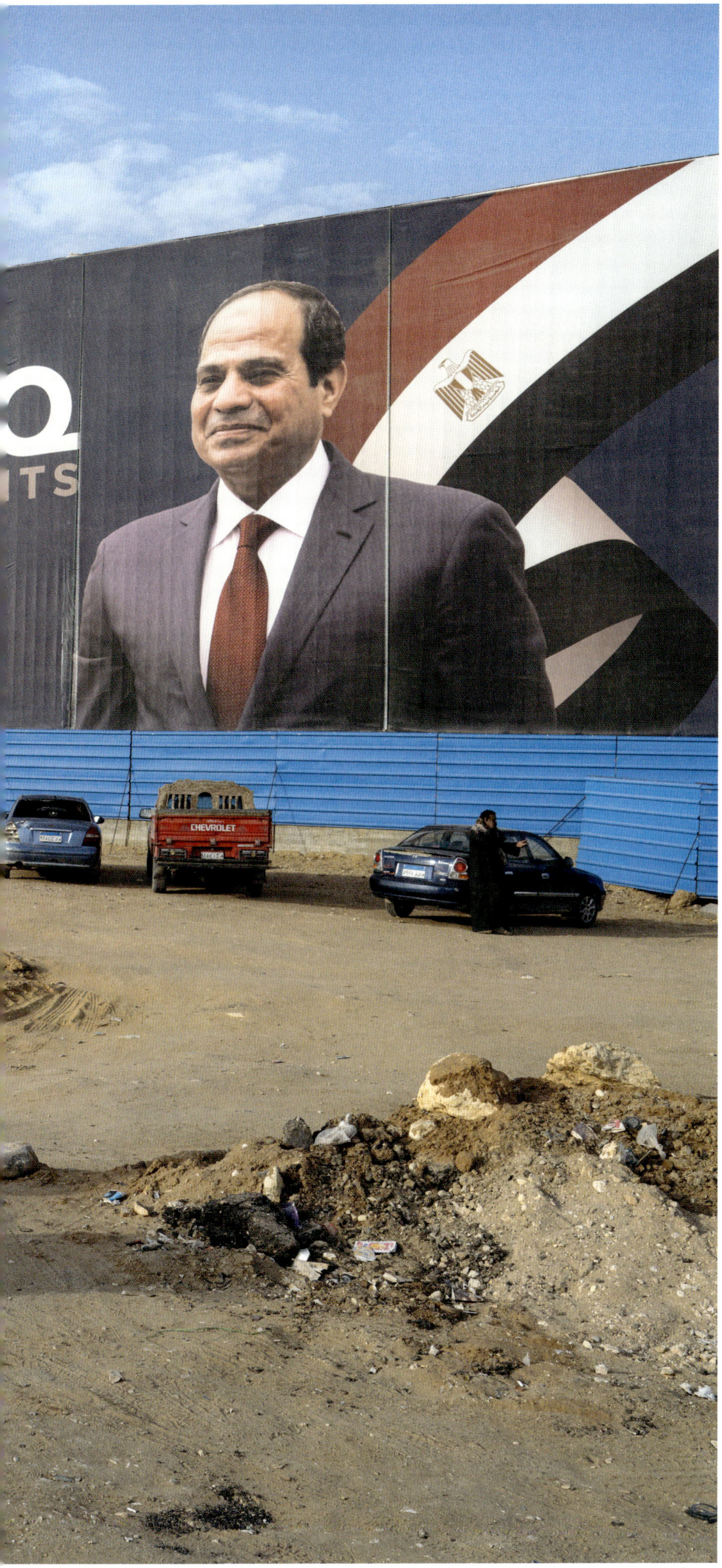

Egyptian real estate company Brouq Developments' billboard depicting President Abdel Fattah el-Sisi.

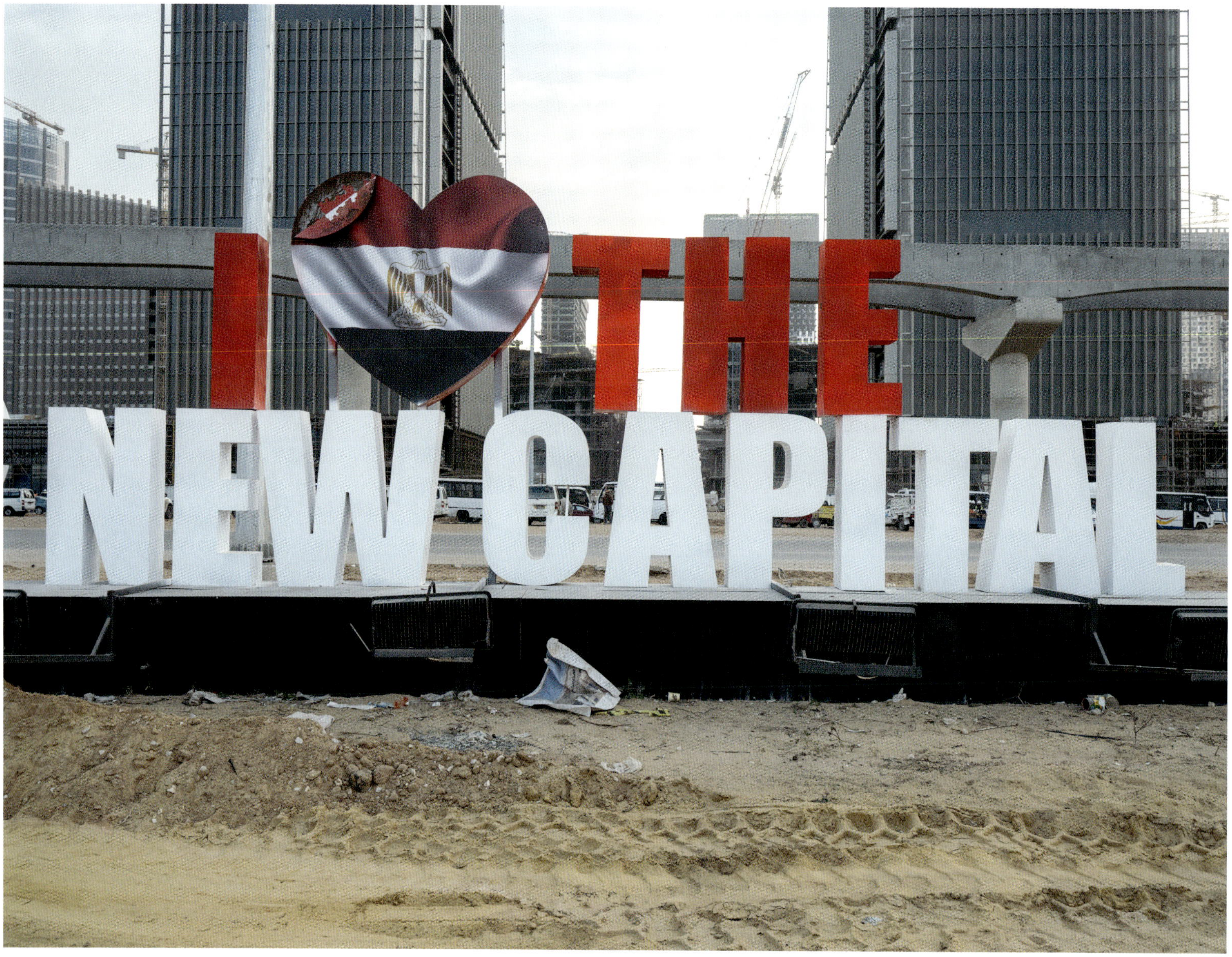

Central Business District.

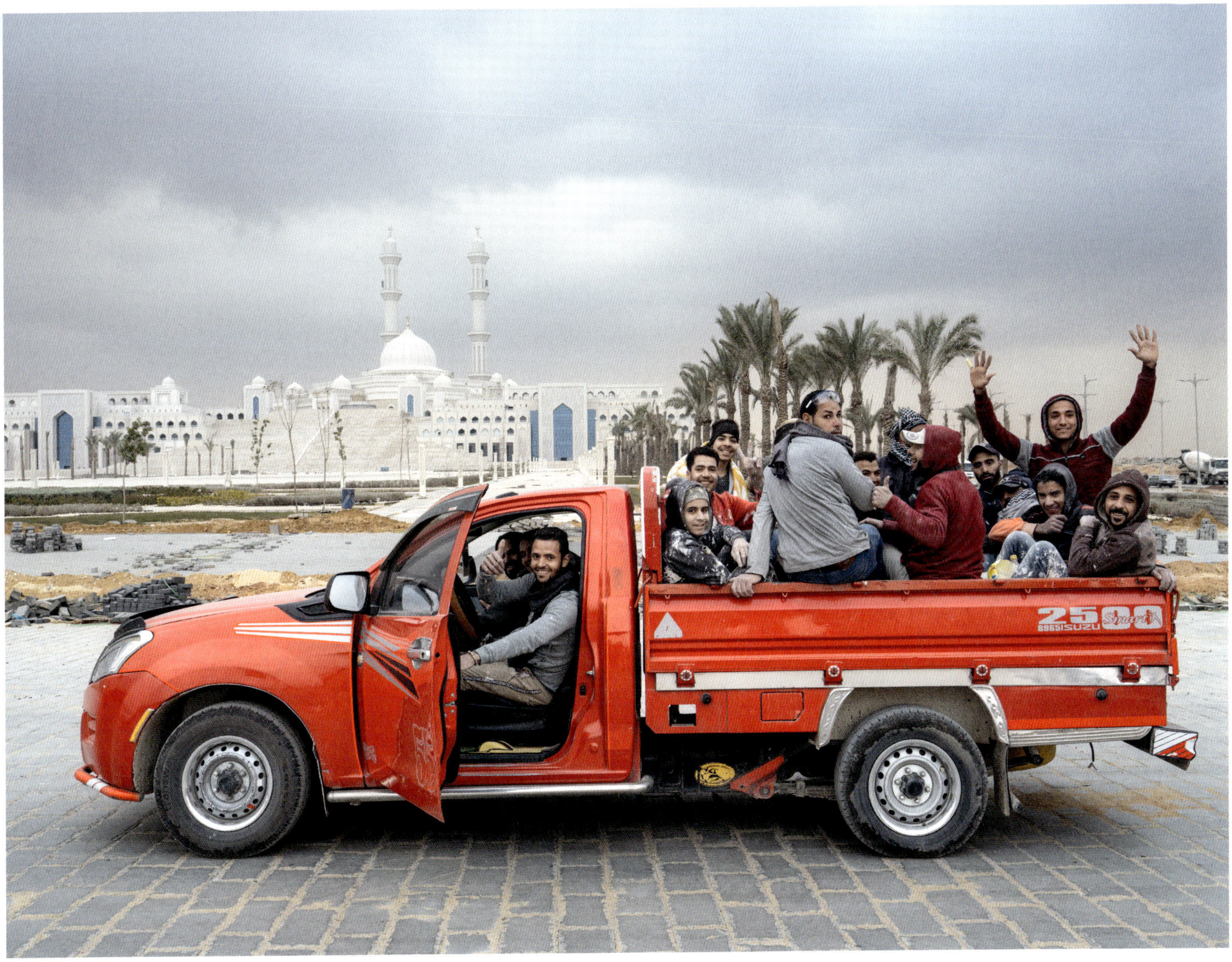

Workers pass the newly built Masjid Misr Mosque, which accommodates 100,000 worshippers.

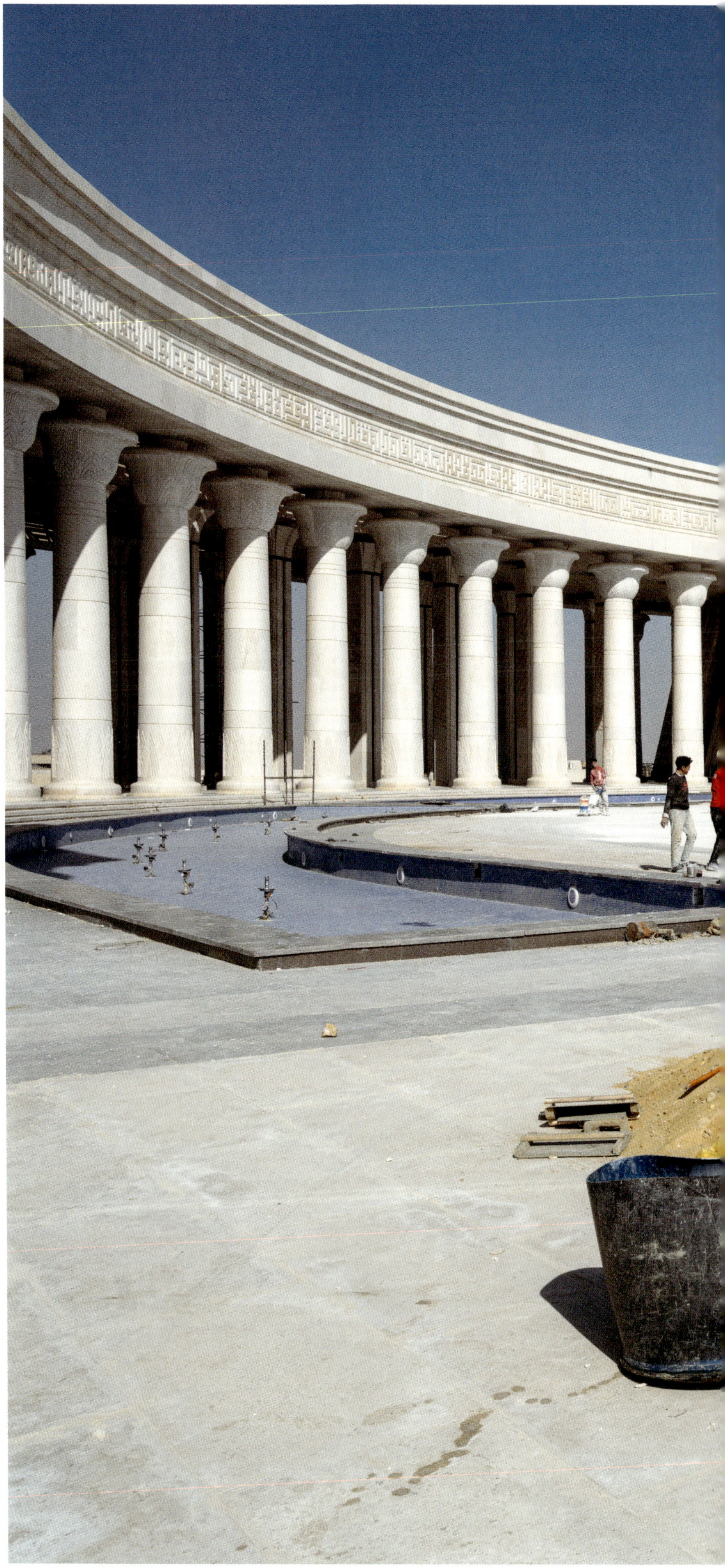

Triumphal Arch.

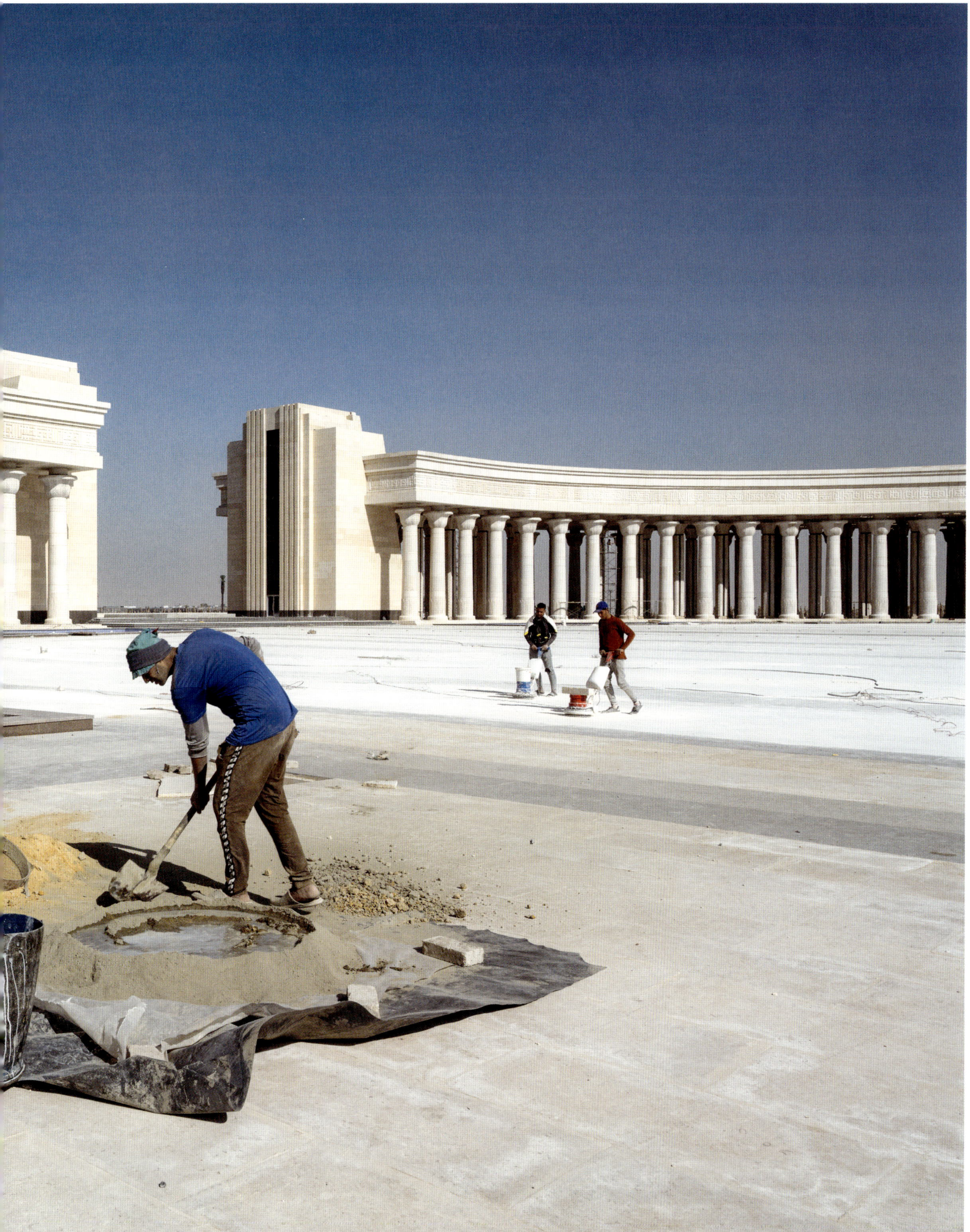

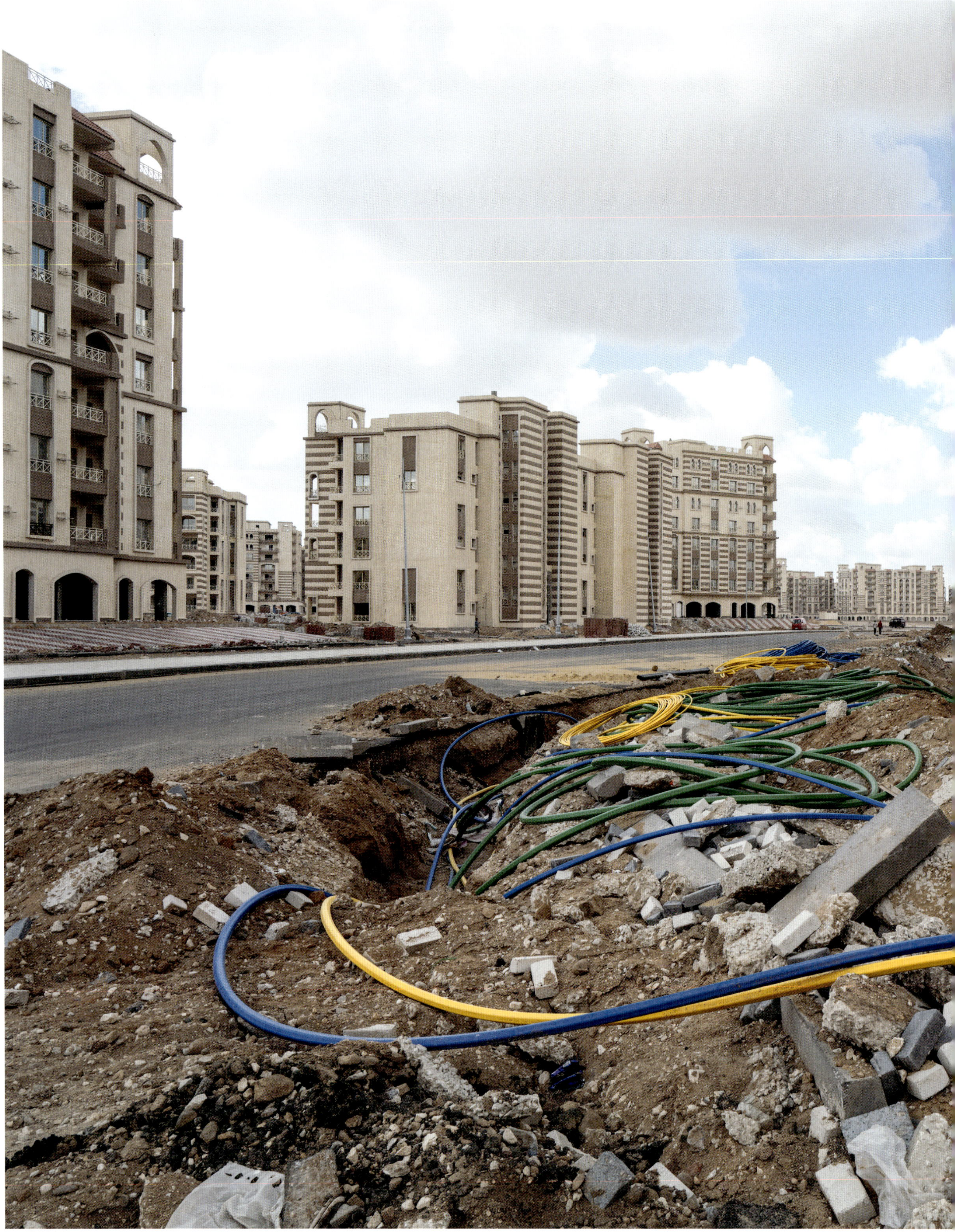

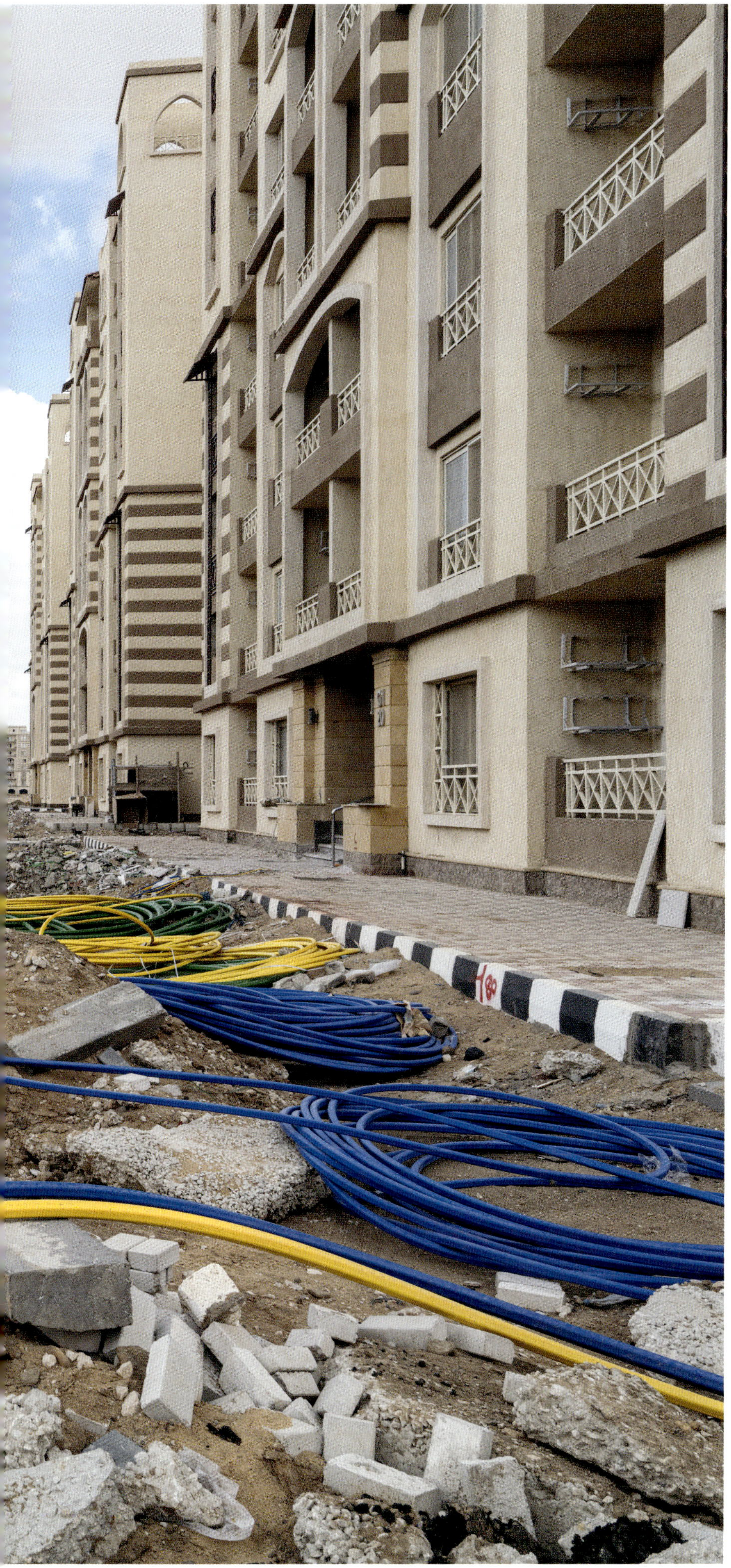

First Residential Neighbourhood (R1).

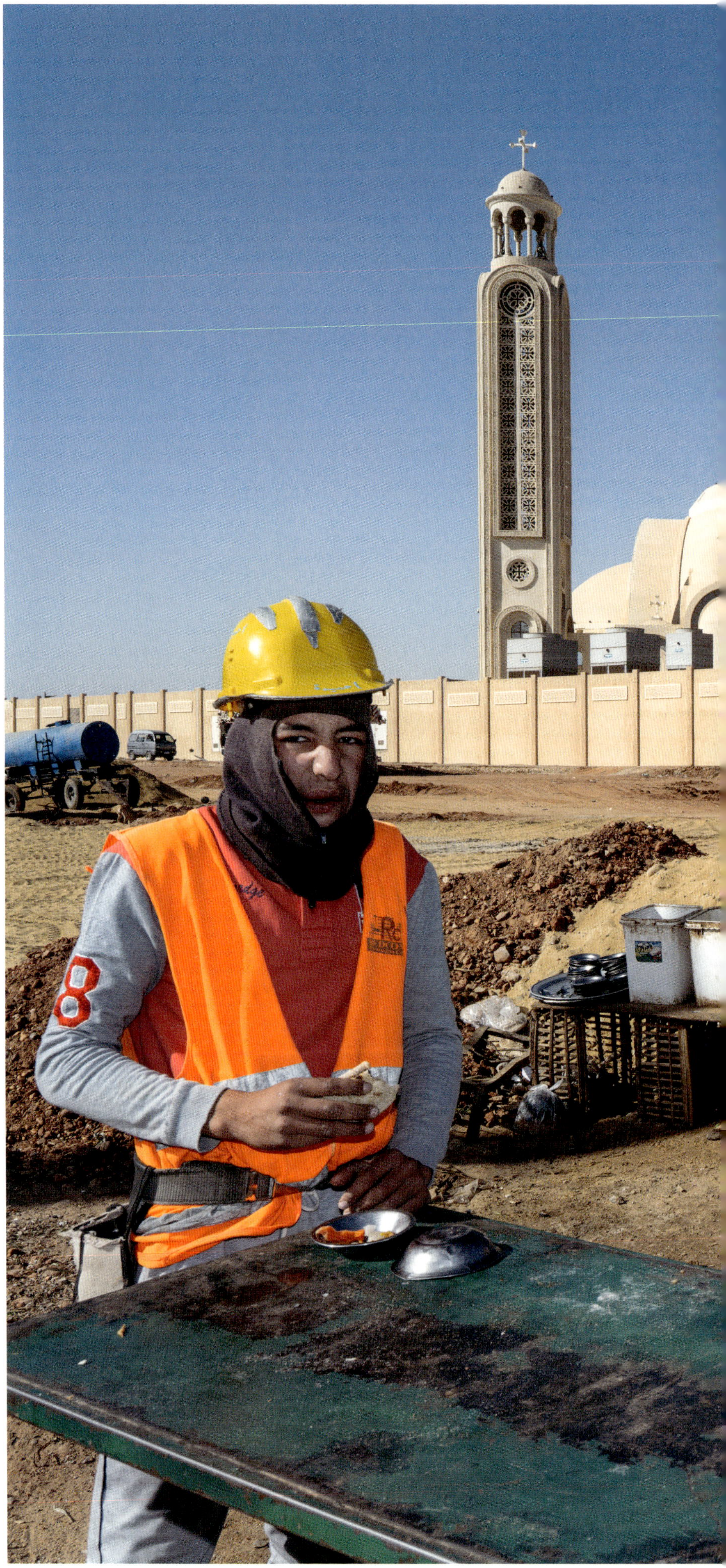

The Cathedral of the Nativity of Christ,
inaugurated in 2019.

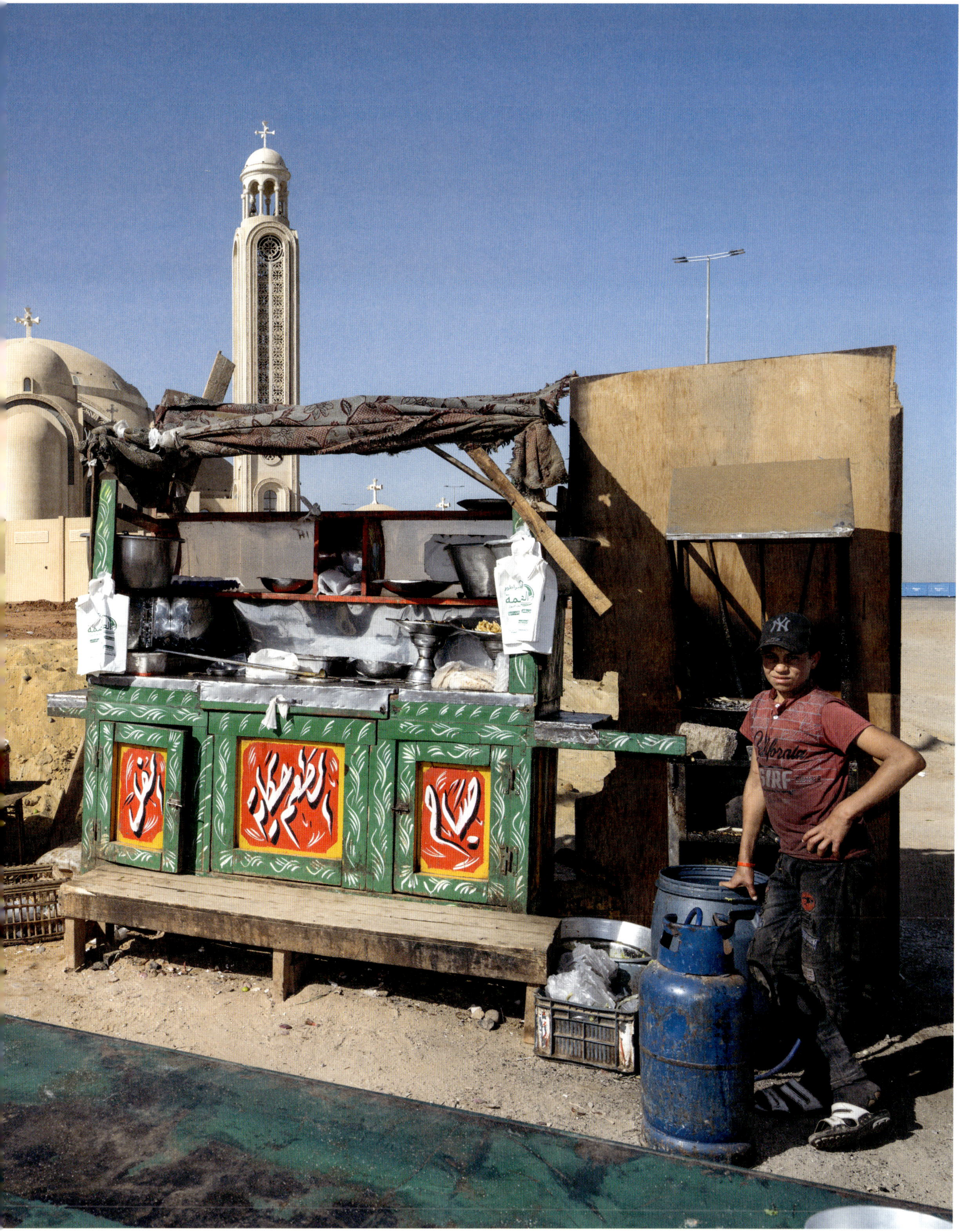

Construction worker.

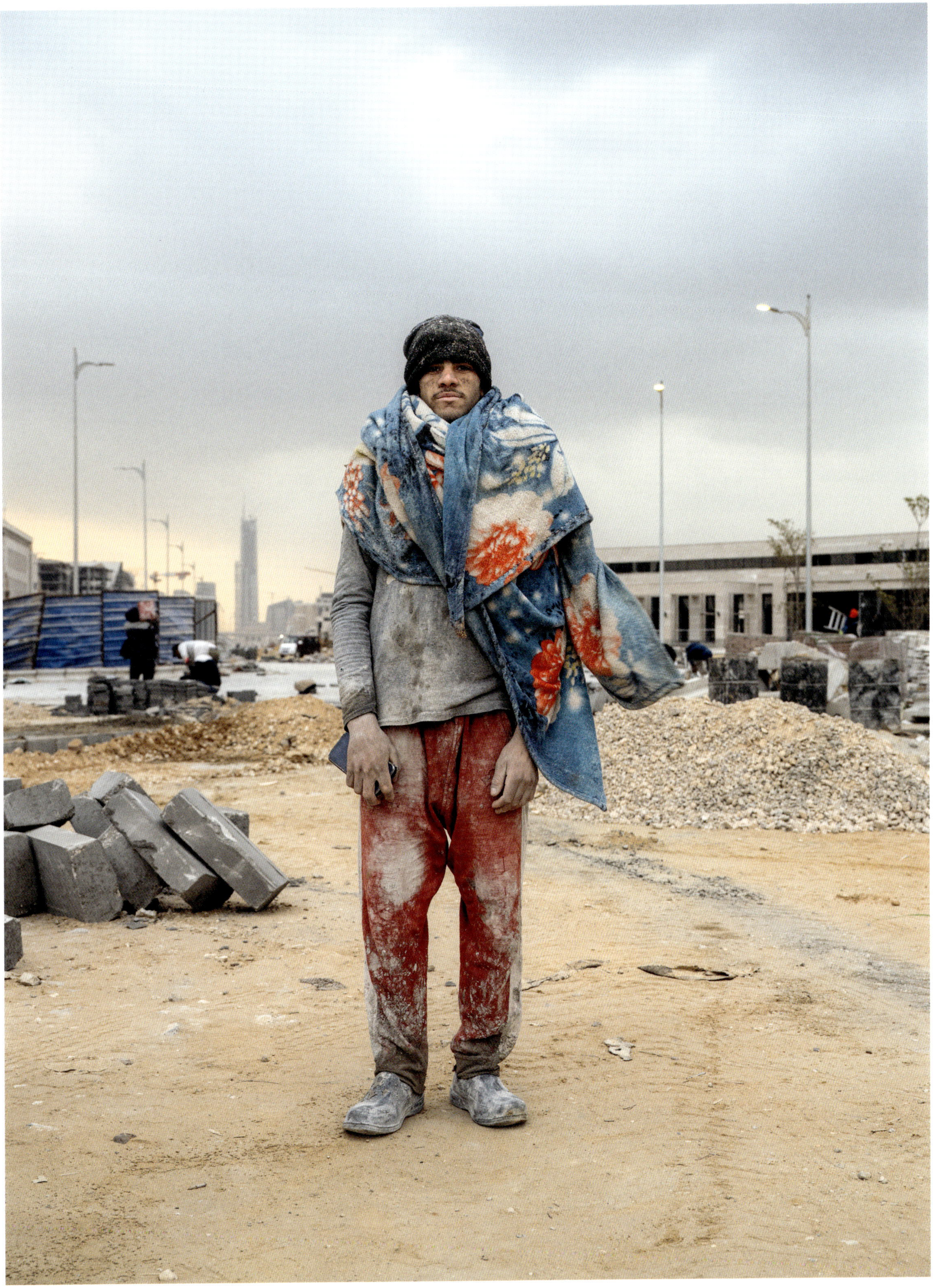

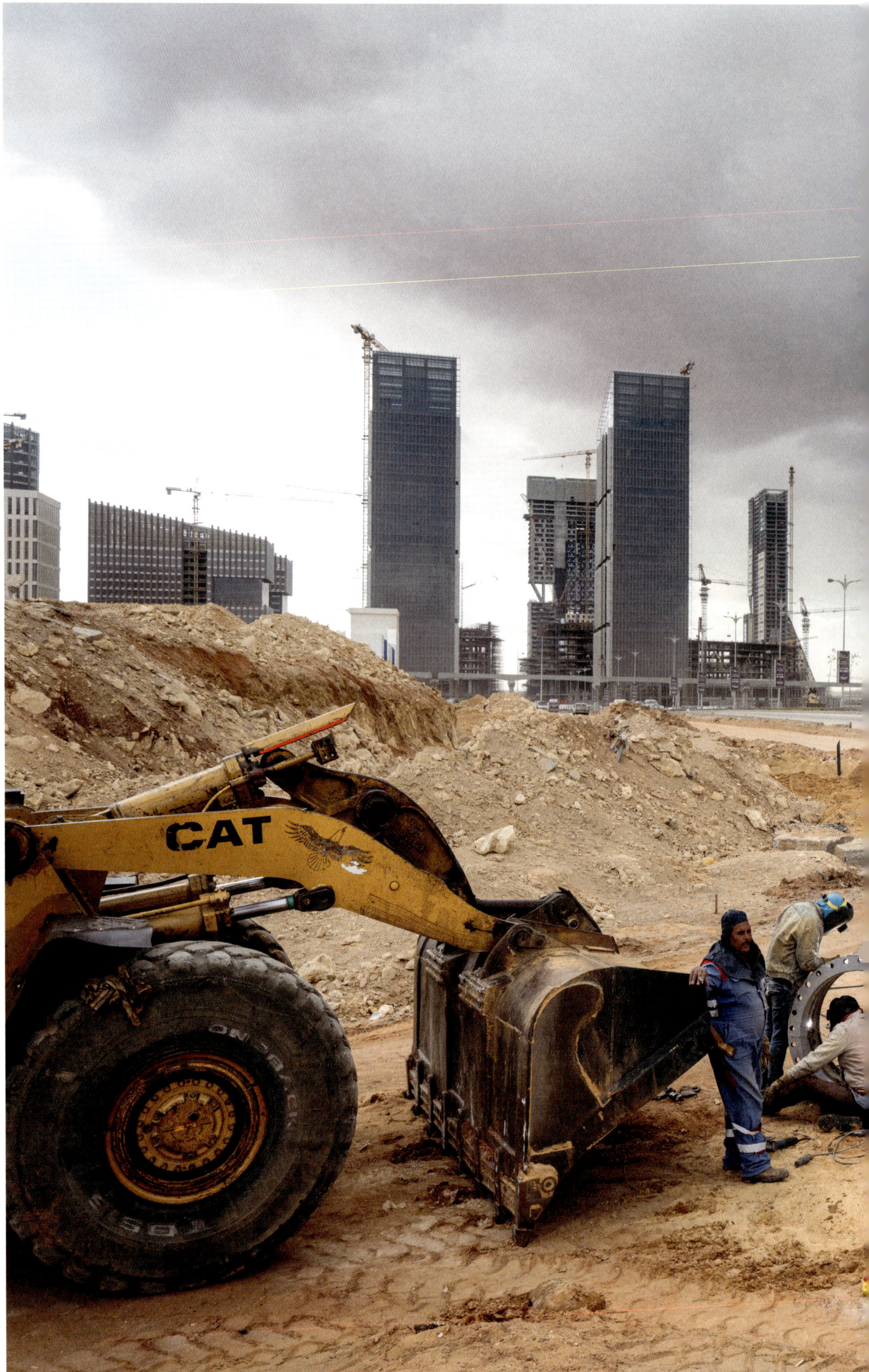

Central Business District,
featuring the 394-metre-high
Iconic Tower under construction.

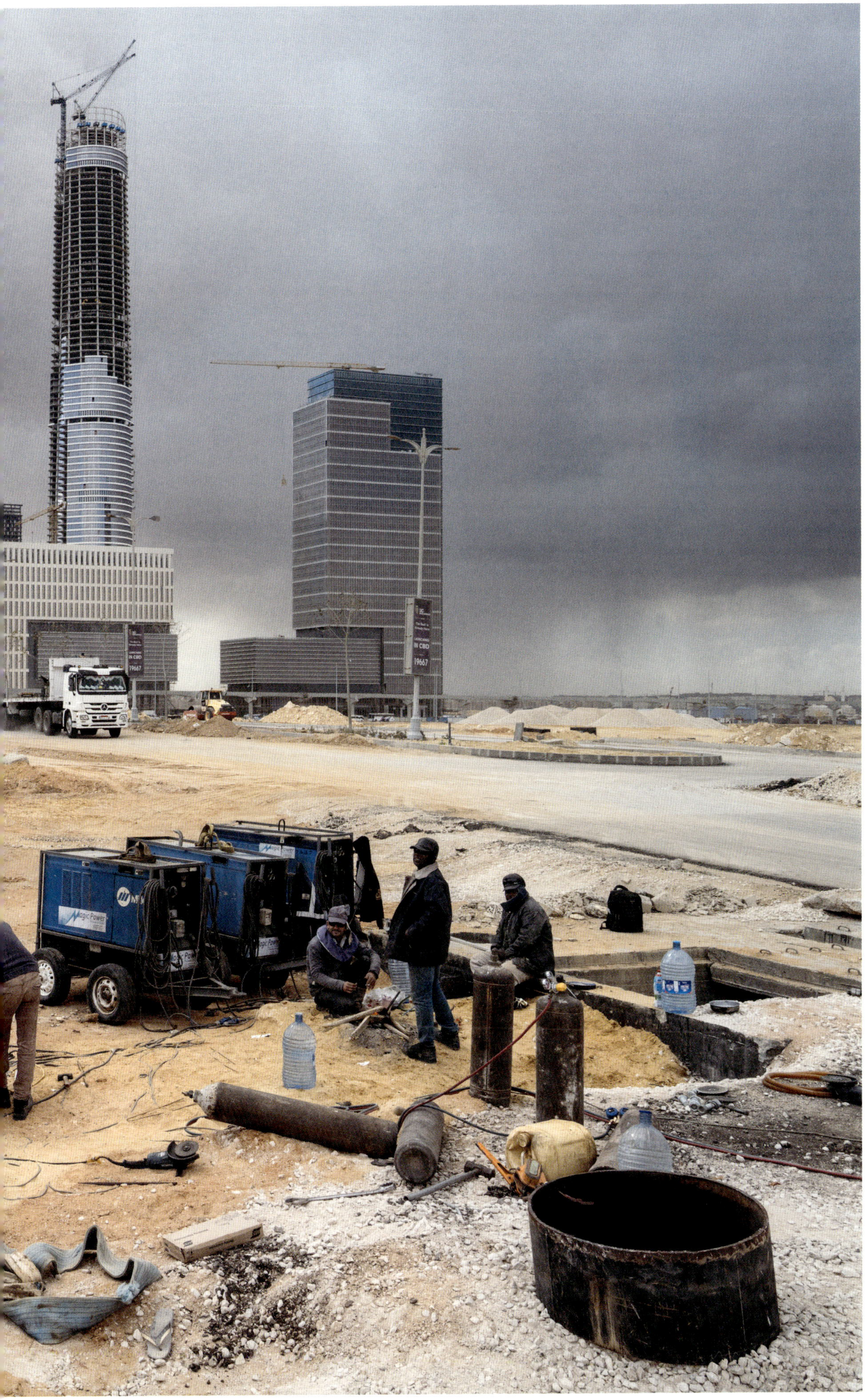
IN CBD
19667
IN CBD
19667

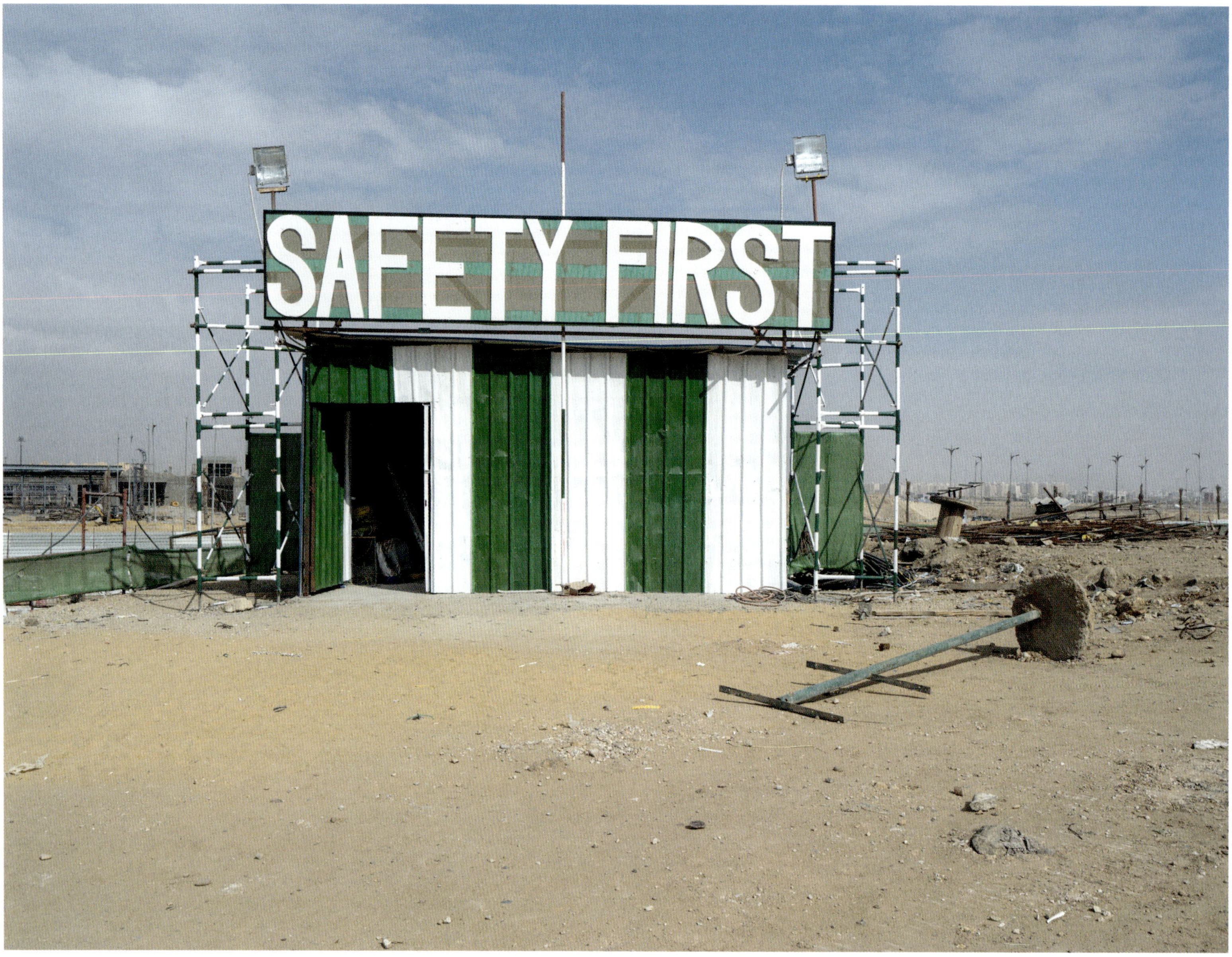

Workers' storage near the Fifth Residential Neighbourhood (R5).

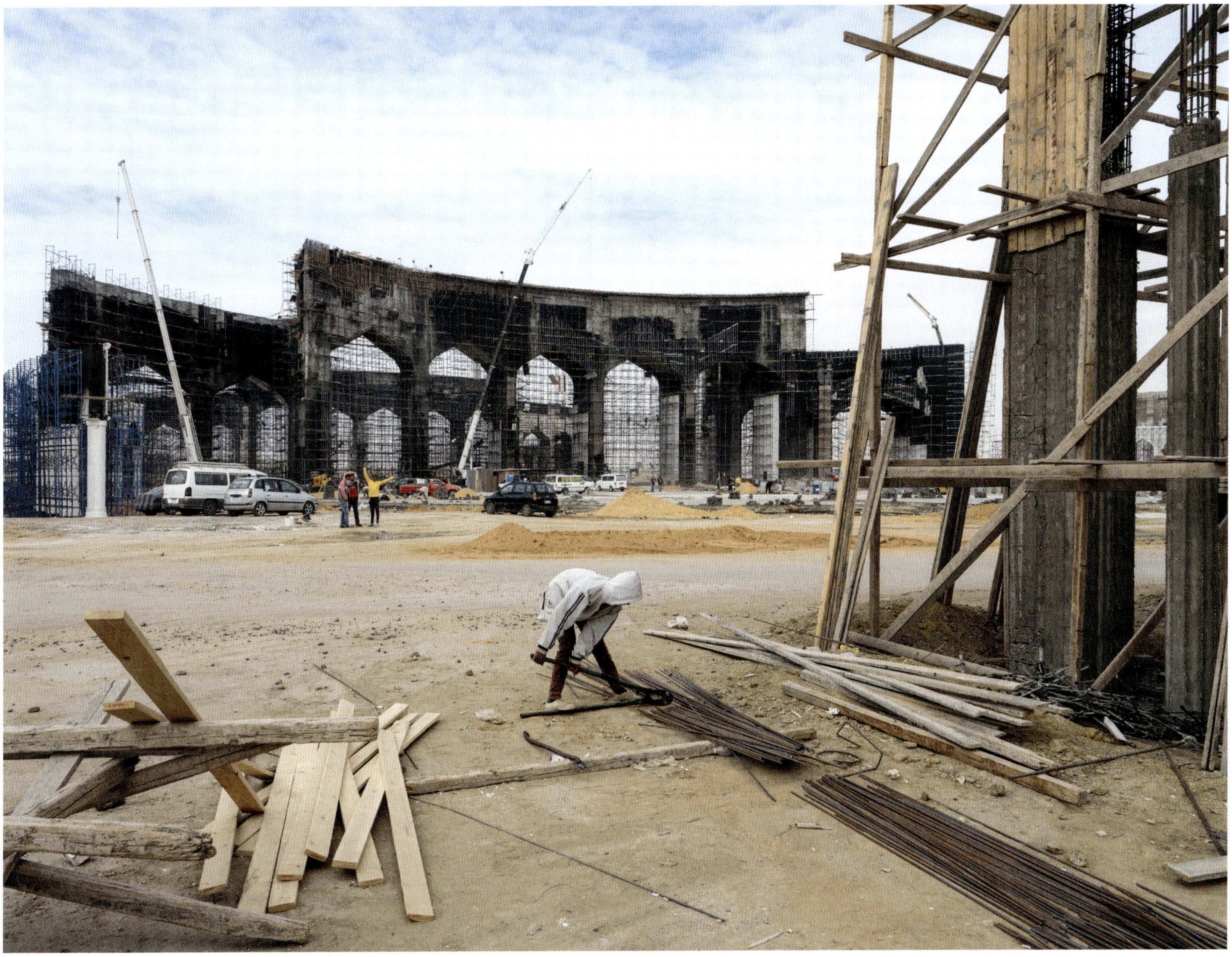

Construction site of the west gate to the NAC.

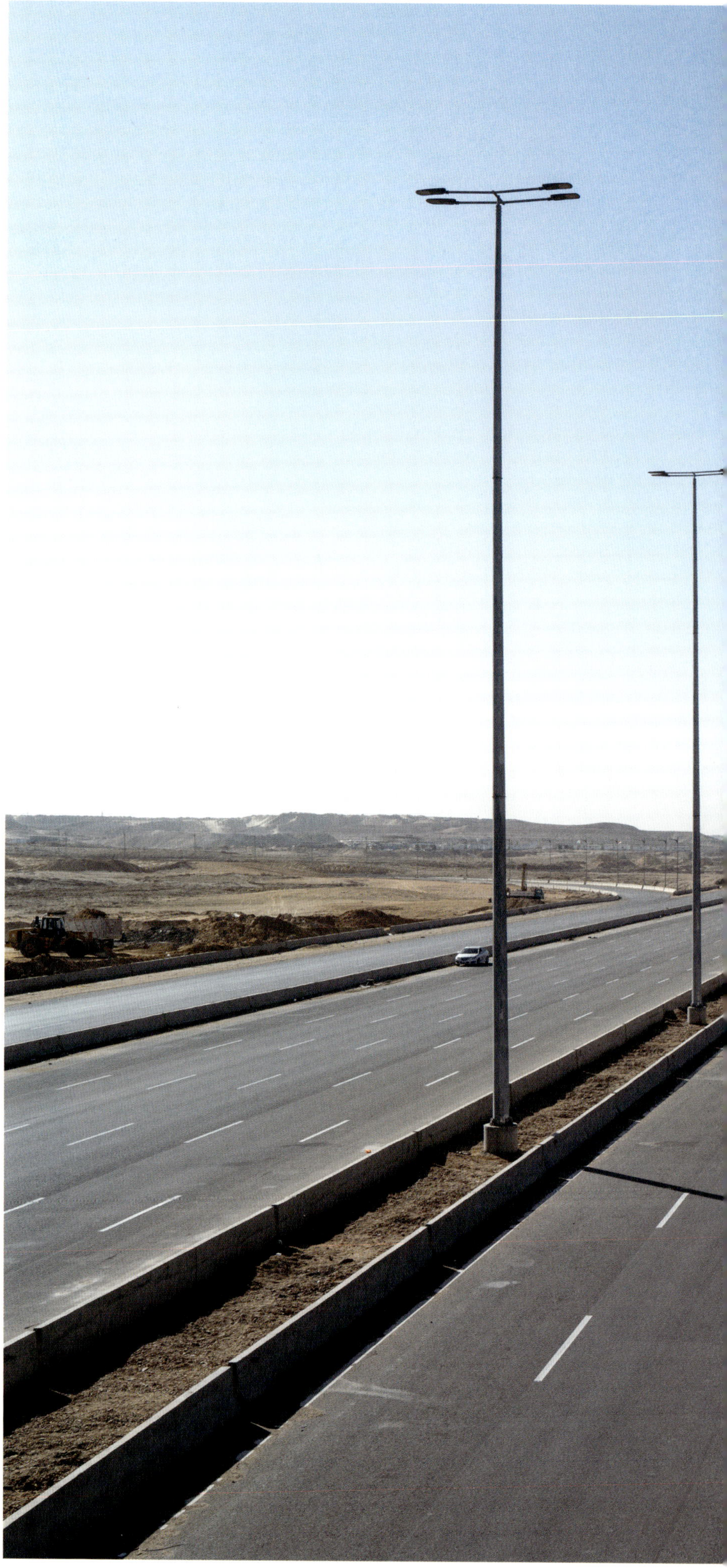

A new regional ring road bisects the NAC.

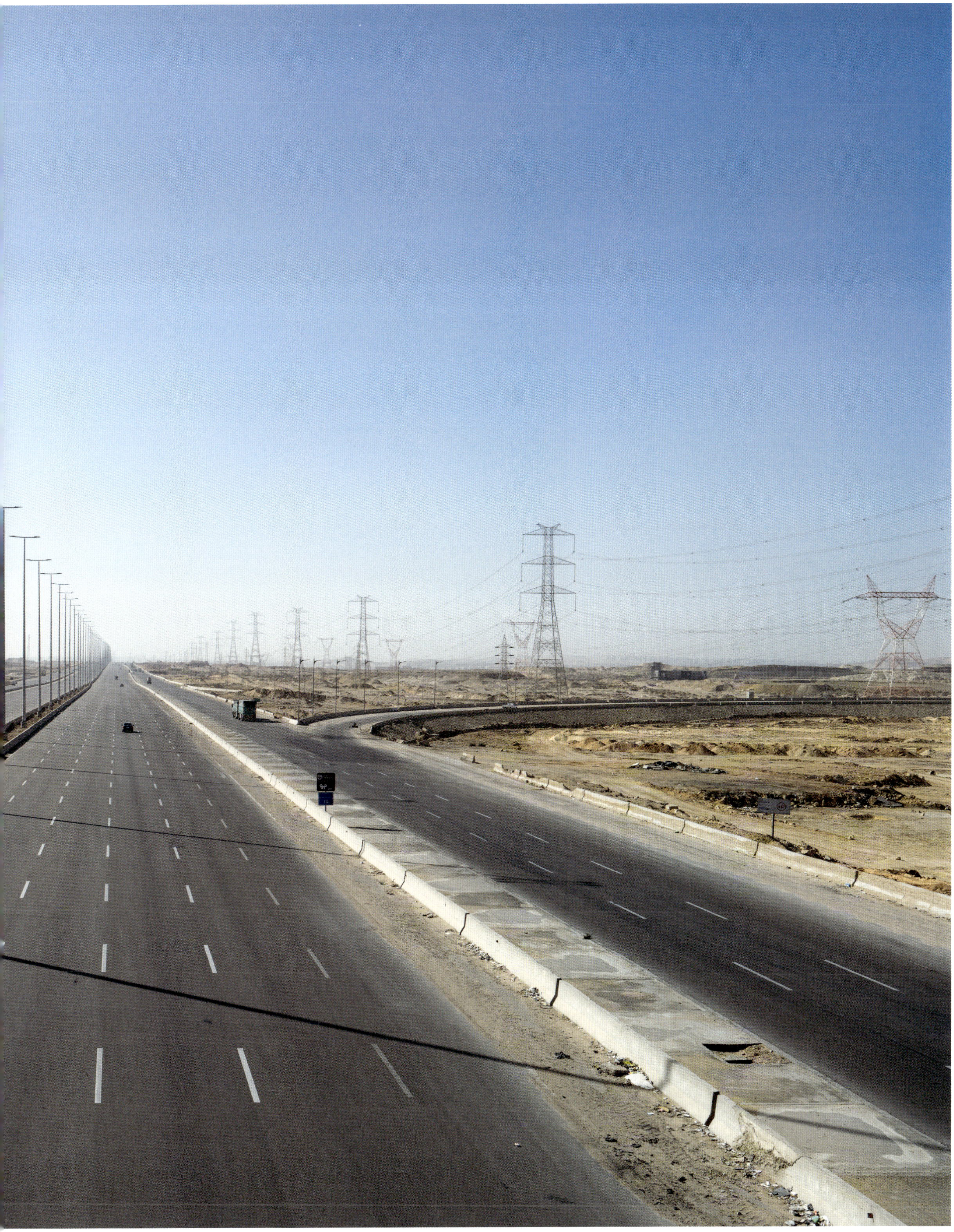

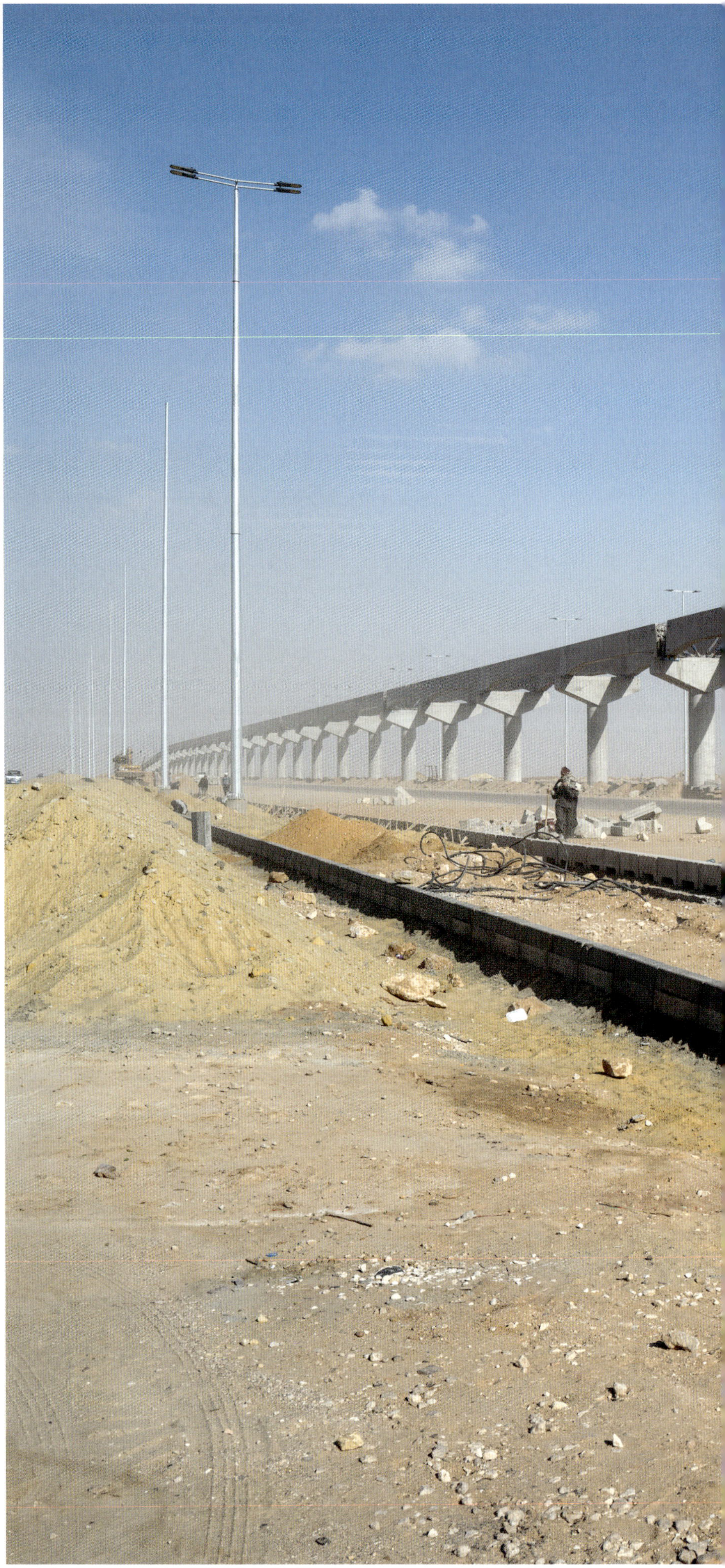

Light rail transit construction site.

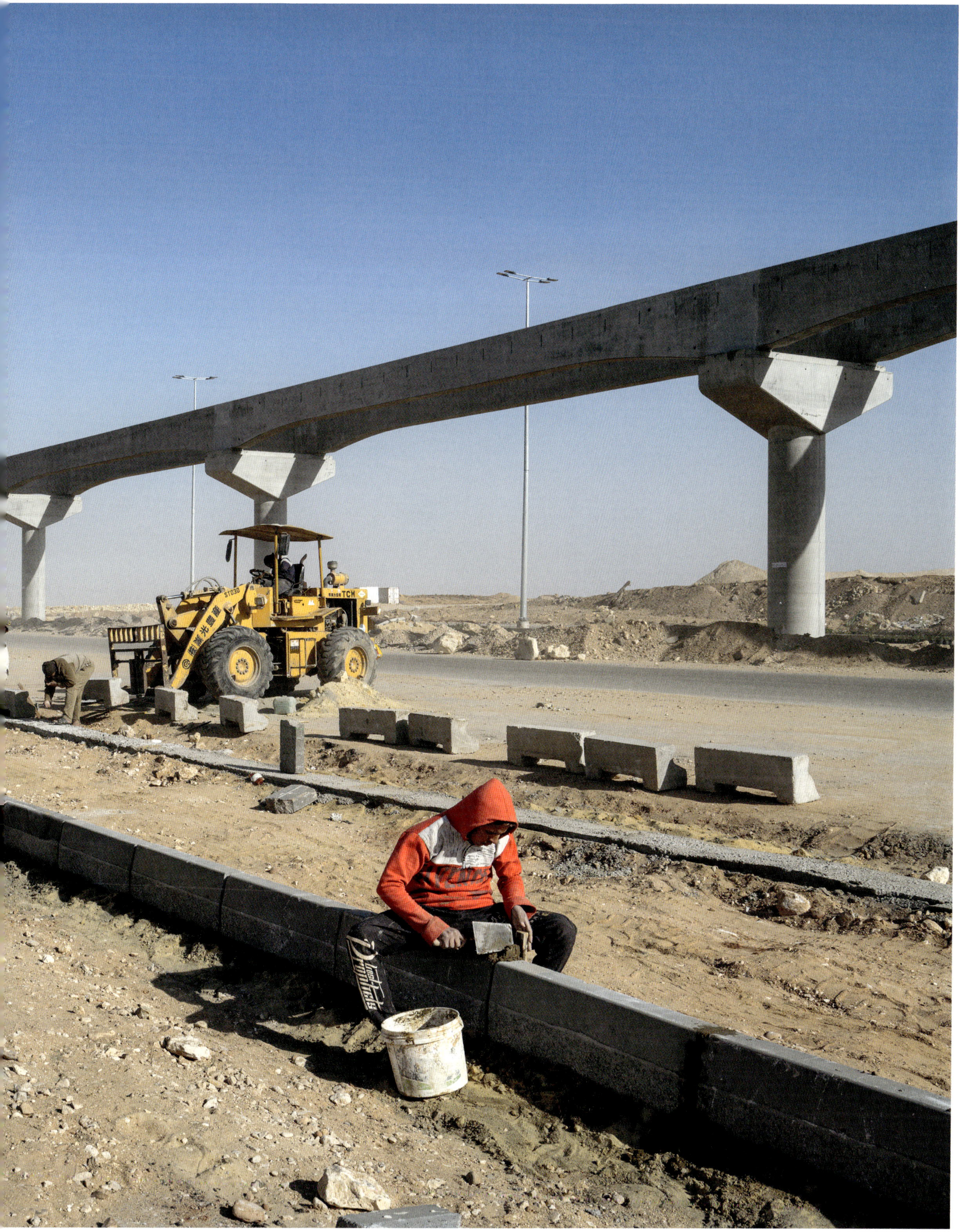

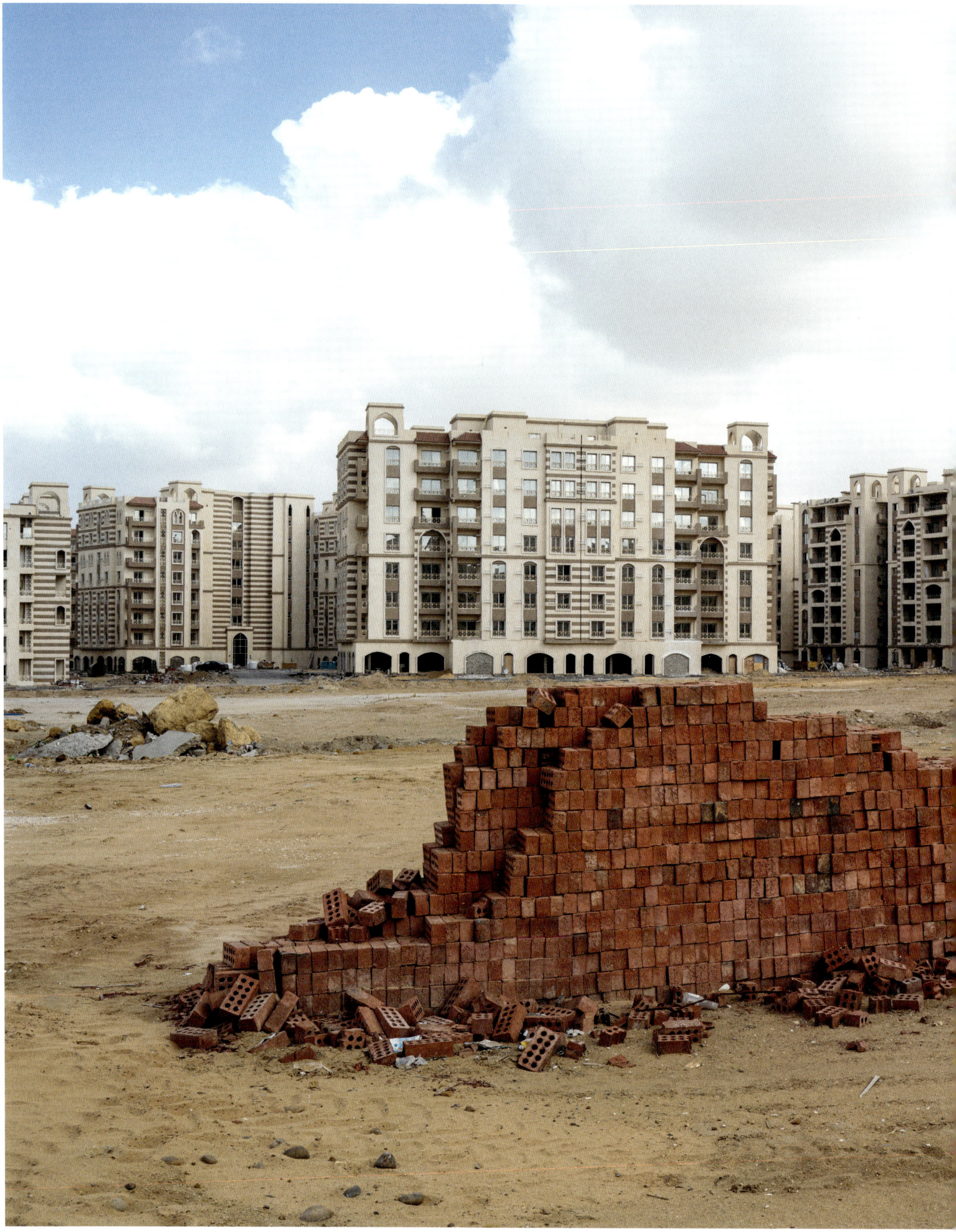

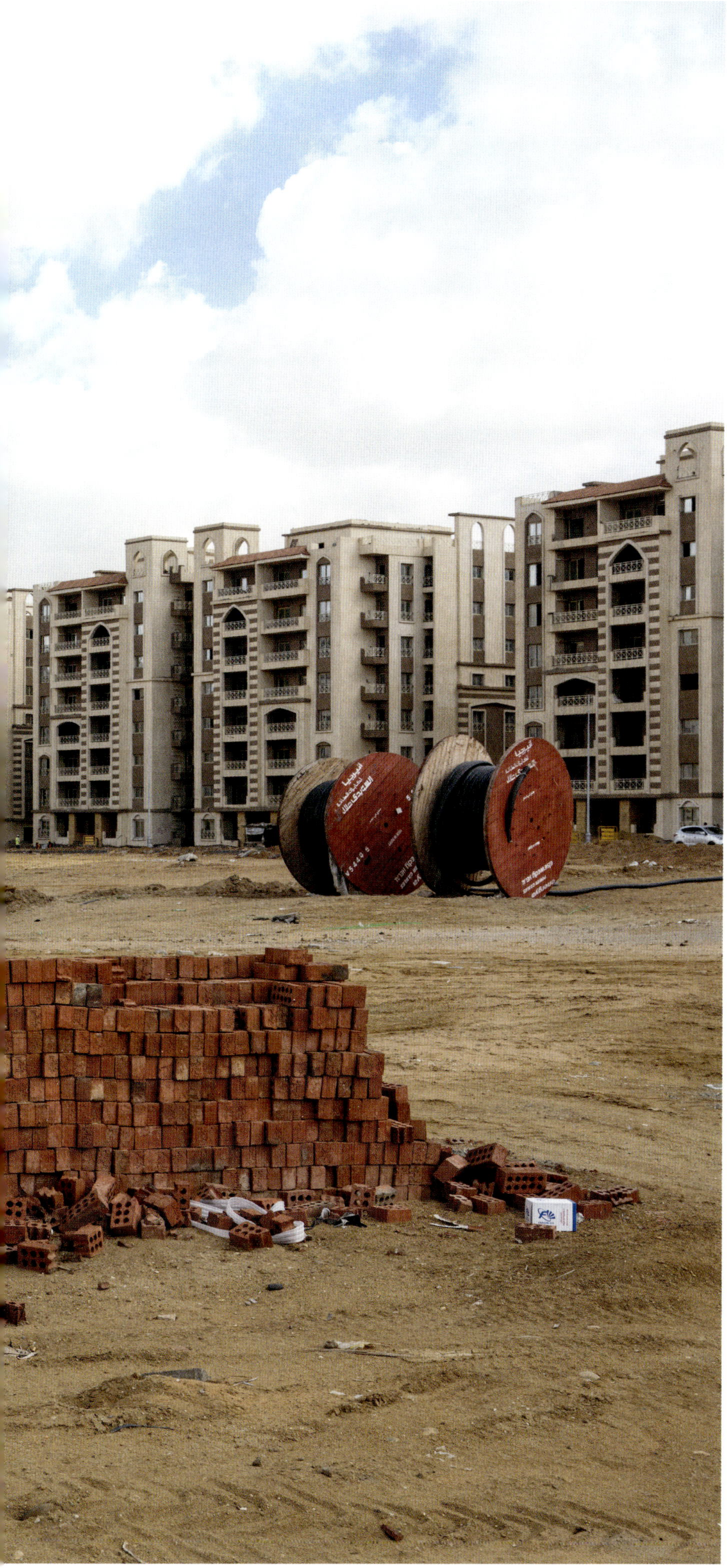

First Residential Neighbourhood (R1).

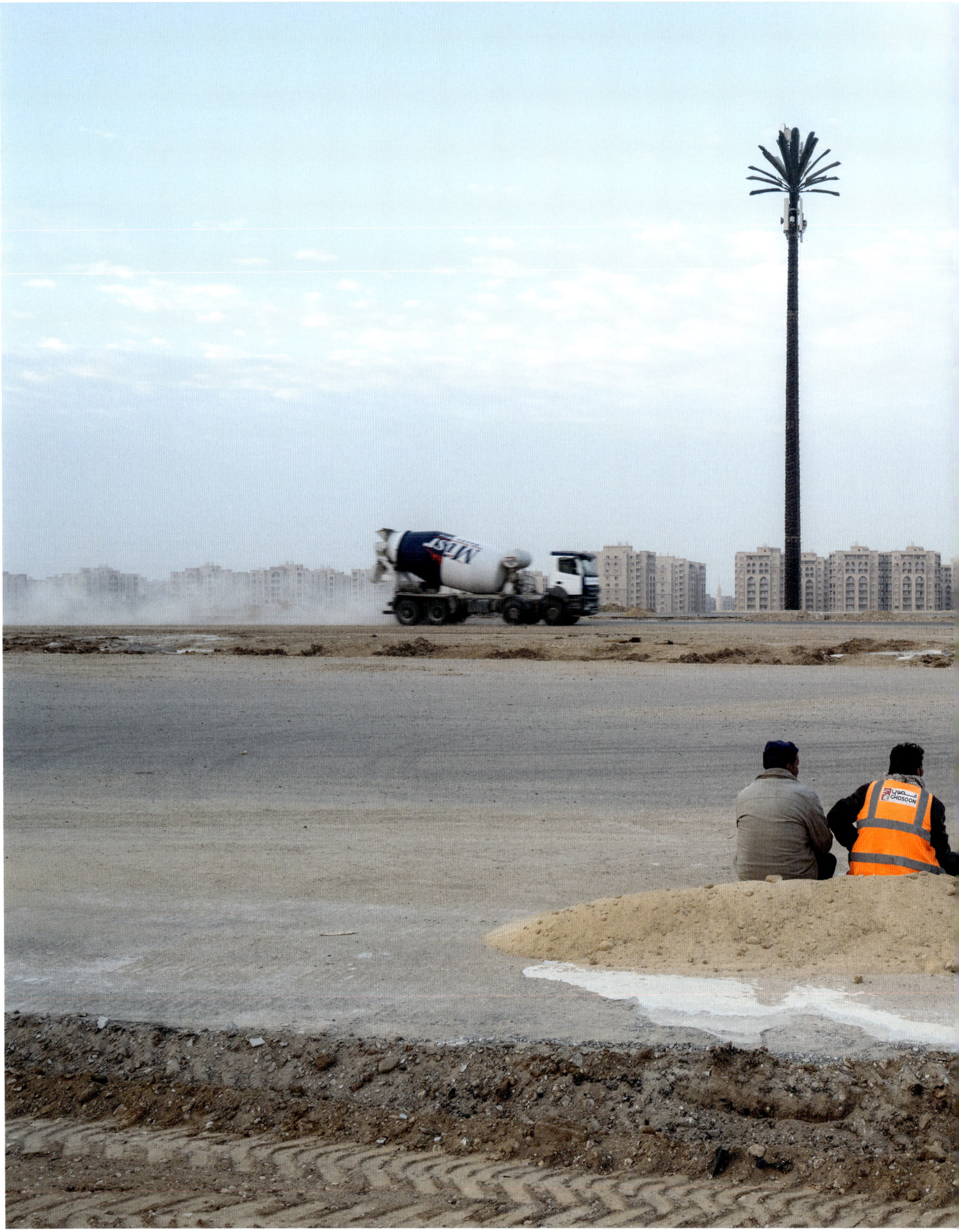
GHOSOON

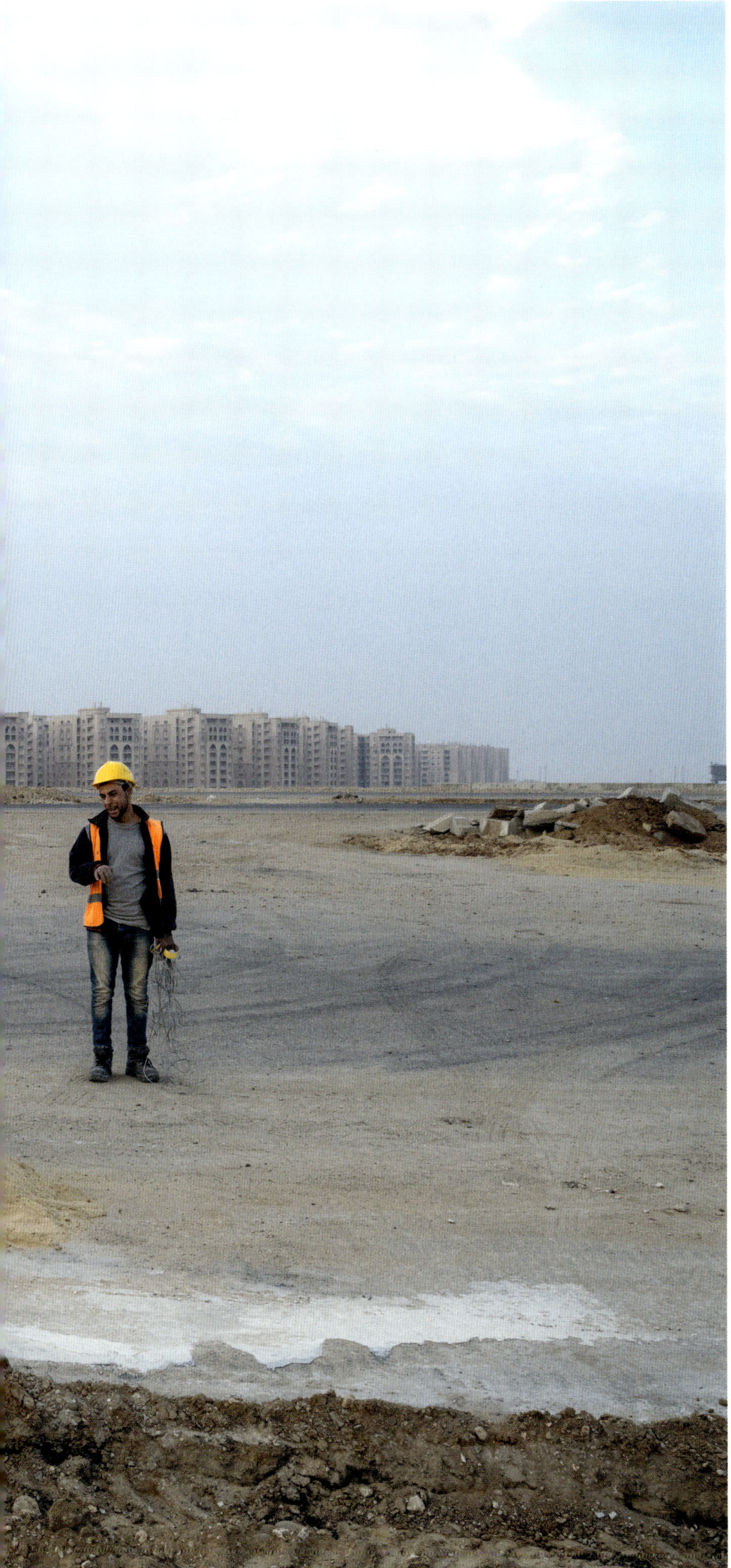

Palm tree-shaped mobile phone antenna.

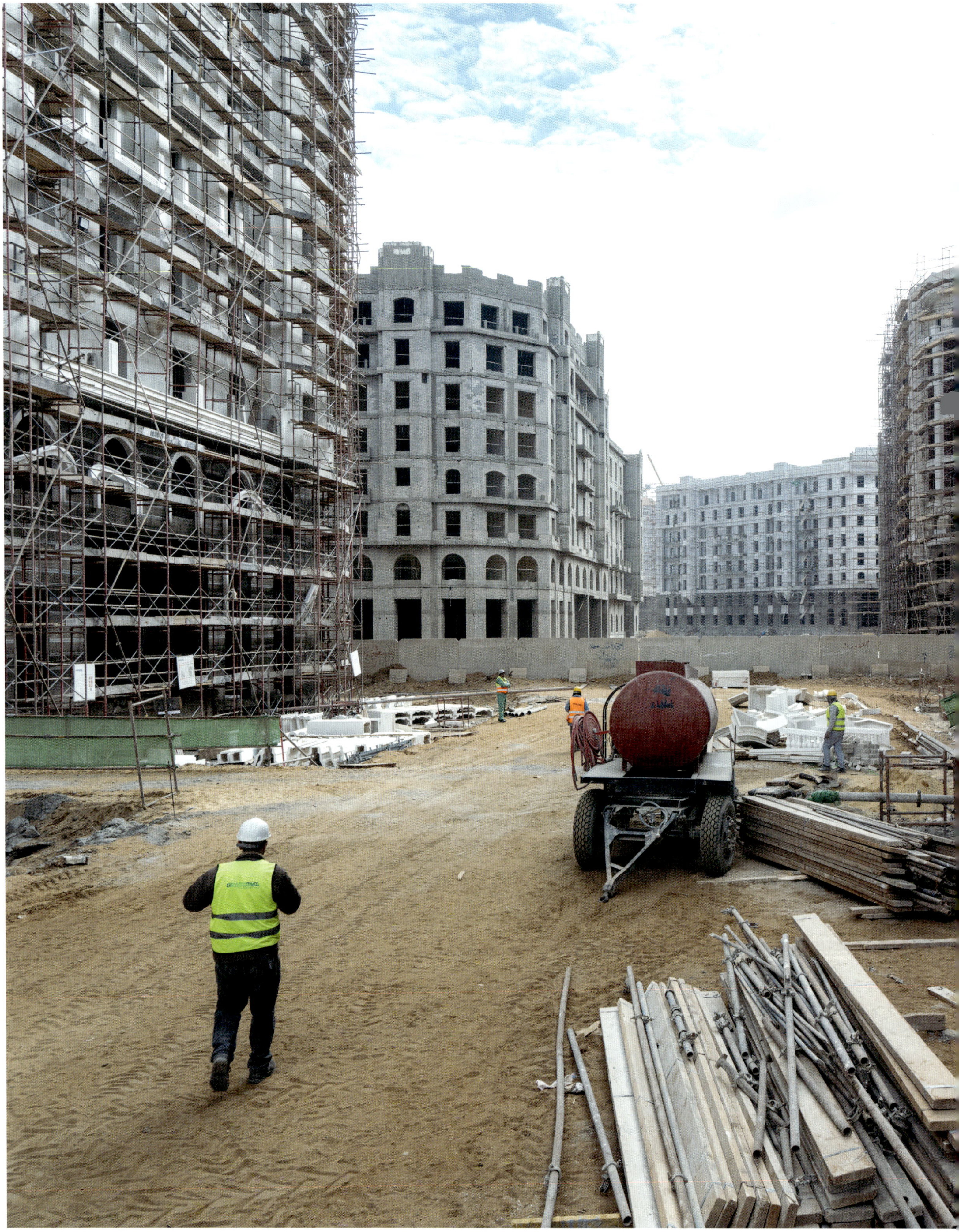

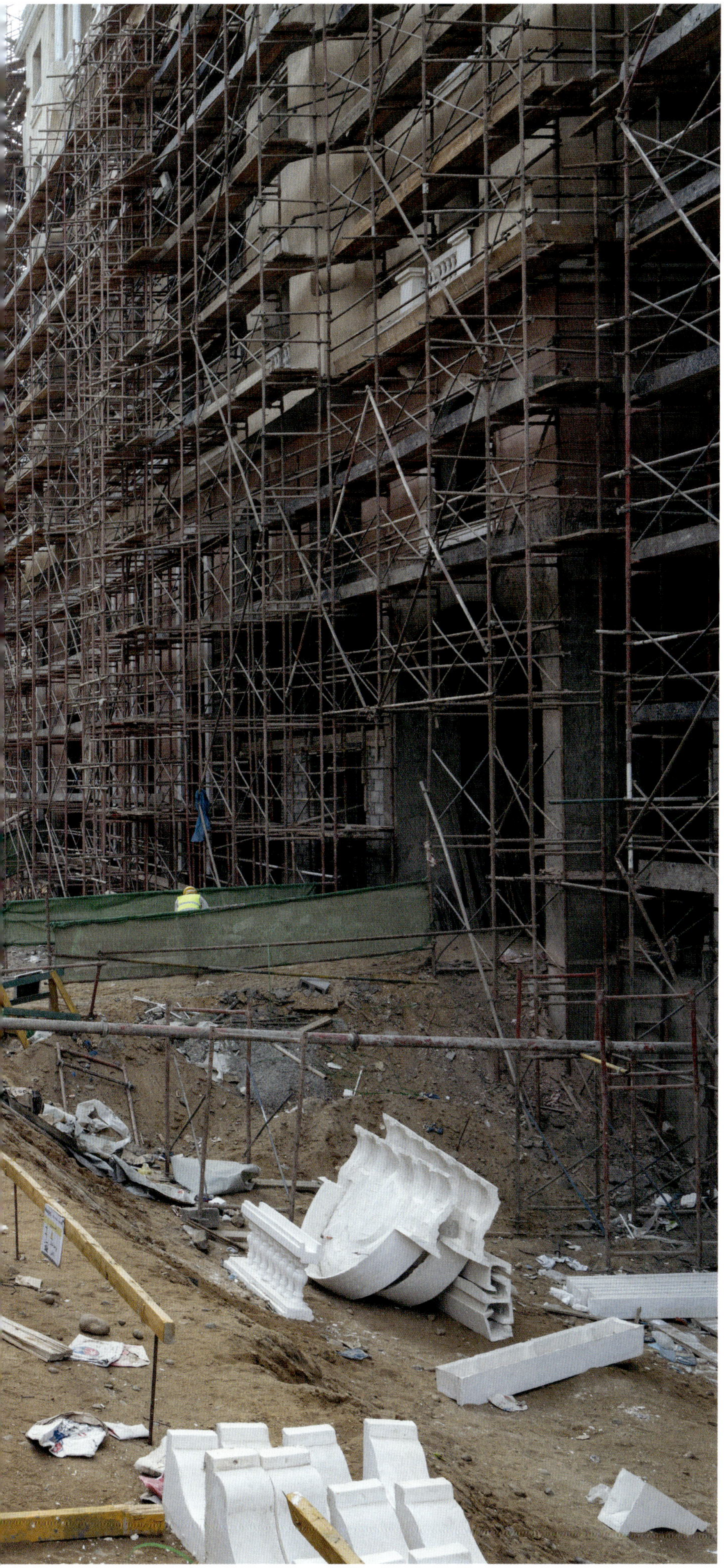

Fifth Residential Neighbourhood (R5).

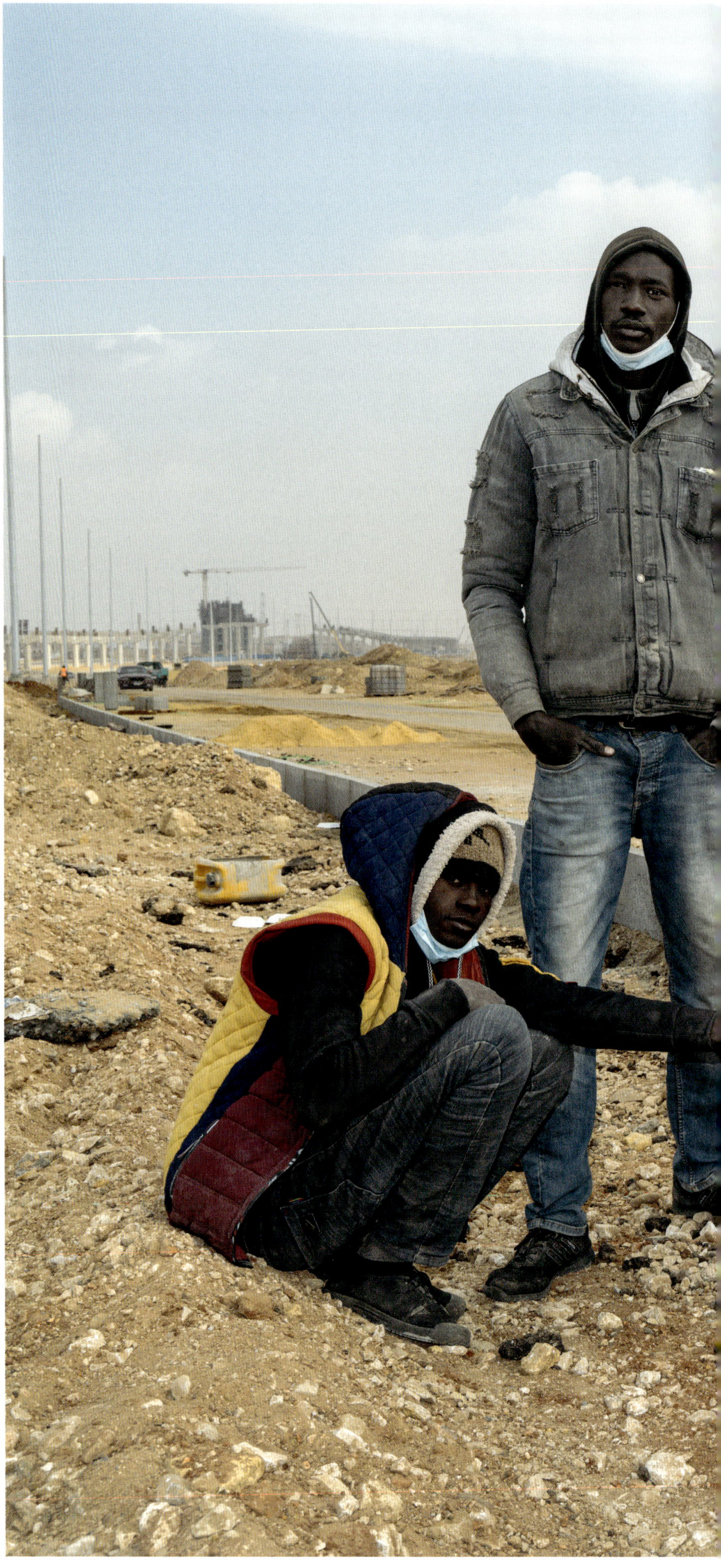

South Sudanese workers in front of the Iconic Tower.

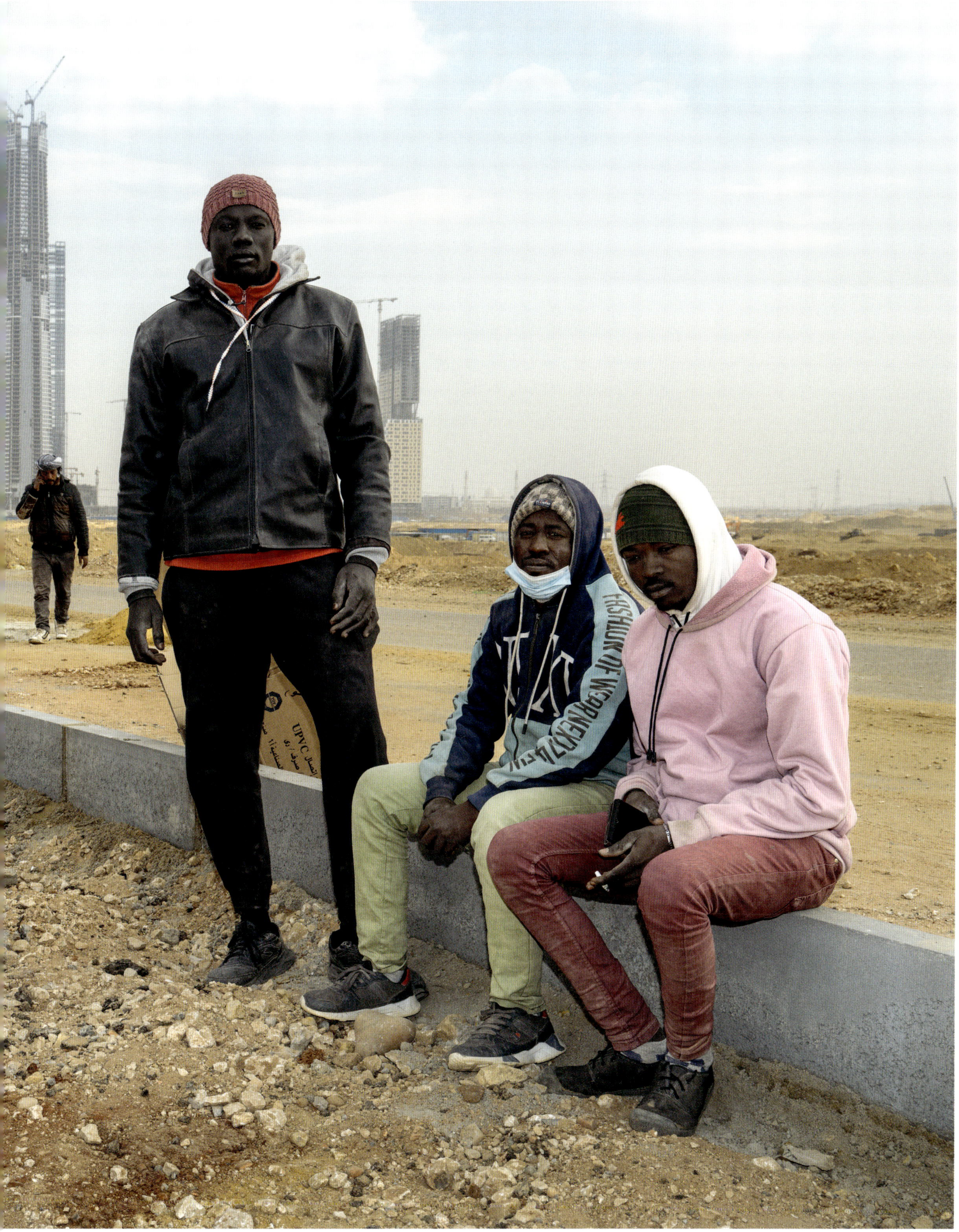
UPVC

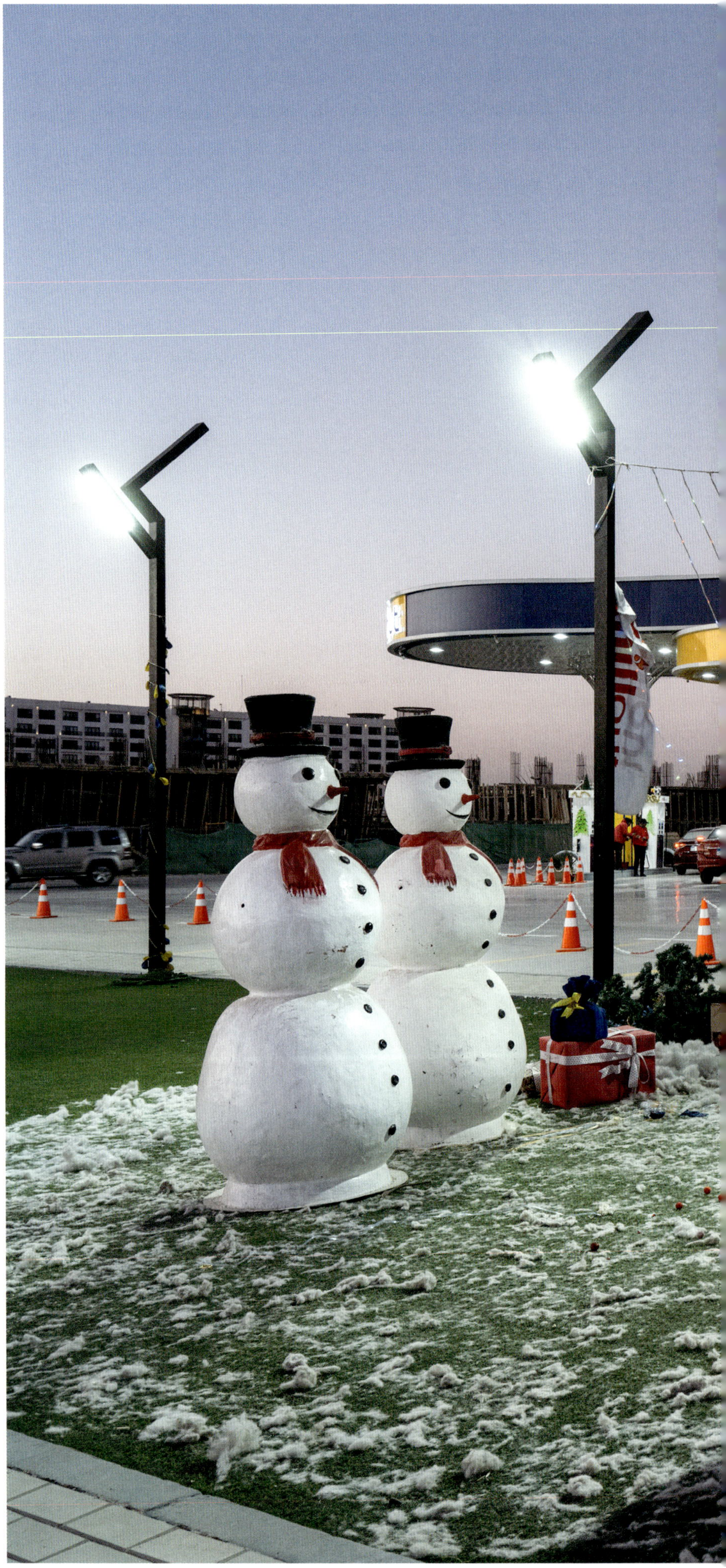

Petrol station in New Cairo, an upscale satellite city east of Cairo, bordering the NAC.

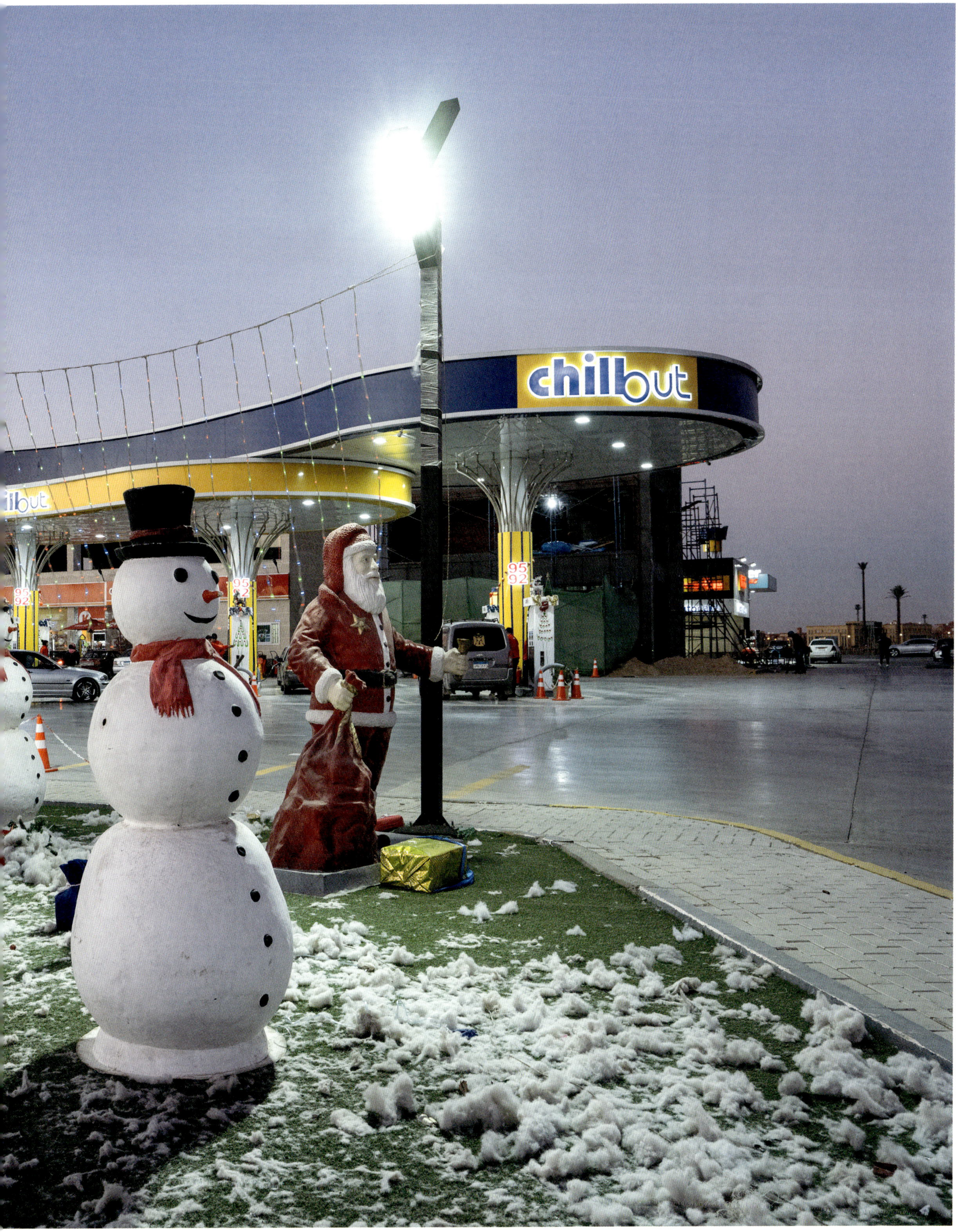
chillout
95
92

INDONESIA

NUSANTARA

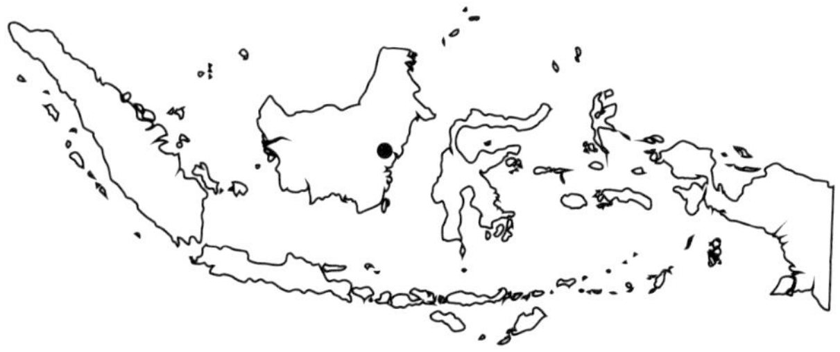

Start of construction: 2022
Inauguration date: 2024 (expected)
Initiated by: President Joko Widodo
Master plan by: URBAN+
Expected population by 2045: 1.9 million
Surface area: 2560 km²
Current capital: Jakarta

40% of the Indonesian capital Jakarta's territory lies geographically below sea level. As a result of massive groundwater abstraction in recent decades, the city is steadily sinking under its own weight. Low-lying sections are already permanently flooded. And while the ground is sinking, sea levels are rising. If the climate crisis is not addressed immediately, much of Jakarta is at risk of becoming uninhabitable over time.

Plans to relocate the troubled capital to safer places are not new. Given the gravity of the situation, the government of Joko Widodo — popularly called Jokowi — decided in 2019 to put its money where its mouth is. An area of 256,000 hectares was demarcated in Borneo's East Kalimantan province, six times larger than Jakarta's current surface area with its 11 million inhabitants.

The new city-to-be was named Nusantara, Old Javanese for 'outer islands'. The design envisages a population of 1.9 million by 2045. Jokowi makes the case that the capital will boost Kalimantan's economic development and shift the political centre of gravity from Java to a more central location in the Indonesian archipelago.

'Building a city from scratch creates an opportunity,' says Sofian Sibarani, managing director of URBAN+, the urban design firm that created the new capital. 'Nusantara will be a sustainable smart city in harmony with nature. No tall skyscrapers but a polycentric layout with functional zoning and skywalk concepts. Just as animals move from treetop to treetop, buildings will be linked by aerial bridges. 75% of the surface area will be green. No virgin rainforest will have to be cut down. This is because the selected area has already been disrupted by large-scale forestry.'

'Nusantara is a classic example of greenwashing,' says Merah Johansyah of the NGO Jaringan Advokasi Tambang, an Indonesian network of communities facing large-scale mining projects. 'Nusantara is totally irresponsible socially, environmentally and financially. There was no public participation, no democratic process, no proper environmental impact study. It is an extremely expensive prestige project that cannot be separated from business interests. The territory of the new city includes 162 concessions for mining and industrial forestry, mainly palm oil and eucalyptus. Quite a few concessionaires have close ties to powerful politicians. They will be richly compensated for the loss of their concessions. In contrast, the local population in the targeted area — 186,000 souls in 72 villages — will lose any future prospects. Unlike the large landowners, most villagers hold no title deeds to the lands they inherited from their ancestors.'

The Sepaku Semoi Dam, which will provide drinking water to future city dwellers, is currently under construction in the village of Sepaku. The local Suku Balik tribe saw its access to the river closed. 'We can no longer fish or sail there,' says farmer Pak Udin. 'In addition, for years the river had been heavily polluted by pesticides from the plantations. The government gave us bags of aluminium sulphate to purify the water. They say we can still consume the water if we mix it with a bit of that powder. But most villagers don't trust it and are forced to buy bottled water.'

'We don't want money or a new house as compensation,' says Pandi, former district mayor of Sepaku. 'We want to preserve our village. A village where everyone knows each other and where the door doesn't have to be locked. There is fear in the air now. We see more and more police and soldiers appearing in our neighbourhood. Soon our house will be in the middle of a tourist recreational park.'

Kalimantan is home to one of the world's oldest rainforests, the habitat of endangered species such as the orangutan, the proboscis monkey and the honey bear. A city of millions on the edge of the forest will have a spillover effect in the surrounding area. New roads will open up natural areas for reclamation and agriculture. Vulnerable mangrove forests in Balikpapan Bay are also threatened. Fishermen complain of smaller catches due to polluting industries and coal transports on the water. The entire region is riddled with (illegal) coal mines. Indonesia is the world's largest coal exporter. Black gold accounts for 60% of Indonesia's electricity generation and 35% of its carbon emissions, after deforestation. It seems difficult to reconcile with the great principles involving sustainability and renewable energy in the carbon-neutral forest city of Nusantara.

August-September 2022

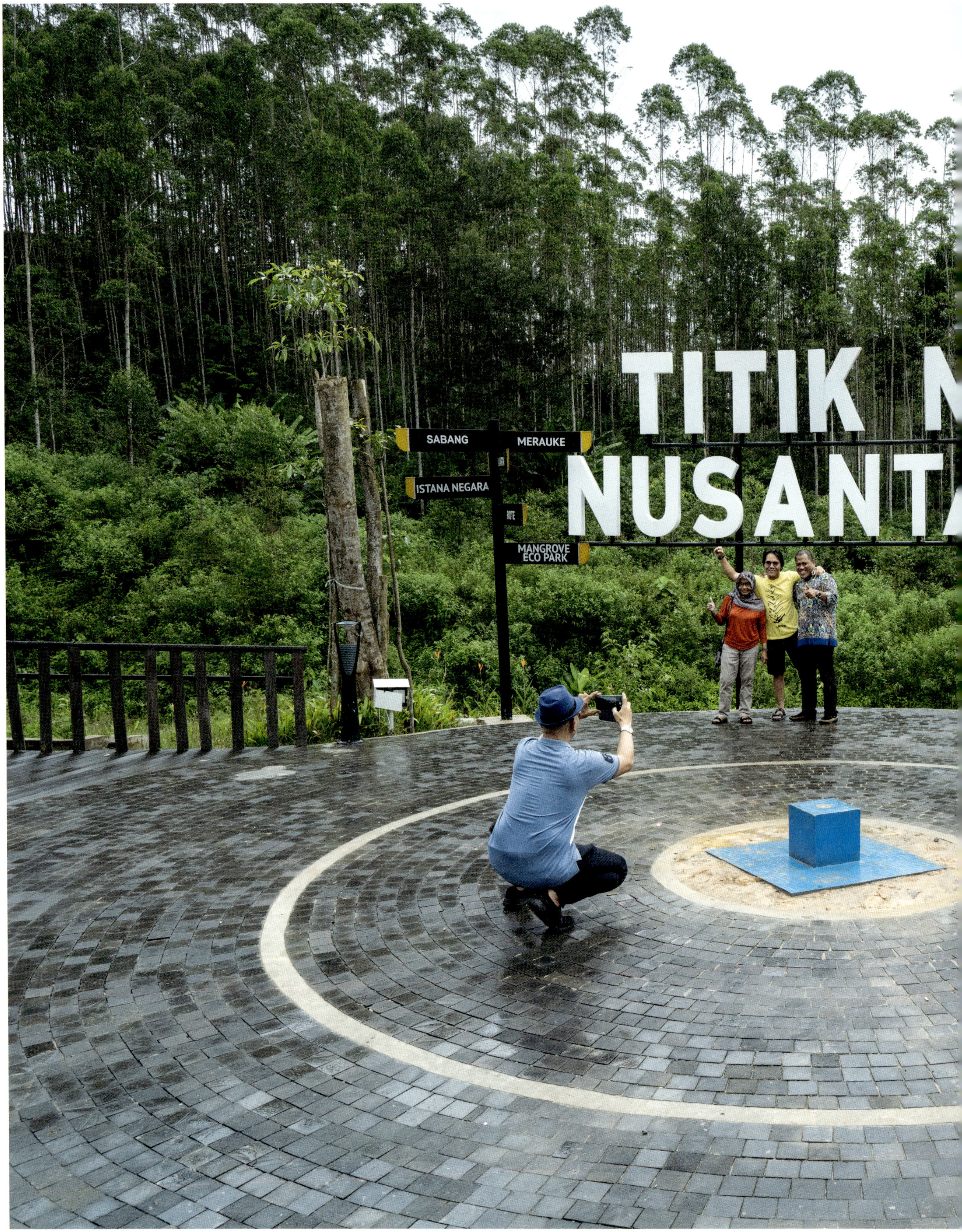

SABANG
MERAUKE
ISTANA NEGARA
MANGROVE ECO PARK

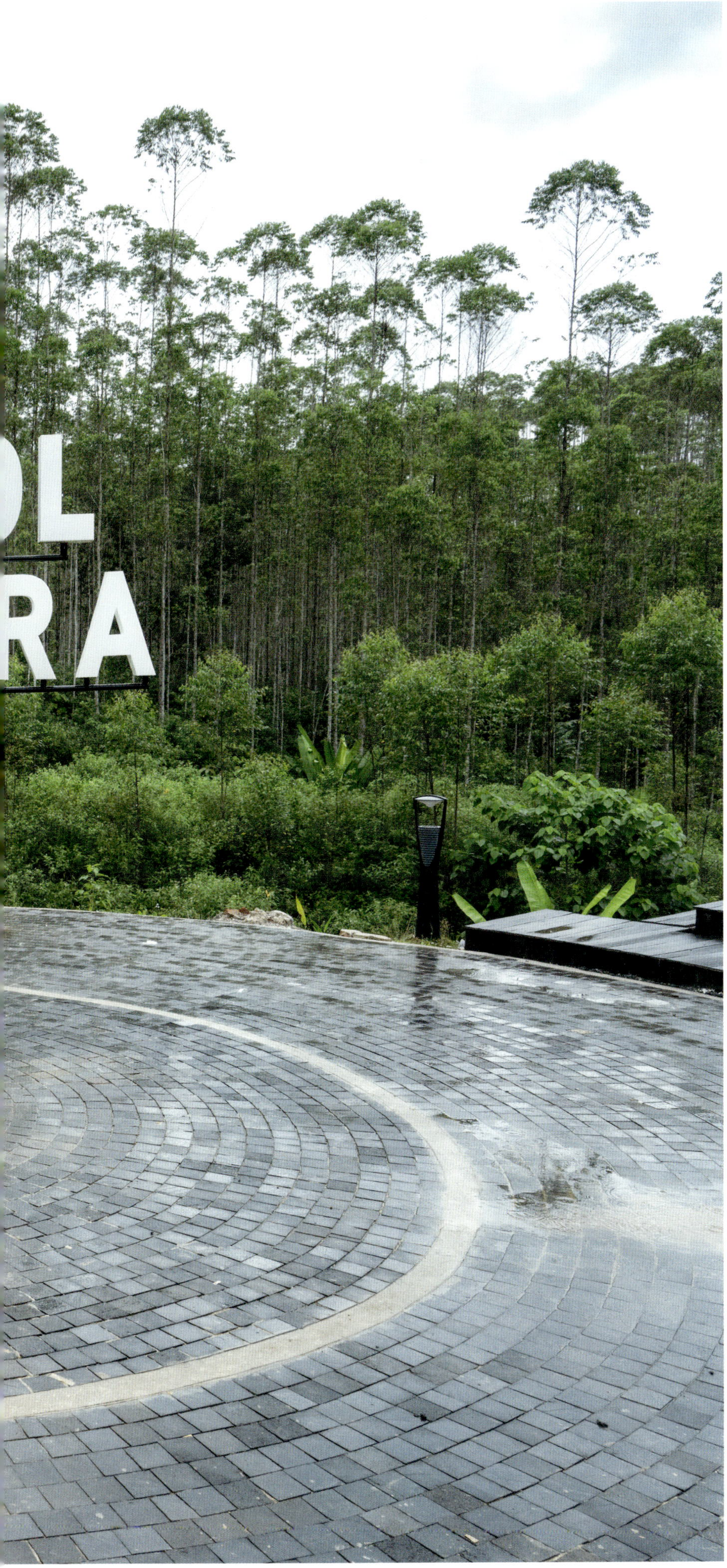

A blue survey column at Titik Nol (Ground Zero) marks the geographic centre of Nusantara.

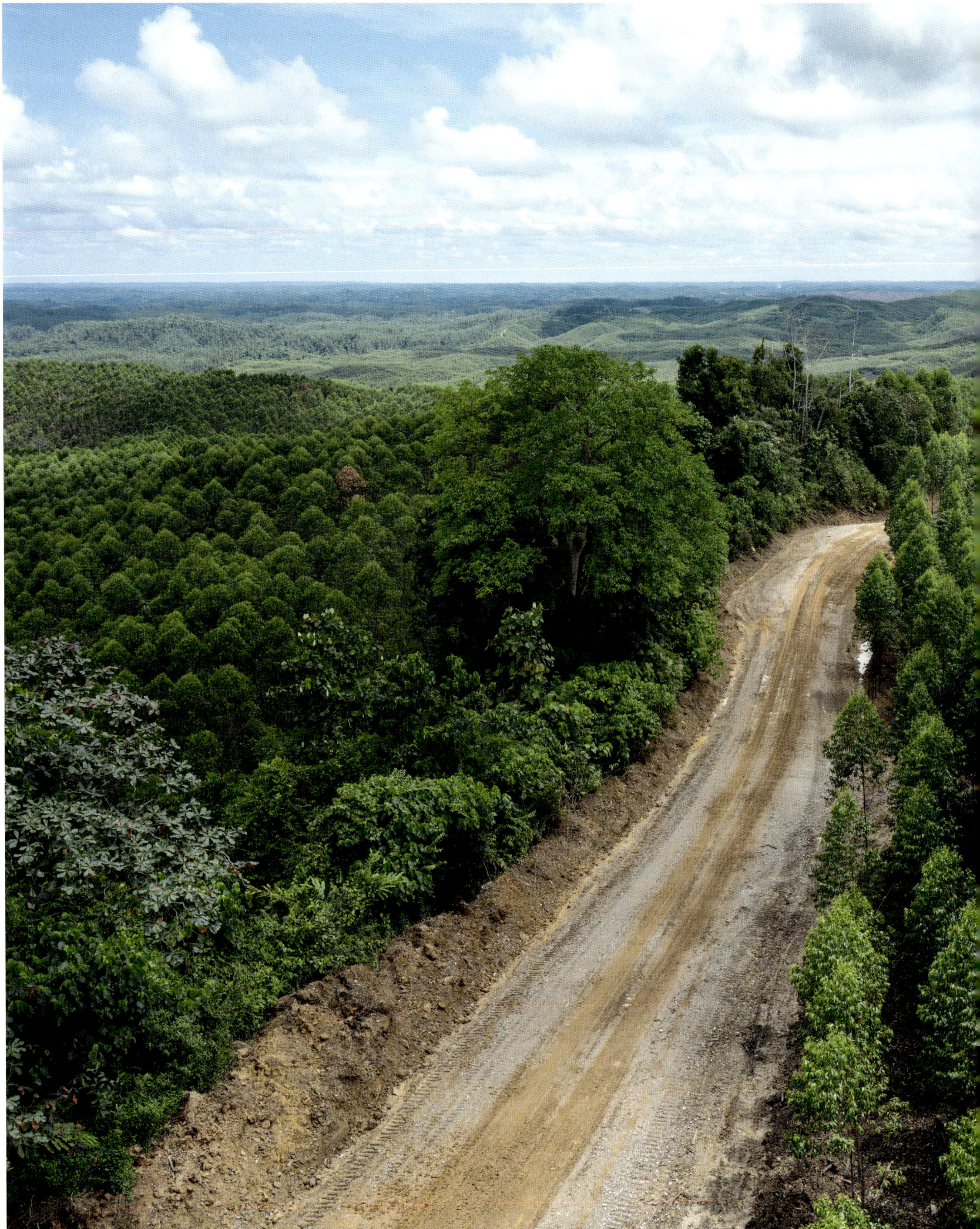

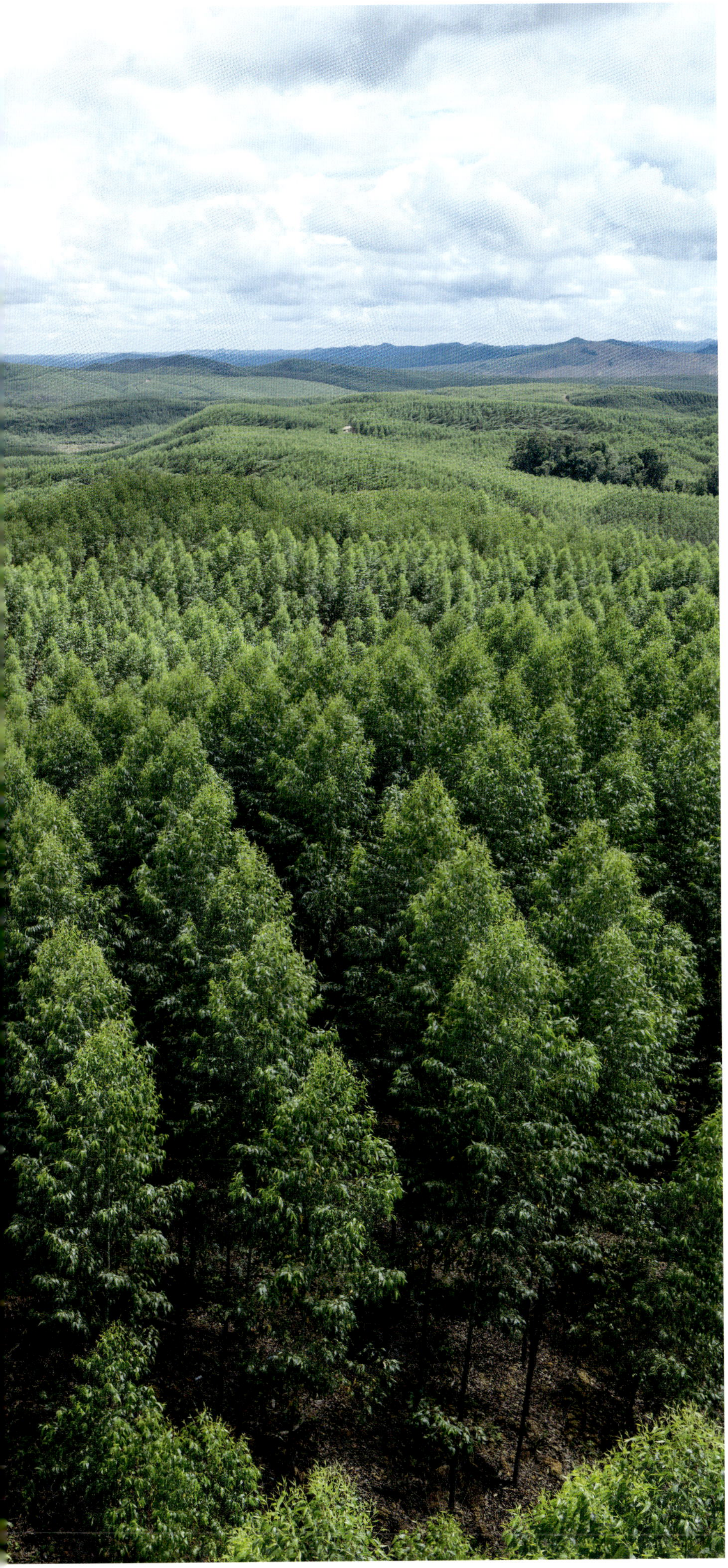

Eucalyptus plantation as seen from the
Sudarmono observation tower near Sepaku,
the core of the future capital.

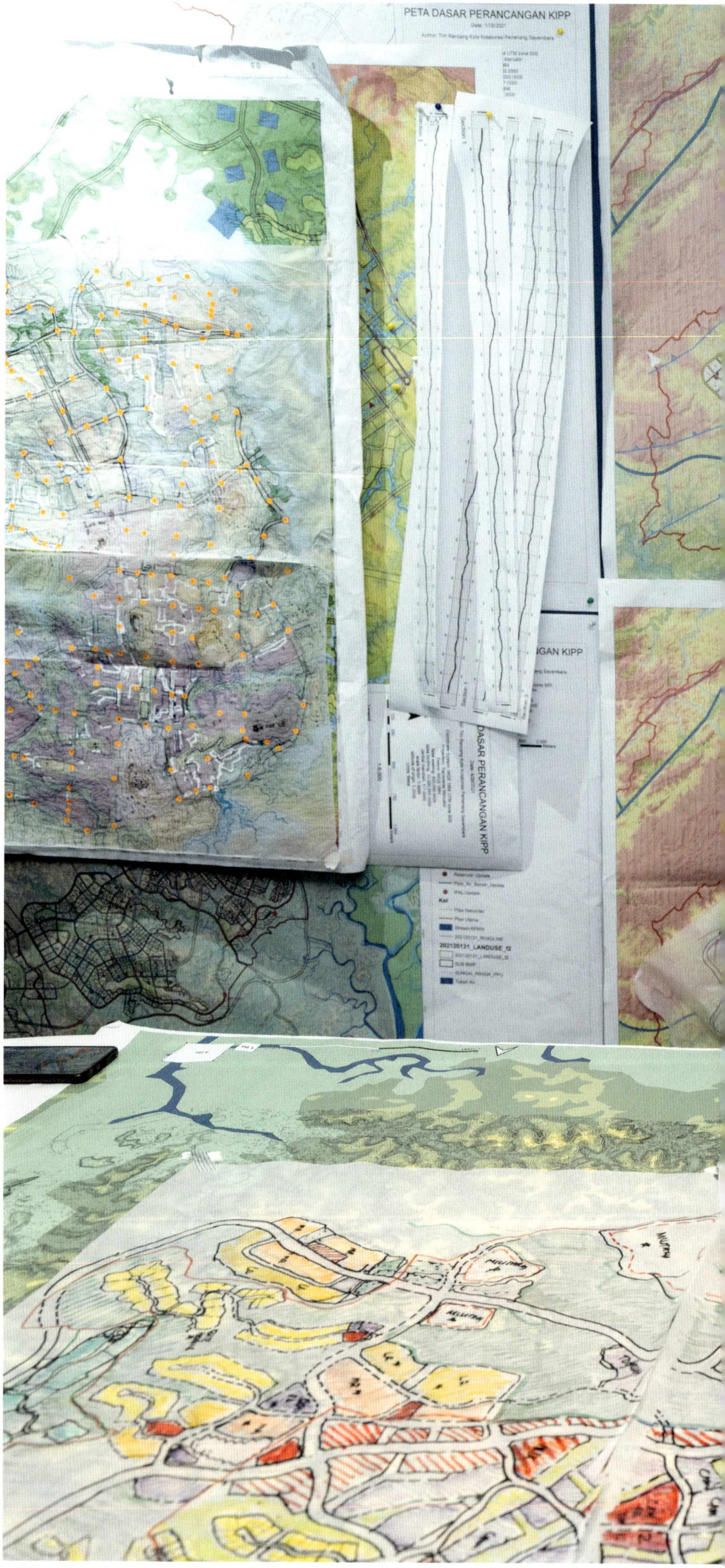

Architect Sibarani Sofian, head of URBAN+, who won the design competition for the new Indonesian capital.

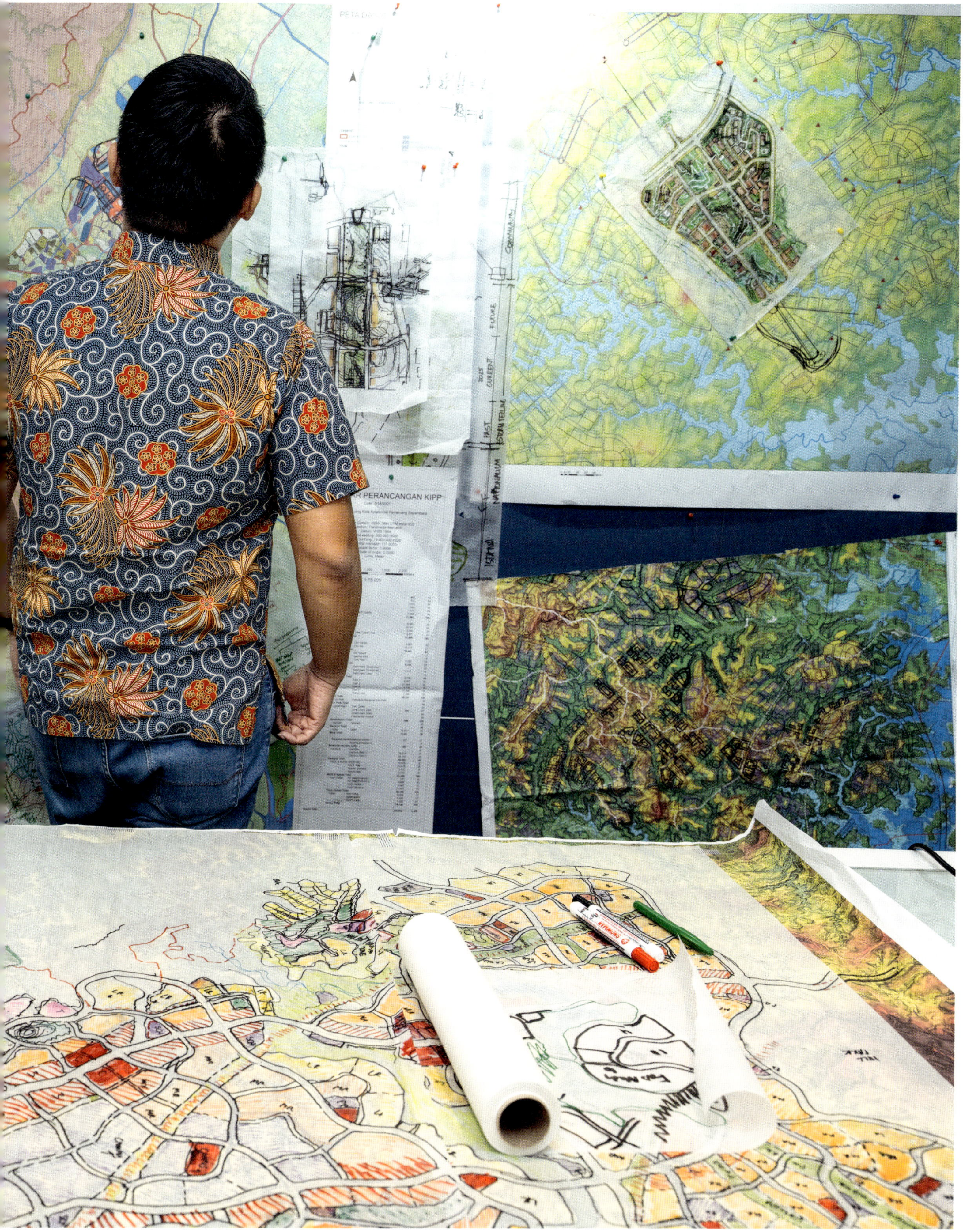
PERANCANGAN KIPP
PAST
CURRENT
FUTURE
2025

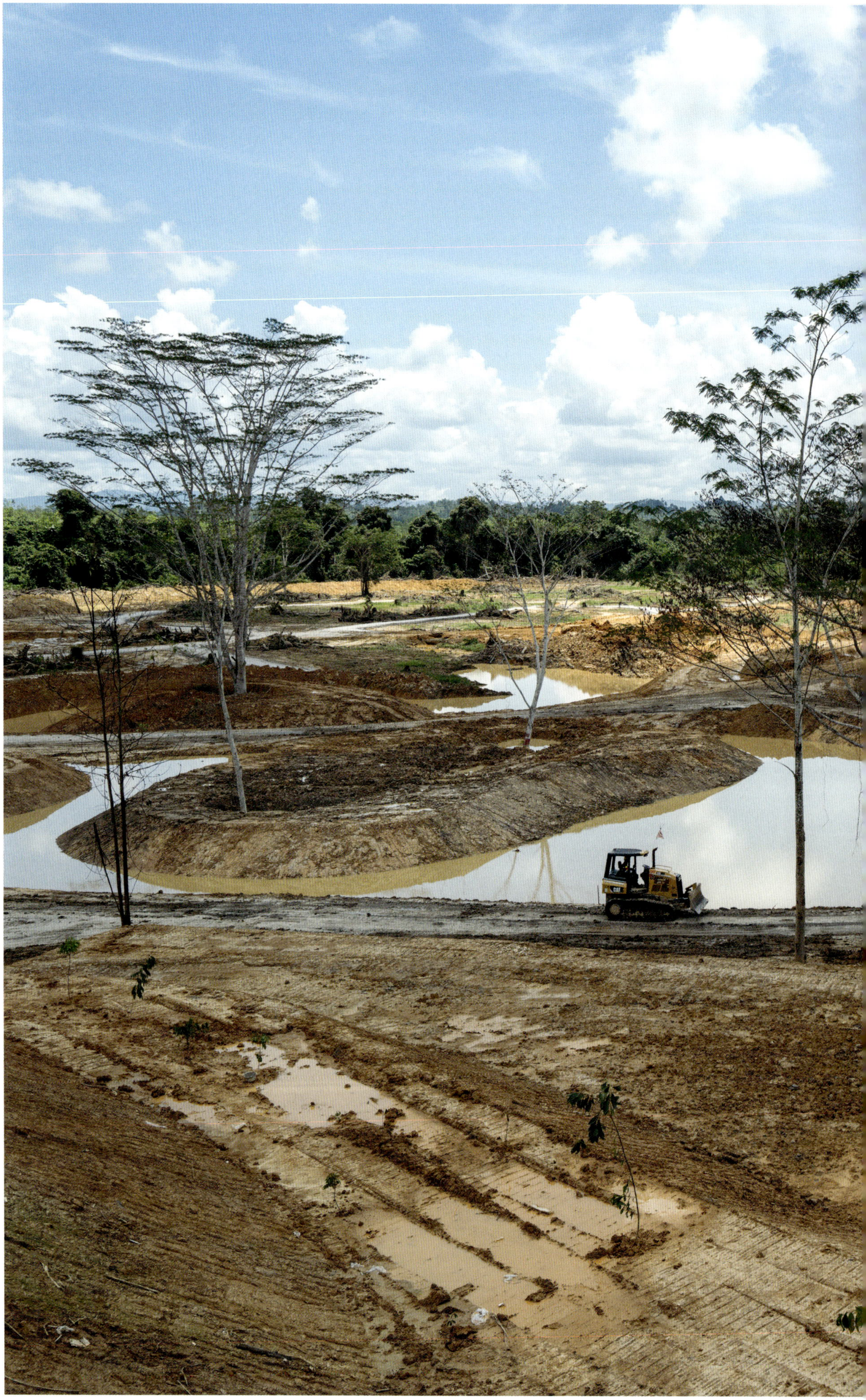

Construction site of Mentawir Nursery, where trees will be grown to be replanted in the new city.

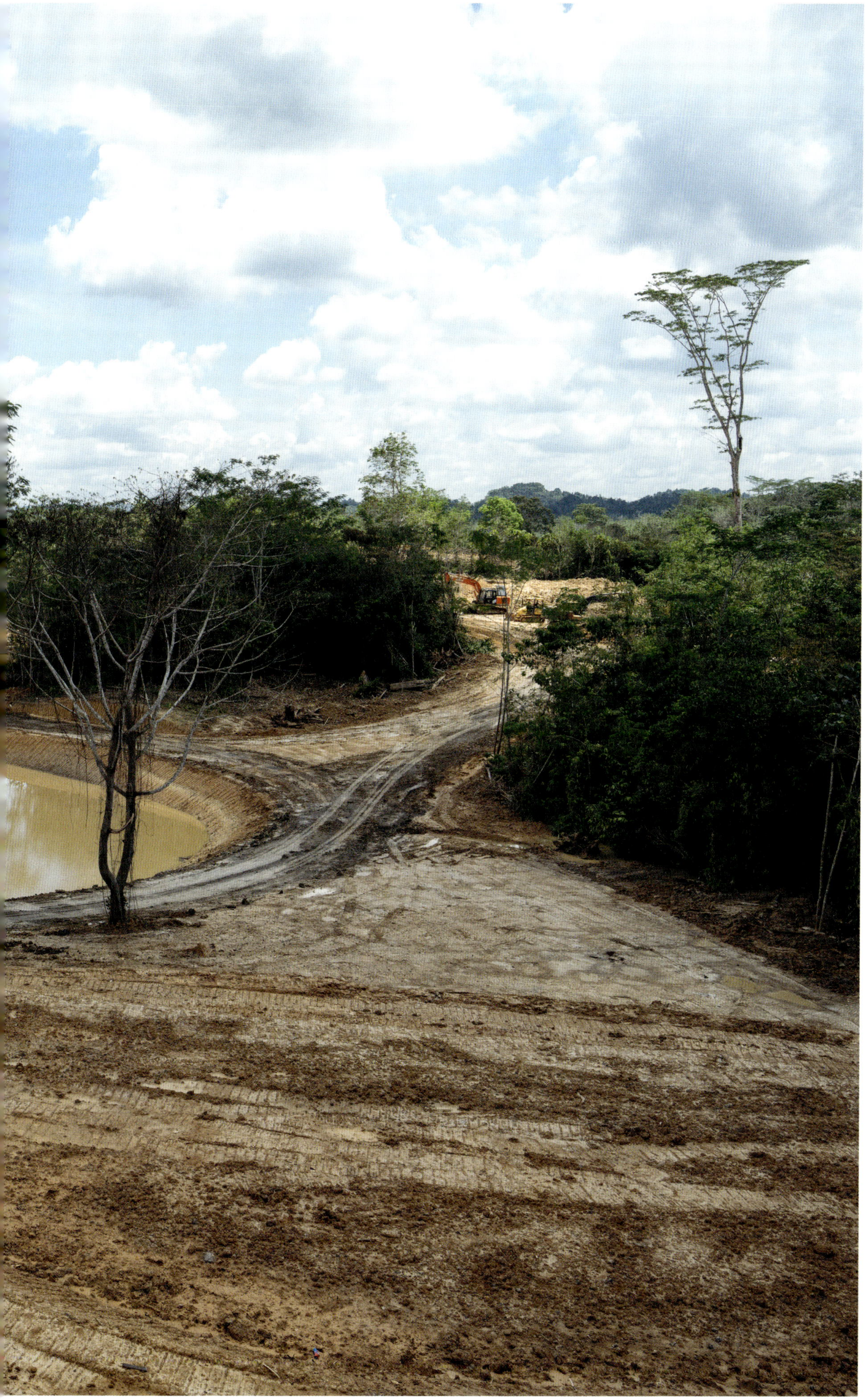

Worker at Mentawir Nursery.

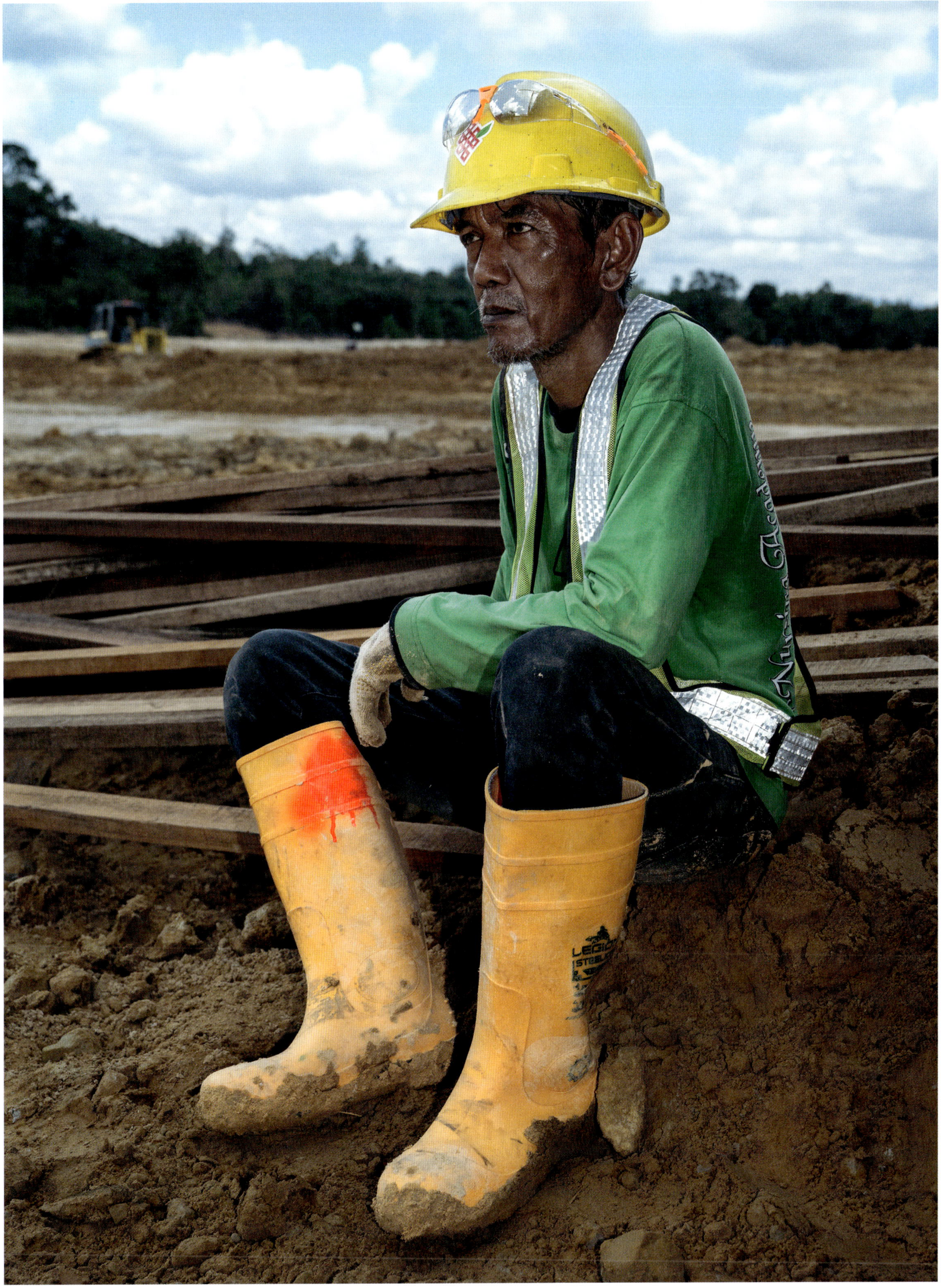

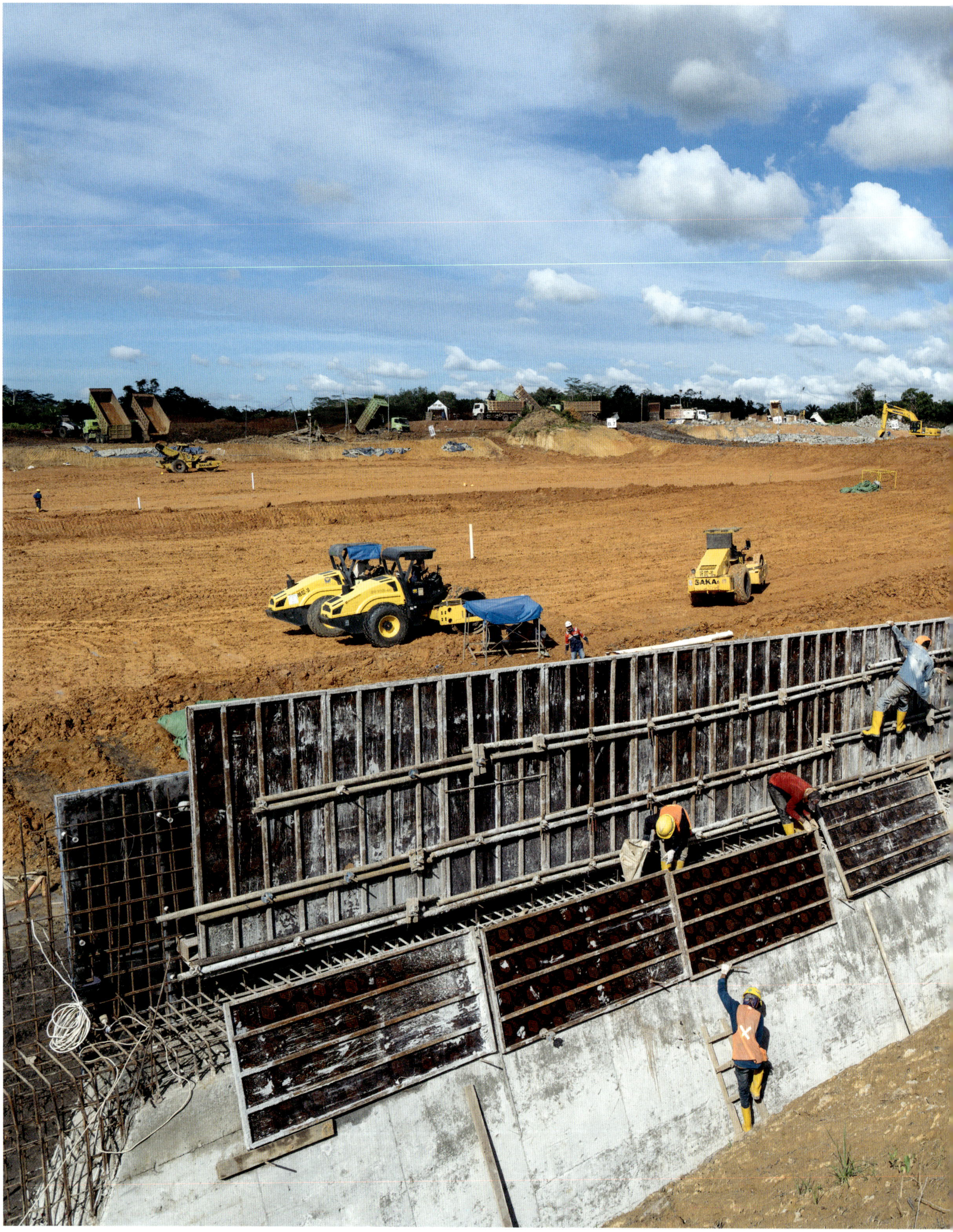
SAKA

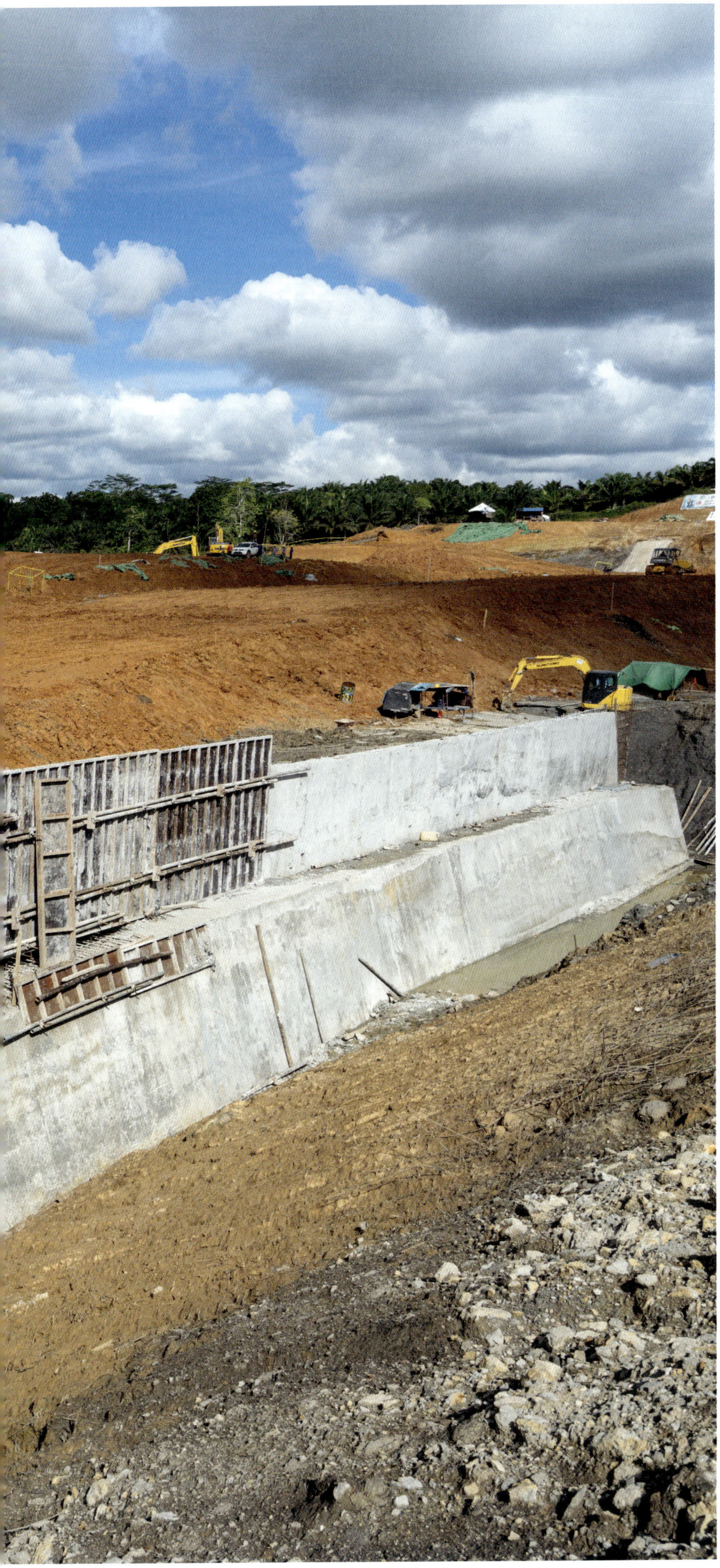

The construction site of the Sepaku Semoi Dam, which will provide water to the new capital.

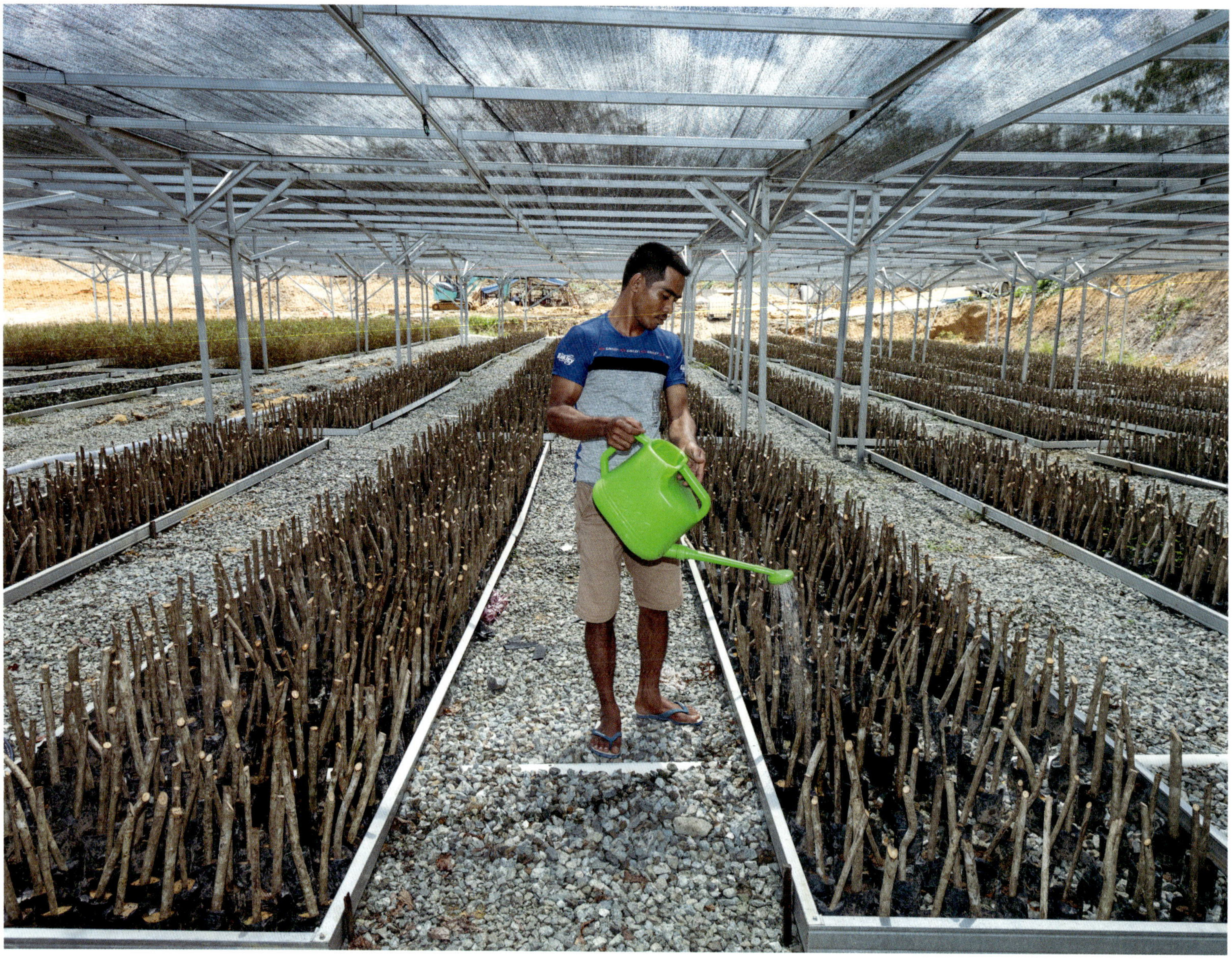

Young *Peronema canescens* trees at Mentawir Nursery.

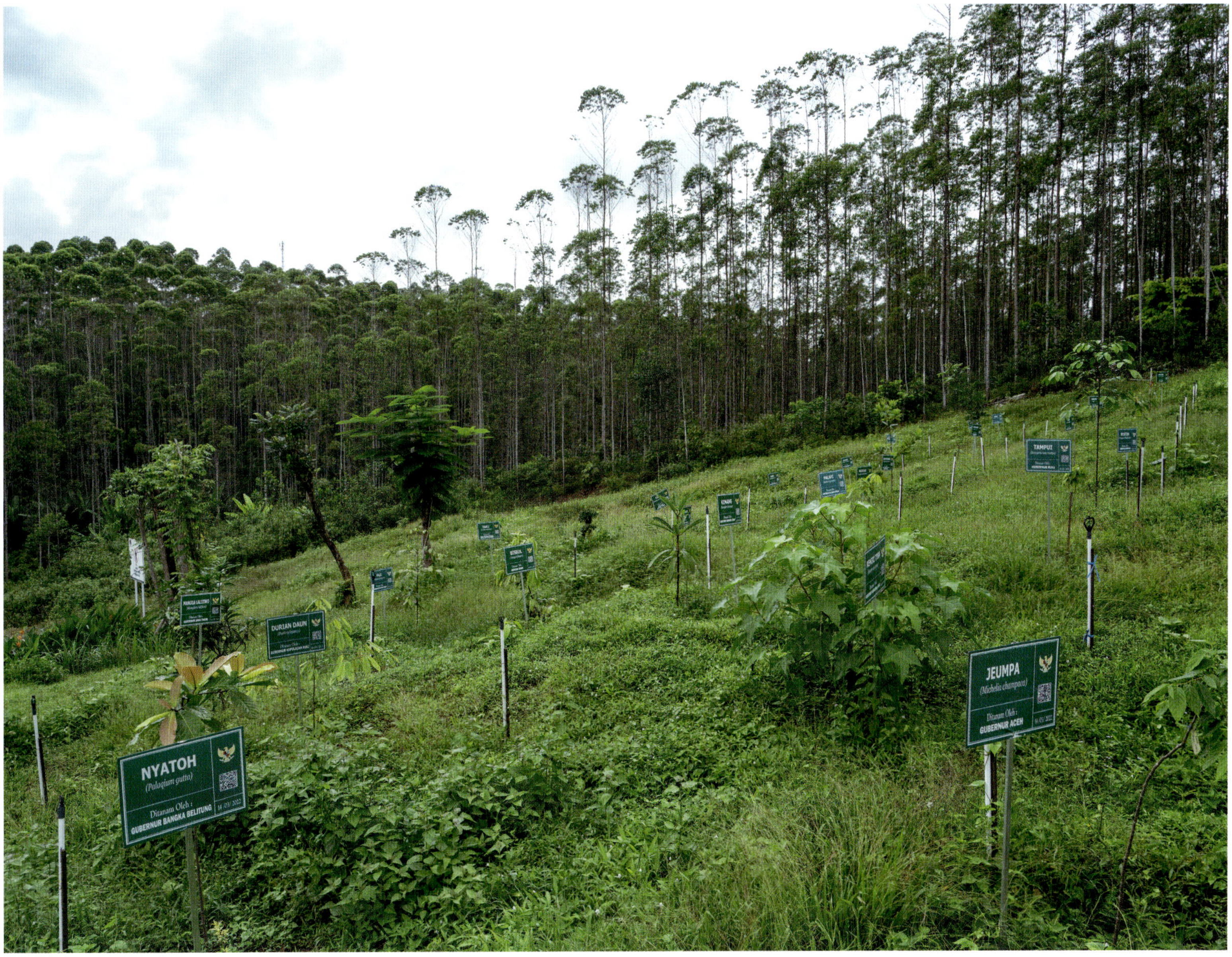

Young trees, symbolically planted by Indonesian governors, at Titik Nol.

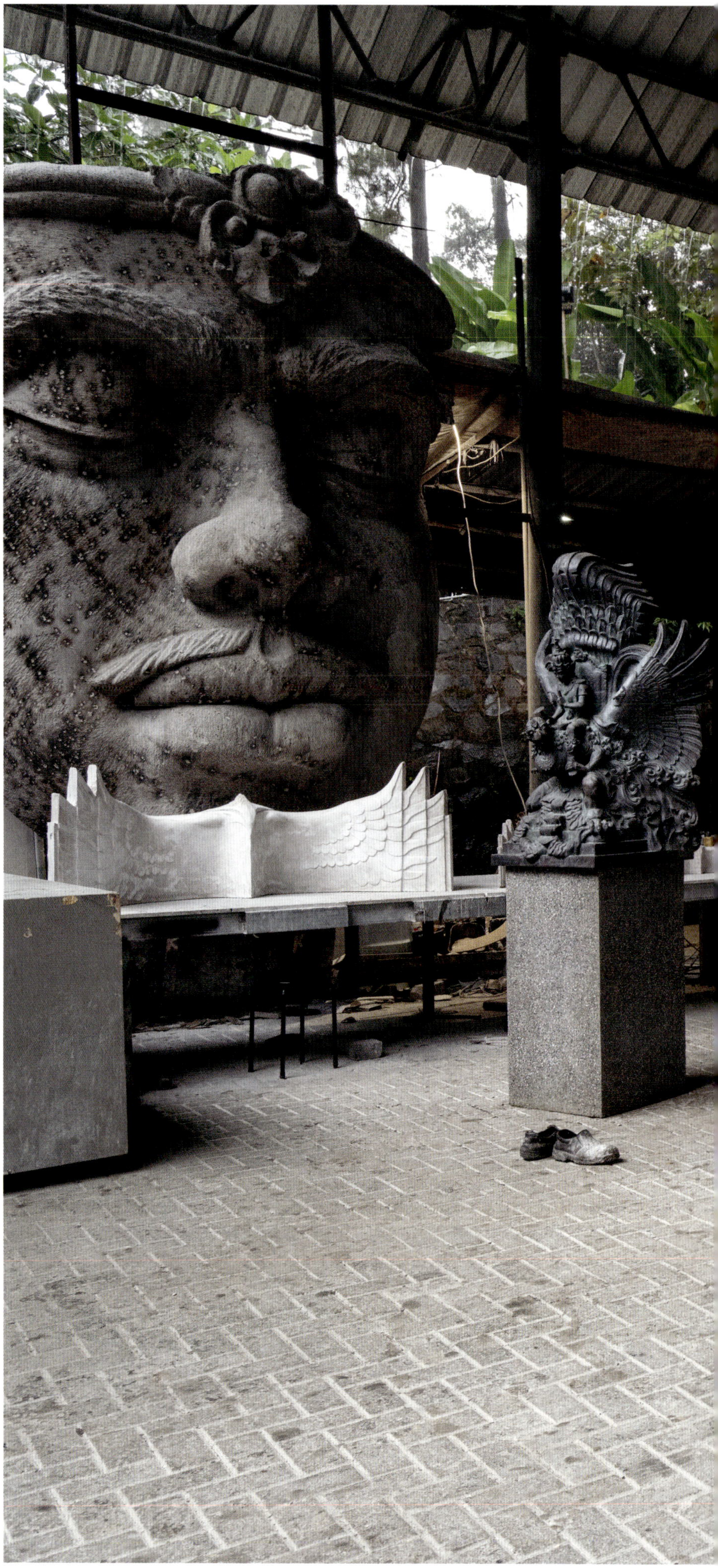

Scale model of the future presidential palace, designed by Indonesian artist Nyoman Nuarta, at NuArt Sculpture Park in Bandung, Java. The palace represents a giant Garuda bird with spread wings, a national emblem of Indonesia.

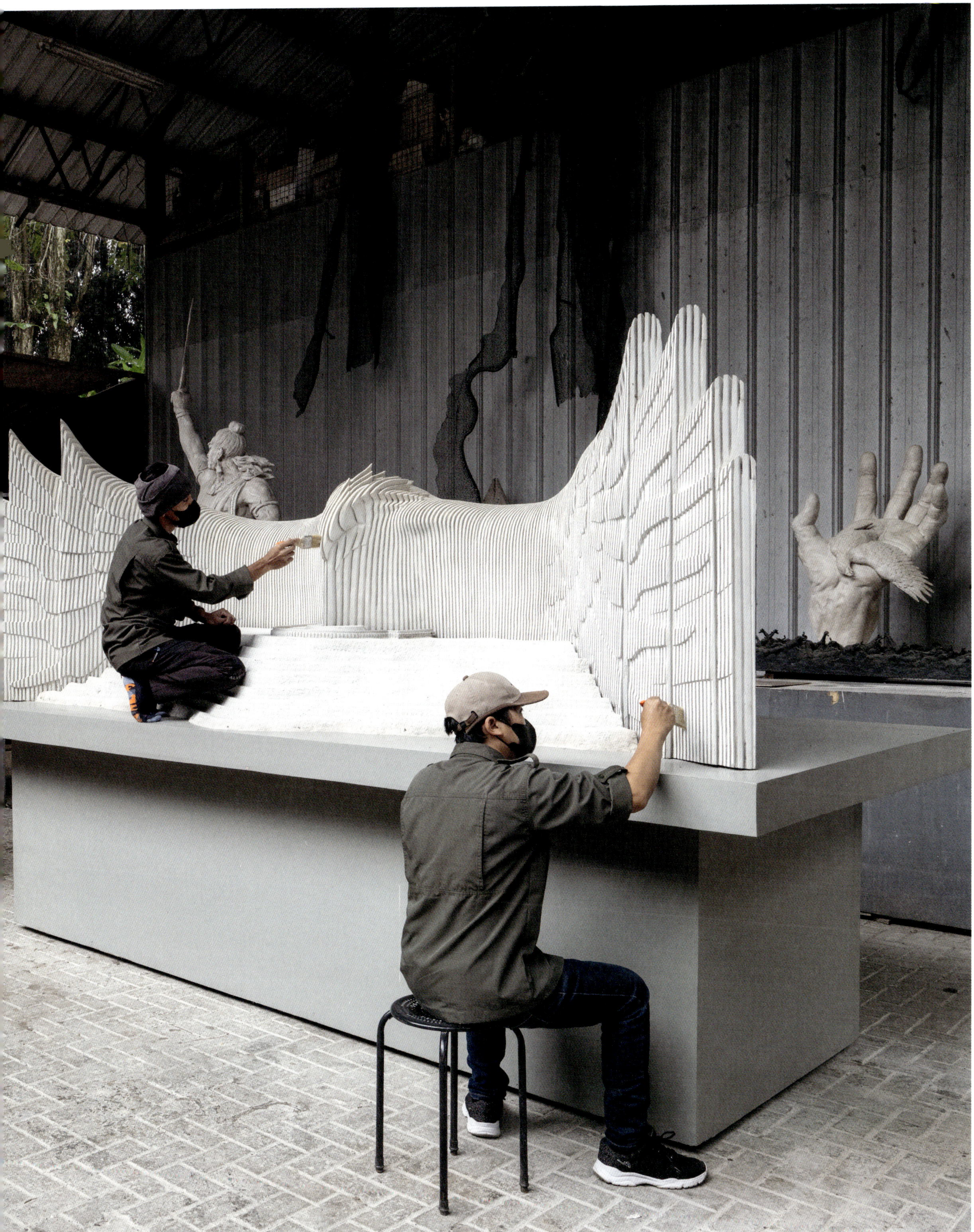

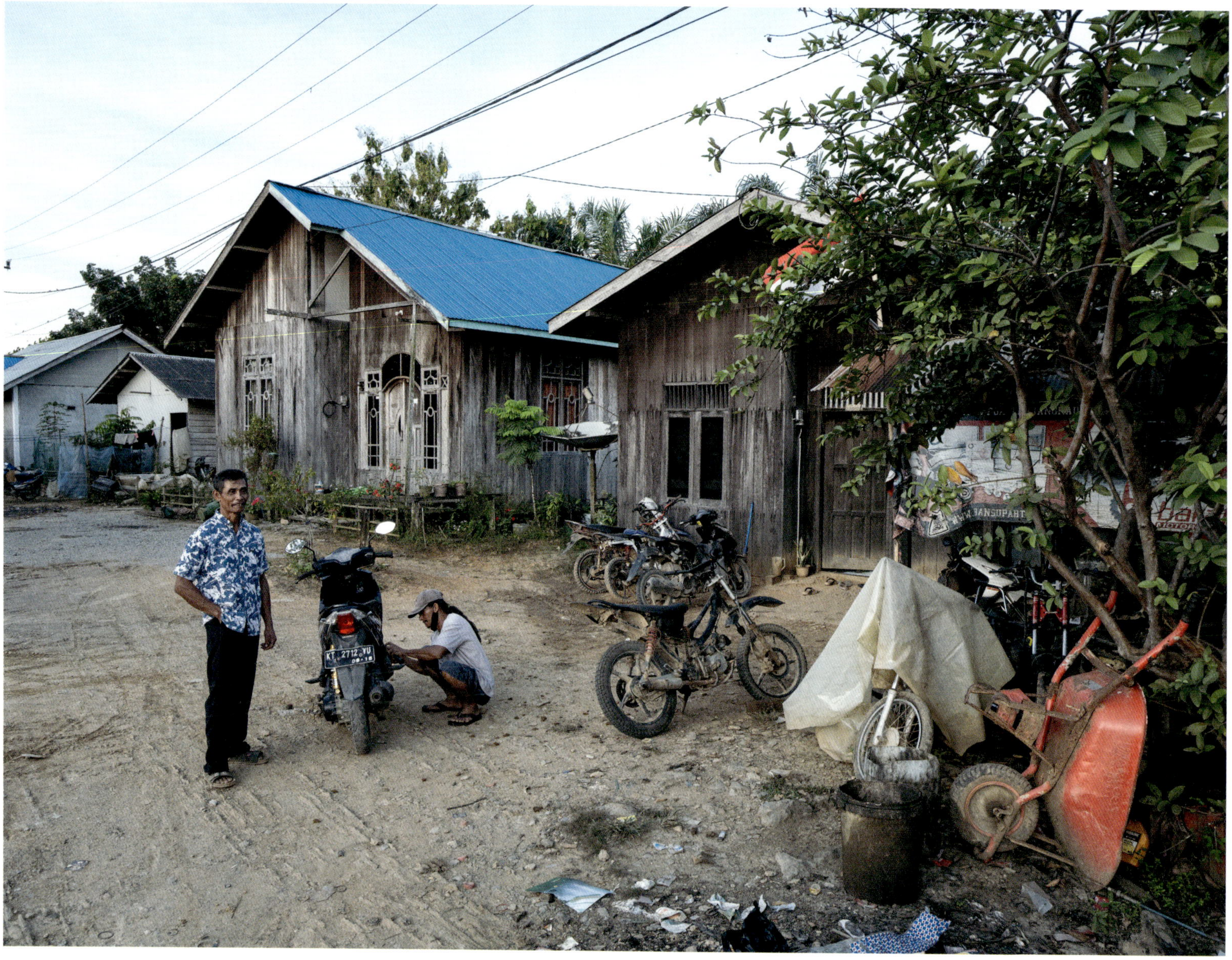

Sepaku village.

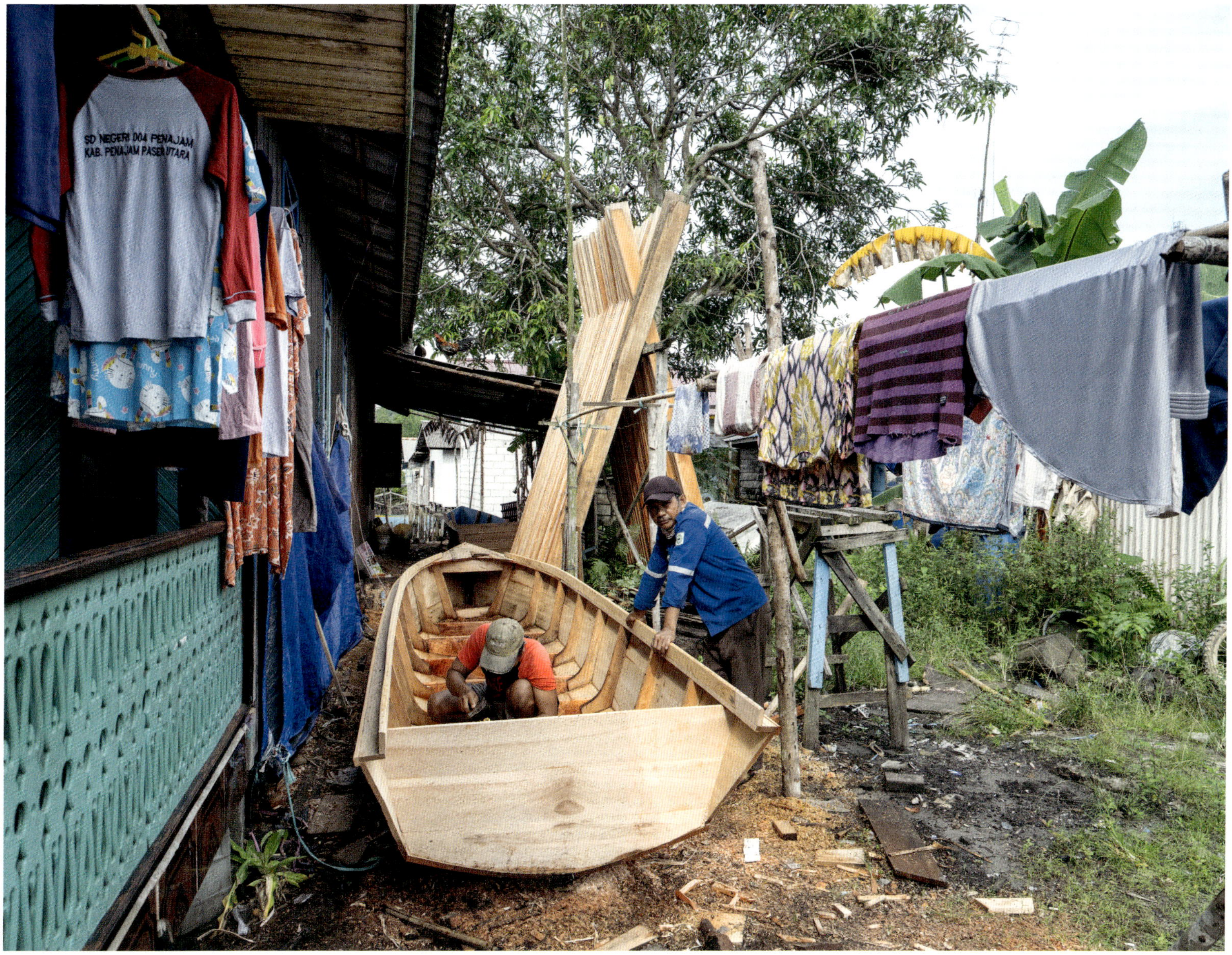

Fishing village Pantai Lango in Balikpapan Bay, the gateway over water to Nusantara.

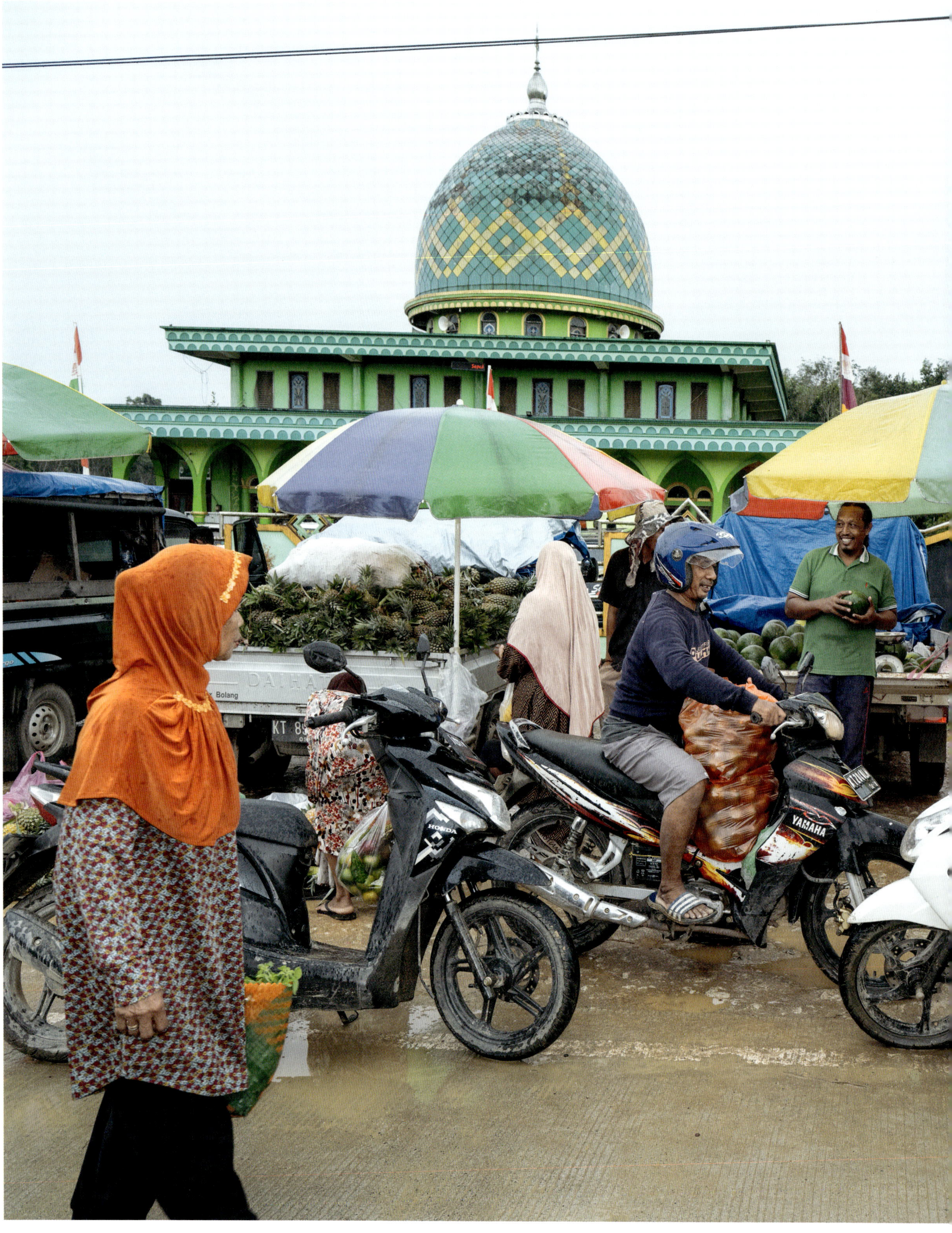
HONDA
YAMAHA

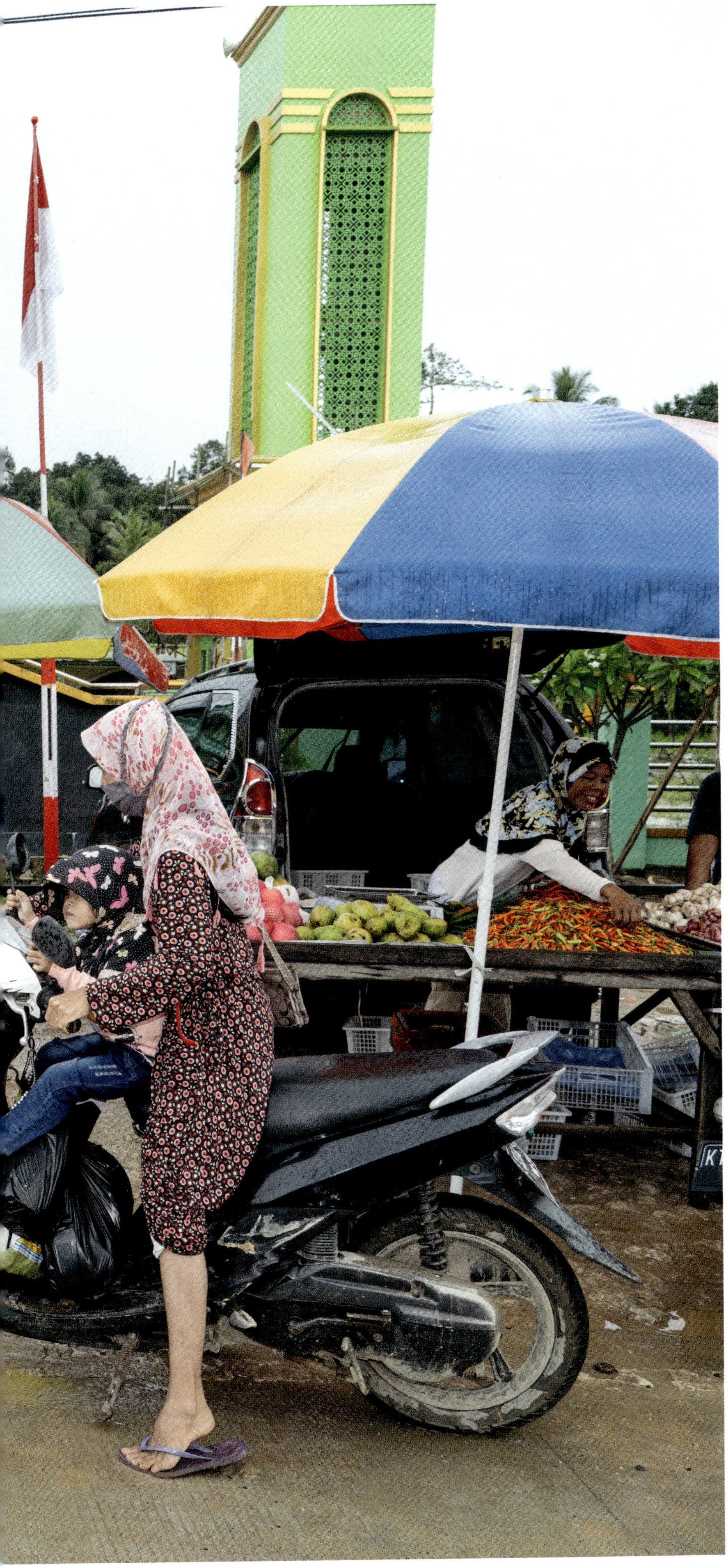

Market day in Sukaraja, Sepaku.

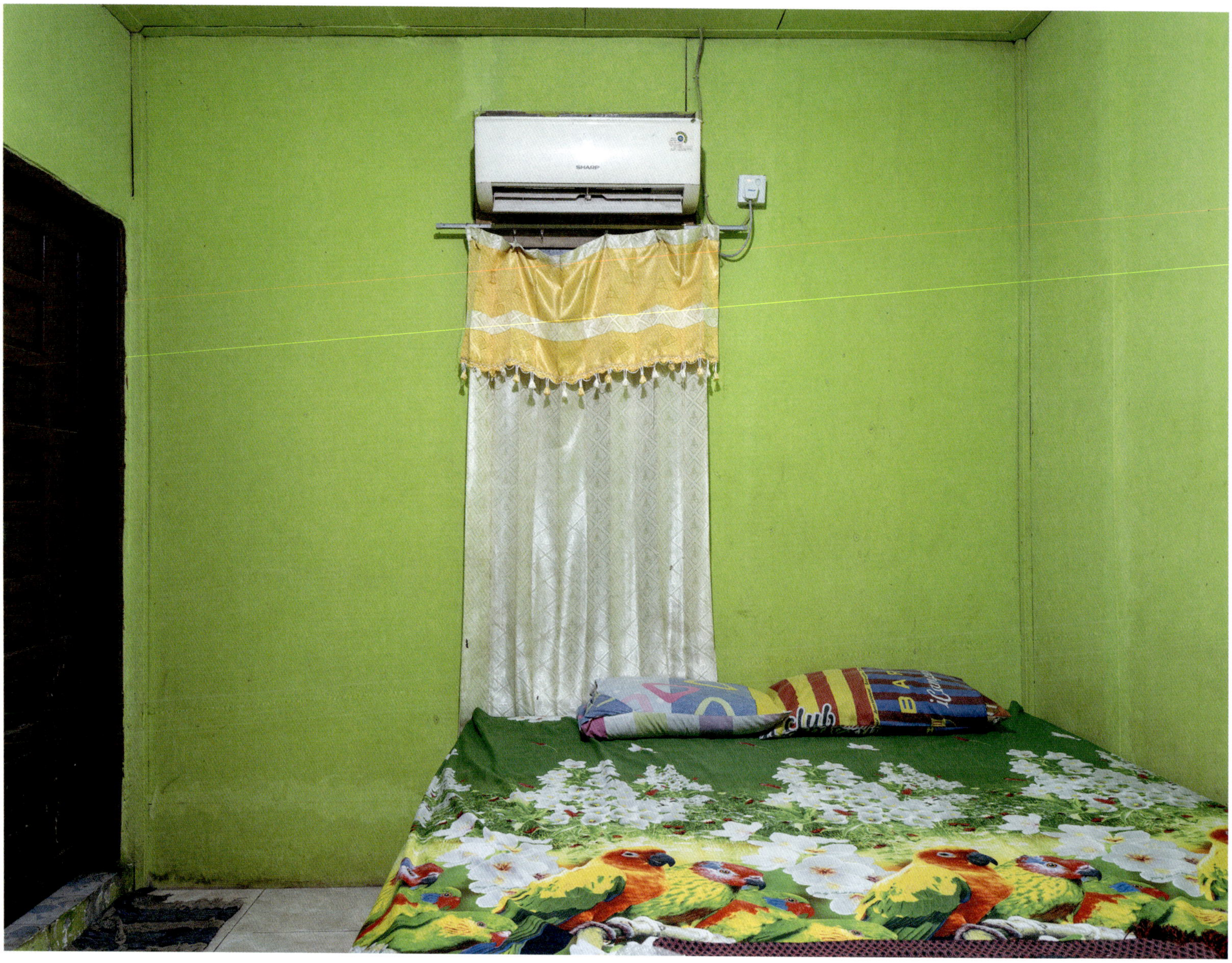

My room at Hotel Wisma Green Parahyangan in Sepaku.

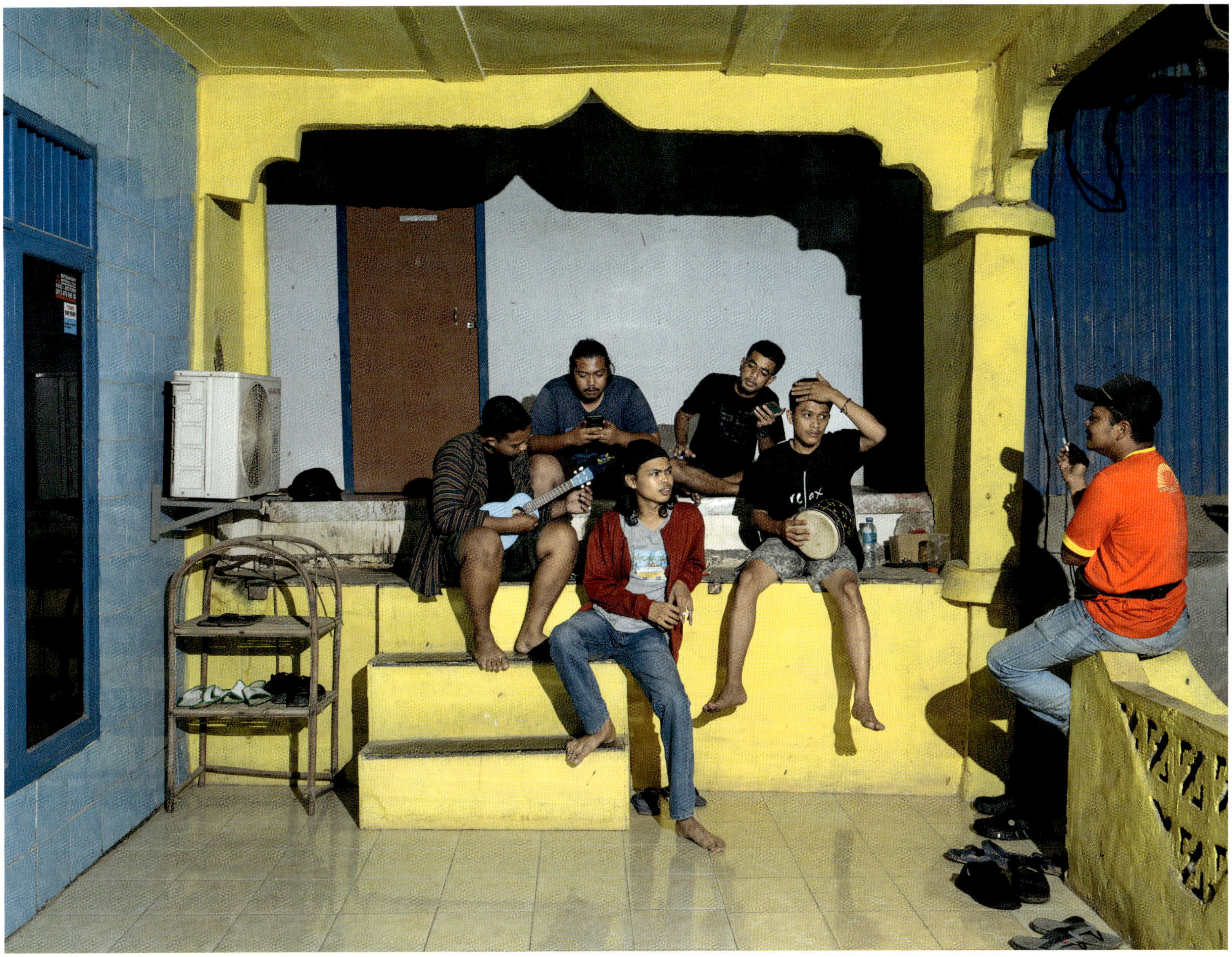

Jam session in Penginapan Nabila guesthouse in Sukaraja, Sepaku.

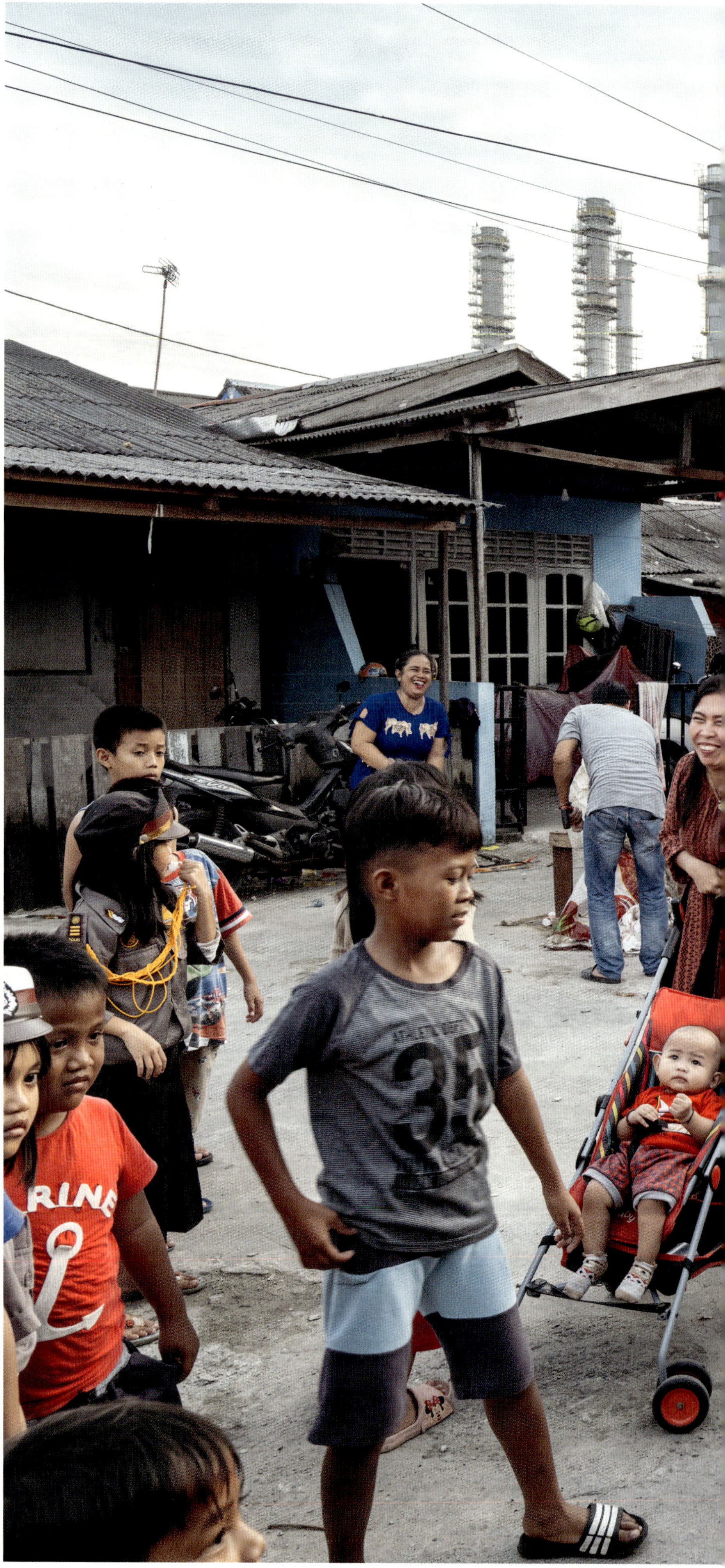

The fishing community of Kampung Baru
in Balikpapan lives near the polluting refinery
of state-owned oil company Pertamina.

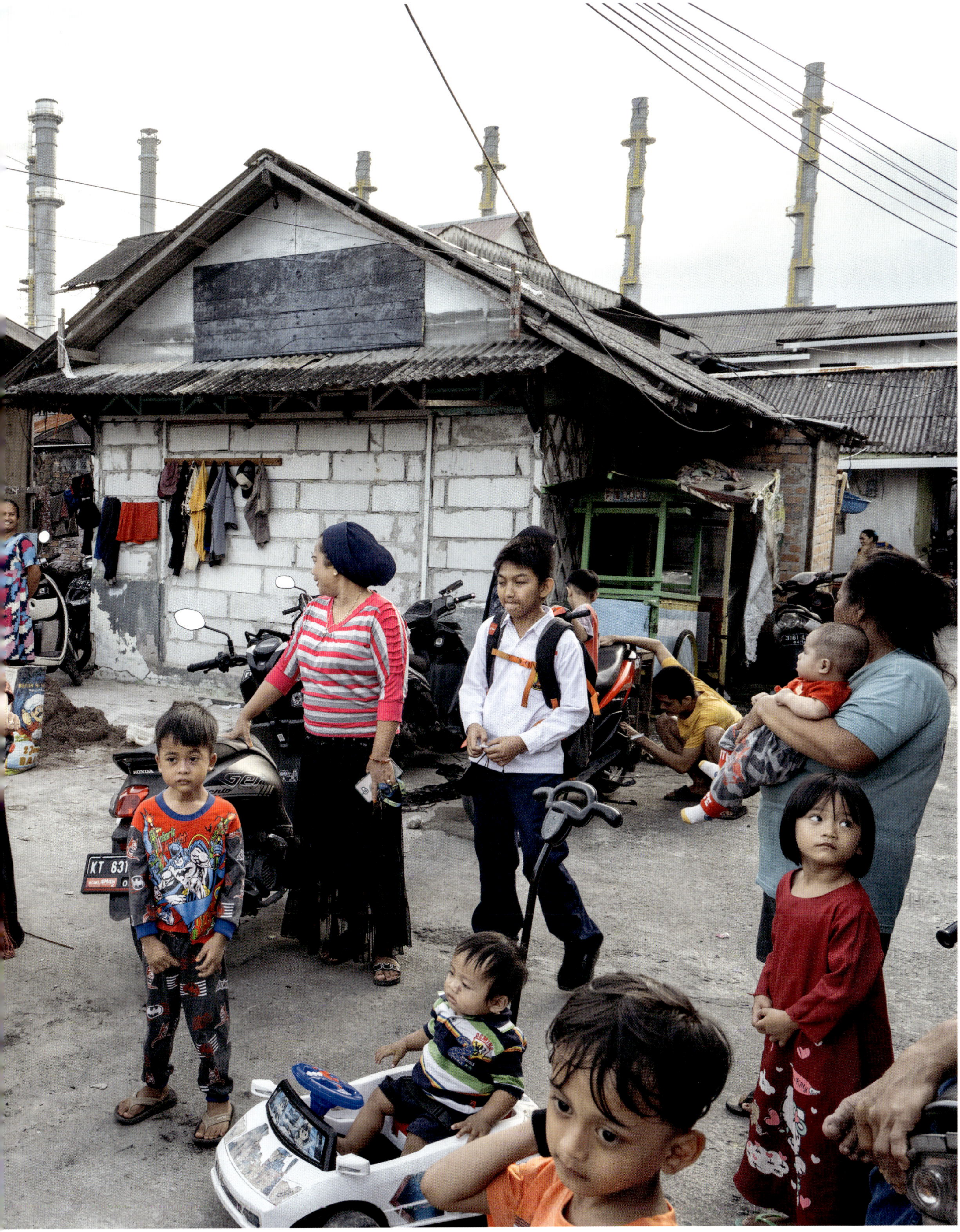
KT 631

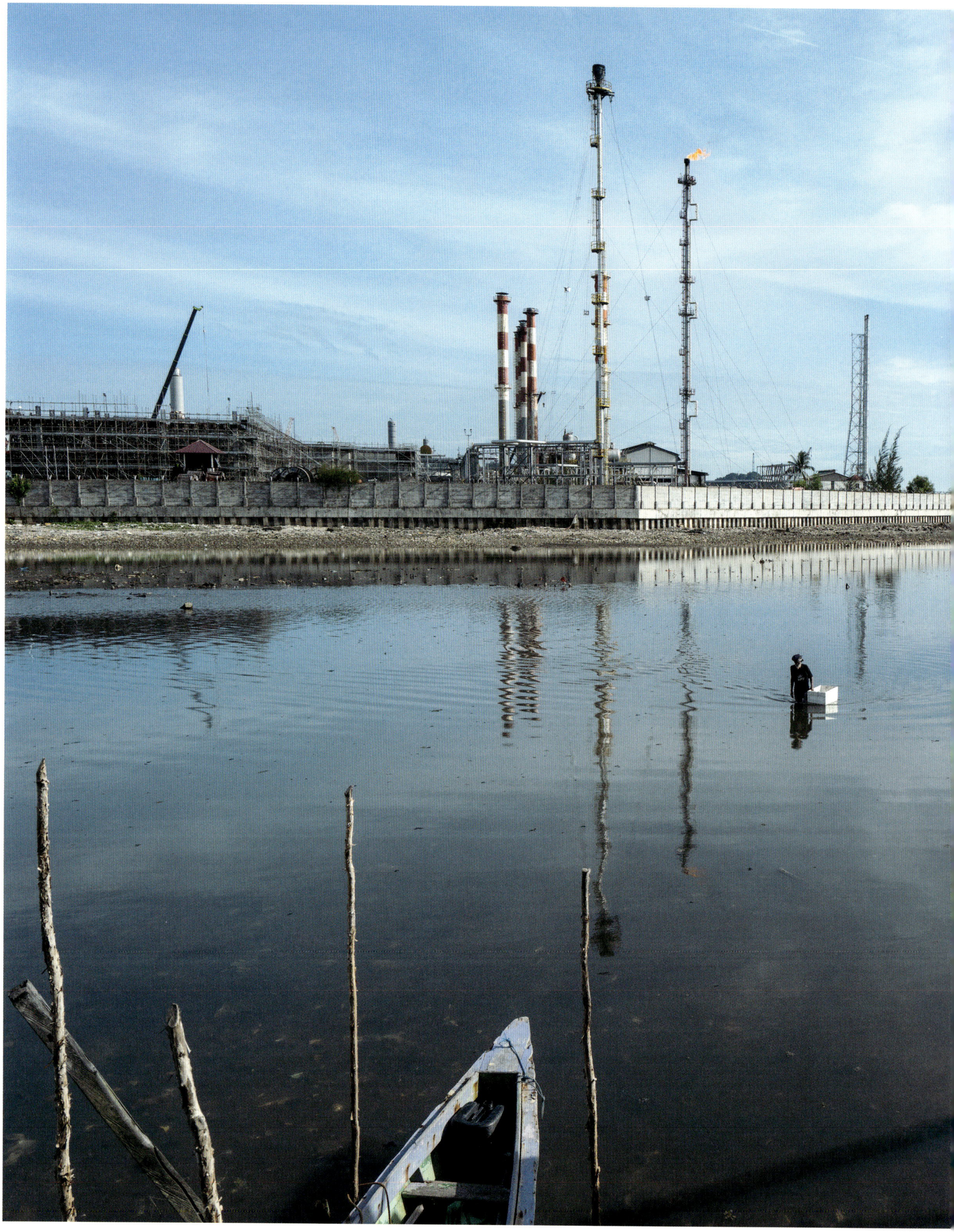

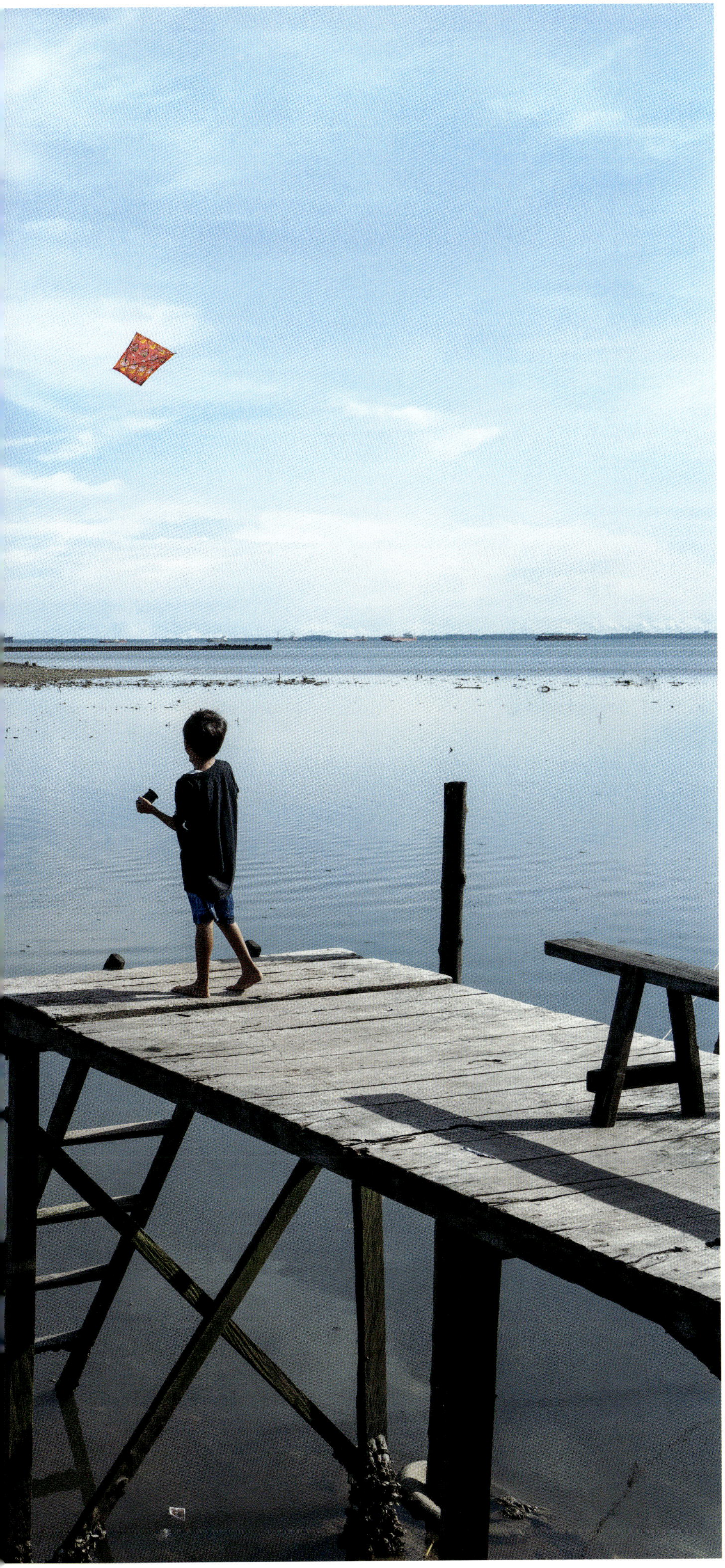

Pertamina refinery in Kampung Baru, Balikpapan.

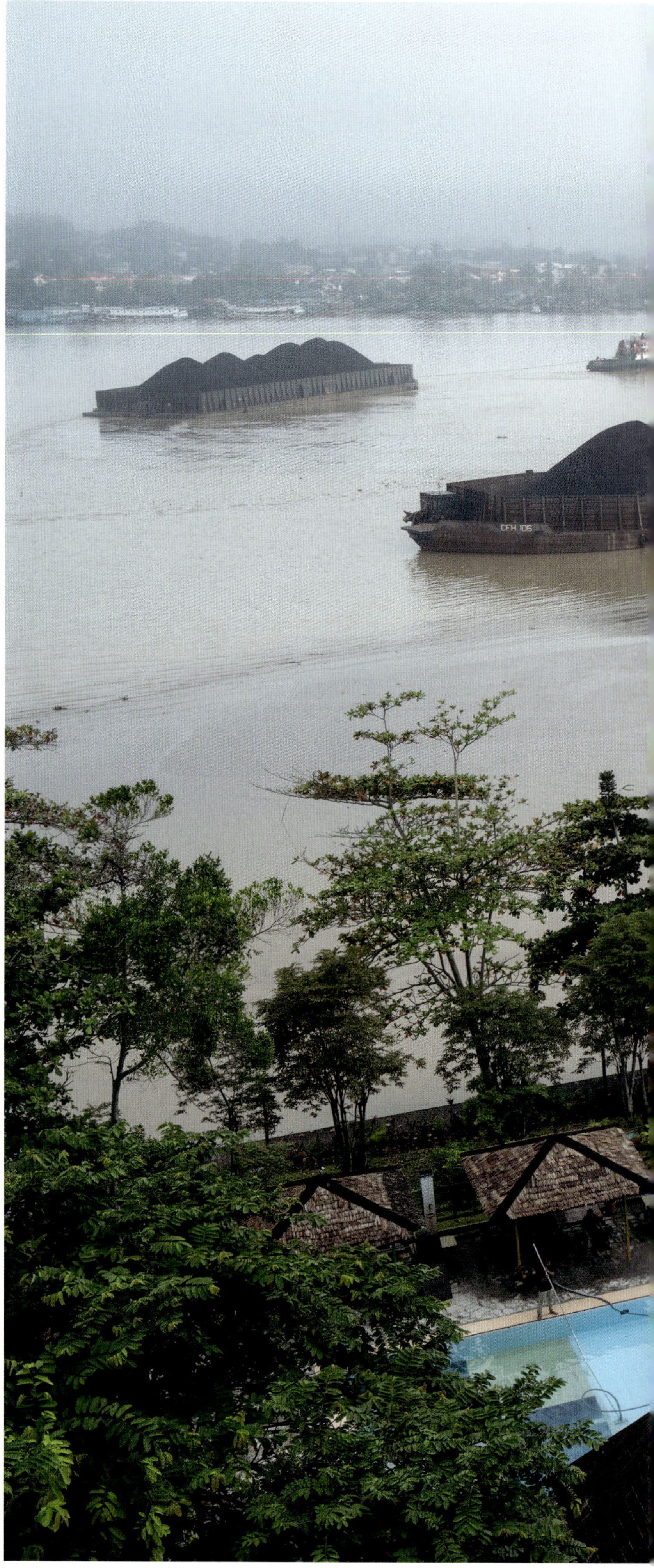

Every morning, dozens of barges loaded with coal sail down the Mahakam River past Samarinda, one of the gateways to the new capital.

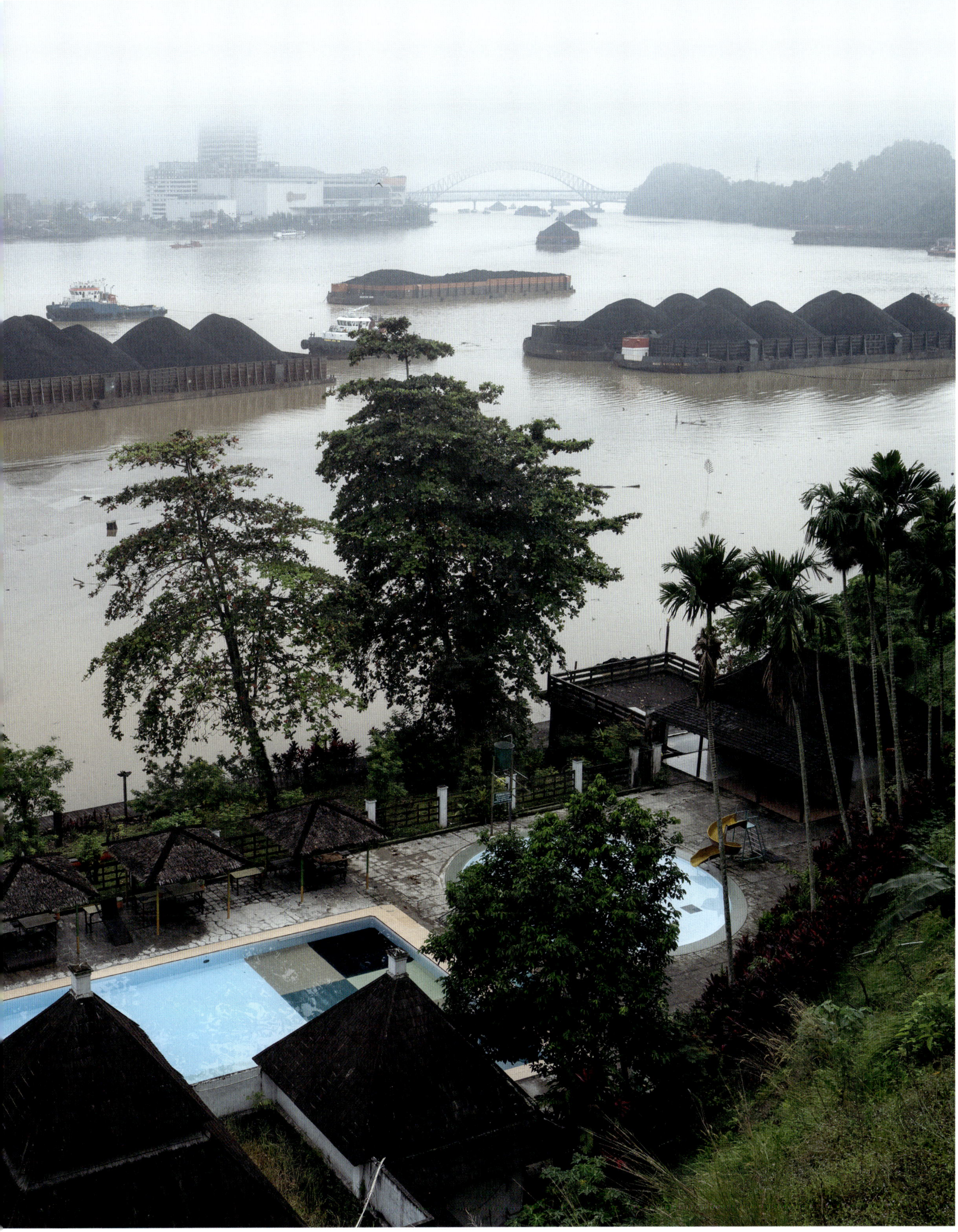

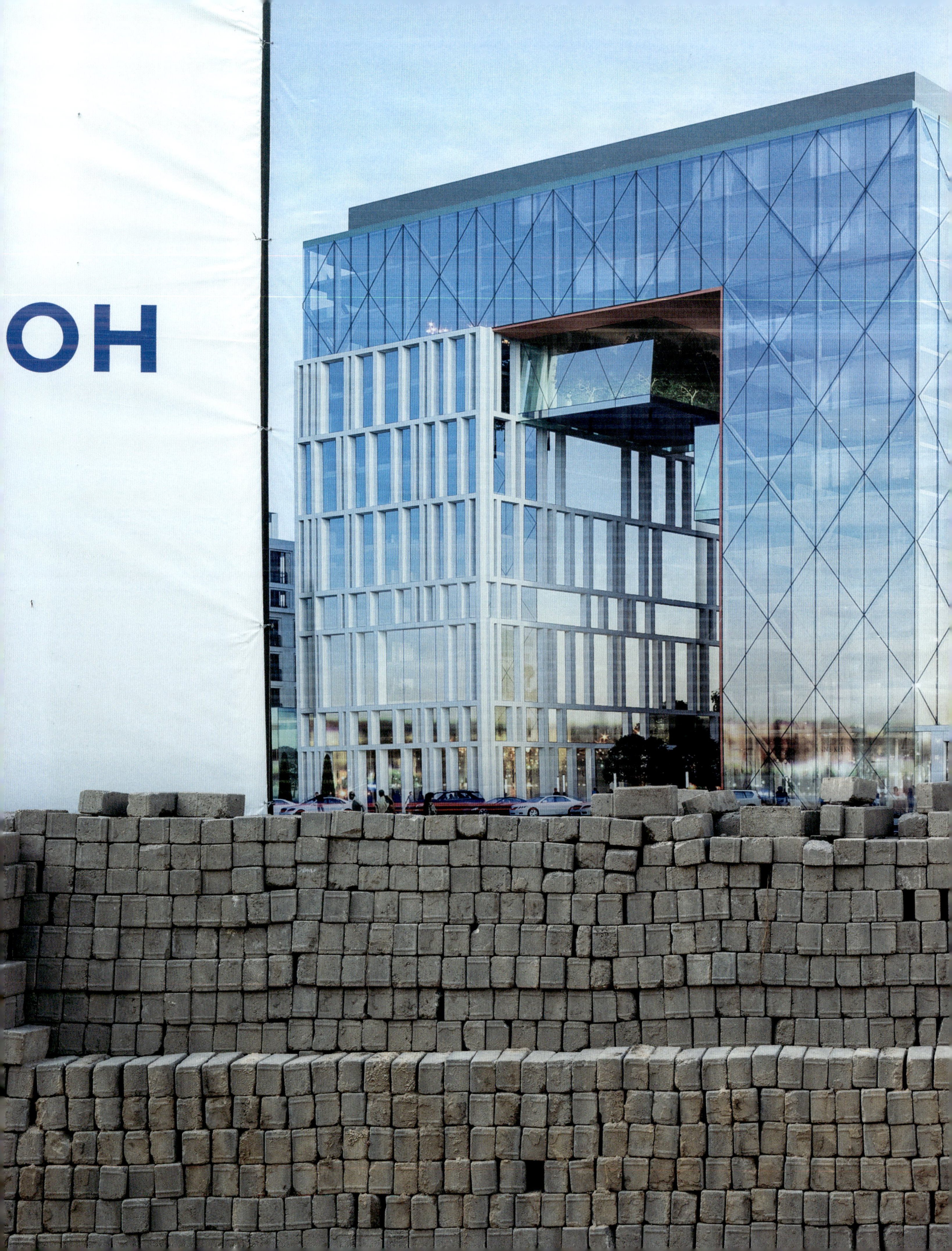
OH

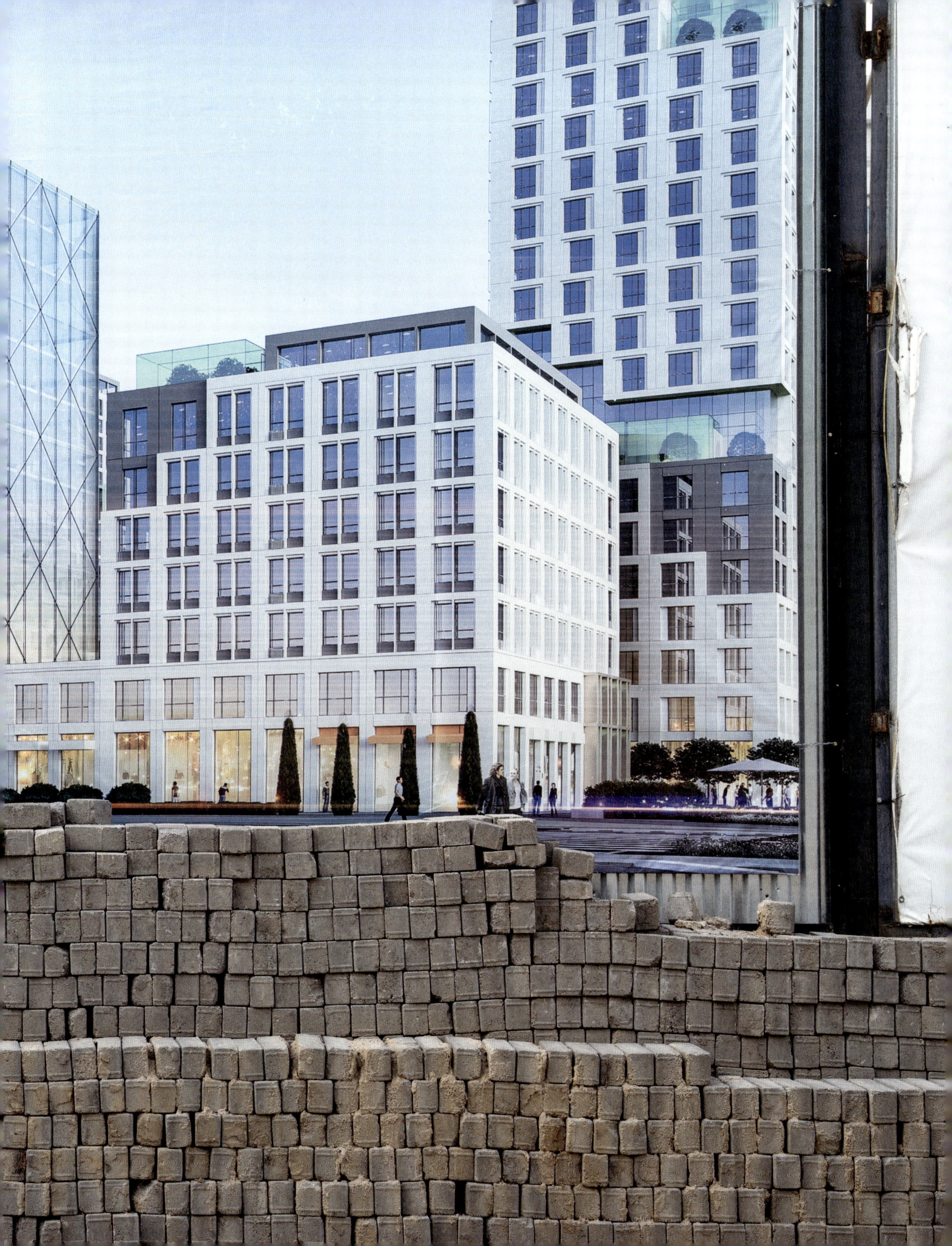

This book is published on the occasion of the exhibition *New Capital* in Be-Part, platform for contemporary art based in Waregem, Belgium, from 16 March to 19 May 2024.

Many thanks to:

Dorina Pojani, Gert Verbelen, Sarah Theerlynck, Astrid Devlaminck, Carolijn Domensino (Lannoo), Patrick Ronse (Be-Part), Milo Profi fotolabo, Jan Desloover *(De Standaard)*, Lieven De Cauter, Panos Pictures, Griet Ivens and Ina Van den Broeck (CC Ter Dilft Bornem), Flemish Government – Flanders Department of Culture, Youth and Media, World Press Photo.

Special gratitude to all the people who assisted me in securing photoshoot permits and who helped me with the logistics of on-site photography.

In Brasília:

Luc Vankrunkelsven (Wervel), Delphine Charles and Dinah Opoczynski (Embassy of Belgium, Brasília)

In Abuja:

David Dawali, Majesty Stiqler, Osaze Efe

In Astana:

Yenlik Tlesheva (Embassy of Kazakhstan in Belgium), Vitaliy Alexandrov (Ministry of Foreign Affairs of the Republic of Kazakhstan)

In Sejong:

Jae-hyun Seok, Jinhee Park, Annie Kim (South Korea Ministry of Land, Infrastructure and Transport), Tim Schilstra, Albert Retief

In NAC:

Ruth Vandewalle, Khaled Al-Husseini (Administrative Capital for Urban Development)

In Nusantara:

Nefertiti Hindratmo and Bramantyo Ardi Wardhana (Embassy of Indonesia in Belgium), Merah Johansyah and Pradarma Rupang (Jaringan Advokasi Tambang), Kris Vanslambrouck (11.11.11), Sibarani Sofian (URBAN+), Cristian Rahadiansyah (JIPFest), Sidik Pramono (Bappenas)

Many thanks to everyone in my photos for their kind cooperation.

Photography:

Nick Hannes

Text:

Nick Hannes, Dorina Pojani

Graphic design:

Gert Verbelen

Translation and editing:

Lyrco

D/2024/45/70 - NUR 653/652

ISBN: 97894014 0376 4

www.lannoo.com

If you have any questions or comments about the material in this book, please do not hesitate to contact our editorial team: art@lannoo.com.

This project was completed with the support of the Flemish Government.

Vlaanderen verbeelding werkt · milo profi · BE-PART